MW00641434

Nature's Perspectives

Nature's Perspectives
Prospects for Ordinal Metaphysics

Edited by

Armen Marsoobian
Kathleen Wallace
Robert S. Corrington

STATE UNIVERSITY OF NEW YORK PRESS

Published by
State University of New York Press, Albany

© 1991 State University of New York

For information, address State University of New York
Press, State University Plaza, Albany, N.Y., 12246

Library of Congress Cataloging in Publication Data

Nature's perspectives : prospects for ordinal metaphysics / edited by
    Armen Marsoobian, Kathleen Wallace, Robert S. Corrington.
        p.   cm.
    Includes bibliographical references.
    ISBN 0-7914-0491-9 (alk. paper). — ISBN 0-7914-0492-7 (pbk. :
alk. paper)
    1. Buchler, Justus, 1914–   —Contributions in metaphysics.
    2. Metaphysics.   3. Order (Philosophy)   4. Naturalism.
    I. Marsoobian, Armen. II. Wallace, Kathleen. III. Corrington,
    Robert S., 1950–
    B945.B7564N38   1991
    110'.092—dc20   90–32137
                                                                          CIP

10 9 8 7 6 5 4 3 2 1

Like as the waves make towards the pebbled shore,
So do our minutes hasten to their end;
Each changing place with that which goes before,
In sequent toil all forwards do contend.
Nativity, once in the main of light,
Crawls to maturity, wherewith being crown'd,
Crooked eclipses 'gainst his glory fight,
And Time that gave doth now his gift confound.
Time doth transfix the flourish set on youth
And delves the parallels in beauty's brow,
Feeds on the rarities of nature's truth,
And nothing stands but for his scythe to mow:
    And yet to times in hope my verse shall stand,
    Praising thy worth, despite his cruel hand.

William Shakespeare, Sonnet LX

Contents

Preface

This is the second major book on the work of Justus Buchler.[1] Our plan has been to gather together in a single volume some of the best essays written to date on Buchler's work. This book, then, is intended, not as a *festschrift*, but as an important resource in ordinal metaphysics for philosophers and scholars.

The volume is evenly divided between previously published work and articles written expressly for this volume. In selecting these papers we had to make difficult critical decisions regarding what to include and what to omit. We have striven to achieve a representative sample of the work being done in this area, drawing from what, in our judgment, are the best articles written over the past thirty years and selecting the most original and suggestive of the recently written papers. Verbal changes in previously published papers have been made at the author's request or to correct or reflect the most up-to-date rendition of passages from Buchler's works. We were also concerned that we achieve breadth in the range of subject matter and kind of analyses represented in the volume. We, therefore, had to omit some very good papers which would have duplicated material already selected. We tried to keep primarily expository material to a minimum, including as much as necessary to allow for the reader not familiar with Buchler's system, to participate in the discussion.

The book also includes a complete up-to-date bibliography of the secondary literature on Buchler. The entries in the index were constructed by combining the indexes of Buchler's five systematic books (TGT, NJ, CM, MNC, ML[2]) and adding proper names and other key terms from the essays.

We would like to acknowledge our appreciation to all those who submitted articles to this volume. We are indebted to Connecticut State University for providing a grant that partially defrayed the costs of preparing this manuscript. Also Southern Connecticut State University, and especially J. Philip Smith, Dean of the School of Arts and Sciences, was of great assistance in providing the resources necessary for completing this project. We thank Jean F. Alberino who most genially and expertly typed the manuscript and Kimberly Landino for her able and unstinting assistance

in preparing the manuscript and index. Finally, our thanks to Dorothy Mc-
Kenzie for her 1979 portrait study of Justus Buchler.

Notes

1. The first is Beth J. Singer's fine study, *Ordinal Naturalism: An Introduction to the Philosophy of Justus Buchler* (Lewisburg: Bucknell University
Press, 1983).

2. Soo "List of Abbreviations" for Buchler's works, p. xiii–xiv.

Acknowledgments

Grateful acknowledgment for permission to reprint is made to the following:

"Toward a Radical Naturalism," by Sidney Gelber, *The Journal of Philosophy* 56:5 (February 26, 1959), pp. 193–199.

"Natural Obligation, Natural Appropriation," by Matthew Lipman, *The Journal of Philosophy* 56:5 (February 26, 1959), pp. 246–252.

"Buchler's Metaphysics," by Richard J. Bernstein, *The Review of Metaphysics* 74:22 (November 1967), pp. 751–770.

"Justus Buchler: Nature, Power and Prospect," by Sidney Gelber and Kathleen Wallace, *Process Studies* 15:2 (Summer 1986), pp. 106–119.

"Substitutes for Substances," by Beth J. Singer, *Modern Schoolman* 53 (November 1975), pp. 19–38.

"The Concept of Identity in Justus Buchler and Mahayana Buddhism," by Marjorie C. Miller, *International Philosophical Quarterly* 16:1 (March 1976), pp. 87–107.

"Aristotle's Categories and the Nature of Categorial Theory," by Abraham Edel, *The Review of Metaphysics* 29:1 (Spring 1975), pp. 45–65.

"Possibility: Three Recent Ontologies," by Phil Weiss, *International Philosophical Quarterly* 20:2 (June 1980), pp. 199–219.

"Review of *The Main of Light*," by I. A. Richards, *Times Literary Supplement* (November 29, 1974), p. 1343. © Times Newspapers Limited, 1974.

"Buchler's Ordinal Metaphysics and Process Theology," by Peter H. Hare and John Ryder, *Process Studies* 10:3–4 (Fall–Winter 1980), pp. 120–129.

"The Fish," by Marianne Moore, in *Collected Poems* (New York: The Macmillan Co., 1951), pp. 37–38. Reprinted also from *The Complete Poems* (London: Faber and Faber, Ltd.)

A poem by Saigyō Hōshi (1118–1190), translated by Arthur Waley in *Japanese Poetry: The 'Uta'* (Honolulu: University Press of Hawaii, 1976), p. 103.

List of Abbreviations

Following Buchler's practice the following abbreviations are in use. The Editors have altered the reference practices of individual authors where necessary to conform to these. Thus, in the text, references to the works of Buchler as listed below will cite simply the abbreviation and page number, chapter or passage.

TGT *TOWARD A GENERAL THEORY OF HUMAN JUDGMENT.* New York: Columbia University Press, 1951; Second, revised edition, New York: Dover Publications, 1979. The 1979 edition preserves the pagination of the 1951 edition, although Buchler made some changes in the text. This edition also includes an introduction written by Buchler.

NJ *NATURE AND JUDGMENT.* New York: Columbia University Press, 1955; New York: Grosset and Dunlap, 1966; Lanham, MD: University Press of America, 1985. All printings have the same pagination.

CM *CONCEPT OF METHOD.* New York: Columbia University Press, 1961; Lanham, MD: University Press of America, 1985. Same pagination in each.

MNC *METAPHYSICS OF NATURAL COMPLEXES.* 1966. Second, expanded edition. Edited by Kathleen Wallace and Armen Marsoobian, with Robert S. Corrington, with an introduction by Kathleen Wallace. Albany: State University of New York Press, 1989. The 1989 edition preserves the pagination of the 1966 edition (New York: Columbia University Press) for the original text. When the reference is to the original text it will read simply MNC and page number; when the reference is to any of the material added to the 2nd expanded edition it will read MNC [1989] and page number.

ML *THE MAIN OF LIGHT: ON THE CONCEPT OF POETRY.* New York: Oxford University Press, 1974.

OCW "On the Concept of the 'World'," *The Review of Metaphysics,* 31:4, June 1978, pp. 555–579. Reprinted in MNC [1989], Appendix III, pp. 224–259. References will cite first *The Review of Metaphysics* then the MNC [1989] page number.

PIN "Probing the Idea of Nature," *Process Studies*, 8:3, Fall 1978, pp. 157–168. Reprinted in MNC [1989] Appendix IV, pp. 260–281. References will cite first the *Process Studies* then the MNC [1989] page number.

A 1976 issue of *The Southern Journal of Philosophy* was devoted to Buchler's philosophy with Beth J. Singer and Joseph G. Grassi as Special Editors. Some of the material from this issue is also reprinted in MNC [1989] Appendix I. When there is a reference to material from this issue the following convention is in use:

SJP *The Southern Journal of Philosophy*, 14:1, Spring 1976. When the material referred to also appears in MNC [1989], the reference will cite first the SJP then the MNC [1989] page number.

Introduction

The current philosophical climate is one that sometimes celebrates the powers of the human imagination, as if the human process were somehow disconnected from nature. Some deconstructive or semiotic theories, for example, in denying the referential status of texts or signs, reinforce the alienation of the self from the world. It is against this background that the philosophically original system developed by Justus Buchler is all the more relevant to reconceptualizing the continuity between human experience and nature. The principles of "ordinality" and "ontological parity"[1] entail that there is no privileged order of nature, including "the human order." The phrase "nature's perspectives" does not imply that nature is constituted by monads of consciousness, a view held by process philosophers, but that all human perspectives are in, of, and about nature. Even when human perspectives are primarily "about" other human perspectives, they are natural. Rather, all perspectives, even the human, are located within wider orders of relevance. The ordinal approach is not equivalent to what has been called philosophical pluralism.

The title of this anthology reflects the commitment of ordinal naturalism to a deepened understanding of the "complexes"[2] of nature and of how nature's innumerable orders support or transform human perspectives.[3] If all perspectives are located in nature and represent one or more order within nature, it follows that no perspective is free-floating or purely arbitrary. The *reality* of a perspective is not necessarily equivalent to its validity. Needless to say, some human perspectives are richer and more compelling than others while some other perspectives may have little relevance for larger human and philosophic concerns. Communal forms of "query"[4] serve to separate out more propitious and generic perspectives from those that have limited scope and power.

The ordinal framework refuses to privilege the traits of the human process and project them onto nature as a whole. Much contemporary thought, whether it goes by the name of deconstruction, neo-Kantianism, or radical hermeneutics insists on magnifying what Buchler would call the manipulative dimension of the human process to the neglect of the assimilative dimension. This book aims to show how the basic principles of ordinal naturalism correct this bias and provide a more judicious account of both human creativity and human limitation and of how human perspectives contribute to, as well as are grounded in orders of community and nature.

Justus Buchler began this project in 1951 with his volume *Toward a General Theory of Human Judgment.* In it and in the volumes that followed, *Nature and Judgment* (1955), *The Concept of Method* (1961)[5], and *The Main of Light: On the Concept of Poetry* (1974)[6], he explored the complexities and relations of "the human-self-in-process" (human nature). These studies are located in an implicit broader theoretical structure which he formally articulated in 1966 in *Metaphysics of Natural Complexes,* his seminal work in general ontology. In many ways this anthology continues the project begun in those works. The essays we have selected represent a series of attempts to further our critical understanding of the structures and implications of Buchler's ordinal approach. They demonstrate in a variety of ways the ramified and ramifying "prospects" for ordinal metaphysics.

I

This volume is evenly divided between reprinted, and now classical papers, and those that were written especially for this volume. We believe that this selection will be (a) of immeasurable value for scholars who already have some familiarity with Buchler's system, as well as (b) of interest to those not familiar with ordinal metaphysics. We have grouped the selected papers into three parts. In the first, called "Critical and Systematic Overview," are grouped essays dealing with either the system as a whole or its pervasive principles or features. The nature of metaphysics, naturalism, and Buchler's systematic principles are explored. The second part, entitled "General Ontology," deals explicitly with aspects and implications of Buchler's broadest categorial investigations, that is, his general ontology. These essays critically explore and compare many of Buchler's central categories and principles with those of classical and contemporary thinkers (e.g., Aristotle, Whitehead, Lewis, Rescher). Substance, identity, possibility, materialism, and even the nature of categorial analysis itself are explored. The final part, entitled "Systematic Extensions and Applications," typifies the breadth of applications and interpretations of Buchler's system. These extensions cover such areas as foundationalism, the theory of poetry and communication, dream analysis, the nature of community, and the redefinition of God (the "divine natures"). A brief glance at the bibliography of secondary literature found at the end of this volume also gives some indication of Buchler's growing influence on the community of philosophic thought.

Buchler's system has not created a school of thought so much as stimulated further query into a broad range of philosophical subject-matters. The concepts developed within ordinal naturalism are remarkably free from bias and provinciality and indications of this fact can be seen in the rich and subtle variations that have emerged from the many assimilations of Buchler's framework. If one of the tests of philosophic worth is the ability of a framework to further and deepen query, then Buchler's thought represents one of the most profound developments within systematic philosophy.

II

Twentieth century philosophy has generated corrosive doubts about its ability to provide a framework for understanding the world in its broadest most general sense. The obsession with epistemology and linguistic analysis has blunted efforts to systematically probe into extralinguistic traits. Ironically, hermeneutic theories have joined hands with analytic philosophies to compress all reflection into the artifacts of human language. Nature, insofar as it remains available, is reduced to a series of self-validating texts that can have little or no relevance for each other. Pantextualism replaces naturalism and drives the principles of human speech and writing into the innumerable orders of the world. The concept of validation is reduced to a mere commentary upon a commentary, which is itself but a prior commentary on something else. The endless chain of signifiers closes in on itself and makes it impossible for community and communication to permeate and guide the human process.

Allied to this metaphysics of the text, which asserts that whatever is in whatever way is a text or an intratextual interpretation, is a belief that all hermeneutic acts are arbitrary on the deepest level. Against this view Buchler speaks of the "deep roots and interests in our pursuit of concepts"[7] which themselves guide the hermeneutic process and insure that the acquisition of meaning serves the larger needs of the community and its members. While many complexes in the world are texts or are translatable into textual terms, many are not. Further, the act of interpretation is always already involved in extratextual needs, desires, and compulsions that are not arbitrary or purely conventional. Buchler corrects the postmodern obsession with textuality by insisting on the ubiquity of ordinality that permeates all orders, whether textual or not.

On the political level, pantextualism has generated a kind of solipsism that makes it impossible to engage in *joint* forms of query and social critique. The *ordinal* framework provides a conceptual vocabulary with which to break out of this solipsism and relativism. While no order will be relevant to *all* other orders, it will be relevant to some. Insofar as orders are relevant to each other they become available for communication and comparison. In the order of human perspectives this availability is a necessary trait for the forms of community that permeate the human process. Solipsism is overcome whenever relevance becomes communication within perspectives. Insofar as the self enters into the innumerable orders of natural and conventional communication, pantextualism, which insists on individual monads of self–reflexivity, is left behind.

It is important to stress that Buchler is not simply adding a new list of categories to the world so much as challenging us to redefine the very process by which philosophers frame and articulate concepts. Categories are not generated to serve purely private or merely aesthetic interests but to provide means by and through which further explorations of the world are possible. Systematic philosophy is distinctive in that it refuses to cling to categories of only regional import. The quest for a truly general conceptual array is deeply related to the concern for interpretive justice. Every gain in breadth should be paralleled by an equal gain in interpretive precision. What many thinkers find especially compelling about Buchler's framework is this combination of sheer breadth with interpretive subtley and precision. The essays contained in this volume are a testament to the philosophically compelling nature of Buchler's system.

Armen Marsoobian
Kathleen Wallace
Robert S. Corrington

Notes

1. For a treatment of these principles see *Metaphysics of Natural Complexes,* 1966, 2nd expanded edition (Albany: State University of New York Press, 1989), chapter 1 and 3 passim. Also the essay by Gelber and Wallace in this volume entitled: "Nature, Power and Prospect: Justus Buchler's System of Philosophy," explicitly treats these principles.

2. "Complex" or "natural complex" is the most generic form of identification for Buchler. See his discussion of the term in *Metaphysics of Natural Complexes,* 1 ff. For a discussion of the tensions between a categorial and precategorial understanding of "natural complex" see, "Conversation Between Justus Buchler and Robert S. Corrington," *Journal of Speculative Philosophy* 3:4 (1989), pp. 261–274.

3. For a treatment of the concept of perspective see *Toward a General Theory of Human Judgment,* 1951, 2nd revised edition (New York: Dover, 1979), chapter 6 passim.

4. For a treatment of query see *Nature and Judgment,* 1955, (Lanham, MD: University Press of America, 1985), chapter 2 passim.

5. *The Concept of Method,* 1961, (Lanham, MD: University Press of America, 1985).

6. *The Main of Light: On the Concept of Poetry* (New York: Oxford University Press, 1974).

7. "Conversation Between Justus Buchler and Robert S. Corrington," p. 269.

Notes and Reflections on Justus Buchler

Sidney Gelber

I think the most striking feature of Justus Buchler's work is the comprehensive scope of his categories. The range of subjects covered in this volume, from possibility to community, from poetry to God, is testimony to the interpretive breadth of his system of thought. But the character of this system is no surprise given Buchler's distinctive background and experience. His interests and work have ranged through literature, history, art, education, curriculum development and, of course, philosophy.

Buchler's interests in literature began at least as early as his undergraduate years at the City College of New York. His first published paper appeared in the City College undergraduate journal *The Lavender* (January 1934). It was entitled "Note on Proust" and, in imitation of Proust, consisted of a single paragraph five pages in length. Shortly after, Buchler wrote a review of Santayana's *Last Puritan*.

Buchler's career at Columbia University was a distinguished one, he earned the Johnsonian Chair in Philosophy in 1959. He was awarded the Butler Silver Medal in 1973. Yet, perhaps one of his most significant contributions was to enhance and sustain Columbia's reputation as a major force in the development of general education in this country. As the administrative and intellectual head of the Contemporary Civilization (C.C.) program at Columbia College (beginning in 1942) he was fully recognized by the many faculty associated with C.C. as the program's guiding spirit and intellectual leader.[1] He was truly its self-critical force, insisting upon annual re-examination of the materials of the program by both students and faculty and requiring the editorial committees to change and improve basic materials on a regular basis. True to Buchler's perception of the self-corrective character of query, the C.C. program was never a "finished" product. As chair of the weekly luncheons held for the entire teaching staff, Buchler was the catalyst, requiring open discussion of ideas and issues pertaining to the C.C. curriculum. A wide range of disciplines were represented: philosophy, economics, history, political science, religion, sociology and anthropology. Buchler was recognized by his colleagues as the figure most responsible for seeing C.C. as a continuing intellectual challenge, compelling its participants to wrestle with the complex inter-actions of the social, political, economic, religious and ideological factors shaping our civilization. Buchler was a proponent of general education which he viewed as a cumulative process by which to understand the world in its complex ways, and to make sense of human activities, purposes and direction.

I have felt that Buchler's notion of judgment has some roots in the C.C. experience. From the early days of his intellectual career, as teacher and head of this influential and critical contribution to curriculum develop-ment, Buchler always had a respect for the complexity of human utterance. In addition to primary text materials by major intellectual figures, the pro-gram included documents, correspondences, accounts of individuals reflect-ing upon events and practices of their day. If Aristotle was pertinent, so were the everyday workings and reflections of common people carrying on their challenge for survival. This healthy respect for the utterances and ac-tions that constitute human animals is embodied in the *parity* of the modes of judgment—active, assertive and exhibitive—in his theory of judgment. Human history and life would be unintelligible if they were all reduced to one mode, or if one mode were assigned priority.

This parity, the equal importance of each of the modes of judgment for understanding human experience and its products, is also exemplified by Buchler's own pursuits. He read widely in literature and poetry, the latter interest culminating in *The Main of Light: On the Concept of Poetry*. He is an avid listener of classical music. He has a great love for the visual and plastic arts, as well as for the sport of baseball. On the one hand, Dona-tello was one of his favorites; on the other, his tastes are hardly provincial or only classical. On the wall of his study in New York is a collage (*papier collé*) of African masks. He created his own unusual three-dimensional work on the wall of his study in Vermont using old iron tools and tree branches, the smooth geometric shapes of the tools placed in sharp contrast to the seemingly uncontrolled bends and twists in the branches. He was for a time an amateur photographer, developing and printing his own pictures, many of them portraits of friends, acquaintances and strangers. He and his wife bought a farmhouse in northern Vermont in the postwar forties. It was a run-down antique colonial house, which they rebuilt and expanded. Much of the work they did themselves, wallpapering, painting, sanding floors, cabinetry. Buchler gained the admiration of the local farmers and artisans, who treated him as a native Vermonter, perhaps recognizing Buchler's re-spect for the reality and value of active judgment. His own life has been illustrative of all the modes of judgment, as is any human life, whatever the specific interests and activities.

Coupled with this breadth and sheer catholicity of intellect and interest was a very strong desire to establish instruments of rational discipline in attempting to understand the recurrent patterns in human action and in the world around us. The breadth and scope of the system, on the one hand, and the rigor of it, on the other, can be seen as the controlled expression of these two urges in Buchler. Students recognized these traits in Buchler and were drawn to work with him. On the one hand, he encouraged adventuresomeness and inventiveness, fostering liberation from the mere adherence to conventional practices and reliance upon conceptually limiting formulations. On the other hand, he consistently exhibited a serious commitment and responsibility to be rigorous in the coherence, organization and persuasiveness of one's work. Students could expect from Buchler, as their dissertation advisor, genuine intellectual challenge as well as responsible, careful criticism at all stages of their work.

Perhaps the fact that Buchler wrote his dissertation on Peirce can give us some clue to the character of Buchler's perception of himself as a philosopher. Peirce is in no way reducible to academic conventions. He was, in both his person and his work, unconventional, not being bound to any specific school of thought or modes of analysis. This, too, is quite characteristic of Buchler. He has never cultivated disciples, nor sought positions of influence or power in conventional organizations and associations within the profession itself, in spite of his serving as chair of the Philosophy Department of Columbia for several years. Buchler was comfortable publishing in *Analysis* and *Mind,* yet chose not to be limited by analytic philosophy in his methods and subjects. He shed light on the genius of Peirce long before Peirce was fashionable. Yet, he chose not to limit himself to pragmatism as a school of thought. He is at home with various and diverse modes of philosophical expression even when he does not share their values. For example, he disagreed with G. E. Moore on almost all major issues but had a high regard for him and his persistent commitment to philosophy. Buchler could expend serious effort on Husserl, with appreciation and understanding of his intellectual concerns without his being dependent upon them as beliefs in shaping his own intellectual conventions. Nor is he a disciple of Dewey, though he appreciates Dewey's sense of eternal challenge in his outreach to a panorama of issues and his ability to reflect his creativity in the very process of teaching itself. Buchler's course syllabi from both Columbia and later, the State University of New York at Stony Brook, are indicative of the reach of his philosophic intellect as are the thirty-five book reviews he wrote between 1936 and 1951.

Perhaps what he respects most in philosophy is the creative process and Plato as the distinctive paradigm of this process. This is probably why he was able to teach such a wide range of philosophic figures without identifying himself with any one. For example, with respect to Whitehead, whom some see as an important precursor to Buchler's work, what he admired most about Whitehead was his ingenuity, the sheer inventiveness of categories, more than his conclusions. The category of query, which is so central to Buchler's theory of judgment and of the human process, is an expression and exemplification of his commitment to the furthering of the inventive life of human beings. Not that query is limited to philosophy. On the contrary, it pervades human life. Not only a Plato or a Spinoza, but also, a Proust, a Mozart, a Martha Graham, a farmer, a carpenter, an athlete, a seamstress, all may engage in the life of query, of methodic and inventive probing of the complexes of nature, of possibilities and actualities. And, of course, the process of education exemplifies query as its *raison d'être*.[2]

Buchler is not only a "renaissance" or "universal" man. As a metaphysician he has always had an eye on persistent traits exhibited universally, in the world at large. And, he had the power of abstracting and conceptualizing those traits to shape the categories of his system. As a system the categories provide us with the opportunity to grasp intellectually, through all modes of judgment, the pervasive and recurrent traits of human life and nature at large. For such traits don't simply reveal themselves to us, in their immediacy appearances are not necessarily intelligible. A philosopher invents and shapes categories in order to render the world more intelligible.

In doing so, Buchler established his philosophic presence independent from conventions of his, indeed of our, time. He has never really been interested in the fashionableness of his ideas. Although he has a great respect for new ideas, he has always been a skeptic. He never takes any idea at face value; it could always be interrogated, questioned, probed, could be subject to some mode of query. In this sense, Buchler's skepticism is not a posture or pose, as it was for Descartes, nor is it an end in itself, as for the Pyrrhonists. Rather, it goes hand in hand with query itself. This skepticism is in part what I had in mind when I characterized his work as exhibiting a "radical naturalism."[3] In Buchler's work nothing is sacred; one can question, interrogate the status of anything, any complex. On the one hand, in the metaphysics of natural complexes nothing is suspended in nonbeing; on the other hand, if every complex is related to at least some other complex(es), then we are challenged to assume the risks of probing, of further discriminating, with its attendant resolutions and disappointments.

Early in his career Buchler worked with Ernest Nagel, who was his dissertation advisor. Buchler started out as a serious and impressive logician, but moved in other directions, away from the involvement with mathematics to the broader issues emerging from the "metaphysics of utterance," such as the nature of meaning and the character and process of human communication. Buchler also rejected Nagel's limiting view of the philosopher's job as essentially to clear up muddiness in thinking and in linguistic expression, the view that speech and thought are like a dirty window and the philosopher's job is to wipe it clean. For Buchler, philosophy is a looking out the window, to extend the analogy, to see what's out there *and* to understand it. If we have to shape categories to understand, to "render intelligible," then one must recognize this to be the task of philosophy. The world understood philosophically is still the same world as the world of science, art or anything else. Every discipline carves out its unique angles of approach and delimits its subject matter without having to place itself outside of human experience and the world. Buchler's great passion has been to understand; philosophy could never be an exercise in taxonomy.

This passion "to understand" characterized his whole approach to the Contemporary Civilization enterprise. C.C. was a way of probing civilization and our history. He was critical of the "great books" approach to general education adopted by the Humanities departments because he felt that an attachment to "great books" *qua* "great books" limited our full understanding of the nature and workings of our civilization. I think he felt that the celebration of a great work—which could take place through the textual analysis of it—was never an end in itself. Rather, its value consisted in how it entered into and furthered the life of query.

For Buchler academic life is not just a life of the mind. While he had the ability to do his writing in solitude, and was totally self-disciplined in his work, he was not a person of the "ivory tower." He engaged in public discussion and lectures on radio and to various lay audiences, as well as providing instruction at the William Alanson White Institute of Psychiatry over a number of years (1958–1960). As already noted, he participated in the community of the university: he took all academic responsibilities seriously; he wrote a history of the tradition of General Education at Columbia College, "Reconstruction in the Liberal Arts,"[4] and served as chair of the Contemporary Civilization program and of the Philosophy Department at different periods of his Columbia career. Academic citizenship was for him as much a part of what it means to be an academic as identification with one's intellectual work. To use Buchler's own categories, as a citizen of the academic world one is giving utterance primarily in the mode of active judgment. It is not surprising, therefore, that students and colleagues recognized in Buchler a continuing and persistent moral sense of commitment and responsibility, to them and to the wider community. As an advisor to students (undergraduate and graduate) he was consistently the compassionate guide, as well as the truly disinterested judge. His stance towards graduate students who were writing dissertations or theses with him was never dogmatic or ideological. As one student put it, "He said, 'You know, I don't have to agree with you; but your work has to be defensible.' "

In this respect he had much in common with John Herman Randall, Jr. The two were to develop between themselves strong personal and intellectual ties, emerging in co-authorship[5] as well as an instructional partnership in Randall's great course in the History of Philosophy. Their intellectual strengths proved to be complementary, each invigorating the other. The power, scope and grasp of Randall's unique comprehension of intellectual history was complemented by Buchler's metaphysical sensibility and an inventive power to develop a persuasive systematic philosophy.

However, in spite of his long and well–established career at Columbia, replete with the achievements and honors measured by usual academic standards, in the early seventies Buchler was prepared to leave the University to continue his work elsewhere. Those who know him well were not surprised that Buchler was willing to make a move to the State University of New York at Stony Brook, a recently established public university and to a department with graduate programs in their nascent stages (the doctoral programs, and the masters program in Philosophic Perspectives). In spite of the rich, impressive accomplishments of Columbia as a university, and the distinctive history of the Department of Philosophy in the shaping of American thought, Buchler had become increasingly disturbed by the overall changes in the University's intellectual climate and the quality of its commitments to general education. In addition, the serious diminution of philosophic pluralism in the Department of Philosophy threatened a decline in its intellectual vitality. The profession as a whole typified what he encountered at Columbia. However, the distinctive ordering of possibilities characterizing Stony Brook appealed to him, representing an oasis for a life of query in an institutional setting. After his retirement he was to reflect upon the excitement, vitality and inventive talent of the graduate students he had come to know and work with at Stony Brook.

True to his own philosophical outlook each moment or stage in his career offered possibilities for further probing and exploration. After completing the comprehensive ontological system in *Metaphysics of Natural Complexes*, Buchler was to see its ramification in an intensive study of poetry, *The Main of Light*. Buchler's intellectual career can perhaps best be appreciated in the light of the unpredictable character of human creativity and inventiveness. We shall never know what other works and contributions were in the offing when a serious illness overwhelmed Justus Buchler and forced him to retire. However, he is ever present to us in his carefully crafted system of thought, and challenging us to confront the risks and satisfactions of a life committed to the boundlessness of query.**

Notes

**(Editors' Note: After reading Sidney Gelber's manuscript, Beth J. Singer provided the editors with the following excerpt from a March 23, 1972 letter which Buchler wrote to her and which corroborates Gelber's independently formulated insights. Buchler was notorious for his resistance to commenting on the influences on and origins of his thought. The following comments constitute a rare exception to his usual practice and we are grateful to Professor Singer for allowing us to quote them.)

In a sense, the philosophic influences that I absorbed stem as much from Plato and Aristotle, Spinoza and Locke, as from American thought. *All* of the influences are piecemeal rather than systematic: a specific insight here, an adaptable concept there, a mode of approach, an emphasis, a happy formulation. My flirtation or adventure with logical positivism came between 1937 and 1939 or 1940. The brevity of this phase is shown, for example, by the fact that my interest in Santayana was strong before this phase and continued strong after it (*Obiter Scripta* was prepared in 1935.). . . .

In 1942 *Philosophy: An Introduction* appeared. In 1951 *Toward a General Theory* appeared. The decade between was crucial for me. In 1942 I began (a) teaching Contemporary Civilization and (b) teaching Contemporary Philosophy. The teaching, reading, editing and (in 1950) administering of CC (the great staff, the discussions, the *esprit*) was *the* most fundamental intellectual experience of my life. On the other side, the teaching of contemporary philosophical trends gave me the first full chance to think recurrently about what were the better and the worse aspects of late 19th and early 20th century philosophy, especially American. By the late 40's *Toward a General Theory* was germinating. Peirce's theory of signs and Royce's theory of interpretation, which attracted me (both of the men idealists, be it noted), were gradually felt by me to be metaphysically inadequate. CC was broadening my awareness, and I think it is true to say that without it I would not have arrived at my sense of what constitutes human *utterance*. Somehow I distinctly remember saying one day in the Contemp. Phil. class (it included Bob Olsen Freddie Sommers, Willard Arnett, and God knows who else) that the pragmatists had tried commendably to understand "judgment" (assertion) in terms of action, but had failed to see that action as such was judicative. Royce's "interpretation" is man's cognitional rendering, in triadic terms, of the world's contents. What impressed me was his suggestion of its pervasiveness and ubiquity. My feeling in general was that sign–theory (Peirce, Royce, Mead, Cassirer) had to be superseded metaphysically by a theory of human production—the basis of our ubiquitous discriminativeness being the way we produce; or conversely, each of our products being our way of discrimination or selecting (judging). I also distinctly remember a CC luncheon (always on Thursday) in which I sat next to Randall and told him I was preparing (it was around 1950) a category that would or could, if necessary, replace the notion of "experience"; that would take Dewey's great broadening and reconstruction of the latter notion for granted, while showing why Dewey could not avoid often lapsing into the views he thought he was abandoning. Randall, chewing vigorously but smiling, kept nodding his head and saying, Yes, yes. . . .

—*Justus Buchler, March 23,1972*
Letter to Beth J. Singer

1. C.C. was the general education program of the Social Science departments.

2. Justus Buchler, "What Is a Discussion?" *The Journal of General Education* 51:2 (October 1954), pp. 7–17.

3. Sidney Gelber, "Toward a Radical Naturalism," *The Journal of Philosophy* 56:5 (February 1959), pp. 193–199, reprinted here, pp. 21–27.

4. Justus Buchler, "Reconstruction in the Liberal Arts" in Buchler, et.al., *A History of Columbia College on Morningside* (New York: Columbia University Press, 1954), pp. 48–135.

5. John Herman Randall Jr. and Justus Buchler, *Philosophy: An Introduction,* Revised Edition (New York: Harper & Row Publishers, Inc., 1971. Original, 1942.)

Part One

Critical and Systematic Overview

Introduction to Part One

We have chosen for this section three essays that reflect critical presentations of Buchler's general philosophical system while at the same time providing insights into what is unique to his method of philosophizing. No mere summary presentation would do justice to the range and depth of his work. The essays included in this part attempt something more modest, that is, to provide the reader with both external and internal guideposts for exploring Buchler's philosophical corpus. The Gelber and Bernstein essays place Buchler's unique philosophical contribution in the context of a tradition of "naturalistic metaphysics." Buchler's system is seen to be *both* radical in the thorough-going nature of its naturalistic commitments *and* categorially rich in the schema provided for understanding this naturalism. The coauthored contribution by Gelber and Wallace explores the internal fabric of Buchler's system in terms of its fundamental philosophical commitments and systematic principles. All the works in this section evidence the fact that Buchler is a philosopher whose commitment to philosophy evinces no lack of timidity in a willingness to radically reconceptualize the terms of philosophic discourse.

Gelber's essay, "Toward a Radical Naturalism," is one of the earliest published pieces to be included in this anthology, having been written before Buchler's major work in general ontology, *Metaphysics of Natural Complexes.* He argues that Buchler's work forces us to rethink many of the assumptions of traditional philosophic naturalism.These approaches often import an implicit psychological perspective into their formulations of man in nature. In contrast Buchler's approach recognizes a truly ontological setting for naturalism, one which accepts the full implications of the "perpetual incompletion" of nature. Gelber contends that Buchler's form of philosophic naturalism can be called radical because it has resisted the temptation to view the "precariousness or the incompleteness of man" as something to be overcome, but rather takes it as "a key to the understanding of the organized human effort necessary to the promotion and elaboration of human life." (p. 22) The concept of "proception" is Buchler's explicit attempt to radicalize a naturalistic treatment of human experience. The traditional naturalist, John Dewey for one, views "incompletion" as "an initial and presumptive circumstance which effective intellectual or moral conduct resolves."(p. 23) Experience viewed as self–completion hides an implicit teleology.[1] The radical naturalist accepts "incompletion" as a perpetual and real condition that is never overcome. Thus perpetual incompletion is an indelible character of the self-in-process (proception) and is inherent in the texture of all human production. Experience is viewed as self–continuation purged of all implicit teleologies.

Bernstein in his essay "Buchler's Metaphysics," explores a number of central categories in Buchler's philosophical system. While concentrating on the categories of proception, judgment, method, query, and natural complex, Bernstein's concern is to show how these categories have been specifically formulated to challenge some long ingrained biases and presuppositions of philosophy. In this light Bernstein identifies the challenges posed by each category to the tradition. For instance, the category of "proception" can be understood as a corrective to the epistemological tradition's hold on the notion of experience, even in such a reformer as John Dewey.[2] Though Buchler's categories are correctives, they are not merely a haphazard attempt at reform. Bernstein demonstrates how they are systematically connected when seen in the light of Buchler's metaphysical principles, in particular, the principle of ontological parity. In this regard Buchler's category of "proception" is formulated so that no type or instance of proception has any more or less reality than any other. Bernstein provides a similar perspective in presenting the other categories in Buchler's system.

Gelber and Wallace in their essay, "Nature, Power, and Prospect: Justus Buchler's System of Philosophy," take a somewhat different approach to presenting Buchler's categorial scheme for philosophizing. Their concern is not primarily to demonstrate how his categories are unique correctives of deadends in philosophy but rather how they are thoroughly consistent nonarbitrary constructions of three deeply held and philosophically defensible systematic principles. These are the principles of ontological parity, ordinality, and commensurateness. These principles, when taken seriously, guard against a common tendency to translate Buchler's categories back into more "traditional" formulations. For example, natural complex cannot be formulated under the traditional conceptions of being or entity, while alescence is not the same as becoming.[3] Buchler's new categories must be seen as ways of systematically translating the systematic principles in an assertive and exhibitive scheme for comprehensive understanding. It is in this sense that Buchler is engaged in systematic metaphysics comparable to the great metaphysicians of the tradition. As with Aristotle, Buchler's categories are interpretable as responses to his predecessors, but they also have a systematic integrity of their own.

One of the familiar criticisms lodged against Buchler is echoed in these essays. This is the charge that his philosophizing is too abstract and obscure, lacking in polemical guideposts for the reader and rarely offering single precise definitions for major concepts and categories. One of the virtues of the essays in this section is that they provide a basis for a definitive rebuttal of such charges. Buchler's own philosophizing is "systematic" and "foundational" in that his general metaphysical principles preclude the treatment of any concept or category, even his own, as fully determinate and complete. As such his categories work together (i.e., systematically) to provide a framework to facilitate the examination, clarification and ramification of the more familiar themes of philosophy. In this sense his work can be seen as "foundational" in its emphasis upon the development of a categorial scheme. This is a "foundationalism" unlike those that have borne the brunt of most postmodernist criticism. Much of what has been written for this volume is the fruit of such a foundational categorial scheme.[4]

Buchler's focus on the construction of this categorial scheme necessarily involves a high level of abstraction. The task of these essays, both in this section and more importantly in the sections that follow, is to make compelling the connection between the abstract ideas of Buchler's system and what is more familiar, both in terms of the products of the philosophical tradition and those of all human endeavor.

—ATM

Notes

1. I have addressed these difficulties of Dewey's metaphysics in a review of Raymond Boisvert's book, *Dewey's Metaphysics,* in *The Journal of Speculative Philosophy* 3:4 (1989), pp. 282–289.

2. For an extended discussion of the difficulties in Dewey's conception of experience see Buchler's "Introduction" to the second, revised edition of TGT, especially pp. xxix–xxxix.

3. For an extended discussion of the difference between alescence and the traditional category of "becoming" see Abraham Edel's contribution to this volume, "The Nature of Categorial Theory," pp. 115—143.

    4. The theoretical issue of "foundationalism" is addressed in a number of places. Buchler himself discusses it in an interview published as "Conversation Between Justus Buchler and Robert S. Corrington," *The Journal of Speculative Philosophy* 3:4, (1989), pp. 261–274. See also Corrington's article, "Justus Buchler's Ordinal Metaphysics and the Eclipse of Foundationalism," *International Philosophical Quarterly* 25:3, (September, 1985), pp. 289–298, and the Gelber-Wallace essay in this section, pp. 49–63.

Toward a Radical Naturalism

Sidney Gelber

A fresh and vital system of ideas has been introduced into the world of contemporary philosophy through Justus Buchler's *Toward a General Theory of Human Judgment* and *Nature and Judgment*. These works present a bold challenge to existing forms of philosophic practice, and offer an exciting blueprint for the future course of our social and humanistic evaluations of man and his works. Buchler's thought, impressive in its power to articulate a novel philosophy of man, is to be located properly within the twentieth century naturalistic renaissance, for his work establishes new directions in its rich heritage.

In the rebirth of any intellectual tradition, polemic against the old orders is fused with a promise of the new. Perhaps prophecy and moral vision are inescapable consequences in the thought of a Bacon, Hegel, or Dewey as they plot, shape and fix the range of new intellectual possibilities. However, without sustained criticism and systematic thought, perpetuated by the heirs of a tradition, moral satiety and intellectual pride may well threaten its basic foundations. Fortunately, Justus Buchler's contribution refuses to pay lip service to its philosophic allegiance, and it moves toward a naturalism that is radical in its pursuit of the consequences of that position.

All naturalists are aware of the irrevocable character of nature's repetitive workings and the inevitable cycles of birth, growth, and death that impinge upon the human figure. Natural piety is an inescapable datum in the intellectual consciousness of the philosophic naturalist. And Buchler, true to the tradition of his predecessors, recognizes that we cannot deny "the precarious tenure of the self in the world and the indefinite boundaries of the self." (TGT 8)[1]

But Buchler's sense of the "precarious" in human life and the implications of an "indefinite" geography and history assigned to the self, upon careful examination, reveal to us a mature naturalism that does not shrink from its radical consequences. Buchler resists the temptation to accept the "precarious" as a form of moral shock to our humanistic disposition or philosophic allegiance. The philosopher has often been an unwitting practitioner of self-deception and illusion. The Epicurean resolved the issue of the "precarious" in terms of a cosmogony of material perfection. The Stoic overcame his sense of the "precarious" through the identification of the self in some macrocosmic mirror of rational love. And the existentialist, though possessing an uncompromising awareness of man's "precarious" status, has achieved this at the cost of a conversion of the human domain into a series of ungratified tensions, where moral paradox and human predicament are the only eternal values. Obviously the ways of settling our moral concern with the natural destiny of the self are many. This total retreat from a radical naturalism is to be observed in Whitehead's allusions to a systematic anthropomorphism; in the harmonic self-sustaining world of internal relations for the idealist; and in the artifice of human experience, created by the recent analysts, to conform to their methods for cognitive safety. And even within the ranks of recent naturalism there appears little desire to come face to face with man's "precarious tenure." Dewey's predilection for overpopulating man's universe in the "foreground" of nature with the sophisticated social instruments for problem-solving may, as Santayana suggested, disguise an unsuspecting "transcendental moralism." But Santayana himself, with all of his honest and accurate vision, would have us turn from a careful delineation of the natural career and destiny of the individual self to a transcendental drama of ideas.

The inability to discourse about man as he is revealed to us in his natural setting cannot contribute towards an effective metaphysics of the individual. Consequently it provides us with no satisfactory image of man as a being whose integral character is ever in the process of being achieved, not in spite of its precariousness or incompleteness, but because of it. The individual has been traditionally reconstructed into a series of discrete acts or thoughts; or his achievements have been celebrated as episodic and fortuitous; or he has been seen only through a dense medium of society, polity, the race, history, or the absolute—despite the fact that these media are, in turn, the temporal products and organized achievements of integral selves. Buchler clearly addresses himself to this point. "The fact that man is characterized by a state of natural debt, by a perpetual incompletion, does not cast doubt on the existence of individuals but emphasizes only the extended nature of individuality, its communicative essence, and the indefinite bounds of its relatedness." (NJ 106) Man's "precarious tenure" for Buchler, therefore, is not an evil of existence, a dilemma to be overcome, thus feeding our hunger for illusory formulas to resolve our moral anxiety. Rather it becomes a key to the understanding of the organized human effort necessary to the promotion and elaboration of human life. Man's own works serve to reveal him in his emergence and cumulative development.

Recognition of our state as one of "perpetual incompletion" uproots certain conventional notions of man and experience. Man completes himself neither in society or history, nor through his ideals or solved problems. His movements and decisions do not pass out of his domain of selfhood into some desert of eternal forgetfulness. Experience is not simply a series of terminal points. For Buchler the direction of experience would entail a process of continuing production, articulated by the self, rather than, as for Dewey, a series of consummatory acts, indicative of the self.

The terminology of "consummatory" acts still relies strongly upon viewing man through the lenses of traditional psychology, through the categories of feeling and memory. An ontological setting for man in the nature of things gives way to a psychological transcription of human experience. As Buchler cautions us, "what an individual assimilates is what he sustains, not what he feels." (NJ 138) And, in spite of the naturalists' endeavor to bring man descriptively back to his natural habitat, this allegiance to a traditional psychological perspective does not permit him to alter significantly the older interpretations of atomism and discretism in experience. It is reproduced on a grand scale in viewing the products and achievements by the individual self without a sense of the continuing relation of one product to another in terms of the common producer. Products become related to the urgencies and exigencies of the conditions that provoked the initial problem and the need for its resolution. But what are these conditions? To argue that they are problematic, unsettled, or unresolved is to beg the question.

For the naturalist, "incompletion" becomes an initial and presumptive circumstance which effective intellectual or moral conduct resolves; it is never a perpetual or real condition. And much of our recent naturalistic tradition has come to accept the problematic, the unresolved, or the indeterminate as circumstantial situations confronting the self, rather than as the indelible character of the self-in-process (proception). Buchler incorporates man's questing and query all within the movement of proception. Query is not simply a stage in reflective thinking towards the resolution of a problem, but a clarification of the ways the proceptive process moves towards its self-continuation. The language of articulation, for Buchler, may share a pragmatic outlook (a methodological pragmatism) with the language of resolution (instrumental pragmatism). However, the latter's orientation is not only narrower, but its instrumental commitment depreciates the actual and elevates the eternal ideality of the settled as good. Perhaps the philosophy of instrumentalism may not be alien to our moral expectations, but it becomes estranged from the world of natural events characterizing the human animal. Instrumentalism has borrowed Darwin's adaptation, as a fact of natural selection, to work as a norm for moral improvement.

A drastic revisionism, or radical stance, for philosophic naturalism implies that man is as he is-in-the-process of revealing himself. Not only are overt or unmasked teleologies swept away, but a philosophy of process, as applicable to this sense of man, becomes necessary. Whether an "active" or "passive" vocabulary is assigned to any particular version of experience, we must, as Locke would remind us, still account for the identity of the individual in terms of his organized self. Furthermore, the recognition of the forward-moving character of the self in time is intimately bound up with the self's unique achievements and directed energies. Buchler's neologism of "proception," indicating "the natural historicity of the individual," clearly points to the fact that man's career "cannot be propulsive and directed without being cumulative." (NJ 114) This thesis brings together the characteristics of motion, organization, and development—all equally important categories for any satisfactory analysis of the human self. "The interplay of the human individual's activities and dimensions, their unitary direction constitutes a process which I shall call proception. The term is designed to suggest a moving union of seeking and receiving, of forward propulsion and patient absorption." (TGT 4) Here is a suggestive kernel of Buchler's radical naturalism. It provides us with a method of analysis considering man as an integral being whose character, movement, and production must be viewed in the light of his unitary career as an individual. Proception, then, indicates the individual's unique, cumulative movement in nature and his relation to it. The individual's world is thus never wholly fixed and settled, nor prepared for such completion. That world may be altered or strengthened by its procepts, but its domain is ever the "summed-up-self-in-process." The proceptive domain is fixed neither spatially nor temporally. The only "here" is theoretically located in the "floating proceptive domain," and the only "now" or "at the moment" is in the "imminent proceptive domain." The traditional dualisms between the actual and the ideal are broken down, since both are incorporated as procepts in the process of man's self-revelation, through his judgments or products. What is and prospectively what ought to be work upon one another, not as antithetical realities, but as diversified procepts within the proceptive domain. What enters into man's productivity is his mirroring of both fact and thought, real and ideal, thing and idea—all are the ingredients making possible our human process.

The image of man as ever reaching out beyond the moment, propulsively set in nature, does just violence to the older Humian version of experience as cyclical and repetitive. Hume's tradition is actually a retreat from even a Hobbesian scheme. Hobbes would regard experience as mechanically additive, but driven prospectively by desire and endeavor. Hobbes at least celebrates man's productive powers in his capacity to shape a

mortal God, whereas Hume can only wonder at the constancy of experience
to repeat itself through habit. Certainly the impact of our social, historical,
and biological modes of awareness from the nineteenth century introduced
categories of alteration and cumulative change as applicable to our interpretation of the human domain. For Hegel man embodies the process of
history, as its agent, through the stages of altered consciousness. But process as forward propulsion is dimmed by the past glories of consciousness.
Precariousness, as a datum of existence, is lost as mind eternalizes itself
through its own enactments. And the hint of a radical vision in Hobbes,
willing to accept and to see man in the uncertainty and fallibility of his
productions, is forsaken by Hegel's retrospective view of man's progressive
contributions to his heritage.

But the response of Dewey and Whitehead is to bring process for human experience back into a natural setting. For Dewey process serves as a
proof of man's naturalness, in the language of interaction and transaction.
The difficulty of this objective is that it is but a preliminary to the successful reconstruction of experience as a total process. Man and nature remain
as entities, though joined by transactional exchange. Man unmistakably enters nature; but how much of nature adheres to man without fully pursuing
the implications of the fact of precariousness? And how much of that natural process becomes a movement of intelligence answering the moral necessity to overcome our social antinomies? For Whitehead process becomes
the organic touchstone against which all things are measured. Entities become undistinguishable from one another by virtue of this generic kinship.
The fact that Whitehead threatens to anthropomorphize all of nature is of
less concern than the inability to apply this process towards a consistent
metaphysics of the integral self. It is process devoid of the facts of human
achievement.[2]

Buchler's advance over his predecessors is clearly observable in the
concept of proception. Process, as characteristic of the human individual,
is not derivable, for Buchler, from the simple motions in nature, as for
Hobbes; nor is it simply a projection of historic time, as maintained by
Hegel; nor does it become equivalent to the exchange relation holding
between man and nature, within Dewey's metaphysic; nor an extension of
organic nature, argued by Whitehead. Process in Buchler's metaphysics is
distinctively a human movement, derived phenomenologically from an
awareness of man as he is in-the-process of revealing himself. The emphasis
is neither upon the genesis nor upon the realized of experience. Buchler,
unlike his naturalistic predecessors, need not set out to demonstrate the natural source of our experience; it is simply affirmed in the very texture
of proception itself. And the teleology implicit in the view of experience
as a process of self-realization would run counter to Buchler's radical

orientation. Man, in the process of revealing himself, for Buchler, is artic-
ulative and evocative and, as such, is a creature of judgment or production.
As a judicative being man is ever in the process of shaping and fixing his
proceptive materials. Though an individual's products may emerge through
various guises—as exhibitive, assertive, and active judgments—they are
all nurtured in the soil of a common proceptive domain. In this judicative
function man demonstrates not only his relation with the structure of nature
impinging upon him, but he also extends his process of utterance to others
through communication, in the conventions of judgment. Thus the concept
of process, as assigned to the human individual, implies a dimension of
extensity that is communicable, examinable, and corrigible. Though individuals are "unitary proceivers" and communities unto themselves, their
powers of productivity establish the milieu for the social community.

To see the human process as a continuity of the process of productivity suggests that our interpretation of products as almost exclusively
assertive requires serious modification. Evaluating man's productive
achievements requires a more accurate accounting of human experience as
we encounter it, and not prefigured in accordance with our antecedent
intellectual commitments. Justus Buchler has opened up new avenues in
philosophic criticism directed towards our multiple products—intellectual,
moral, and aesthetic. We cannot relegate products, other than perhaps
the purely "cognitive," to the shadows of non-rational discourse without
doing violence to the reality of the self. The classical antinomies of reason-
emotion and rational-empirical have drawn up some order of pure intel-
ligibleness against which are measured the less than pure human accomplishments. We have so thoroughly depreciated the world of experience that
only by the deliberate intervention of some "external" order, or method,
imposed on the random and unformed, do we believe that experience can
become productive. And we ignore completely the fact that the methodic is
present in experience by virtue of man's evocative nature. How adequate is
our understanding of man's apparent success in utterance and production if
we turn our studies of method into programs and prescriptions for intellectual performance?

Appreciating man as a producer, rather than simply as a maker or
knower, is to recognize the human process as prospective and viable. An
individual's proceptive wealth, to paraphrase Adam Smith, lies not in what
he has collected but in what he is to produce. Our view of experience advances from one of simple accumulation to that of cumulative productivity.
This radical stance sees man as forward-moving rather than backward-
looking. What Buchler is celebrating here is ultimately in harmony not only
with the heritage of naturalism, but with the deep sources of our humanistic
tradition. This is the tradition that makes the power of the person central,

and implies a metaphysics of pluralism among men. Each man becomes the source and center for his own possible achievements. His works can never escape the marks of his own identity. And human life achieves power through the constancy of its self–affirmations, though the precarious and uncertain can never be masked from the reality of our mortal destiny.

Notes

1. See "List of Abbreviations" for Buchler's works, p. xiii–xiv.

2. In terms of Buchler's clear recognition of such achievement, in his categories of "judgment" or "product," his concept of proception stands apart from Whitehead's notion of process. Further, since not all natural complexes are procepts, it is difficult to understand Edwin Garlan's criticism that Buchler's treatment of experience, like Whitehead's, "would seem to apply to any organized process whatever, human or not." (Review of *Nature and Judgment, The Journal of Philosophy* 54:20, (Sept. 26,1957), p. 620.

Buchler's Metaphysics

Richard J. Bernstein

In 1951, Justus Buchler published *Toward a General Theory of Human Judgment,* an essay which he declared might have been described as "a metaphysics of utterance, were it not for the mischievous associations of the former term and the narrowness of the province suggested by the latter." (TGT vii)[1] Since then, three other short books have appeared: *Nature and Judgment* (1955), *The Concept of Method* (1961), and, most recently, *Metaphysics of Natural Complexes* (1966). We are told that each of these essays can be read independently, but it is clear that each of them may also be read as a chapter within a larger structure, as stages in a single project to outline a comprehensive categorial scheme for understanding man and nature.

In attempting to understand and assess what Buchler is saying, doing, and making, we are immediately confronted with a difficult problem of locating a perspective or context for judgment. One's immediate impression of the fabric of Buchler's thought is that it is radically different in tone, method, and terminology from most of the philosophy written during the same period. Most philosophic writing during the past fifteen years has been "school philosophy." By this I mean that in the different areas of philosophy, a cluster of distinctions, problems, and strategies have come into the foreground of discussion. The philosopher who seeks to contribute to ongoing philosophic inquiry has addressed himself directly to these clusters in order to show where distinctions and problems are illuminating or misleading, or how they can be given new applications or need to be modified in some important way. The advantage of this mode of philosophizing is that there is a closely knit dialectic of refining, clarifying, and amending an inherited body of knowledge and opinion. But the danger of this approach is that the "problems" and "solutions" can become sterile.

A philosopher like Buchler who attempts to break away from "school philosophy" is taking a serious risk. With the introduction of novel terminology, categories, and distinctions, we may be left hanging in mid–air, unable or unwilling to see their relevance to what has become familiar and accepted in philosophic investigation. And yet this philosophic uneasiness may be the beginning of illumination and a fundamental questioning of pre- suppositions which are only dimly perceived and rarely criticized. Being forced to think in new ways may enable us to return to the familiar with fresh perspective and insight. In laying bare the skeleton of Buchler's com- prehensive categorial scheme I shall focus on four interrelated concepts, each of which plays a major role in one of his four books: proception, judgment, method, and natural complexes.

Proception

Proception is the first major category that Buchler introduces.[2] "The interplay of the human individual's activities and dimensions, their unitary direction, constitutes a process which I shall call *proception*." (TGT 4) The category of proception is intended to suggest a "moving union of seeking and receiving" (TGT 4), which are the essential characteristics of the human individual. The two dimensions of proception are manipulation and assimilation: each of these processes presupposes the other. Typically, Buchler stretches the meanings of these concepts so that they possess the greatest generality. Manipulation is not to be identified with adjustment, although active adjustment is one variety of manipulation. In the manipula- tive dimension, the human individual is actor and agent, and the varieties of acting, shaping, molding are indefinite. There is a corresponding gen- erality in the assimilative dimension, for while man is spectator, sufferer, and patient, assimilation does not necessarily involve conscious awareness. "We assimilate not just sensible qualities, but advancing age, changes of modes of thought, and the ethical temper of a society." (TGT 18) Anything that affects our proceptive direction can be said to be assimilated by the proceiver. Manipulation and assimilation are involved in all proception, and they are ontologically inseparable. We never manipulate without assimilat- ing, nor do we assimilate without manipulating. Man is never simply agent or patient, he is always both together.

What are we to make of the notion of proceptive *direction?* Buchler disavows two misconceptions that come to mind. Proceptive direction does not presuppose that there is an overreaching teleological order, nor does it presuppose that specific purposes inhere in all proception. "Proceptive di- rection concerns the potential course and outcome of what at any moment is the net integral effect of an individual's history." (TGT 22) "To say that an individual necessarily has a proceptive direction means, then, that certain potentialities of doing, making, and saying, and certain potential relations to other things, are excluded from his future while others are included in it, all by virtue of the cumulative power of his past in total relation to the world." (NJ 114)

Anything, or more technically, any natural complex which is present to an individual—which actually modifies or reinforces his proceptive direction—is part of his *proceptive domain*. And anything discriminated within a proceptive domain is a *procept*. Not every fact related to an individual is a procept (although it is a natural complex), for it may not be related to him *as* a proceiver. When we speak of an individual proceiving, we are using the verb intransitively, for the individual proceives nothing less than his *world;* his world is not something independent of the process of proception, it is the individual's proceptive domain. We can actually distinguish three "worlds": "the world that includes both complexes related to and complexes unrelated to a given individual; the world that includes only the complexes related to him; and the world that includes only the complexes related to him uniquely."(NJ 120) Although theoretically the first world might be identical with the second world and both are *proceivable,* the three worlds are concentrically related to one another. The first world is the entire actual and possible world: past, present and future; the second is the world without which an individual would not be; the third is the world without which an individual would not be *the* individual that he is.

Restricting ourselves to the proceptive domain, we can distinguish three perspectives. There is the *gross domain,* which comprises everything that belongs to the individual's make-up; the *floating domain,* which "represents the summed-up self or proceiver within a given situation," and the *imminent domain,* which comprises all that is present to or available to the proceiver at a given moment. Once again, these three domains are concentrically related to one another. When we add that the gross domain is a segment of the totality of natural complexes (the first world) we begin to see how Buchler locates the human individual.

But now we can ask the point of introducing this category of proception with its accompanying terminology and distinctions. We have already briefly indicated Buchler's own justification for his general procedure (see note 2). But even if we are convinced of the necessity or desirability of introducing new categories, we want to know the purpose of introducing this specific category. One answer is that Buchler shares with Whitehead the conviction that the meaning and justification of a category cannot be fully explicated and warranted in a few key definitions or propositions, but only by following how it is used with other categories in providing a comprehensive, coherent, adequate scheme for understanding and exhibiting the essential traits of man in the world.

But there is another way in which we can determine the significance of the category of proception: by comparing it with closely related philosophic concepts. From what we have said thus far, it would seem that what Buchler calls "proception" is very close to what Dewey called "experience," especially when Dewey characterized experience as an organic interaction or transaction. Buchler is not only aware of the resemblance; he discusses it in order to clarify the distinguishing features of proception. Like Dewey, Buchler is critical of the dualistic and dichotomizing tendency that has influenced so much modern thought, whether it takes the form of opposing subject and object, mental and physical, private and public, or individual and social. Not that these distinctions are intrinsically misleading or useless; but they lend themselves to abuse when philosophers reify them and divide the world into epistemological or ontological dualisms. The *roles* that these distinctions play are functional when used to discriminate aspects or phases of proception. Like Dewey, Buchler is reacting against, and critical of, the Cartesian framework of modern philosophy with its search for ultimate epistemological or ontological foundations and its excessive preoccupation with man primarily as knower and spectator. The adumbration of the category of proception can be viewed as a search for a more general perspective within which traditional distinctions are given their just due.

But although Dewey (and Peirce) persistently attacked and exposed the varieties of claims to immediate knowledge, Buchler thinks that they are tainted by the very tradition they were attacking, at least insofar as they attached special significance to "felt immediacy" or "immediate experience." "The theory of proception requires a very different approach to the issue of 'closeness' than does the pseudospatial notion of immediate experience."(TGT 24) The distinction between the immediate and the mediate is a "treacherous and deceptive one" because it suggests that "the world unjudged or merely felt and the world judged or interpreted are of disparate ontological status." (TGT 25) But nothing more nor less is "given" to the proceiver than the totality of his proceptive domain. Even when we distinguish the perspective of the "imminent domain," we are not isolating a domain that has a special "closeness" to the proceiver; it is a "slice" of the total or gross domain.

Furthermore, Buchler claims that the category of proception enables us to purify another vestige of the epistemological tradition that persists in Dewey's concept of experience. While Dewey showed us how much more there is to human experience than is found in the emasculated concept of experience of the modern epistemological tradition, Dewey "persisted in regarding 'thought' or 'reflection' as the fullest and most genuine manifestation of 'experience'." (NJ 103) But *an* experience, or more generally, any instance of proception, is neither more nor less complete, real, or genuine than any other instance. Intelligence does bring a certain moral power to experience, but intelligence is not a condition for the maximum being of the process. Buchler is here employing a principle that is fundamental for his entire metaphysical approach, one which is used in the first three books, but specified in detail only in his systematic investigation of natural complexes. It is the "principle of ontological parity," and he contrasts it with "a principle of ontological priority—which has flourished from Parmenides to Whitehead and Heidegger, and which continues to flourish in unsuspected ways." (MNC 30) According to the latter principle, some aspect or segment of reality, experience, or nature is singled out as being "more real," "more genuine," or "more authentic" than some other. But according to the principle of ontological parity, "whatever is discriminated in any way (whether it is 'encountered' or produced or otherwise related to) is a natural complex, and no complex is more 'real,' more 'natural,' more 'genuine,' or more 'ultimate,' than any other." (MNC 31) Individuals, universals, fictions, anything at all that can be discriminated are just what they are and do not have any more or less reality than anything else. Consequently, since proception is a natural complex, no type or instance of proception has any more or less reality than any other. One might think that this principle is innocuous, but it has important consequences for the theory of proception as well as for Buchler's entire metaphysical program. One of the driving thrusts of Buchler's exploration is to unmask the priorities that philosophers have assigned to types of experiences and natural complexes, and to exhibit basic similarities without smuggling in moral, epistemological, or ontological priorities. While the category of proception encompasses the "truth" ingredient in the theory of experience developed in the American naturalistic tradition, it avoids the eulogistic connotations of "experience." By introducing a new term, Buchler hopes to emphasize its neutrality and the ontological parity of all instances of proception. As we shall see, the principle also operates eminently in Buchler's theory of judgment; for all saying, doing, and making is *judging*—each of these modes of judging is just as fundamental and *irreducible* as the others.

Judgment

Whereas the introduction of the category of proception illustrates the way in which Buchler uses a new term in order to avoid misleading associations of closely related concepts, the use that Buchler makes of "judgment" shows how a traditional concept is assigned a more general meaning. Proception as a process issues in products. Although we ordinarily think of producing as an intermittent activity, there is, according to Buchler, a more fundamental sense in which we are always and continuously producing. As long as we are alive, we are always saying, doing, or making. Anything that is the result of saying, doing, or making (even if the result is not intended) is a product. A product actualizes a relation between an individual (proceiver) and natural complexes. And Buchler classifies *all* products of proception as judgments or utterances. Assertion, then, is only one species of judgment. A dance, a moral act, a work of art, anything at all that is the result of the manipulative dimension of proceiving is a judgment. This does not simply mean that whatever we do or make involves or presupposes judgments; the products *are* judgments, and the processes by which these results are achieved are modes of judging. But what does Buchler mean by judgment, and what is the point of extending this concept to cover *all* products of the individual?

Every judgment is a *pronouncement* on some phase of the individual's world. To pronounce is to apply an attitude or to bring a natural complex within the range of an attitude or perspective. "We bring things into relation to us, we render them more determinate in a given respect, by doing something to them, *or* by making something out of them, *or* by saying something about them." (NJ 13) All saying, doing, making involves selectivity or discrimination, a selectivity that at once expresses and shapes what we are. At the same time that every act of judgment is a pronouncement, it is also an *appraisal*. In all proception, there is at least a tacit appraisal of some traits as relevant and some as irrelevant. Neither pronouncing nor appraising is solely or even primarily an intellectual function of the individual. The way or style in which we do and make things (even when we are not aware of what we are doing or making) is as much a pronouncement and appraisal of natural complexes as what we say. Collectively an individual's judgments mirror what he is, although a proceiver as a center of potentialities is always more than the actual judgments he produces.

The claim that all products of proception are judgments may strike the reader as so wild that he may be perplexed why any philosopher would seriously defend it. Yet, I think we can appreciate Buchler's contention if we reflect upon the history of the phenomenological movement. For in this tradition, especially in Hegel himself, we can see a perspective developed in which man's products are not simply viewed as objects external to him, but as the direct expression, the objectification of what he is. Just as Hegel would maintain that an individual is and is not the totality of his objectifications (judgments), so Buchler claims that although the totality of an individual's judgments mirror the self, they do not exhaust the powers and potentialities of the individual. Buchler humanizes and naturalizes this phenomenological insight, and he strips it of its intellectual pretensions. For, according to Buchler, although Hegel shows us that all human products can by understood as human judgments (although strictly speaking for Hegel they are objectifications of *Geist*), Hegel's paradigm of judgment is conscious assertion, whereas for Buchler assertion is only one species of judgment. Here too the principle of ontological parity is at work, for there is no ontological hierarchy of saying, doing, and making.

Buchler classifies judgments according to the three modes of human production: judgments are active, exhibitive, or assertive. These distinctions are functional rather than structural. Whether a product is interpreted as an assertion, exhibition, or action depends on the context in which it is uttered, not on any intrinsic properties of the utterance. Normally we use words to make assertions, but we can make assertions without using words when, for example, we make a significant gesture such as a nod of approval. Although a poem consists of words, its primary function may be to make an exhibitive judgment rather than to assert something. We might not normally think of our actions as making exhibitive judgments, but the total effect of a dance can be exhibitive.

Although the distinction between active, exhibitive, and assertive judgments is not clear and distinct, and any particular utterance may function in all three ways, we can make a rough differentiation. Assertive judgments include all those products where we can ask, is it true or false? (or apply related epistemic concepts such as "probable" or "necessary"). "Exhibitive judgments include all products which result from the shaping and arranging of materials. . . . Active judgments comprise all instances of conduct to which the terms 'act' or 'action' are ordinarily applied." (TGT 48) Nor is it the case that only one variety of judgments—assertions—are cognitive or have meaning. Every judgment is open to interpretation and can communicate to another proceiver. Meaning is not restricted to assertions; we can legitimately ask for the meaning of active and exhibitive judgments.

Furthermore, a judgment is not a discrete event independent and separable from everything else. Every judgment reflects something more than itself "by virtue of which indeed it is the judgment that it is and has the meaning or communicative effect that it has." (TGT 113) Every judgment is uttered within a larger framework, point of view, or *perspective*. The properties attributed to a judgment belong to it by virtue of some perspective. A system of mathematics, a social code, an artistic style may all serve as perspectives within which individual judgments are uttered. Perspectives can be shared by different proceivers (although not all perspectives are sharable), and it is because perspectives are sharable that there can be communication by the various types of judgment. Not only can perspectives be shared; they can be adopted, modified, or abandoned. And a particular utterance can function within different perspectives. However, as human proceivers we never escape from making judgments within *some* perspective, no matter how precise or vague it may be.

We can now understand how these reflections on the nature of judgment dovetail with the analysis of proception. Buchler joins many contemporary thinkers in criticizing the philosophic distortion of man as primarily a knower or sayer. We are still feeling the effects today of the philosophic rebellion against this view of man. But when philosophers rebel, there is a tendency to move to dialectical extremes. The result has been a variety of "philosophies of action" and "philosophies of immediacy" which have proliferated in reaction to more traditional "philosophies of knowledge." All of these philosophies, with their special emphases, are guilty of the same mistaken principle of ontological priority whereby one dimension of human existence is seized upon and assigned a special status. But whether we are acting, making, or doing we are engaged in distinctively human processes, and whereas, for specific purposes in specific contexts, one of these modes may be more important than the others, from the perspective of a metaphysics of human utterance, all are equally basic and irreducible. Furthermore, as judgments, all three modes share generic features.

Perhaps the most interesting consequence of Buchler's theory of judgment is its significance for understanding the nature of philosophy (and especially Buchler's own). Philosophy uses both assertive and exhibitive judgments, and as an activity it is a form of active judgment. To appreciate the nature of philosophy we must understand all three of its functions.

Philosophy shares features with both science and art. Like art, it constructs, it shapes by bringing "together a number of categories and develops them by analogy and metaphor and definition." (TGT 122) But while philosophy has an important exhibitive function, it is not a "free creation." Philosophy constructs and is at the same time a commentary on its construction: "it examines alternatives, excludes supposed implications, and justifies the categorial configurations in terms that do not make use of the categories." (TGT 122) However, we must not think of philosophy as consisting of two parts, but rather as a single judgment-complex. Philosophy both *says* and *shows;* it asserts and exhibits. This emphasis on the mutual reinforcement of assertion and exhibition provides an orientation for understanding what Buchler himself is doing. His investigations do not take a direct argumentative form in which key premises are made explicit and inferences drawn from them. By the use of metaphor, analogy, definition, comparison, commentary, and argument, he weaves an elaborate tapestry of interconnecting categories which is intended as a general interpretive scheme for revealing basic similarities and differences among natural complexes. Buchler's emphasis on the exhibitive or "showing" function of philosophy has direct consequences for the evaluation of a philosophic perspective. Such a perspective is developed as one which is to be shared and criticized, which is offered to compel assent. This assent is not simply a matter of accepting assertions as true; indeed "the minimal requirement of achievement in philosophy is that it compel imaginative assent and arouse the sense of encompassment even where it fails of cognitive acceptance." (TGT 134)

While philosophy consists of the interplay of assertive and exhibitive judgments, as a form of query—"the interrogative spirit methodically directed"—it is an activity:

> Art, science, and philosophy are (at least) protracted action, and they each subdivide into habits and techniques of action. Action as such, it is commonly believed, does not question; it simply occurs and exists. But this is an error. We question as much by our actions as by our words. . . . What we do in a given instance may challenge the stability or value of our present situation, suspend an aspiration, create a pair of alternatives for someone else, impose demands and conditions—and in general, by active commentary on present existence, complicate the future course of utterance in any mode. We are never, to be sure, actors purely and simply; but then, neither are we ever discoursers or contrivers purely and simply. (NJ 63)

Philosophy is composed of assertive, exhibitive, and active judgments; each of these three modes is equally integral to philosophy. The exhibitive and active functions of philosophy are not secondary or accidental features.

An important distinction has been lurking in our discussion. According to Buchler, any product of a proceiver is a judgment, whether it is the result of design or purpose or is an "accidental" by-product. Throwing a piece of paper in a waste basket is no more or less a judgment than designing a complicated experiment. Idle doodling is a judgment, as is the creation of a masterpiece. Uttering nonsense syllables is a judgment, just as much as working out an elegant mathematical proof. All these instances of production are instances of judgment, but some are pursued methodically while others are not. We must be careful here, for many types of activity, whether doodling, uttering nonsense syllables, or throwing away scraps of paper, *can* be performed methodically. But to advance our understanding of the metaphysics of utterance, we must explore the concept of method and its correlative concept, query.

Method

The best succinct statement of what Buchler means by "methodic" and "query" is given in a footnote to *Metaphysics of Natural Complexes:*

> Methodic activity is the purposive ramification of judgment in any of its modes—assertive, active, exhibitive. When methodic activity is

informed by the interrogative spirit, by invention and probing, it constitutes *query*. Query is the genus of which inquiry or science is one species—the species concerned with the ramification and validation of assertive judgment. (MNC 187)

Just as the concept of judgment is generalized to encompass doing and making, so also are the corresponding concepts of method and query. But it is easy to miss the point of what Buchler is claiming. He is not claiming that inquiry (which is concerned with the ramification and validation of *assertive* judgments) is necessarily involved in all doing and making, but rather that there are forms of method and query distinctively appropriate to our doing and making. When an artist selects and arranges his material, he can do this purposively and thereby ramify his exhibitive judgments. The process of artistic creation can be informed by probing and invention, so that it becomes a form of query. So too with our active judgments. A good mechanic will tinker with an engine methodically in order to locate a source of trouble; his activity is methodical and is informed by the "interrogative spirit."

"A method is a power of manipulating natural complexes, purposively and recognizably, within a reproducible order of utterance: and methodic activity is the translation of such a power into the pursuit of an end—an end implied by the reproduction." (CM 135) Method does not simply arise from need, it arises as much from "zest and even prodigality." Men deliberately attempt to limit their world in some respects and to make it more abundant in others; method arises from the basic ability to control and direct the world within which the proceiver finds himself. Thus the basic concept for understanding method is that of *power*, for method is a human power.

Echoing the Lockean notion of power, which he seeks to revive as a legitimate and essential philosophic concept, Buchler tells us that "[a] power may be described as a possibility that has been actualized in some degree and can be recognized as generic in the next instance of actualization."(CM 100)[3] This concept of method as a power has close affinities with Peirce's concept of thirdness, especially when Peirce emphasizes that although a third is manifested in particular and discrete acts, a third is never exhausted in any of its manifestations. Method as a power cannot be reduced to a prior body of rules or instruments, for these "do not motivate and direct themselves."(CM 100) And although method is a human power, it does not reside solely in agents, "but in a natural complex that embraces agents and other component complexes."(CM 101)

Although method is essentially purposive, the goal to be achieved can have almost any degree of specificity or indefiniteness. We must be careful

not to smuggle in any eulogistic or moralistic overtones in this general account of method, for the varieties of method are indefinite: There can be
methods for suppressing knowledge as well as methods for achieving
knowledge, methods for destroying life as well as for saving it, methods for
stifling creativity as well as methods for fostering it. Furthermore, methods
can be routine, habitual, and arbitrary. If I select a group of people from a
class by picking all those whose last names begin with ''B'', I am perform-
ing a methodic activity, but there is nothing inventive or novel about it.
Method becomes inventive only when it becomes query. In query there is
indefinitely *continuing* ramification. ''The primary effort of method is repeatedly to complete its instances; of query, to deepen each instance.
Method without query can destroy mankind and its own laborious progeny.
Method informed by query is the essential expression of reason. Reason is
query aiming to grow and flourish forever.'' (CM 114)

If we take this last suggestion seriously, as Buchler certainly wants us
to take it, then a life of reason can be expressed in what we do and make as
well as in what we say. Once again the dominant thrust of Buchler's philosophy is evident. Throughout the exploration of the concepts of judgment,
method, and query, he has attempted to show the relevance of these concepts to our saying, doing, making. And he has challenged any claim to
assign one of these modes of judgment greater significance than the other
two. Man as a unitary rational being can live a life of reason by cultivating
query in all its modes.

Buchler's first three books develop a comprehensive picture of man as
an individual and in community. He presents us with a judgment-complex
which is both assertive and exhibitive, one which builds upon and modifies
the naturalistic tradition in American thought as exemplified in Peirce,
James, Santayana, Mead, Dewey, and Whitehead. Man as a proceiver
is understood as a creature who is continuously assimilating and manipulating. He interacts with the world as doer, sayer, and maker. Buchler emphasizes over and over again that these three modes of producing are equally
basic for a metaphysical understanding of man. And he attempts to elaborate a categorial scheme that both captures and underscores this essential
understanding. In classifying all human products as judgments, Buchler
wants to show that in everything man produces he is making a pronouncement and assessment of natural complexes whereby the human self is
expressed and shaped. We are what we do, say, and make. At the same
time, he seeks to restore the applicability of the concept of human power
which is never exhausted in any set of actual judgments. Furthermore, when
man becomes self-conscious of his capacity to manipulate, he can act
methodically and, consequently, purposively ramify his judgments. He can
do this with imagination and invention; he can inform his producing with

the "interrogative spirit." And the new perspective that emerges enables us to assign a new meaning to man as a rational creature. In a spirit reminiscent of the Platonic conception of *eros,* Buchler tells us that "[r]eason is a form of love. . . . It is love of inventive communication. Nothing is more foundational for all value than query, and reason is devotion to query." (TGT 168)

Natural Complexes

If Buchler had ended his inquiry after his first three books, his project of sketching a comprehensive metaphysical scheme would have been radically incomplete. The dominant emphasis in these three books is on the human individual, his role in community and his interactions in the world. Yet in the opening pages of Buchler's first book, in the definition of proception, Buchler introduces the concept of natural complexes. Although this concept plays an important role in his first three studies, it is only in his most recent book that Buchler turns his attention to an explicit analysis. The movement of his speculation is from a metaphysics of human utterance or judgment, to a more general metaphysics of natural complexes. The analysis he offers is at once more general, more abstract, and more argumentative than that found in the preceding books:

> Whatever is, in whatever way, is a natural complex. . . . Relations, structures, processes, societies, human individuals, human products, physical bodies, words and bodies of discourse, ideas, qualities, contradictions, meanings, possibilities, myths, laws, duties, feelings, illusions, reasonings, dreams—all are natural complexes. All of these terms bespeak discriminations of some kind, and whatever is discriminated in any respect or in any degree is a natural complex (for short "complex"). (MNC 1)

"Natural complex" is Buchler's most general and abstract metaphysical category; it designates everything that is, in whatever way. And this includes not just actualities, but possibilities, and even contradictions. In defending the employment of this new category, Buchler argues that none of the competing traditional terms, such as "existence", "being", "reality", "entity", have the scope and integrity of the generic term, "natural complex."

What then are the characteristics of "natural complexes?" Everything that is or can be discriminated (we do not know if all natural complexes are humanly discriminable) is a complex. There are no basic, pure, atomic simples. Every natural complex is related to other complexes and is located in some order; it affects and is affected by other complexes. This is not a doctrine of internal relations. For although every natural complex is related to other natural complexes, it does not follow that every natural complex is related to *every* other natural complex. The contrast of "simples" and "complexes" *can* have a use within some perspective or order, but the notion of absolute ontological simples is a myth paralleled by the epistemological myth of the pure given. This entails that every natural complex has subaltern complexes and is subaltern to some other complexes. And although these subaltern complexes or "traits" are further discriminations within a complex, Buchler rejects traditional notions for understanding this relation of complexes and subaltern complexes. They are not "contained" as a box contains things or as a substance has attributes or as a cluster consists of discrete traits. As Buchler himself notes, his formulations can be viewed as a "generalization and neutralization of the maxim of Anaxagoras, 'Neither is there a least of what is small, but there is always a less. . . . But there is always a greater than what is great'." (MNC 14)

There are two important consequences of this theory of natural complexes. First, it is a doctrine of pluralism and openness. Everything is a natural complex; there is no single "stuff" to which these can all be reduced. Natural complexes are in different irreducible orders. Secondly, this metaphysical doctrine is closely related to Buchler's conception of query. For although a particular query has beginning points and terminal points, there are no absolute beginnings or endings of query in any of its modes. There are no ultimate foundations, and no ultimate terminus to query. Such notions as *complete* description, explanation, or analysis turn out to be vacuous. At best there can be completeness of query only within a limited and well-defined order or perspective. This conviction about the *essential* inexhaustibleness of complexes and query (which is also a natural complex) has self-referential consequences for Buchler's own philosophic method. For his investigations constantly exhibit the sense of man *in medias res* involved in a configuration of natural complexes.

The use of the term "natural" in natural complex is more difficult to pin down. We are told that "natural" is not set up to be contrasted with nonnatural, or supernatural, but it is not entirely clear what the positive meaning of natural is in this context. Natural complex is used to designate "all discriminanda generically." (MNC 2) Consequently, even the concept of God, *if* it is thought of as a metaphysically viable concept, signifies a natural complex. The proper question about anything that we discriminate is *not* whether it is or is not a natural complex, but rather what kind of complex it is, what are its generic and specific features.

Every natural complex has *integrity, scope,* and *contour.* "[A]ny complex has just the status, just the relations, just the constitution that it has."

(MNC 21-22) This *is* its *integrity,* and integrity entails both uniqueness and commonness. The *scope* of a complex has various forms, including comprehensiveness, pervasiveness, and inclusiveness. And the *contour* of a natural complex is "the continuity and totality of its locations, the interrelation of its integrities."(MNC 22)

Every natural complex is characterized by its *prevalence* and *alescence.* Buchler, more stridently than in his other books, argues that traditional metaphysical distinctions are inadequate for describing the generic features of natural complexes, and he boldly introduces a new and strange terminology. The minimal sense of claiming that every natural complex *prevails* is that every complex obtains, it has "an inviolability merely as such." (MNC 53) Furthermore, in saying that every natural complex prevails "we are implying that it is ineluctable; that it has a sphere of primacy and domination; that it is restrictive and exclusive of other complexes." (MNC 53) Every natural complex is prevalent *in some respect;* it is also not prevalent in certain respects and orders. Every complex then is not only prevalent; it is also *alescent.* This term is suggested by the Latin *alescere* and is introduced to suggest "coming about," or "taking place." Alescence can also take the form of deviation or variation. A complex "is prevalent in so far as it excludes traits from its contour. A complex is alescent in so far as it admits traits into its contour." (MNC 56) Although the terminology is new, we might think that Buchler is merely rebaptizing old distinctions. But he explicitly discusses a number of these distinctions, including "permanence and change;" "being and becoming;" "regularity and irregularity;" "determinateness and indeterminateness;" "the intelligible and the unintelligible" in order to show that none of these correspond to the distinction of "prevalence and alescence."

The most interesting and forceful use of these highly abstract metaphysical concepts occurs in Buchler's discussion of possibility and actuality. For even if we are not completely satisfied with Buchler's positive doctrine, he raises challenging criticisms of many contemporary and traditional accounts of possibility and actuality. It should be clear that both actualities and potentialities are natural complexes. Consequently, both possibilities and actualities exhibit prevalence and alescence. As natural complexes they are necessarily related to other complexes; there are no "pure" possibilities, just as there are no "pure" actualities. Possibilities are always possibilities *of* and *for* natural complexes.

Just as actualities cannot be conceived apart from their relation to possibilities, so too possibilities cannot be conceived without relation to actualities. "A possibility cannot be said to prevail or to arise if it is unrelated to any actualities, nor can an actuality be said to prevail or arise if it is unrelated to any possibility." (MNC 133) Buchler attempts to show that many of the traditional ways of distinguishing actualities from possibilities fail. Thus the contrast of the physical and the nonphysical won't do, for there are actualities like "aims, thoughts, or poems" (MNC 143) which are not exclusively physical, but are actualities. Nor can we distinguish actualities by saying that they "come to pass," for "tonal relations, physical ratios, and space, which have not come to pass . . . are as actual as physical bodies and wars are." (MNC 144) Nor is it the case that only actualities are encountered, for we encounter possibilities. "When our friend lies gravely ill, we encounter the possibility of death. . . . Possibilities may have an impact, even as actualities may, and it may be a dull or vivid impact." (MNC 145) And it turns out that both possibilities and actualities can be efficacious. But then how are we to distinguish them?

> Consider two contradictory traits. They are sometimes both found to prevail as possibilities in one and the same order of complexes. They are never both found to prevail as actualities in one and the same order. A given tree will possibly grow to 100 feet and possibly not grow to 100 feet. It never will actually grow to 100 feet and actually not grow to 100 feet. The principal consideration with respect to actuality is that if mutually contradictory complexes are actual, they never prevail in the same order; if mutually contradictory complexes prevail in the same order they are not actualities. (MNC 156)

The basis then for distinguishing actualities from possibilities pivots on the way in which each of these are exclusive and restrictive. Whereas all prevalences restrict and exclude, actualities do this in a different way than possibilities, for mutually contradictory actualities *cannot* prevail in the same order, while "[c]ontradictory traits *may* prevail as possibilities in the sense that both are actualiz*able*, both are eligible for actualization, given certain conditions that obtain." (MNC 157)

Buchler's treatment of possibility and actuality illustrates a facet of his thought which we mentioned earlier. For throughout, he is attempting to break away from many of the biases and unquestioned presuppositions that have conditioned so much of the discussion of issues. There is a tendency, especially in contemporary philosophy, to think of possibilities on the model of discrete "entities" or "things" that are like discrete actual things, except that they don't exist. We then debate whether we are or are not to "countenance" such entities in our ontology. When the issue is formulated in this way, all kinds of queer questions arise concerning such possibilities. Where are they? Do they come into being? and pass away? Understandably, philosophers who think that the paradigm of a "real" entity is a concrete physical thing are loath to count such ethereal entities as part of their ontology. But, as Peirce remarked long ago, such a way of viewing the issue reflects deeply ingrained nominalistic prejudices. For whether we decide to accept or not accept such "entities," we are thinking of them as sharp-edge, discrete "things." Buchler's point is that this approach is not only unsatisfactory for formulating issues concerning the nature of possibilities, it is unsatisfactory for understanding the characteristics of actualities as well. He is challenging this entire "thing" framework and attempting to show us a more illuminating way of understanding the intimate interrelationships of actualities and possibilities, which escapes the strained discussion of what kind of queer "entities" possibilities are.

Queries

Earlier we raised the question of the proper context for understanding and assessing Buchler's philosophy. I believe that we can now answer that question. For Buchler's metaphysics is best understood against the background of the American naturalistic tradition. Although his metaphysics echoes many of the themes developed by Peirce, James, Santayana, Dewey, and Whitehead, he is also sharply critical of these philosophers on specific points. Nevertheless, he shares the same metaphysical temper in his attempt to elaborate a comprehensive perspective for understanding nature and man as an integral part of nature. The pluralism, the essential inexhaustibility of nature, the anti-Cartesianism, the suspicion of any philosophic appeal to epistemological "givens" or ontological "simples," the ongoing, self-corrective, and ramifying nature of query, the philosophic sensitivity to man as doer and maker as well as "knower" are incorporated and explored in his metaphysics. Furthermore, many of the most lasting insights that have resulted from the more fashionable analytic and phenomenological movements are encompassed in his total perspective. Philosophers fascinated by new phenomenological investigations of experience frequently fall into the trap of thinking that the only alternatives to the phenomenological concept of experience are those of traditional empiricists and rationalists. They fail to realize that there has been a persistent attempt, from Peirce to Buchler, to develop a more adequate theory of experience which shares many of the important characteristics of the phenomenological "field" and "world" and yet views experience as continuous with and encompassed by the rest of nature. Or consider some of the recent developments in analytic philosophy, such as the attack on the myth of the given, the exposé of the foundation metaphor, the probing critique of concepts of pure description and neutral observation. All of these themes have been developed by the "classical" American philosophers and have been explored by Buchler in novel ways.

There is also an important point of contact with the recent emerging "philosophy of mind." Negatively, much of the enthusiasm for this "new" field has developed from the increasing realization of the inadequacies of traditional empiricism and reductive behavioristic approaches. Positively, there has been increasing sensitivity to the distinctive nature of human activity and the change of philosophic perspective that takes place when we view man as an *agent*. Here too, one will find these themes developed by Buchler, especially in his appreciation of the manipulative dimension of proception and its consequences for man as doer and maker. But although these remarks may help to clarify the context for appreciating Buchler's metaphysical investigations, there remains the complex task of assessing Buchler's distinctive contribution.

First there are internal questions to be raised. Despite Buchler's attempt to develop a comprehensive interpretative scheme, it is disturbing to realize how many basic issues still remain to be confronted. Fundamental to Buchler's thought is the claim that human agents are causally efficacious, but there is no sustained and detailed analysis of the meaning and role of causation (although there is an illuminating discussion of the closely related concepts of power and potentiality). And I doubt if Buchler's brief discussion of God will satisfy the most sympathetic reader. We may well agree that "[t]he critical question must be, not whether God exists, nor whether there is an 'entity' which satisfies the scheme of traits by which the concept of God is perpetuated, but in what way a natural complex thus discriminated is to be understood, analyzed,and experientially cncompassed; or, in what way it is to be further discriminated and found related." (MNC 8) But if this is the critical question, the answer is not to be found in Buchler's four books. Again, one finds a detailed discussion of actuality and possibility, but the concept of necessity is barely discussed. Or, consider the long metaphysical tradition of disputes about nominalism and realism. Here Buchler incisively comments on the confusions that have pervaded the discussion. And he carefully notes the misleading analogies that obscure our understanding of "traits or subaltern complexes" as "constituents" of a complex. But if we try to pin down the precise sense (senses) in which a trait is a constituent of a complex, the concept turns out to be elusive. Further, although Buchler is skeptical of the Whiteheadian view that "every actual entity [or individual] is present in every other actual entity" and claims that we must avoid the two extreme positions: "That of anthropomorphism, by limiting 'experience' to human individuals; and that of the doctrine of internal relations, by not merely admitting degrees of relevance . . . but so couching the conception of experience as to recognize a meaning for irrelevance," (NJ 106-107) the precise metaphysical relations between human individuals and other individuals—the toughest problem for any viable naturalism—is not precisely specified. Perhaps these and related issues will be explored in greater detail in future studies, but they suggest "external" questions about the verification or validation of Buchler's metaphysical scheme.

In the preface to his first book (of this series), Buchler boldly stated the goal of a philosophic theory and the conditions for its acceptability:

> Every theory aims, in the last analysis, to exhibit a structure among data ordinarily regarded as disparate: by the use of a relatively small number of categories a scheme is devised which requires to be self-consistent and consistent with other schemes that have come to be thought part of the fabric of knowledge. The burden a philosophic theory in particular bears is likely to be great; for beyond these primal requirements it dedicates itself to the difficult union of a high level of generality with interpretative justice. In the case of such a theory the circumstances of verification are usually very complex, and *the acceptability of the result depends ultimately, perhaps, upon the presence of a sense of philosophic satisfaction in the reader, who is both spectator and participant.* (TGT xi; italics added)

It would be a radical perversion of these claims to think that Buchler is saying that ultimately the acceptability of a philosophic scheme is merely a matter of taste. For the philosopher, like any individual, is not entitled to whatever he utters. "He must substantiate; he must validate or render secure the products that emanate from his own perspectives." (TGT 160) And such validation requires constant critical query. But it is just here that *this* reader remains unsatisfied. This is not to deny (as I have tried to show) that Buchler's investigations are rich in insight, challenges, new perspectives, and forceful arguments. But at times the level of analysis is so abstract and so condensed that there is no sense of compulsion for accepting just *this* categorial scheme. In part, this is because Buchler has tried to cover so much ground in what is, comparatively speaking, a very short space. And, in part, this is perhaps the consequence of attempting to delineate new categories and stretch the meaning of familiar concepts. But the gap between the familiar and the unfamiliar is frequently too great to warrant philosophic satisfaction. Buchler is most forceful when he descends to more familiar philosophic problems and distinctions and carefully tries to show us in detail what is muddled and inadequate about these, and then proceeds to show us why his analysis is superior. (Cf. his discussion of "basic judgments" TGT 81 ff.) But such a detailed critique of alternative philosophic doctrines is all too rare. One hopes that, in future studies, Buchler will not only fill in the gaps in his categorial scheme, but will pursue the careful dialectical treatment of more familiar problems, solutions, and distinctions which will produce in the reader that philosophic compulsion which Buchler's total philosophic perspective demands.

Notes

1. See "List of Abbreviations" for Buchler's works, p. xiii–xiv.

2. Buchler justifies the introduction of new categories and the expansion of the meaning of traditional terminology as follows: "The philosopher must either coin new terms, or stretch the 'meaning' of terms in current usage, or combine existing terms in unfamiliar ways. Each of these procedures has its pitfalls and excesses. But there are no other alternatives short of utter vacuity. The problem is to determine the optimum uses and the apt occasions of each procedure. The philosopher estimates the linguistic technique which will convey his concepts without sacrifice of their substance. . . . The responsible introduction or extension of terms, whether in philosophy or science, reflects a conceptual need and serves a conceptual purpose. . . . The unfamiliar philosophic category that has justified itself to its user must counter one resistance by another—the inertia of easy usage by the resistance to oversimplification. The growth of nomenclature, provided that it issues from the urgency of query, is a positive good, not a necessary evil." (NJ 108-109)

3. This quotation reflects Buchler's emendation to his original formulation made in the 1968 second printing of CM. Bernstein, writing in 1967, quoted the earlier formulation: "[a] power may be described as a possibility that has been realized at least once and that can be recognized as generic in the next instance of realization." (CM 100) [Eds.]

Nature, Power and Prospect: Justus Buchler's System of Philosophy

Sidney Gelber and *Kathleen Wallace*

I

The work of Justus Buchler is systematic philosophy akin to that of Aristotle, Spinoza, Whitehead, and Hegel. By systematic we mean not that some traditional set of problems has been covered, but rather that the philosophical product is the deliberate and methodic interrelation of its constituents, *viz.,* its concepts, categories, and principles in a structure which supports broad inferences and extensions or applications of the conceptual scheme. Note that this means that no system is complete or exhaustive. No set of categories or systematic project is without further ramification. Therefore, the achievement of "system," while finished by its author, docs not mean the end of philosophy. A system is, in a sense, a beginning of beginnings.

We want to emphasize that systematic philosophy constructs categories to articulate its subject matter. Categories are not necessarily "transcendental abstractions" which distort or make impossible "lived experience" intelligible. No description can be pure; categorial description can be as valid, in the relevant respect(s), as any other. Assumptions in philosophy are not mere preferences, but commitments which are worked out in and through categorial development. Systematic philosophy is defined not so much by the scope of its subject matter or by any one kind of system, as by the deliberate achievement of a conceptual array within which themes and categories recur and facilitate theoretical development and ramification. Thus, it is not necessary to think of systematic philosophy as synonymous with or as necessarily based on an ontology. Husserl, for example, is as systematic in his "theory" of consciousness as Aristotle is in his metaphysics of being.

Systematic principles or concepts are "foundational," that is, when explicitly formulated by a categorial structure, they can become an explicit basis for or, better, a framework of further categorizing. The interpretive scope of a categorial structure is determined in part by its subject matter. A general ontology is wider in scope than a more specific theory.

But to say that a more general categorial structure *frames* a less general or more specific one does not mean that from generality as such we can deduce or derive what would be specifically apt. Rather, the more general principle or structure *frames* in the sense that it provides possibilities of interpretation; it involves a commitment to what it entails. Spinoza's commitment to what is entailed by his definitions and axioms is vividly shown by his methodic scheme. Aristotle cannot assert something of the soul (*psyche*) or employ special systematic principles which would entail consequences contrary to his more general ontological principles. The priority Aristotle assigns to substance (*ousia*) is a recurrent—systematic—commitment exemplified in certain kinds of characteristic inferences which are tolerated and compelled by the system. Hegel's dialectic—the movement of the concept—is a pervasive, systematic theme which resonates through his analysis of any subject matter. Given his commitment to what Whitehead calls the reformed subjectivist principle, any being (actual entity) *is* becoming, that is, the becoming of experience. In Buchler's system, a principle of ontological parity is a commitment which pervades the analyses in both the general ontology and the more specific metaphysics of what Buchler calls human utterance.[1] For Buchler, that no one of the three modes of human judgment is any more of a judgment than any other is also an exemplification of the more general principle of ontological parity.

The implications of this view of "foundational" for Buchler's philosophical method are revealing, especially if we contrast it with Spinoza's explicit methodological principle. What Spinoza means by foundation is a *necessary* starting point: definitions are foundations for axioms, axioms for theorems, and so on. While Spinoza does not necessarily reveal what his aims and strategy are, his highly formalized method is supposed not only to guide but to show that the inferential consequences are also necessary, given the necessary first starting point.

In light of the fact that he wrote an entire book devoted to the concept of method, the reader may be initially puzzled that, unlike either Spinoza or Whitehead, Buchler does not explicitly or formally specify methodological principles at the outset of any of his works. As exasperating as this may sometimes seem, Buchler's method of "plunging in" is part of a deliberate systematic strategy. Buchler's starting points are not necessary in Spinoza's sense, but neither are they arbitrary. Rather, they are starting points because they are conducive to the growth of systematic aims and goals. A starting point is congenial as a beginning, but it cannot prescribe all that is to follow. What is "foundational" is what is categorially wrought, not the raw materials.

Philosophical query[2] does not require a *necessary* first starting point itself either indubitable or axiomatic. A philosopher starts with what is compelling; what is categorially "foundational" is wrought by and furthers query. Systematic philosophy is not just a set of assertions or claims, but is exhibitive as well as assertive. It is a pattern of concepts and interrelated themes which unfolds much as a Bach fugue does. The product *is* the unfolding and is of indefinite richness in variation and applicability. In this respect, Buchler is an admirer of Plato as the exemplar of philosophical query:

> The Socratic method is indeed a *method*, the very antithesis of timorous caution. Its boldness of movement can never be clear to those who think of the Platonic dialogues as a mass of astute but noncommittal propositions. For it renders its products not by simple affirmation but assertively, exhibitively, and actively, in subtle proportions. It is in a sense the paragon of query, being masterful in all the modes of judgment. (NJ 77)

Instead of interweaving characters as well as ideas, Buchler's drama is mainly one of ideas. Ideas, themes, principles are introduced, developed; they recede into the wings only to reemerge in another context, from another angle. Buchler, like Plato, does not *explain* that this is what he is doing or why, because he holds the view that the work speaks for itself; that it is the product, not the author, which determines meaning. If the chance intersections of history are favorable, it is through one's product(s) that immortality is achieved.

Once we have noted the systematic character of Buchler's method of "plunging in," we see that his foundational principles are clearly earmarked and defined. Buchler's work consists of a general ontology (a metaphysics of being), a metaphysics of human utterance (a theory of human being *qua* human) and a theory of poetry. The most general or "foundational" principles which pervade all of his work are, as one might expect, found most perspicuously in the general ontology. It should be noted, although we will not treat it in this essay, that poetry is singled out by Buchler because he regards it as a humanly fundamental mode of articulation. Poetry's unique ability to penetrate and portray the prevalences of the world[3] without making assertive claims of truth or falsity gives poetry a power of expression unmatched certainly by any other linguistic mode of utterance.

There are at least three "foundational" or systematic commitments throughout Buchler's work. While "naturalism" is not a term used explicitly by Buchler, it prefigures an idea which is basic to his work. Naturalism is a commitment to the view that there is no being or reality which is wholly different from and discontinuous with any other being. In rejecting the notion of "the supernatural" as meaning that which "in itself" is wholly prior to or other in being than "the natural," a naturalistic view does not necessarily deny that there is a being such as God, but only that way of categorizing such a being. Buchler transforms this somewhat negative formulation of naturalism into a positive ontological principle— namely, the principle of ontological parity. Ontological parity is not only a rejection of the notion of wholly discontinuous realms or kinds of being— some more real than others; it is a commitment to the equal reality of all beings. There are no degrees of reality or being (even though there are many degrees of other kinds). Thus God, in whatever its supremacy may consist, is not more real, is not more of a being, than anything else.

A second ontological principle in Buchler's work is the principle of ordinality, that is, that every being is both determinate and indeterminate, and therefore that every being is complex. There are no ontological simples. Because any being is determinately and indeterminately complex, it is, in principle, accessible or related to some other beings, which may include human beings. In using the term "natural complex" rather than "being" as the generic term of identification, Buchler is exhibiting the pervasiveness of these two principles. Any [natural] complex is an order and any order is a complex.

The first two principles are explicitly articulated by Buchler. We would identify a third, what we call a systematic commitment to a principle of commensurateness. Beings are determinate, but they are *specifically* determinate. Commensurateness provides for what Buchler calls the [gross] integrity of a complex. While any complex is plurally located, it is not plurality without limit (even if its limits are indefinite, revisable, or difficult to define). What is actual of, or possible for a complex is determined by the complex, by its relations. There are, therefore, no "pure possibilities" nor "pure actualities." Every being, possibility or actuality, is relative to some other being, is conditioned by and conditions other beings. A complex is delimited from other complexes by the commensurateness of its constituents. Even if not every trait of a complex is related to every other trait, it must be related to at least some other trait and between those which are unrelated there must be mediating traits which mark the commensurability of these as the constituents of *this* complex or order.[4]

A principle of commensurateness also means that there is no single form of determination (or of being) for all beings. To say with Buchler that all beings are natural complexes (complexes, for short) is not to ascribe some generic or universal form of determinateness to them, but is rather to affirm that the conditions of being at all are ordinal. Whatever those conditions are, none has more (or less) being (or is more or less real) than any other. Let us examine how these principles resonate in the work.

Buchler says at the beginning of *Toward A General Theory of Human Judgment* that his work is a "metaphysics of utterance." This is a potentially misleading statement—for his metaphysics of human-self-in-process encompasses more than even what Buchler means by utterance (or judgment). Furthermore, it would be misleading if the reader takes him to be characterizing his work as a whole, including the general ontology. Even in *Toward A General Theory of Human Judgment* and *Nature and Judgment,* the metaphysics of utterance is transcended by more general principles. It is located in an implicit broader theoretical structure with which the more specific structure resonates, but which is not derived from the specific principles of the theory of human nature (or process). Indeed, it is Buchler's contention that in order to adequately develop a just theory of human life, one must be aware that the human is always located in some natural and social framework which transcends any one individual or group. (This is an embodiment of the principles of both ordinality and commensurateness.) Similarly, the theory of human judgment is not merely a specification or instantiation of the more general theory. A more specific theory has its own independence and integrity; it is not a mere appendage of or auxiliary to something more encompassing, but has its specific determinations and scope which are defined by its subject matter and not exclusively by a prior theory. They are distinct but related.[5] For example, that a moral ideal is ontologically or generically a possibility would not mean that its character (integrity) as ideal is derivable from or reducible to the meaning of possibility. The *kind* of possibility an ideal is is determined by specific relations, such as human need, striving, and anticipated conditions for betterment or perfection.

We will focus initially on the systematic structure of *Metaphysics of Natural Complexes* where the general foundational principles are most explicitly articulated. A systematic trend or principle is articulated through a categorial structure, a pattern of interrelated ideas and concepts. From the principle of ontological parity are developed what we will call the categories of "being," *viz.,* prevalence and alescence. Corresponding to the principle of ordinality are the categories of determinateness, *viz.,* ordinality and relation (with the subaltern categories of strong and weak relevance). Finally, the principle of commensurateness is most obvious in what we will call the categories of natural definition, *viz.,* actuality and possibility.

Of course, in a certain sense each category helps to articulate the system as a whole. Hence, none is defined exclusively in terms of any one trend, even if one trend is more emphatically relevant than another. Furthermore, we note that the categories are developed by Buchler in the order we have indicated and that the sequence is crucial. For example, prevalence and alescence are indispensable to the formulation of possibility and actuality while the reverse is not the case. In addition, as we have already indicated, "natural complex" is the term of universal identification and hence is precategorial. Buchler also introduces a group of intermediary categories of identification by means of which the unity and distinctness of, the similarity and difference between complexes can be articulated. These are: trait, integrity, contour, scope, and identity. (See MNC 12ff., 22, 35–39) While these are cumulatively defined throughout the work in terms of the categorial structure, their stipulative use from the outset serves the precategorial function of establishing a conceptual language with which to shape the systematic structure.

What it means "to be" is formulated by the pair of concepts, prevalence and alescence. If there are no degrees of being or reality, then a given complex is no more or less real than any other. Yet, to say simply that everything is would not adequately distinguish relevant differences in ways, even if not degrees, of being. Buchler criticizes what others have singled out as the relevant ontological differences: "being and becoming," "permanence and change," "the static and the dynamic," "stability and instability," "determinateness and indeterminateness." Buchler conceptualizes the differences in terms of prevalence and alescence, which together are meant to be exhaustive of what it means "to be."

Every complex prevails, is alescent, or both (in different respects), that is, a complex excludes traits, admits traits, or both in different respects. The purpose of this distinction is to distinguish the nascent, deviant, augmentative, or spoliative character of a complex from its sphere of dominance while at the same time consigning neither to the status of lesser reality. Prevalence and alescence are modes or dimensions of being. Thus, in whatever way a complex is—prevails or is alescent—it is no more or less real in that respect than it is in any other. Thus, the house which prevails in my visual field is as real as the same house which prevails in its geographic location. The house which is being torn down is alescent and is as real as the house which prevails whole and entire in my memory. In keeping with the principle of ontological parity, God prevails but is no more real than the alescent house.

The principle of ordinality means that every complex, that every prevalence or alescence, is determinate. To be determinate means to be ordinally located. To be ordinally located means to be related to some other complex(es) in some respect. To prevail is always to prevail in an order. (Similarly for alescence.) Thus, the house in my visual field is located (prevails) in a visual order in which I as perceiver also prevail. In a visual order I am relevant to the perceived house, and the house is relevant to me. Determinateness (relatedness) is always reciprocal. The house has the trait of being visible and of being perceived. I have the trait of vision and of "house-seeing." Two people, each looking at the house, would be located in the visual order, and each could be reciprocally related to the other in that order. If they were, they would each be either strongly or weakly relevant to the other as house perceiver (however they might be relevant or not to each other in other respects, i.e., orders).[6]

In the order of marriage, each partner is strongly relevant to the other as spouse—the determinate character, the integrity, of each as spouse is determined by the other. Yet, in another order, for example, as house perceivers, they may be irrelevant, strongly relevant, or weakly relevant to each other. Spouses may be strongly relevant (indispensable) to one another as spouses, but weakly relevant (dispensable) to one another's career, each to the other as friend to a third, and irrelevant (determinative in no respect) to one another as potential victims of nuclear fallout.

To prevail or be alescent as determinate is to be plurally located, to be reciprocally related. To be related is to determine as well as to be determined. Every complex is also an order; it locates other complexes, at the least, its own constituent traits. If God prevails, God is determinate, that is, determines and is determined by other complexes. God, therefore, is not wholly self-determined, because no complex has only one ordinal location. God is no more real than any other complex, because God's prevalence is no more (or less) determinate than that of any other complex.

If the boundaries between complexes are sometimes difficult to discriminate, that does not mean that there are none. The principle of commensurateness means that no complex is relevant to (determinative of) every other. Complexes (orders) have limits. Where commensurateness ceases, where there are no mediating traits, there is the limit of an order (MNC 96). In order to conceptualize the meaning of a limit or "natural definition," Buchler introduces the categories of actuality and possibility.

Every trait of a complex is an actuality or a possibility. The traits of actuality define its current situation; those of possibility define a prospect for itself.[7] A prospect is not necessarily the future, but is a continuation or extension of the complex. A possibility, like an actuality, is a relative limit, immanent in (determined by) the relevant traits of the complex. If the traits of a complex, its actualities and possibilities, are commensurate with one another, then not just anything conceivable can prevail or be alescent as a possibility for it.

To illustrate: Suppose we ask whether it is possible for an insect to talk.[8] That would mean that an insect in an order of biological existence cannot talk, and in an order of fantasy can talk. This would be a contradiction in respect to talking. If in the same respect (talking) presumed traits contradict one another, then the traits are not commensurate with one another. Therefore, if one possibility is a trait of the complex, the other cannot be. For contradiction means that there are no mediating traits, and thus that not both are limits of, can define a prospect for, a complex.

Since not every complex can be relevant to every other, not all complexes have the same possibilities. If possibilities are those commensurate traits of a complex which define its prospect, then not all possibilities "always were" (MNC 165). However, since [some] complexes may be located in the same order, complexes may have a possibility or some possibilities in common; they may share a prospect. All possibilities as well as actualities are "empirical," i.e., commensurate with relevant conditions or traits. Therefore, no possibility is by definition "pure" (independent of any conditions) or "eternal"(guaranteed to prevail no matter what the conditions).

If possibility is always of a complex, then there is no realm or world of possibility, nor one of actuality. Recalling the principles of ordinality and commensuarateness, there is no single order "the World," for there can be no single order determinative of all complexes, actual and possible. The World means exhaustively and distributively [all] the innumerable natural complexes (OCW 574). But, the World is not innumerable complexes collectively identifiable: "all" is not a determinate trait. Therefore, the World is not an order, not a complex. For even though the World is distributively exhaustive, "it" is never complete, whole or *a* totality, because "it" is indefinitely extended. That the World is indefinitely extended does not mean that its limits are ambiguous or vague. "It" has no limits, for since "it" distributively "includes" everything, "it" has no principle of exclusion (of limitation).

The physical universe is not equivalent to the World; it is a world, albeit one of unimaginably great scope.[9] But, it does not *include* every other world, i.e., it does not define the conditions and traits of every other complex or order (which would be a denial of the principle of commensurateness). Thus, a world of literature is not necessarily "located in" the order, the physical universe, even though books in some respects are. For the possibilities and actualities of literature as such are not necessarily determined by the conditions of the physical universe. Nor is the relation of any work of literature to the world of literature necessarily determined by the physical universe.

If all possibilities are "empirical," then moral ideals are ordinal, relative to the relevant conditions. Ideals can be formulated as being both humanly relevant and "objective," that is, available in a plurality of orders. To say that ideals, or values for that matter, are relative, is not to admit that they are merely preferences, the morally arbitrary results of a cultural or subjective relativism. Rather, their genesis as well as their merit is conditional. Love is an ideal because of the kind of relation it is and because of the kind of impact, intense but rare, it can have on human life and aspirations. The fifty-five mph speed limit is a value of and for highway driving, because it reduces the risk of highway accident (and hence exemplifies the value of preserving human life). It also conserves gasoline. Only if it did *not* accomplish those aims would its continued enforcement be arbitrary. Its merit is relative (ordinal), and therefore objective (commensurate with its goals and with other values).[10]

> The merest breath a man takes favors one possibility and renders others obsolete. . . . At the other end of his scale, where he is unique in the manner of his kind, he methodically actualizes possibilities that he has produced or apprehended. In so doing, he also keeps actualizing himself. He is not the sole or even the most basic determinant of his own actualization. His is not the only kind of complex that is continually in process of actualization. His kind alone, however, is able to dwell with the possibilities, and this is crucial for his degradation or salvation. (MNC 184f.)

II

We can now trace the resonance of general principles in the metaphysics of human utterance. Man is ontologically no more or less real than any other kind of complex, *and* human orders are continuous with other orders of nature. (Naturalism, or the principle of ontological parity.) However, continuity does not mean similarity in all respects, nor does it preclude discontinuities. While a man is biological, man is not merely biological. Thus, human life is not a depletion of possibilities (genetically defined) all resident at the start of a life. Rather, potentialities and possibilities arise and expire—life is not a process of moving from indeterminateness to determinateness. That life is always determinate and indeterminate exemplifies the principle of ordinality.[11] "Man is born in a state of natural debt" (NJ 3), but his possibilities and actualities are not all "generic." (Principle of commensurateness.) That is, individuality requires that a complex also have specific and unique possibilities.

What is distinctive of an individual is not what is "internal" to it, but what is strongly relevant to it. Strong (or weak) relevance is not a matter of degree, but one of difference in kind. Both strong and weak traits are equally determinate of what a being is. To illustrate: a human being is a spatiotemporal, existing being, even though it is not *distinctively* human in virtue of that trait. (Spatial and temporal relations as such are weakly relevant to human beings *qua* human.) However, it is not any *less* determinate with regard to space and time than being (complex) for which such relation is presumably distinctive. It is no less determinate as existing than it is determinate as rational (or, for Buchler, judging), *even though* the latter is strongly relevant to it *as human*. (Principles of commensurateness and ontological parity.)

These systematic resonances do not, of course, establish the specific principles and categories pertinent to human nature. Buchler's theory of proception and judgment articulates, in a descriptive sense, what is categorially distinctive of human nature, or rather for Buchler, human process. But, in addition to descriptive categorization, a philosophical theory of human nature or process also aims to categorize what it means to be distinctively human in the best sense. In other words, a metaphysics of human process would be incomplete if it did not provide a categorial identification of what is generically normative. What it means to be human in the best sense requires an additional category, not the introduction of degrees into what is generically descriptive. For example, *if* man were defined as essentially a rational animal, rationality could not admit of degrees, and "more" of it would not constitute a norm or an ideal, without entailing that some human beings are less "human" than others. Rather, the normative is a question of what is the *distinctive* qualification of a function as an ideal. We will focus our discussion of human process on the question of the generically normative, articulated by Buchler as *query*.

Buchler develops a theory of the human self in several works.[12] The individual is a whole-self-in-the-process-of-becoming. Distinctively human becoming is judging (uttering or producing).[13] The self *is* its products. "Becoming" in this sense is not an "internal" process of achieving self-consciousness. We become, the self judges, whether aware of doing so or not. Becoming is a relational process and therefore the self is not the sole determinant of its products. Its products and therefore itself are also determined by other complexes. The self is spread out in space as well as in time. The historical and spatial spread of the self-in-process, of the judging self, is the rudimentary basis for association.

> Man is born in a state of natural debt, being antecedently committed to the execution or the furtherance of acts that will largely determine his individual existence. (NJ 3)

> The fact that man is characterized by a state of natural debt, by a perpetual incompletion, . . . emphasizes . . . the extended nature of individuality, its communicative essence, and the indefinite bounds of its relatedness. (NJ 106)

The spread of the self is both something we find ourselves "in" and something which we forge, extend, and ramify through our products (judgments, utterances). Judgment "allows the individual to transcend himself. Through each product the individual is literally multiplied." (TGT 53)

Buchler introduces query through a discussion of the self's spread and association. (NJ 56–58) Why? Because association is indispensable to an understanding of the achievement of the best of human possibilities, such as art, science, philosophy, religion, society. These ongoing achievements make association into civilization. Civilization is the product of the ramifications of query. Through query human individuals become civilized, that is, they become capable of producing systematically and inventively. Judgment becomes query.

The self is an unfolding. It is a ramified spread-out self. We, in self-unfolding, also produce civilization. How is that process to be understood both individually and collectively? The Hegelian approach would say it is the necessary dialectical development of reason. Santayana[14] would say that it is a natural process; at a certain level of biological or organic complication more "refined" possibilities yield more refined results, even though they are thoroughly continuous with more primitive levels of nature. For each, Hegel and Santayana, civilization is a historical development. But do these approaches capture the distinguishing traits of that process? Rationality as the distinguishing generic feature is both too broad (would tolerate inclusion of judgments and events which are rational, but actually or potentially destructive of an individual or of a civilization) and too narrow (since not all civilizing processes and possibilities are necessarily rational). On the other hand, neither perfection of function nor civilization is a "merely natural" development—that is too general, or too narrow if by "natural" one means "biological" or "organic." Now, of course science, for example, is rational activity, but Buchler wants a category which will distinguish rational activity that produces civilization from that which destroys it; the difference between a Hegel and a Hitler.

> Query, whether collaborative or not, presupposes reflexive communication. It is the interrogative spirit methodically directed. *As the most powerful force making for civilization.* . . . (NJ 66; our emphasis)

Query is a perpetual human possibility. So, too, is the destruction of civilization, reversion to a "state of nature." Query does not guarantee historical or individual progress, but without it progress of any significant kind would be inconceivable.

Query is the activity not of a special faculty (for example, Reason), but of a whole self. It is not the mind of the mathematician which probes; it is the mathematician who has focused his/her powers in a given direction. If query is the process of being searchingly and inventively reasonable, it is not only that. "Rational" activity is an instance of, but is not exhaustive

of, query. Query is constructive and inventive probing which also initiates
and promotes self (reflexive) communication.[15] Love can be an exemplification of query; perfecting a swimming stroke can be an instance; symbolic
inventiveness in a wedding ceremony; political maneuvering, legislative
policy, voting *can* all be instances of query, even though it would be difficult to describe all of these as primarily or generically "rational." Through
the reflexive communication facilitated by query the limits of the self are
extended. By this is meant not only that the self continues to be extended
temporally and spatially, but that its possibilities are augmented, its boundaries are redefined, in such a way as to allow for further query. If there is
an absence of the very possibility of query, the action and results of a Hitler
should not be surprising.

That query is generically normative does not mean that it is the highest or best specific value for every individual in any situation. If we abstract
from the vicissitudes of life, which often require that we make choices between alternatives none of which exemplify query, what recurrently signifies the best, humanly speaking, is query. If this is the case, then is there
not a sense in which query could play a role in ordering all specific aims
and purposes? For even if every choice is not one between the life of query
and its absence, it may be that it is only through query that we are *best* able
to determine what the relatively best choice or goal is. Even this may not be
a safe generalization, for there may be situations in which "instinct"
(which for Buchler would issue in judgment) is as reliable as or more reliable than query (systematic and inventive probing) in responding to the
situation. So, even if through query we can train our instincts, it would not
be the case that query is always the best determinant of value. This exemplifies the principles of ordinality and commensurateness (the ontological
bases for articulating a theory of value as both relative and objective).

But the life of query is recurrently prized for being that kind of life
which does reliably promote the civilizing process—for an individual as
well as a society. Art, science, philosophy, religion, political institutions,
these are the distinctive achievements of humankind. Human beings are at
their best when they transcend themselves through query. The life of query
may in one respect have an impact on an individual and in another respect
be a civilizing force. An athlete who breaks a world record in the 100-
meter dash has not only achieved a goal for himself in surpassing a limit,
but has defined a new historical limit, available to and a challenge for others. Here, through query, our possibilities of judgment in respect to athlet-
ics have been extended. The philosopher who is personally satisfied by her
work has also contributed to the intellectual life, defining new and foreclos-
ing other pathways for query. The interrogative temper is infectious. Without query human life would not be much better than a Hobbesian state of

nature. As Hobbes points out, human nature is productive, not just avaricious. If the theories of a Hobbes, a Hegel, and a Santayana are richer in detail and closer in spirit to the lived experience as it were of query, Buchler's theory is a categorial challenge to the traditional ways of conceptualizing that experience.

The elusiveness of query in Buchler's system rests in part on the fact that the reader is not explicitly alerted to its function, but more importantly on the absence of systematic detail in its explication. There may also be another factor, and that is Buchler's use of language. Language is the tool of philosophy. Philosophy is query and hence may require linguistic as well as conceptual inventiveness. Language even in philosophy is subordinate to query. The philosopher is not bound by language, but rather, must employ language responsibly in pursuit of query.

Buchler often uses language to evoke a rich texture of meanings, rather than to offer a single precise definition for any concept or idea.[16] (This style is more prevalent in the works on human process than in MNC.) This is due in part to his notion of philosophy as exhibitive judgment. Not every sentence asserts or makes a claim; it may instead (or also) be embedded in a pattern of sentences which shows the possibilities of an idea. The intent is to extend interpretive possibilities; the risk is that the ideas may sometimes be elusive. But if it is the responsibility of the philosopher to promote the life of query, then it is a very fine line one treads. For if an idea were indeed *perfectly* clear, if all its implications were drawn out, then query would be terminated, until and unless new ideas were introduced. On the other hand, if an idea resists interrogation, it becomes a stumbling block to query.

Buchler's systematic philosophy is not so much polemically provocative as it is a shock. While MNC is spare and abstract, it is quite accessible, in part because general ontology may not depend on detail of applicability and relevance for its persuasiveness or intelligibility. But in a metaphysics of human process one expects a certain kind of systematic detail in establishing the theoretical aptness of the ideas for what is typically found to be immediately relevant—e.g., reason, mind, body, emotion, morality. The kind of conceptual leap required by the reader is not what one suspects is needed. It is the level of abstractness and the absence of strategic clarification in the metaphysics of human process which quite literally shock. While Buchler uses familiar examples, their conceptual translation is sometimes difficult to follow.

Now there is probably no philosophic work which has not been condemned as obscure, unclear, or irrelevant at some time or other. The important question is how remediable the alleged obscurity is. In Buchler's case it is not endemic. The connection between the ideas and what is found to be familiarly the case can be made compelling, even if Buchler himself does not do so.

The spareness of Buchler's system, his systematic strategy and style of expression might disorient the reader who is unfamiliar with systematic philosophy. From the economy of thought manifest in his works, it is evident that Buchler's focus was the development of a categorial structure, not the elaboration of detail in application. From the point of view of the scheme, nothing has been omitted which is required on theoretical grounds, even though much could be added which would be felicitous. As we pointed out at the outset, the *relative* completeness of Buchler's system does not preclude development. If we take the idea of query seriously, then the merit of a philosophical system rests in its capacity to promote query, not in its completion as defined by its author. This means that its merit is never absolutely established, even if its integrity can never be annulled.

> Reason is a form of love, as love (in an equally just perspective) is a form of reason. It is love of inventive communication. Nothing is more foundational for all value than query, and reason is devotion to query. . . . It is for reason to discover and appraise itself from time to time and, like the god that it was early said to be, find that its work is good. Sometimes the progress of reason is more easily measured by the discernment of unreason and by the struggle that it is destined to undergo in order to prevent the fruitless death of its possibilities. (TGT 168, 169)

Notes

1. TGT (1979) Preface, xi.

2. See pages 59ff. for a discussion of query, one of Buchler's distinctive categories of human process.

3. See Justus Buchler, *The Main of Light: On the Concept of Poetry* (ML).

4. See also Beth J. Singer, *Ordinal Naturalism: An Introduction to the Philosophy of Justus Buchler* (Lewisburg: Bucknell University Press, 1983), p. 168 for a discussion of commensurateness in terms of "mediated relatedness."

5. Buchler makes the related point that a theory is a formalized perspective which may tolerate some subperspectives and not others, may urge some subperspectives and be incompatible with others (TGT 71). But a subperspective is still a perspective and has an integrity as well as being subaltern to a broader perspective or theory.

6. MNC 104–128 for a full treatment of strong and weak relevance.

7. Buchler formulates the mode of natural definition of or by a possibility as "prefinition" (MNC 165–170).

8. OCW 576, in MNC [1989] 255. (This example is also discussed in the Weiss ["Possibility: Three Recent Ontologies"] and Wallace ["Ordinal Possibility: A Metaphysical Concept"] contributions to this volume.[Eds.])

9. "The World" is something which exceeds the self or any self which would suggest that it is the physical (public) world *only if* we were to assume that it had to be contrasted with mental, self-centered, and private selves. Note that such a world could not include such a self.

10. Compulsion and convention, dimensions of judgment, would also be important in rendering an intelligible account of the conditions and genesis of value. (See TGT, Chs. 3 and 4.)

11. This suggests that the so-called alternatives of free will and determinism are not necessarily metaphysical distinctions. To be "free" is also to be determinate and to be "determined" is also to be indeterminate. Hobbes, in rejecting the notion of the will as a separate faculty, is making a related point.

12. TGT, NJ, CM, ML. In the last book, Buchler weaves together the general ontology and the metaphysics of human process in a philosophical account of poetry.

13. The notion of judgment for Buchler is not limited to inferential or logical processes. Judgment is the generic category identifying that which is distinctively human. Thus, emotion, action, prayer, preference—anything we say, do, or contrive, consciously or not, which discriminates traits and defines where one stands, is judgment. See NJ, Ch. 1; TGT 46–57.

14. George Santayana's *The Life of Reason; or the Phases of Human Progress* (New York: Scribner's 1905–06), can be seen as a naturalization of the Hegelian phenomenology. Reason itself is a natural development. The "phases" are common sense, art, society, religion, and science.

15. Chapter 2 of NJ is entitled "Query." The idea is developed, however, throughout Buchler's work. See TGT 54, 66–81, 166–169; CM 114–115, 141–144. In CM, the idea of query becomes explicitly normative.

16. This is an observation on Buchler's method, not an exclusion of clarity from query. In Buchler's case, clarity or precision of statement is embedded, so to speak, in a dramatic structure.

Part Two

General Ontology

Introduction to Part Two

Unlike contemporary views which eschew the possibility of genuine cognitive gain in philosophy in general, Buchler's view exemplifies a commitment to philosophy and metaphysics in particular as legitimate and indispensable disciplines in human intellectual life. But this is not a naive faith. Those views which reject the very possibility of knowledge, and of philosophy especially, are themselves based on *metaphysical* assumptions about the nature of mind, thought, the world, criteria of justification and the like.[1] In shaping the categories of ordinal metaphysics, Buchler is, in effect, launching an extended critique of prevailing contemporary metaphysical assumptions. Sometimes he addresses himself explicitly to them. Thus, in the Introduction to the second, revised edition of *Toward A General Theory of Human Judgment*, Buchler reviews the problems with the concept of experience which his theory of proception and judgment is designed to overcome. This is a procedure not dissimilar to that of Aristotle's when he catalogues his predecessors' views of change and why they are inadequate. Similarly, in the first chapter of *Metaphysics of Natural Complexes*, "Rudimentary Considerations," Buchler attacks what he regards as longstanding philosophical assumptions, for example, the concept of ontological simples. But, more often Buchler concentrates his efforts on developing his positive categorial alternative. The papers in this section are meant to give some indication of the kind of alternative Buchler's work represents.

Along with new papers written for this volume we have selected several previously published papers. Each of the papers deals with a specific aspect of Buchler's system. Four of the papers compare and contrast Buchler's approach with other philosophical positions (Singer, Miller, Edel and Weiss). The Wallace and Ryder papers draw out the implications of Buchler's view for logical possibility and materialism, respectively.

Singer's paper, "Substitutes for Substances," is an analysis and critical comparison Whitehead and Buchler, two recent metaphysicians each of whom has attempted to elaborate a set of categories as an alternative to traditional substance-quality metaphysics. Singer begins with an incisive analysis of the traditional doctrine pointing out that among its several key assumptions is the principle of ontological priority (against which the Buchlerian principle of ontological parity is specifically formulated).[2] While Whitehead rejects several of the key principles of substance-quality metaphysics, most notably, the principal of substantial identity, Buchler's metaphysics of natural complexes is more thoroughgoing as an experiment in categorial innovation. Singer argues that not only does Buchler's system successfully avoid the pitfalls of substance–quality metaphysics, but it *consistently* sustains its radical systematic commitments.

"The Concept of Identity in Justus Buchler and Mahayana Buddhism" by Miller starts with a comparison of the general metaphysical outlook of each and in the specific discussion of the concept of identity focuses on the unconventional character of Buchler's view. Identity is a derivative metaphysical concept, meaning that it is a concept which is dependent upon prior metaphysical assumptions and categories. Because there are no privileged beings or *complexes* in the Buchlerian system, identity is freed from its association with entities or substances. The key idea for identity in Buchler's view is "continuous relation," not unalterability as such. Therefore, identity cannot be denied to a complex; every complex (e.g., a thing, an event, a law, a musical score, a rainstorm . . . "whatever is") has ontological identity.

The first two parts of Edel's paper, "The Nature of Categorial Theory," were published separately as "Aristotle's Categories and the Nature of Categorial Theory" in *The Review of Metaphysics* (Spring 1975). Edel argues that the adequacy of categories is validated by how they advance concrete work in various fields in the history of thought. In the third part of his paper, Edel analyzes two of Buchler's most original categories, proception and alescence. In the analysis of alescence, Edel suggests that, in consort with its paired category, prevalence, alescence does, in a more generalized way, what Aristotle was doing with the concept of change. Alescence (and prevalence) are designed to work in a more modern intellectualized setting, i.e., in a world which has abandoned natural teleology and the concept of the isolated subject-substance. He faults Buchler, however, for not carrying through exactly how the categories work in the diversified intellectual arena.[3]

The Weiss and Wallace articles on possibility provide two rather different avenues of access to Buchler's highly original theory of possibility. In his article, "Possibility: Three Recent Ontologies," Weiss contrasts Buchler's view with those of David Lewis and Nicholas Rescher. He argues that the latter views reduce possibility to some kind of misplaced, defective or "hypothetical" actuality. Buchler's, on the other hand, is a robust theory of possibility, allowing for the integrity and full reality (the ontological parity) of possibility as such. Wallace's paper, "Ordinal Possibility: A Metaphysical Concept," analyzes the place of the concept of possibility in the Buchlerian system and follows out the implications for the notion of logical possibility. Weiss and Wallace disagree on the consequences of the ordinal view for logical possibility and we have included their discussion written just for this volume in which they articulate what is at stake in their respective interpretations.

Ryder, in his paper, "Ordinality and Materialism," extends the principles of ontological parity and ordinality to an analysis of contemporary materialism. If, as Ryder points out, contemporary materialism has overcome its atomistic and reductionist past, then one can explore the possibility of an "ordinal materialism." Ryder argues that Buchler's principles are effective for constructing a more adequate materialist ontology. But, as Ryder admits, a materialist ontology is committed to the primacy of matter in at least some ontological sense. He then goes on to argue for a "less dependent" status of the material order which would still be consistent with the spirit of ordinality.

We have devoted an entire section to General Ontology because the principles and categories of the metaphysics of natural complexes are presupposed by and exemplified in Buchler's other works. Yet all the books of the Buchlerian system are in metaphysics. Metaphysics then must not be equivalent to general ontology. What then is the difference?

General ontology is the, but not the only, subject matter of metaphysics. Others could be human process (as treated by Buchler, for example in *Toward A General Theory of Human Judgment* and *Nature and Judgment*), poetry (as in Buchler's *The Main of Light*), God (with Spinoza for example), knowledge or change (both of which were treated by Aristotle). In other words, we can have a metaphysics (a categorial analysis) of each of these subject matters. Thus, on the one hand, metaphysics is wider in scope than general ontology. On the other hand, some subject matters are broader or more general than others. Buchler's "self–as–judger" is a more general conception of the human self than Aristotle's "self-as-knower."[4] General ontology is the broadest subject matter; it is the concern with being *qua* being, or being in its most general terms. In Buchler's categories, that would mean being *qua* [natural] complex. General ontology is also the broadest in the sense that the categories which articulate being or natural complex as such have the widest application, wider than categories of lesser scope, such as proception.

A metaphysics is a system of categories, it is an arrangement of concepts.[5] Metaphysics, or a categorial structure, is a basis or, better, a framework for further "categorizing," for extending our efforts to render the world intelligible. More general or pervasive and comprehensive categories are presupposed by less general ones. In this sense, the categories of general ontology are fundamental to those of lesser breadth. For example, the metaphysics of human process is located in, is "framed by," a broader categorial perspective, namely, the metaphysics of natural complexes.[6] No one of Buchler's three modes of judgment is any more of a judgment than any other, nor is any mode more distinctively human than another. This categorial fact exemplifies the more general principle of ontological parity. Buchler's ontological category of *contour* (or, *gross integrity*) is broader than and is exemplified by the category *proceptive domain*. The latter, in turn, fleshes out the meaning of the more general concept and both are fundamental to (or, "frame") the concept *guiding moral tone*.[7] Neither the metaphysics of natural complexes nor the metaphysics of human process can be directly inferred from the other; the categories of each have their own integrity. *But*, the more general principles and concepts of the metaphysics of natural complexes are present in both and are explicitly worked out *as a categorial structure* in *Metaphysics of Natural Complexes*.

This is a non- or antifoundationalist view of metaphysics. Buchler, in commenting on his rejection of traditional versions of foundationalism, puts it this way:

> there are broader concepts; there are narrower concepts. There are concepts which are more suggestive, concepts which are less; but no concept needs to be final in the sense that there's nothing which moves it, touches it, affects it. It seems to me that that's a species of fanaticism and a great barrier to a successful expansion of metaphysics.[8]

> the disapproval I expressed of foundationalism does not imply that we can't make a distinction between concepts which are broader and concepts which are narrower in scope. . . . the progressive advancement and encompassment of ideas by more pervasive ideas is very fundamental to the method of metaphysics; and that, of course—just to repeat once more—that does not imply the necessity or inevitability of any final idea, which somehow I associate with the tacit assumptions, at least, of Husserl.[9]

I would like to conclude this introduction with a brief look at what it means to say that a category *frames* a less general concept. Take Buchler's category of possibility. As a natural complex any possibility or kind of possibility is ordinally located. That means that there are no "pure" possibilities (i.e., possibilities unrelated to any actuality or other possibility). We have two papers on possibility included here, so rather than discuss in detail Buchler's theory of possibility per se, I'll focus on what this view of possibility would commit one to in some other, more familiar, context or order.

The categorial commitments of ordinal metaphysics would entail that a moral ideal is a possibility. It is a natural complex, a complex constituted by relations between human need, striving and craving (themselves natural complexes) and some other complex which is the "object" of that striving in some respect. The ideal (or possibility) *qua* complex is not the mere product of human need or whatever, but has an independent and plural integrity. For since every complex is plurally, i.e., ordinally, located, it cannot be determined by a single relation or location. The "object" becomes a possibility—in this case, an ideal—through the unique relation (prefinition)[10] it has to the complex, the human situation. Therefore, a moral ideal is not an eternal or absolute good. It is not a good at all if it is not, in fact, in some respect (order), a possible good. Nor is it a *mere* reflection of human needs and desires; it is not reducible to a single order of needs or desires. Rather, it is a complex which is an ideal (possibility) *because* it prefines another complex (i.e., human situation) in some respect. Thus, ideals can be interpreted as being both humanly relevant, "subjective," and "objective," that is, available in a plurality of orders.

A theory of moral ideals, framed by the ordinal conception of possibility, should be able to *positively* overcome a naive relativism (since no ideal could be the product solely of human phantasizing) without making ideals inefficacious essences, remote from the conditions of human striving and imagination. Such a theory of moral ideals would be an instance of the category of possibility "at work" in rendering a specific subject matter intelligible. If Edel is right about validation of categories, while the *specific* traits of ideals *qua* ideals are not deducible from or necessarily validated as ideals by their general or ontological status as possibilities, the ontology provides a theoretical context in light of which one can discriminate more special traits, a context for devising a nonreductive and judicious rendering of moral ideals.

—*KAW*

Notes

1. I have pursued some of these issues elsewhere. See Kathleen Wallace, "Making Categories or Making Worlds," *The Journal of Speculative Philosophy* 2:4 (1988) pp. 322–327; "Making Categories or Making Worlds, II" *Texas A & M*

Studies in American Philosophy 1 (1990); "Metaphysics and Validation," in *Antifoundationalism: Old and New*, ed. Thomas Rockmore and Beth J. Singer, Temple University Press, 1991.

2. The others which she identifies are: the principle of atomicity, the principle of substantial identity, the principle of independence, the principle concreteness, the principle of universality and the principle of simplicity.

3. One of our aims in gathering the papers for this volume has been to show the categories "at work"—as the basis for advancing work in other areas (see, for example, Wachter, "Exhibitive Judgment and Freud: Toward a New Interpretation of Dreams," and Corrington, "Ordinality and the Divine Natures" both in Part III), or as a way of overcoming longstanding philosophic problems (see, for example, Singer, "Substitutes for Substances," Weiss, "Possibility: Three Recent Ontologies," both in Part II, Cahoone, "Relativism and Metaphysics: On Justus Buchler and Richard Rorty," and Marsoobian, "Reference, Interpretation and Articulation: Rethinking Meaning in the Arts" in Part III).

4. Edel makes a similar observation in his paper included in this volume.

5. Also see Justus Buchler, "Reply to Greenlee: Philosophy and Exhibitive Judgment," SJP 140, in MNC [1989] 208 for a discussion of what he calls metaphysical awareness and metaphysics.

6. Of course, at the time TGT was written the system of general ontology had not been fully worked out, but it is implicit in the structure of TGT.

7. Justus Buchler, "Russell and the Principles of Ethics," in *The Philosophy of Bertrand Russell*, ed. Paul Arthur Schilpp (Evanston and Chicago: Northwestern University Press, 1944), pp. 513–535.

8. "Conversation between Justus Buchler and Robert S. Corrington," *The Journal of Speculative Philosophy* 3:4 (1989), p. 264. (This conversation took place on August 18, 1982. The text is taken from a tape recording made at that time and transcribed. Buchler's comments are rendered verbatim.)

9. Ibid., 266.

10. This is a formal concept in Buchler's system, MNC Chapter 4. See also Weiss's paper, "Possibility: Three Recent Ontologies," here, p. 163ff.., and my paper, "Ordinal Possibility: A Metaphysical Concept," here, p. 178ff.

Substitutes for Substances

Beth J. Singer

All modern philosophy hinges round the difficulty of describing the world in terms of subject and predicate, substance and quality, particular and universal. The result always does violence to that immediate experience which we express in our actions, our hopes, our sympathies, our purposes, and which we enjoy in spite of our lack of phrases for its verbal analysis. We find ourselves in a buzzing world, amid a democracy of fellow creatures; whereas, under some disguise or other, orthodox philosophy can only introduce us to solitary substances, each enjoying an illusory experience: "Oh Bottom, thou art changed! what do I see on thee?"

(Alfred North Whitehead)[1]

I

As Whitehead points out, traditional substance-quality metaphysics is so deeply embedded in our conventions of perceiving and thinking and so intimately associated with Western language and logic that it is difficult even to find terms in which to criticize it, terms which do not presuppose it. Nevertheless, a number of recent American philosophers have rejected substance-quality metaphysics. Serious questions have been raised by Dewey, by A. E. Murphy, by John Herman Randall, Jr., by Stephen Pepper, Justus Buchler, and others. But Whitehead is one of a limited number of philosophers of any period to have elaborated an alternative system of categories. Others who have done so include Buchler and Randall. Randall attempts to modify Aristotle's metaphysics in the light of certain doctrines derived from Dewey and Woodbridge. He does not eliminate the category of substance but redefines it as "a cooperation of processes."[2] Buchler's "metaphysics of natural complexes" rests upon a radically different concept, and not only employs new terminology but obliterates certain hard and fast distinctions essential to the substance–quality doctrine.[3] Buchler's system also contrasts sharply with that of Whitehead and I believe it will be illuminating to compare these two systems in the light of an analysis of the traditional doctrine.

Implicit in any version of the metaphysics of substance and quality are a number of interrelated assumptions. Perhaps the most fundamental of these assumptions is that of *atomicity*, i.e., the principle that there are discrete individuals or, in a stronger version, that the ultimate constituents of the world are discrete individuals. Substance-quality metaphysics involves the assumption that to be a substance is to be an atomic individual. For example, Descartes' mental substances are atomic (and consequently isolated from one another and the corporeal world). Spinoza, arguing that there can be only one substance, presupposes that any substance must be an atomic individual. (Were it not, its existence would presuppose that of related elements.) The same principle of atomicity is applied by some philosophers to qualities, with the result that they must posit an infinity of simple or undefinable qualities.

On the hypothesis of atomicity, individuals are assumed to be what they are intrinsically and essentially, regardless of any relations in which they may be implicated or contexts in which they may be located. As a corollary, substances are held to retain their identity while undergoing changes in their traits. We may call this the *principle of substantial identity*. In Newtonian physics, the same principle is applied to the elements. The principle which Whitehead condemns as the fallacy of simple (spatiotemporal) location rests upon this principle.

According to Aristotle, the existence of a substance is requisite for the existence of qualities, but not vice versa. According to Descartes, substance is a thing which needs nothing else in order to exist. Both principles assert the *independence* of substances. Despite the superficial plausibilty of Aristotle's principle, it is not at all clear in what way a substance is independent of its qualities; and the meaning of "needing nothing else in order to exist" is questionable.

The principle of independence often goes hand in hand with a principle of *ontological priority*.[4] Substances, being supposed independent, are thereby taken to be "fundamental," "ultimate" or "absolute," whereas the qualities and relations of substances, the wider complexes in which substances are included, the processes in which substances are implicated, the powers they exercise, or the potentialities they possess, are taken to be "secondary" or "relative." Thus Strawson says, "in our conceptual scheme as it is, particulars of these two categories [material bodies and persons] are the basic or fundamental particulars . . . the concepts of other types of particulars must be seen as secondary in relation to the concepts of these."[5]

Substances are held to be *concrete*. There is some ambiguity in the concept of concreteness. For instance, G. F. Stout says,

Concrete things are diverse from each other in a way which cannot be resolved into difference of kind. . . . What is concrete is a subject to which characters belong and which cannot itself be a character of anything else.[6]

In criticizing Stout, G. E. Moore points out that "every event is quite as incapable of being predicated of anything else as is a concrete thing or concrete individual or substance."[7] Events are here contrasted with concrete things; yet events are not mere abstractions to Moore, but are "substantives":

All events . . . are . . . "substantives proper"—a category which excludes their being "characters," for the very reason that no "substantive proper" is predicable of anything else. But though all events are "substantives proper," it appears to me . . . a mere misuse of language to call events, as Dr. McTaggart does, "substances."[8]

Whereas Stout seems to use "concrete" as the antonym of "abstract," it does not always have this meaning. Etymologically, "concrete" means "composite" or "compound." In ordinary language, it has come to mean "specific" or "solid." It is in the latter sense that Moore seems to understand "concrete things." The term "concrete" is also applied to facts, which seems to give it the meaning of "actual." But if, by a "fact," we mean the fact that something is or was, rather than the thing or occurrence itself, a fact is an abstraction rather than a concrete actuality.

Substance-quality metaphysics in most of its formulations incorporates the principle that qualities, attributes, or characters are *universal*, in contrast to the particularity, as well as the concreteness, of substances. That is, the same quality may belong to several substances, so that substances are describable in terms of their qualities, but not vice versa. So-called "simple" qualities are strictly not describable at all. Though not necessarily presupposed by substance-quality metaphysics, the *principle of simplicity* is often associated with it and, as has been suggested above, rests upon the same principle of atomicity. It gives to simple qualities a kind of ultimacy analogous to the ultimacy of atomic substances.

To summarize, the metaphysics of substance and quality presupposes the following principles: the principle of atomicity; the principle of substantial identity; the principle of independence; the principle of ontological priority; the principle of concreteness; the principle of universality. The principle of simplicity is also an assumption commonly made by proponents of substance-quality metaphysics. While this list does not exhaust the assumptions of substance-quality metaphysics, it includes those which I believe are most central to it and most widely made. It also contains principles which are rejected by Whitehead or Buchler or both. In comparing the concepts which these philosophers propose as substitutes for the concepts of substance and quality, I will try to show how each accepts, rejects, or modifies these assumptions, and I will indicate a number of problems which seem to me to be raised by the alternatives they adopt.

II

While he does not deny that they are faithful and even indispensable to our ways of thinking and talking, Whitehead finds the traditional versions of substance-quality metaphysics inadequate as analyses of what we actually experience. The substance–quality doctrine is an instance of the "fallacy of misplaced concreteness."[9] As this criticism implies, Whitehead does not deny that there are concrete, substantial actualities. Rather, he attributes concreteness to entities other than those traditionally identified as substances and redefines what it is to be a substance. In *Science and the Modern World*, the term "substance" is employed for the "underlying substantial activity of individualisation" which is named "creativity."[10] In *Process and Reality* Whitehead says that "the notion of 'substance' is transformed into that of 'actual entity'."[11] In this paper I shall be mainly concerned with the slightly narrower concept of actual occasion.

Contending that the "substances" of tradition, the things which endure and change, are abstractions, Whitehead affirms the individuality and concreteness of the "final real things of which the world is made up." Correlatively, he affirms the abstractness, objectivity, and immutability of forms. For the solitary individual substance, persisting identically through successive qualifications by universal attributes, Whitehead substitutes a perceiving (feeling or experiencing) subject, constituting itself once and for all in a single act of experience.

The act whereby an actual occasion creates itself (prehension or perception in the mode of causal efficacy) is a process in which the entire world is brought into a novel unity. Through this process each occasion is internally related to every entity in the universe except its contemporaries. Its relations thus enter into its constitution and Whitehead thereby negates the principle of substantial identity. But despite the fact that actual occasions are internally related, Whitehead does not reject the principle of atomicity. Like Leibniz, he combines a doctrine of internal relations with a view of substances as atomic. In *Process and Reality*, "atomism" is said to be "the ultimate metaphysical truth."[12] Each actual occasion is said to "atomize" the universe. While actual occasions are analyzable, like each of Leibniz's monads, each occasion is atomic in the sense that it is an elementary and unitary entity which is indivisible as well as unique. Whitehead states, in *Adventures of Ideas*, that "as used here the words 'individual' and 'atom' have the same meaning, that they apply to composite things with an absolute reality which their components lack."[13] Thus not only does Whitehead adopt a principle of atomicity, but in giving his actual occasions an absolute reality which their components lack, he gives atomic individuals ontological priority.

Whitehead's atomic substances are also independent in the Cartesian sense. When an actual occasion achieves its "satisfaction" as "its particular individual self," Whitehead says, it "requir[es] nothing but itself in order to exist."[14] Since the entire world enters into its nature, this would seem to be contradictory. But Whitehead's claim is that, having attained its satisfaction every occasion "has attained its individual separation from other things."[15] In becoming, it becomes atomic; having become, it is independent. An actual occasion is independent in a second sense as well. As a subject "presiding over" its own becoming, each occasion is self-creative and *causa sui*. The doctrine of self-causation reflects the teleology Whitehead sees in the underlying creativity of the universe. Concrescence has a vectorial character: rather than being a passive mirroring of the given, it is a purposive enrichment of the inherited world. Self-causation does not mean arising *ex nihilo*, but rather that in the becoming of any actual occasion there is some degree of freedom. To be actual, for Whitehead, is to experience creatively, in his special sense of "experience." To be self-creative is to become a self that never was and thereby to introduce novelty into the world.

The determinative factor in self-causation is the "subjective aim" of the concrescent individual.[16] Whitehead says that the subjective aim is "this subject itself determining its own self-creation as one creature."[17] Through selective "conceptual" prehension or "valuation" of the multiplicity of eternal objects, each occasion determines the way in which it actualizes the possibilities of its primary datum.

According to Whitehead's "Ontological Principle," there must be an actual reason for everything actual. Whitehead locates the reason or cause of the subjective aim of an occasion partly in God's primordial nature and partly in the occasion itself.[18] But this seems equivalent to saying that it is inexplicable or that it has no reason, since there is no factor in the concrescent occasion which accounts for the subjective aim taking the direction it does. Whitehead himself, in discussing the conceptual valuation which is the condition of originality, appears to negate the doctrine of freedom. Originality has its source in the "mental pole" of an occasion (its prehension of eternal objects), in the phase Whitehead calls the phase of "conceptual reversion," distinguishing this from "conceptual reproduction."[19] But on pages 381–382 of *Process and Reality* [1929][20] we find the following passage:

> The question, how, and in what sense, one unrealized eternal object can be more, or less, proximate to an eternal object in realized ingression—that is to say, in comparison with any other unfelt eternal object—is left unanswered by this Category of Reversion. In conformity with the ontological principle, this question can be answered only by reference to some actual entity. Every eternal object has entered into the conceptual feelings of God. Thus, a more fundamental account must ascribe the reverted conceptual feeling in a temporal subject to its conceptual feeling derived, according to Category IV, from the hybrid physical feeling of the relevancies conceptually ordered in God's experience. In this way, by the recognition of God's characterization of the creative act, a more complete rational explanation is attained. The Category of Reversion is then abolished. . . .

If this is indeed Whitehead's doctrine (for other contexts refute it), then the principle of the independence of an actual occasion, in the sense of its being *causa sui*, would be negated.

The structure of ontological priority in Whitehead's system is complex. One aspect of it is the principle that "the prime fact is the prehensive unity of volume," whereas "space-time cannot in reality be considered as a self-subsistent entity."[21] The distinction of "final real things" is also a distinction of ontological priority as is the conception of grades of concreteness. Actual entities, their constituent prehensions, and the groupings or nexūs of actual entities are all said by Whitehead to be concrete, but actual entities are the *most* concrete entities in the universe. Their most concrete components, prehensions, are not as concrete as the entities themselves.[22] Nexūs are also less concrete than their component occasions. There are ambiguities in Whitehead's concept of concreteness and it is not clear to me what he means by "more" and "less" concrete, or precisely what the connection is between concreteness and concrescence.

In *Adventures of Ideas*, Whitehead states that "concrescence is useful to convey the notion of many things acquiring complete complex unity."[23] He points out, in the same place, that "the participle 'concrete' is familiarly used for the notion of complete physical reality." But in Whitehead's system complexity is not a sufficient condition of concreteness: there are complex forms or eternal objects. Since prehensions and nexūs are "individual and particular" in the same sense as actual occasions, they would seem to be equally unities. But (abstract) eternal objects are similarly individual and particular. ("Every so-called 'universal' is particular in the sense of being just what it is, diverse from everything else.")[24] Thus neither complexity nor unity accounts for concreteness or for degrees of concreteness.

The concept of completeness seems to be a key to what Whitehead means by "concrete" and to illumine the concept of grades or degrees of concreteness. While a given form might be the form of some incomplete thing, the notion of incompleteness is inapplicable to forms per se (the indeterminateness of eternal objects with regard to particulars is not incompleteness). By definition, a prehension is incomplete in the sense that it is not independent: its subjective form is not proper to it but is provided by the actual occasion of which it is a component.[25] This would not apply to eternal objects, but a nexus might be said to be incomplete in the same sense, namely that it has no subjective form of its own. On this interpretation, whereas an actual occasion would be complete and therefore concrete, both nexūs and prehensions, being incomplete, could be said to be imperfectly concrete. Against this it can be argued that Whitehead says that a society (a social nexus) "is its own reason."[26]

If a nexus were only a perceived grouping (and this is one way in which Whitehead employs the term)[27] then it would be wholly abstract. But a nexus is defined as "a set of actual entities in the unity of the relatedness constituted by their prehensions of each other, or —what is the same thing conversely expressed—constituted by their objectifications in each other."[28] Thus a nexus comprises both the "intrinsic" and "extrinsic" reality of its constituent occasions,[29] their concrete actuality as well as their objectification. It would seem, therefore, as concrete as its constituents. However, a nexus, like a prehension, is not *causa sui*. But if "concrete" means being *causa sui* (or if, as certain contexts seem to imply, it means "concrescent") the question may still be raised whether a prehension or a nexus should be said to be concrete at all.

In moving away from a metaphysics of substance and quality to a metaphysics of experient actuality, Whitehead does not abandon the distinction between concrete actuality and abstract quality or possibility. And he does not eliminate a distinction between substance and accident, although he reinterprets the distinction. There is, Whitehead says in *Process and Reality*, only one substance in the sense of "ultimate subject":

In all philosophic theory there is an ultimate which is actual in virtue of its accidents. It is only then capable of characterization through its actual embodiments, and apart from these accidents is devoid of actuality. In the philosophy of organism this ultimate is termed 'creativity' and God is its primordial, non-temporal accident.[30]

In *Science and the Modern World*, creativity is said to be analogous to Spinoza's substance, "the one activity of realisation individualising itself into an interlocked plurality of modes."[31] Actual events are identified with "the individualisations or modes of Spinoza's one substance."[32] But in *Process and Reality* it is asserted that actual entities are "sheer actualities" and not merely modes of substance.[33] These concrete actualities, the substantial individuals of Whitehead's system, are nevertheless "accidents" of the ultimate subject–accidents without which it would not be actual.

While rejecting the notion of "a collection of primary substances qualified by universal qualities,"[34] Whitehead distinguishes between actual entities, prehensions, and nexūs on the one hand as "ultimate facts," ontologically prior to other real things, and on the other, the forms or pure possibilities (eternal objects) which are actualized in real things. Yet eternal objects seem to be as "ultimate" as actual entities, and in other contexts Whitehead grants special, final existential status to both actual entities and eternal objects, giving to all other types of entity "a certain intermediate character,"[35] a lesser ontological worth, which seems to correspond to their place on the continuum from concrete to abstract.

The distinction between actual entities and eternal objects is not the traditional distinction between particulars and universals but it resembles the traditional view in distinguishing substantial entities from formal ones and concrete entities from abstract ones. Since actual entities enter into the constitution of other actual entities, no actual entity can be described in terms of universals. What were formerly taken to be universals, to Whitehead are particular possibilities; they are unique, identical, and distinct, although they are so "eternally." Still, the distinction between substance and form remains sharp and is central to Whitehead's philosophy, although certain functions and traits of substances and forms have been reversed. "In the philosophy of organism," Whitehead states, "it is not 'substance' which is permanent, but 'form.' Forms suffer changing relations; actual entities 'perpetually perish' subjectively, but are immortal objectively."[36]

Whitehead says that forms suffer changing relations. Eternal objects are conceptually prehended by different actualities, with the result that they acquire new relations to actualities. Therefore, it seems to me, in the actual world new relations arise among the forms themselves. But according to Whitehead, the ingression of eternal objects takes place without any change in the essence of eternal objects (such a change would produce a different eternal object). That is, while the relation of ingression is "internal" to the concrescent occasion, it is "external" to the eternal object. There is a similar asymmetry in the relation between God's primordial nature, which is actual, and actual occasions. The primordial nature of God conditions all occasions but is unconditioned and unaffected by the creative advance. Whitehead explicitly states that "a relationship is a fact which concerns all the implicated relata, and cannot be isolated as if involving only one of the relata."[37] But an external relation does not affect the relata, raising a question as to precisely what Whitehead means by "relation."

Even though Whitehead rejects the more traditional versions of substance-quality metaphysics, it should be apparent by now that a number of its fundamental principles are basic to his system. In the first place, while asserting the interrelation of actual occasions, Whitehead affirms the principle of atomicity. In asserting that an actual occasion is uniquely atomic and that it is *causa sui*, Whitehead is asserting its independence. An actual entity is still contrasted with an eternal object as a substance is contrasted with a quality. In retaining the distinction between substance and form, despite his elaborate qualification of the traditional distinction and of the functions assigned to each, Whitehead does not depart far from the principle of universality: eternal objects are abstract, unchanging, and ingredient in many particulars. They are pure potentials, and actual events have no relevance for them as such.

In making the distinction of more and less concrete, Whitehead is making a distinction of ontological priority. In some contexts, he also makes actual entities more fundamental than, and hence ontologically prior to, eternal objects. He also accepts, though in a limited context, the concept of simples: despite the relational essence of an eternal object, there are simple as well as complex eternal objects.[38]

Of the assumptions of substance–quality metaphysics which Whitehead rejects, perhaps the most conspicuous is the principle of substantial identity. He denies that an actual entity is what it is apart from its relations, that they are intrinsic to it, or that it remains the same while its traits change; he strongly repudiates the fallacy of simple location. But this analysis is not applied in a thoroughgoing way to eternal objects; their relational traits (i.e., their relations to actualities) change with their ingression into actuality, yet in themselves they remain the same. Furthermore, the complex form which is common to the members of a social nexus remains the same through the process of transition. Thus the principle of substantial identity, which does not apply to actual occasions, does hold for eternal objects.

III

In contrast to Whitehead, rather than searching for "final real things," Justus Buchler has sought, in *Metaphysics of Natural Complexes* (MNC), to define a generic concept which can serve as the basis for categoreal interpretation of all the kinds or ways of being which we recognize, and which does not rule out the possibility of other kinds or ways of being:

> The concept of natural complex permits the identification of all discriminanda generically, without prejudicing the pursuit and analysis of differences, of further similarities within the differences, of further differences within these similarities.[39]

For Buchler, "whatever is, in whatever way, is a natural complex."[40] In large measure, MNC is an expansion of this statement.

The category of natural complex excludes nothing nameable or imaginable, nothing encounterable or producible, nothing which could be, whether humanly conceivable or not. The term is applied univocally by Buchler to anything actual or possible. "Relations, structures, processes, societies, human individuals, human products, physical bodies, words and bodies of discourse, ideas, qualities, contradictions, meanings, possibilities, myths, laws, duties, feelings, illusions, reasonings, dreams—all are natural complexes."[41] While they may differ in other ways, all natural complexes are equally real and no type of complex is ontologically more ultimate or more fundamental than any other.[42] This principle of ontological parity is central to Buchler's metaphysics. It is not an arbitrary assumption but is a corollary of the principle that whatever is, is a natural complex.

That whatever is, in whatever way, is a natural complex means (1) that there is nothing which could be meaningfully regarded as non–natural,[43] and (2) that there are no simples. But it means more than this. (3) It means that whatever is, is *a* complex; it has a unity based upon fact that it is not merely a collection of traits but is an *order*. (4) In addition, it is part of the definition of "natural complex" that whatever is, is located in some natural order, an order which is itself a natural complex.

(1) The term "natural complex" as used by Buchler has no meaningful opposite. Buchler introduces the concept of God in *Metaphysics of Natural Complexes* to indicate the scope of "natural complex" and to show that the concept of the natural does not presuppose or require the concept of the supernatural.[44] God, in this scheme, is a natural complex, and the analysis of "natural complex" is applicable to God in the same way as to any other complex. (The reader may wish to make a comparison with Whitehead.)

(2) Buchler gives a number of arguments to prove that there can be no simples (no unanalyzable or relationless traits) and that simples, having by definition no relations, could not constitute a complex. For him, whatever is has traits or constituents. These traits are themselves complexes, with traits or constituents of their own.

(3) Any natural complex is a constellation of natural complexes, an "order" of "subaltern" complexes which are said to be "located in" that order. To be located in an order is not to be contained in it as in a class or a box or to be included in it as in a cluster; it is not to be attached to that order as an "attribute." To be located in an order is to be related to other complexes which also constitute that order. An order, for Buchler (i.e., a natural complex), is not a substance. An order is a locus or "sphere" of relatedness and relevance.[45] Viewed as having traits, every natural complex is an order.

(4) Buchler also argues that every complex is located in some other complex.[46] Every complex, like every trait of a complex, has relations, be they only the relations which differentiate it from other complexes. Its relations are among the constituents of that complex. But it is only as located in an inclusive order, within which that relation is defined, that two complexes can be related. More generally, it is only under certain conditions— i.e., within a given order—that a natural complex has just the relations, just the constitution, just the possibilities, just the status that it does.[47] The status of a complex in an order, its constitution, the way in which it is *both* similar to and different from other complexes, Buchler calls the *integrity* of the complex. A natural complex has an integrity in every order in which it is located. For instance a human being may be a woman, a mother, a teacher: these are all integrities in different orders.

An order is not a substance but a natural complex. Its traits are not universals, but are also natural complexes which, in turn, are also orders of natural complexes. The inclusive order itself is located in at least one other order or complex of related complexes. This is Buchler's *principle of ordinality*: every natural complex is both an order of subaltern complexes and subaltern to (located in) other orders. It is this principle which grounds Buchler's principle of ontological parity. Whatever is, is a natural complex in precisely the same sense as anything else: it is an order of traits and is a trait or constituent of some other order or orders. There are no complexes which can be only traits and none which can be only orders. Thus no complex is intrinsically more fundamental or more ultimate than any other. Therefore there is no complex which is independent in either the Aristotelian or the Cartesian sense. For any complex to be presupposes both that its constituents and the order or orders in which it is located also are.

The principle of ontological parity and the principle of ordinality together enable Buchler to account for complicated interrelationships which are unintelligible in terms of substance–quality metaphysics. For instance, as a citizen a man is a constituent (a trait) of a society. Yet since citizenship is one of the man's traits and the society is a constituent of his citizenship, the society itself is a constituent of the man. This presents no problem for

the metaphysics of natural complexes and neither society nor citizenship is
relegated to a secondary or ideal status. To see a man as a constituent of a
society is to see both in an order in which that relation obtains. To see the
society as a constituent of the man is to see them in another order, an order
which is systematically related to the first and yet distinct from it.

Every natural complex is inevitably located in an indefinite number of
orders, for each trait of a complex involves relations to other complexes.
For instance, a tree has traits which relate it to the sun, to the soil, to the
air, to the colors of the spectrum. Each of these relations implies an order
of relatedness. The same tree has traits which locate it in an order of botanical classification; it may also have traits which (potentially or actually)
locate it in a selection of trees to be cut for pulpwood or to be included in
a photograph.

The traits of a complex in a given order may differ from its traits in
another order; its traits in various orders may nevertheless overlap. Thus
maleness is a trait of some human individuals in a biological order; maleness may also feature as a trait of a person in a political order (for instance
in a state in which only men are enfranchised). But the color of his eyes,
which is a biological trait of a man, is not among his traits as a political
complex; and his political affiliation has no relation to his eye color. While
according to the principle of ordinality there is no complex which has no
relations, this is not a doctrine of internal relatedness. In the first place, a
natural complex has relations only in the orders in which it is located. Second, two complexes which are related in one order may be unrelated in
some other order. For example two siblings, reared apart, may not be in
communication with one another. Third, a natural complex is not necessarily related to all of the complexes which are located in the same order. For
example in a group (an order) of friends, there may be two individuals who
have friends in common but are not acquainted with one another.

Buchler's contention that there is irrelevance and unrelatedness in the
world is linked to a careful definition of what it means for natural complexes to be related. His theory of relation rests upon a distinction between
the integrity and the scope of a natural complex. As we saw, Buchler defines the integrity of a complex as its status in an order, defined by the
traits which, within that order, constitute it as just that complex. A natural
complex may have other traits which do not determine its integrity, traits
whose absence would not change its status. For instance, while sandiness is
a trait of a certain beach, neither the number of grains of sand nor any
particular grain of sand affects its being a beach, or its being a sandy
beach, or its being that particular beach. Traits of a complex which do not
determine its integrity belong to the scope of that complex.[48] There cannot
be a complex without both integrity and scope.

As Buchler sees it, for two natural complexes to be related, each must be a constituent of the scope of the other. It may also be a constituent of the other's integrity. When a natural complex is a constituent of the scope of a second complex, it is *weakly relevant* to the second. When it is a constituent of the integrity of the second, it is *strongly relevant* to that complex. In either case, the two complexes are related. For example, an ordinary man, moving into a city, will enlarge the scope of that city (weak relevance), whereas a new city manager may, in addition to enlarging its scope, alter some aspect of the city's integrity (strong relevance). In both cases the man and the city are related.

No complex can affect either the scope or the integrity of another without being included in the scope of the second, i.e., without the two being mutually related. However, whereas weak relevance is always symmetrical, strong relevance is not. One complex may be a determinant of the integrity of a second without its own integrity being also affected. For our purposes here, it is only important to note that, given two complexes, if neither is included in the scope of the other, the two are unrelated. It is on the basis of this theory of relation that Buchler rejects a universe of internal relatedness.

We noted that a natural complex may have distinct integrities in diverse orders in which it is located. This implies that it may, in a given order, be unrelated to a complex to which, in another order, it is related. It also has consequences for the theory of *identity*. Buchler rejects the principle of substantial identity. In the first place, no natural complex is identifiable in itself but only in terms of its integrity in some order in which it is located. To identify a tree as a redwood presupposes a botanical order. To identify a man as Socrates is to recognize his location in an order of dialecticians or of social critics, and so on. In the second place, for Buchler the identity of a complex is itself complex and is subject to variation and ramification. As we saw, a natural complex has an integrity in each order in which it is located. The totality of its integrities in all of its ordinal locations is the *gross integrity* or *contour* of that complex. Its *identity* is neither its integrity nor its contour but is the continuous relation between the contour and any of its integrities.[49] The "sameness" of a natural complex is provided, not by the persistence of any one constituent, but by the fact that each integrity is a constituent of the same contour. Thus it is the same complex in each of its locations. Even if a complex ceases to be located in a given order or acquires new ordinal locations and new integrities, it still remains the same complex.

According to the principle of ontological parity, relations and possibilities are natural complexes in the same sense in which anything else is a natural complex. As such, relations and possibilities are traits of other complexes. Relations, therefore, are never external to the complexes related; but they may be determinants of their scope alone and not of their integrity. In the case of possibilities, Buchler's principle of ordinality entails that there can be no "pure" or "abstract" possibilities. In Buchler's terminology, the traits of a complex "define" its contour. Crudely stated, possibilities are traits of a natural complex which define the ways in which the contour of that complex may (or may not) continue or be extended.[50] So conceived, there can be no possibilities which are not possibilities of and for the complexes of which they are extensions. This is why there can be no "pure" possibilities.

Buchler maintains that possibilities are no less "basic" to the integrity of a natural complex than are its traits of actuality; this is another expression of his principle of ontological parity. Possibility and actuality are interdependent; possibilities are actualized (although some may never be) and actualities generate possibilities. Possibilities, *qua* possible, permit certain additional possibilities and preclude others. For instance, the possibility of rain on a given day permits the possibility of flooding due to the rain. The actualization of a given possibility may give rise to new possibilities or to the nullification of others.

To this doctrine it may be objected that over and above the "real" possibilities to which it refers, there is an infinity of pure or abstract possibilities, since "anything at all is always possible." On Buchler's view a pure or abstract possibility would be one which does not affect either the scope or the integrity of any natural complex. Therefore a pure possibility would not be related to any natural complex and would be totally irrelevant. But an irrelevant possibility, one which makes no difference in any way, is not a possibility at all.

It also follows from Buchler's principle of ordinality that there can be no independent realm or "bare disjunction" of forms. Thus Buchler does not speak of *the* order of possibility. It seems to me, however, that when we make general statements about possibilities, we are referring to the class of possibilities, and a class must be a natural complex and hence must, by definition, be an order. Furthermore, if there is no single, inclusive order of possibility, then either general statements about possibilities are only statements about the term "possibility," or a class is an order of discourse only and the statements refer merely to the class and not to the possibilities themselves. But this, too, is problematic since, on Buchler's view, the possibilities themselves are located in this order of discourse (as the constituents of the class), as well as being located in the orders of which they are possibilities.

Clearly, Buchler must reject the principles of atomicity and independence. There are no isolated, irreducible, or wholly independent elements in this system. Even nature is not a single, self-existent complex. There is no single order of nature here as there is in Whitehead. It would be more apt to speak of nature as complexity than as a complex. Buchler speaks of nature in terms of "the provision and availability of complexes," avoiding any suggestion of fixed limitation, of completeness, or of absolute boundedness.[51]

Except in speaking about other metaphysical systems, Buchler avoids the term "concrete." He points out that if we wish to call attention to the particularity, the determinateness, the constancy, the completeness, or the relative independence of certain complexes, or if we wish to discriminate the concrete from the abstract or from the general, we are not making distinctions of primary and secondary ontological status or distinctions of degree of reality.[52] If we were to distinguish concrete actualities from any other actualities, we would still not be distinguishing anything which is more actual, or which *is* in any honorific sense of "to be." He does not deny that individuals, bodies, persons, have different traits from other types of complex. But he does deny that they are more ultimate or more real than other complexes and he denies that there is anything which is either more or less natural or more or less a complex than any other.

We may ask whether this principle of ontological parity does justice to the common sense conviction of the distinction between solid objects and attributes or parts, or abstract or ideal complexes. For example, it seems odd to say that a child is no more ultimate a reality than his name, his hands, his hunger, his color, or his fantasies. But it seems just as unsatisfactory to me to say, as we would on the traditional doctrine of substances, that the child's clothing, consisting of spatio-temporal individuals, is more ultimate or more real than his personality, his hunger, or the nightmares which grip him in terror.

In accordance with the principle of ontological parity, Buchler rejects the absolute distinctions between substance and quality and between particular and universal which mark substance-quality metaphysics. Buchler does have a doctrine of universals. He denies that only particulars "exist" in any sense of that term,[53] but both particulars and universals are complexes and there is no absolute distinction between the two. According to *Metaphysics of Natural Complexes*, a universal is a type of possibility. Buchler points out that a relation of similarity may prevail among complexes. This relation prevails as an actual trait of both actualities and possibilities (another consequence of ontological parity). It would be nonsense to say, for example, that the possibility that a person will marry is only possibly similar to the possibility that another person will marry. A universal, for Buchler, is a possibility of (actual) similarity: it is "the possibility of different complexes having traits that are similar in a given respect."[54] Thus a universal is a possibility which may be repeatedly actualized.

At least in connection with the factors I have examined in this preliminary survey of the two systems, Buchler departs more radically from traditional substance-quality metaphysics than does Whitehead. Buchler rejects the principle of atomicity altogether, whereas Whitehead combines a version of this doctrine with the doctrine of internal relatedness. While Whitehead denies that there can be actualities apart from the world, he asserts the independence of an actual occasion both as atomic, in his special sense, and as *causa sui*. For Buchler there is no complex which is independent but every complex is implicated in a network of intersecting constellations of complexes. At the same time, it is Buchler who insists that while there is no complex which has no relations, there are actualities as well as possibilities which are mutually unrelated; whereas in Whitehead's system, despite the doctrine of independence which he espouses, both actual occasions and eternal objects are internally related and every actual occasion is in some sense related to the entire universe.

Buchler abandons the traditional principle of substantial identity. Identity, for him, is not the unchanging "thisness" of something which persists unalterably through less fundamental change. Identity is now a relation between the gross integrity of a complex and any of its constituent integrities; it may undergo changes in the form of addition or subtraction of constituent integrities. For Whitehead, on the other hand, while an actual occasion is not a thing which remains the same through change, its identity is established irrevocably; it differs from the identity of a substance in that it is not independent of any of its traits or relations. On the other hand, the identity of an eternal object does remain the same even though the eternal object undergoes changing relations to actuality. This implies that there can be entities some of whose relations are not among their traits. This is in strong contrast to Buchler's doctrine that relations, like possibilities, are as much traits of any complex as its traits of actuality, potentiality, or power, or its traits of quantity, quality, or spatio-temporal location.

Buchler, though he accepts many kinds of priority and posteriority, of course rejects any principle of *ontological* priority and is highly critical of the principle of priority inherent in Whitehead's doctrines of actuality and concreteness.[55] Whitehead's substitute for substance, actual occasion, is concrete. Buchler's natural complex cannot be said to be concrete or abstract, and Buchler himself seriously doubts the viability of the concept of concreteness. Whitehead, like Buchler, modifies the traditional distinction between universal and particular. Where Whitehead preserves the notion of simples in connection with eternal objects, Buchler repudiates the principle of simplicity altogether. Finally, whereas Whitehead retains the distinction between substance and form, Buchler has abandoned the substance-quality orientation completely.

Notes

1. Alfred North Whitehead, *Process and Reality* (New York: Macmillan Company, 1929), pp. 78–79. Free Press Paperback edition, 1957, p. 64. Corrected Edition, edited by David Ray Griffin and Donald Sherburne (New York: The Free Press, 1978), pp. 49–50. Hereafter, PR with 1929, 1957 and 1978 page reference as in PR [1929] 78–79, [1957] 64, [1978] 49–50.

2. John Herman Randall, Jr., *Nature and Historical Experience* (New York: Columbia University Press, 1958).

3. Justus Buchler, *Metaphysics of Natural Complexes.* For full citation see "List of Abbreviations," p. xiii–xiv. Hereafter MNC.

4. On the concept of ontological priority see Buchler, MNC 30–31.

5. P. F. Strawson, *Individuals: An Essay in Descriptive Metaphysics* (London: Methuen and Co., Ltd., 1959), p. 11.

6. G. E. Moore, G. F. Stout, and G. Dawes Hicks, "Are the Characteristics of Particular Things Universal or Particular?" Richard J. Van Iten, ed., *The Problem of Universals* (New York: Appleton-Century-Crofts, 1970), pp. 156–174; passage quoted, p. 166.

7. Ibid., p. 158.

8. Ibid.

9. Alfred North Whitehead, *Science and the Modern World* (New York: The Macmillan Company, 1925, reprinted, Free Press Paperback Edition, 1967, same pagination), pp. 51–52. Hereafter, SMW followed by page number.

10. SMW 123.

11. PR [1929] 28, [1957] 23, [1978] 19.

12. PR [1929] 53, PR [1957] 41, PR [1978] 35.

13. Alfred North Whitehead, *Adventures of Ideas* (New York: Macmillan Co., 1933), p. 227. Hereafter, AI followed by page number. Note that at PR [1929] 29, PR [1957] 24, PR [1978] 20, Whitehead calls a nexus an individual.

14. PR [1929] 233, PR [1957] 178, PR [1978] 154.

15. Ibid.

16. George Kline, in a persuasive paper, distinguishes the actual occasion as concrescent, which he calls the "concrescence," from the actual occasion as "the *product* of the concrescent process," which he calls the "concretum." Each plays a different role in the process of transition. As I use it here, the term "actual occasion" refers to "the actuality of the atomic entity which is *both process and*

outcome." PR [1929] 129, PR [1957] 102, PR [1978] 84; italics added. See George L. Kline, "Form, Concrescence, and Concretum: A Neo-Whiteheadian Analysis," *The Southern Journal of Philosophy* 7:4 (Winter 1969–70), pp. 351–360.

17. PR [1929] 108, PR [1957] 86, PR [1978] 69.

18. PR [1929] 373, PR [1957] 285, PR [1978] 244.

19. PR [1929] 380, PR [1957] 290–291, PR [1978] 248–249. "The mental pole introduces the subject as a determinant of its own concrescence." Ibid. "[The category of reversion] is the category by which novelty enters the world." PR [1929] 381, PR [1957] 291, PR [1978] 249.

20. PR [1957] 291–292, PR [1978] 249–250.

21. SMW 64; 65.

22. PR [1929] 28, PR [1957] 23, PR [1978] 19.

23. AI 303.

24. PR [1929] 76, PR [1957] 62, PR [1978] 48.

25. PR [1929] 29, 359; PR [1957] 23, 274; PR [1978] 19, 235.

26. AI 261.

27. AI 258.

28. PR [1929] 35, PR [1957] 28, PR [1978] 24.

29. Cf. SMW 103.

30. PR [1929] 10–11, PR [1957] 10, PR [1978] 7.

31. SMW 70.

32. SMW 123–124.

33. PR [1929] 10, PR [1957] 10, PR [1978] 7.

34. PR [1929] 240, PR [1957] 184, PR [1978] 158.

35. PR [1929] 33, PR [1957] 27, PR [1978] 22.

36. PR [1929] 44, PR [1957] 34, PR [1978] 29.

37. SMW 161.

38. Cf. SMW 166.

39. MNC 2. Unless otherwise stated, all further page references are to this book.

40. MNC 1.

41. MNC 1.

42. Buchler distinguishes two generic ways of being, "prevalence" and "alescence." Although these concepts are of major importance to his metaphysics, it is not possible to deal with them in a paper of this length. But in so far as Buchler maintains that any complex whatsoever may be prevalent or alescent in the same senses of these terms, and that neither prevalence nor alescence is the more fundamental, the distinction between them has no special relevance for the thesis of this paper.

43. "It eliminates the idea that [anything] can be regarded as 'non-natural,' as intrinsically and necessarily discontinuous with any of the possibilities or actualities of the world . . . " ML 104.

44. MNC 6–10.

45. MNC 93–95.

46. MNC 12–17.

47. MNC 21–22.

48. The distinction between the integrity and scope of a natural complex is roughly analogous to the logical distinction between the meaning and scope of a term.

49. MNC 22. (See also MNC [1989], Appendix II, "Notes on the Contour of a Natural Complex," pp. 215–223. [Eds.])

50. MNC 162. Buchler introduces the word "prefinition" for this mode of "natural definition." Cf. MNC 161–163.

51. MNC 3.

52. Cf. MNC 41–47.

53. "Existence" is not a category in Buchler's system. See note 42 above.

54. MNC 180.

55. Cf. Justus Buchler, "On a Strain of Arbitrariness in Whitehead's System," *The Journal of Philosophy* 66:19 (Oct. 2, 1969), pp. 589–601.

The Concept of Identity in Justus Buchler and Mahayana Buddhism

Marjorie Cantor Miller

The metaphysical category of identity is necessarily a derivative category. It is one which cannot be adequately discussed or clarified apart from other fundamental categories to which it is related and whose significance and ramifications must be worked out within particular systematic contexts. A fruitful comparison of Buddhist views of this concept and those of Professor Buchler therefore requires three comparisons: (1) of basic metaphysical outlook, (2) of fundamental categories, and finally, (3) of the definition, functioning, and ramifications of the concept of identity within each of these systematic approaches. In the course of these three comparisons I hope to make clear the pervasive similarities in the two views of the nature of identity, and finally to show their ultimate incompatibility due to the different projects of the two systems.

I

A basic standpoint, the fundamental metaphysical principle for Professor Buchler, is that of "ontological parity."[1] It is a principle which in some sense sets a ground rule for all the metaphysical analyses which he undertakes: that is, if a metaphysical system is to be adequate, it must be broad enough to deal with all which *is*—and nothing we may dream, imagine, consider, encounter, etc., may be ruled out in advance as having less "being" or less "reality" than any other. This principle may be clarified if we pause to examine the term "natural complex."[2]

"Natural complex" is the term used in Buchler's system to refer to everything which in any way may be referred to (in his terms, "discriminated"). It is a replacement for the awkward categories "thing" or "entity," terms used for the same purpose of universal identification, but which tend in their very formulation to carry connotations of individuality, substantiality, and so forth: all of which connotations prejudge issues, thus standing in the way of further metaphysical analysis.

To identify complexes in a way which declares or implies that only "substances," or "moments," or "actualities," or "possibilities," or "processes," or "eternally unchanging objects" are *real*, is to distort reality by *a priori* declarations of its nature. It is to preclude intelligent exploration of all those discriminanda which do not "fit" into "reality" as thus identified. Such predeterminations of reality result in the philosophical absurdities of "unreal entities," "existing, subsisting and nonexisting entities," and so forth.

Degrees of Reality, degrees of Being have no place in the identification of natural complexes. Priority and posteriority, relative importance and unimportance, significance and triviality may indeed be predicated of complexes, but only as they are or may be located in specified orders—within which such comparisons are made or discovered. It is never with regard to their being or reality that complexes are prior or posterior, but only with regard to some specifiable criterion or set of criteria (themselves natural complexes, of course) which are discriminated as traits of a given order (itself a natural complex).

One of the consequences of the principle of ontological parity is the denial of the dichotomy between "appearance" and "reality": there is no really "Real," no Reality "behind" or "beneath" phenomena. This is not, however, to deny the distinction between fact and illusion in a spatiotemporal order. That is, if I see railroad tracks converging on the horizon, and I walk up to confirm my sighting and discover that the tracks are in fact parallel and do not converge—I simply discover that the complex of the converging tracks is a *real* visual illusion concerning the *real* parallel tracks: tracks whose parallelism is a fact in the spatio-temporal order. The illusion is no less a *real* illusion, no less a *real* complex, than the parallel tracks are *real* tracks. Further, part of the nature of the tracks, as natural complex, is to converge when viewed from a certain spatial perspective and to be parallel when viewed from another spatial perspective or when evaluated by mathematical or physical means. Neither of these aspects of the railroad tracks is more truly *the* tracks than the other. One is no more and no less fundamental than the other. One has no more being than the other. Each complex has just the kinds of relations that *it* has, just the consequences, just the causes, just the possibilities, actualities, etc. that *it* has—no more and no less than the other.

Professor Buchler's metaphysical system, based on the principles of ontological parity, is an attempt to develop a categorial apparatus broad enough to deal with every natural complex which may be encountered or produced; its emphasis is upon framing categories which are applicable to *every* discriminandum so that every complex may be seen as open to further query, amenable to manipulation and clarification by means of these

categories. Buchler's philosophical wrath, as it were, is directed against
dominant Western views which distort reality—limit what we may "legitimately" encounter or produce—by antecedently deciding that only certain
"realms of being," certain "levels of reality" are really "Real."

At first glance, there is much in the history of Buddhist metaphysics
which would encourage one to see it as an obvious exemplification of a
system founded on ontological *priority*: there are many references to
appearance-reality distinctions, to realms of being, etc. I would contend,
however, that the development of Buddhism in the Mahayana tradition (particularly in the Prajnaparamitâ Sutras, in the Madhyamikâ school and in
Zen) is exactly an attempt to overcome the problems of the principle of
ontological priority and to replace it with a principle of ontological parity.
That is, the distinctions between the "conditioned" and the "unconditioned" realms, between the "world of becoming" and the "world of Being," between *samsara* and *Nirvana*, were found to lead to much the sort of
distortions which Buchler identifies. To rule *samsara* out of "existence," in
favor of *Nirvana* as the only Reality, is to miss the meaning of both.

For Buchler, the principle of ontological parity means that there is
no ontological "Absolute" or "Ultimate": since every complex is a complex located in an order of complexes, and has constituent traits which are
themselves complexes with constitutive subaltern complexes, there is no
final resting place for query. The process of query never produces "ultimately first" or "ultimately last" points which are open to no further investigation. This is not to say, however, that, given particular purposes or
projects, no completion is ever possible. On the contrary: given the project
of building a house, writing a poem, determining the nature of the relations
between two complexes, or investigating the facts relevant to a particular
question, the building, writing, determining, and investigating are each
open to exactly the type of completion which their integrities in the given
orders permit. The principle of ontological parity applies only to the
mistaken attempt to find "Ultimately Ultimates" and "Absolutely final
Absolutes."

In the same way, various schools or groups of Buddhist philosophers
have emphasized various discriminations or descriptions as final, but as
Nâgârjunâ makes clear in his *Mûlamadhyamakakârikâ*[3] (and later schools
enlarge upon) these descriptions of finalities are only *relatively* final, given
certain projects; ontologically we must ultimately recognize no finalities at
all. From the broadest metaphysical perspective there is no final resting
point: no "One," no "Many," no "things," no "void":

The Lord replied: Nirvâna, Kâsyapa, is a consequence of understanding that all laws (things) are equal.[4]

The doctrine of *sunyata* is the principle in Mahayana Buddhism which functions, in some respects, as does Buchler's principle of ontological parity. As the latter notes that the predicates "being" and "real" must be attributed to all complexes alike if reality is not to be illegitimately distorted, Robinson describes *sunyata* (emptiness) as "the common predicate of all things:"[5]

> The perfection of wisdom consists in the direct realization that all the dharmas, whether conditioned or unconditioned, are empty. Transmigration is empty, and nirvâna is empty; the Buddhas are empty, and the beings whom they guide are empty. Thus there is no essential difference between the relative and the absolute.[6]

For Mahayana, then, as for Buchler, metaphysics must begin with at least one universal predicate: a predicate which applies without distinctions of degree or ultimacy to all which may be discriminated in any way. Thus for the Mahayanist a fruit fly, a bit of excrement, a human being, Mt. Fuji, the Buddha—all are equally empty. None is more "fundamentally" or "ultimately"empty than the others; such comparative terms do not even make sense in this context. For Buchler also God, man, puzzles, poems, and dreams are real equally, each existing in the mode and manner appropriate to it, but each having no more and no less being or reality than any other.

The Madhyamika doctrine of *sunyata* is, in a sense, a name for Buchler's principle of ontological parity: all discriminations have validity *only* within given perspectives. Considered ontologically, all things are equally empty. There is a genuine and impressive metaphysical principle which is common to these two approaches. Its utilization in the development and refinement of metaphysical categories, however, produces quite different results. The difference is attributable to fundamentally different purposes in the development of metaphysical doctrine.

II

It is in the movement from this basic principle to the categories that the difference of purpose must be examined. For Buchler, while we want nothing to be excluded from the realm of query, we proceed to query—to investigate, ramify, discover and analyze—by a process of precise discrimination. Metaphysical generalization must be broad enough to enable us to utilize well formulated categories in the making of careful and fruitful distinctions. Generalization is not, for Buchler, an end in itself. It is a tool which leads to ever more pointed distinctions: only thus is it a fruitful philosophic enterprise. "Precise generalization is twin to precise differentiation. Neither is possible alone for very long." (MNC 3)

For the Buddhist, on the other hand, the very process of discrimination stands in the way of the ultimate aim of knowledge. The aim of Buddhist philosophy is not simply to acquire greater clarity in the assimilation and manipulation of complexes, but is rather the religious goal of "transforming"[7] man's habitual way of "taking" himself and his world: it is to help him to recognize his being in the world, to achieve "awakening," enlightenment, *satori*. The doctrine of ontological parity is a prolegomenon to the development of adequate metaphysical categories; the doctrine of *sunyata* is a counterweight to the falsifying process of categorization.

While the Mahayana doctrine of *sunyata* resembles the Buchlerian doctrine of *ontological* parity in preserving the notion of a single reality, not divisible into realms having more or less being, reality, or ultimacy, it does permit a kind of *epistemological* priority: there are degrees of ultimacy with regard to truths, to approaches to the one reality. The experiences of *avidya* (ignorance) are experiences which recognize individuals, selves, birth, death, change, and duration. The development of metaphysical doctrine helps to counteract the errors of ignorance. Ultimately, however, true wisdom is the correction of metaphysics itself. It requires the hundred-fold negation,[8] or the quadruple logic of Nâgârjunâ:[9] the negation of the negation, the negation of the assertion, the negation of the asserted conjunction of negation and assertion, and the negation of the denial of the conjunction of negation and assertion. The metaphysical categories which represent epistemological progress over the views of ignorance are themselves transcended in ultimate knowledge.

The doctrine of *sunyata* (emptiness) applies not only to "things," but also to every category which attempts to organize or to interpret such "things." The categories developed by Buddhist thinkers represent insightful, progressive means of understanding the "things" which we frame and encounter, but they remain *means* to increased understanding. When we turn towards them as principles (as sorts of "things"), taking them as existents in a world of framed and encountered existents, we must recognize—according to the Mahayanists—that they, too, are *sunya* (empty).

In discussing the Buddhist metaphysical categories which bear upon the concept of identity, then, it must be remembered that these categories are useful only so long as they are not taken to be ultimately valid: they have reference only to an intermediate level of truth, to reality viewed from a particular perspective. In the last analysis their validity dissolves when the perspective itself is transcended.

The categories to be explored include three characteristics: *anâtman* (nonself), *anitya* (nonpermanence), and *duhkha* (suffering, "the universal nature of the hindrance-ridden being''[10]); the constituent factors of existence or *dharmas*; and the principle of relational origination[11] or *pratityasamutpâda*. In the final section of the paper the categories of *svabhava* (own-being) and *asvabhava* (non-own-being) will be explored as they refer to identity.

Anâtman is a fundamental ontological characteristic of beings: there is no "self," no individual ego nor "I," no "me" or "mine," there is no "belonging to me." Ultimately this categorical characteristic is a denial of a substance-attribute view of beings, or of an essence-attribute, or even a "container-trait" view of existence. There is no substantial "I" which "underlies" attributes or in which these attributes "inhere"; there is no "me" to whom traits "belong," or in which they may be found.

Given this fundamental description of the characteristic of *anâtman*, various Buddhist schools interpret it differently. For the Abhidharmists[12] and the Sautrantika-yogacarins[13] for example, a distinction is maintained between the false "appearance" of a self and the "reality" of *anâtman*. In the Madhyamika[14] tradition, however, neither *âtman* nor *anâtman* is more *real* than the other: ultimately both characteristics are *sunya*. The characteristic of *anâtman* is accepted as a higher "truth," a more productive concept, a better perspective from which to comprehend being—but ultimately all truths, concepts and perspectives are *sunya* (void). In Zen, on the other hand, the attempt is made to realize the metaphysical characteristic of *anâtman* in the very experience of or appearance of *âtman*: it is not to deny the reality of the self but to understand it differently—nonegoistically.

While the characteristic of *anâtman* applies particularly to conscious beings, it is related, through the characteristic of *anitya* (nonpermanence), to all that is. This term is applied to the "world of ten thousand things," to all "thought-created being," and in so doing involves an implied contrast to Nirvana, or nonthought created-being, or some other such absolute term which would represent permanence, eternality, etc. In fact, however, this is not the case: the development of Buddhism is a record of the attempt to overcome this linguistically created dichotomy, this "either-or" sort of opposition.

Anitya is a category which helps to prevent reification or entification: the "freezing" of reality into things, entities or beings. It makes change, becoming, process the characteristics of all that in any sense *is*. There are no Forms or substances which underlie or direct change, there is only change itself. Further, there are no *things* which change, there are only interrelated factors which may be investigated in any changing complex. This doctrine, too, is a corrective for the unenlightened perspective which takes "things" as having relative degrees of duration and permanence, and thus ranks them in hierarchies of significance by virtue of their substantiality; this view too, however, has *its* corrective, and that is that ultimately all is *sunya* or the One Mind. In fact, nothing changes, everything is as it always was: empty. This is *not* to say that there is a permanence which "underlies" all things, a "Being" which is more fundamental than the becoming. There is a shift in perspective that enables one to understand that all is changing, and all change is no-change.

The third characteristic, *duhkha*, is rendered variously as suffering,[15] turmoil,[16] and in a particularly useful fashion, as "the universal nature of hindrance-ridden being."[17] While as suffering and turmoil it is an extremely significant category in terms of Buddhist theory and practice, it seems to me that its ontological significance is best captured in Inada's rendering. That is, it is a further emphasis on the nonisolated, nonself-dependent, nonentified nature of what is. All that is is "hindrance-ridden." There is constant mutual "interference" of all the factors of existence, such that no "thing" can exist with all its traits contained "in" it. Although this description of *duhkha* barely scratches the surface of its range of meanings and significances, it is sufficient to show the emphasis being developed here against isolated, self-dependent, durable "things." *Duhkha* again focusses on the interrelationships, the mutual dependencies, the nonpermanent nature, the complexity of all that is.

The category of *dharma* (in its metaphysical sense rather than in its general meaning as "law" or "teaching") is an extremely difficult one to analyze. It refers to what Streng calls "the factors of existence."[18] Inada points out that the more common Western translation (since Warren) has been "elements of existence,"[19] and that this has led to the erroneous classification of Buddhist metaphysics as a radical pluralism.[20] The pluralist view takes *dharmas* to be the ultimately simple components, the real elements which give rise to phenomenal appearances. Stcherbatsky sees them as the irreducible point-instants of reality, unutterable because each is totally unique.[21]

If one pursues the elements-as-components view of *dharma*, one is able to draw out a well-developed metaphysical system which has interesting parallels and contrasts with Western metaphysical systems, and which is thus readily open to further philosophical analysis on classic Western lines. If one takes this view as an adequate representation of the Buddhist spirit, however, one surely misses the mark. For it is exactly the overcoming of the dichotomies of one/many, transcendental/phenomenal, simple/compound, etc., that the development of Buddhism is about.

If, on the other hand, we take *dharmas* to be the *constituents* of complexes rather than components, if we consider them to be the factors of existence in the sense that existence is always taken to be open to further ramification and exploration in terms of the *dharmas* which constitute it, then we begin to be closer to the Buddhist spirit. Inada summarizes this difference of approach as follows:

> This, in other words, is not to assert the existence of separate elements of existence first and then to see them in aggregation. The *dharmas* do not have any *a priori* status. Rather, it is to indicate the existential nature of so-called 'elements' *(dharmas)* in the matrix of relatedness. Thus one's experience is a fact of unique relatedness but at the same time the particular experience can be factored into different aspects. In this sense, the *dharmas* give a pluralistically factored nature or conception to experience and never the other way around, i.e., that they, the *dharmas*, underline experience in terms of an interplay or an aggregated construction out of them.[22]

Taken in this sense, *dharmas* are quite similar to what Buchler calls "traits."[23] They are the subaltern complexes which constitute a given complex without necessarily being components or parts: they are not absolute "simples," not "atoms," not elements whose transcendental "reality" could be opposed to the phenomenal ideality of experience. Rather, the category of *dharma* may be taken as a direction for analysis: every complex is composed of *dharmas*, or sub-complexes; every complex is related, has traits, which constitute it. Traits and relations are in turn complexes which may be factored—no existence of any sort is ultimately "complete" or absolutely simple; all are composite in some sense, all may be seen to be analyzable, ramifiable in terms of their *dharmas*.

The category of *dharma* is again a corrective to that stance or perspective which views existence as composed of substantial entities endowed with personal, individual existence. In the light of *dharma* theory it is clear that there is no substantial entity to be postulated as *having* the *dharmas*, to which the *dharmas* could belong. There are only *dharmas*, organized and related and *taken* to be things or persons, "I" or "mine." If one changes one's perspective or stance, examines existence from within another order, one finds "only" *dharmas*. As with all the categories discussed so far, however, this one too is—from yet another order or perspective—ultimately empty. There is neither complex nor simple, neither "things" nor "no-things," nor the constituents of things.

The final category to be considered is *pratîtyasamutpâda*, relational origination.[24] This category is fundamental to Buddhist ontology, but is most difficult to interpret adequately. It has been referred to as a theory of causation,[25] dependent arising,[26] and relativity.[27] According to Inada:

It should be interpreted in the total ontological sense which means that the rise of an experiential event is spread both "spatially" and "temporally" in a dynamic sense. That is to say, the relational structure is not static but underscored by the co-arising phenomenon of the total nature of things, although some elements at play are significantly present while others remain insignificant . . . the term, relational, . . . simultaneously . . . refers to a lateral, horizontal, and vertical relational structure to the moment in question. There is no reliance on anything alien nor an imposition by an alien force in the process because the moment is a moment by virtue of its own creative or constructive *(karmaic)* process. Thus the term, relational, makes way for both the active and the passive functions of the so-called "subject" in question. And the term, origination, refers to the arising of a novel moment by virtue of the total relational structure impelled by a natural dynamics of its own.[28]

Perhaps the most important point to stress concerning this category, with regard to the question of identity which is the project of this paper, is the nonisolated, nonindependent nature of any "thing" to be considered. Any "thing" will be found to be related in an indefinite number of ways to an indefinitely large order of "things" as such. Every experiential moment is not a substantial "thing," nor *of* a substantial "thing," but is rather a relational moment coordinated with an indefinitely large number of other such moments: it is passively constituted in the sense that every other moment which has a bearing on it has either contributed to it positively or contributed to it by not interfering with it. It is actively constituting in that some of the factors which constitute it are its own past moments, moments related to it in a compact temporal series; and its direction, its status, is the result of its own past and the seed of its future. This discussion, however, is distorting in that there have been references to "its" as if there were frozen entities—existences or subsistencies which are characterizable in and of themselves. In fact, the whole point of the *pratītyasamutpāda* doctrine is to undermine the "it-ness" of any moment, to see it as a moment in the multidimensional flow of the whole. In order to consider a "thing" it is necessary to view it as a nexus of codependent arisings: to see "it" as having whatever nature it has in relation to its location in a variety of orders— temporal, spatial, and causal.

Further, it is necessary to realize that whatever "nature" a "thing" has, in the multidimensional sense referred to above, will cease—as nature—when its co-ordinated moments cease. If, at any point, we stop mis-taking an object for an *object*, the "objects" which depend upon that mis-taken one will no longer be mis-taken. Every arising (as every ceasing-to-arise) has consequences; and no "object" can be understood apart from its conditions and consequences: indeed, in some sense, an object *is* its conditions and consequences.

A final point which should be noted is that every moment, of whatever description, enters into, is part of, this relational network. Thus sensing, consciousings, fantasies, lies, truths, persons, places, laws, relations, traits, objects, etc. *all* have causes and consequences. All are equally conditioned arisings. References to the unconditioned realm, to *Nirvana* as the unconditioned, are ultimately references to a perspective which *understands* the conditioned realm *as conditioned*. Again, in the enlightened perspective there is no dichotomy between conditioned and unconditioned, *samsara* and *Nirvana*. The *meaning* of both is *sunya*.

Turning now to Professor Buchler's categories, those we must consider include natural complex, order, relation, integrity, and contour. "Natural complex" was discussed at some length in the first section of this paper: we may simply reiterate here that whatever in any sense *is* is a natural complex. All natural complexes are orders, are located within more comprehensive orders, and have constituent traits which—relative to any given complex—are subaltern complexes. Further, any subaltern complex relative to any given complex is itself a complex and therefore an order with its own subaltern complexes: "Every complex is an order and belongs to an order of complexes. Thus orders are inclusive and belong to more inclusive orders." (MNC 93)

Buchler defines an order as "a sphere of (or for) relatedness." (MNC 95) In this sense, a complex (as an order) is not simply a nexus of relations, but is rather a context or framework for actual and possible relations. It is that which locates and limits the complex in terms of the commensurateness of traits.

Relations "are complexes which obtain 'between' or 'among' other complexes."(MNC 104) That is, they may obtain between or among two or more complexes viewed as separate, or between a complex and complexes viewed as subaltern to it. For two complexes to be related, each must be "at least a condition of the scope of the other; that is, of the other's comprehensiveness or pervasiveness. Each is a determinant, a determining trait, of the other's scope." (MNC 104)

To be related is to be relevant, but relevance may be divided into two kinds: strong relevance, and weak relevance. A relation which has bearing on the scope of a complex but not on the integrity of that complex is weakly relevant to it. A relation, on the other hand, that affects the integrity of a complex is strongly relevant to it.

The concept of "integrity" is quite obviously crucial to Buchler's metaphysics, but it is one of the most difficult to pin down. In the section of his work in which he focusses on the concept as it functions with regard to relations [29] he offers three negative cautions: (1) "Integrity cannot imply unique traits alone, for this means that a complex would be utterly unconnected with any other." (MNC 105) That is, an integrity of a complex cannot be viewed as that in it which is totally unique. While it is the case that every complex will have some unique traits, absolute uniqueness would render the complex opaque to any sort of discrimination—by definition it would be totally unrecognizable. (2) "The integrity of a complex does not lie in the totality of its traits." (MNC 106) For if integrity were viewed in this manner the changing of any trait whatsoever would result in a change of the integrity of a complex, and Buchler does not wish to use the category in this essentially evanescent fashion. (3) "Integrity is not to be equated with 'individuality,'" (MNC 106) since many complexes are not individuals (i.e., relations, processes, possibilities, etc.) and yet do have integrities.

Professor Buchler follows these three negative points with a positive suggestion which refers to the minimum conditions of an integrity: i.e., " . . . the minimal condition of an integrity is the location of a complex in a given order. To every complex there are related certain others which affect its location (its presence) in a given order, and therefore its integrity. Any such complexes will be called *strongly relevant* to it." (MNC 107, emphasis in original)

In an earlier section of *Metaphysics of Natural Complexes* "integrity" is defined as follows:

> Whatever the boundaries or limits of complexes may happen to be, whatever may be the conditions under which these limits obtain, wherever these limits may lie, any complex has just the status, just the relations, just the constitution that it has. This is its integrity, that in which its being "a" complex and "that" complex consists. Integrity entails both uniqueness and commonness. . . . The integrity of a complex is always conditional, in the sense that it is minimally determined by the location of the complex in this or that order of complexes. A complex has an *integrity* for each of its ordinal locations. (MNC 21–22)

Thus, as the concept emerges, it refers to the sense in which any complex as found, made, or encountered is in some sense a whole—a complex to be reckoned with *qua* a "this." However amorphous or precise the definition, whether consciously or unconsciously encountered, whether fantasized, sensed, or methodically developed—the "this" that we deal with is an integrity of a complex, it is the location of a complex within an order with all the traits and relations that its location in that order makes available for query.

Further, the very definition of integrity includes within it, as Buchler points out, the suggestion of "an integrity in the formation of which man has had a part. Discriminations are, so to speak, framings of complexes from the welter of complexes. They may or may not be conscious." (MNC 22–23)

The final category to be considered is "contour." The concept of contour is dependent upon "integrity" and "ordinality." That is, as we noted earlier, every complex may be located in an indefinitely large number of orders (i.e., spheres of or for relatedness). Every complex also has an integrity for each order in which it is located.

> The continuity and totality of its locations, the interrelation of its integrities, is the *contour* of the complex. The contour is itself an integrity, the gross integrity of that which is plurally located, whether successively or simultaneously. A contour is the integrity of a complex not in so far as the complex transcends all orders but in so far as it belongs to many orders. (MNC 22)

It should be stressed here that the contour of a complex, as its gross integrity, is *both* "the continuity *and* totality of its locations." That is, the contour should not be viewed as a mere aggregate of the integrities of a complex, nor yet as the aggregate of all actual and potential integrities: it is also the *continuity* of these locations. Further, the contour involves "the interrelation of its integrities." As "the continuity and the totality of its locations, the interrelations of its integrities," the contour of a complex can be seen to have a fluidity, a plasticity, which varies in degree depending upon the sort of a complex which it is.

For example, a complex such as the law of gravity will have a relatively stable contour: the orders in which it functions (the order of the relations between physical bodies, the order of formulations in the physical sciences, the order of linguistically expressible concepts, etc.) are relatively persistent orders; integrities of the law of gravity are not likely to arise or to cease in great number or with great frequency. This does not, however, imply that the contour of the complex "the law of gravity" is fixed for all time. On the contrary, new integrities, new orders in which this law may be located, may indeed emerge—and, if they were to do so, each new location would involve the arising of new possibilities as well as new actualities for the complex, and in so doing might cause previously existing possibilities and/or actualities to cease to prevail. Thus the contour—the totality and interrelationship of the integrities—would change. The change, however, would not be from a "this" to a "that."Rather, it expresses new locations for the "this"—the law of gravity. The continuity of the integrities of the complex is not impaired by the addition or deletion of an integrity: the continuity of the integrities, as a factor in the contour, is what permits flexibility in the contour as a whole.

The same principle would, of course, hold true if we consider a second example, one which generally has a less stable contour than the law of gravity. Let us consider a human complex: a man, Mr. Jones. The contour once again is the continuity and the totality of his locations, the interrelation of his integrities. His contour, his gross integrity, includes his integrity as a human animal, as a husband, a father, a wage-earner, an apartment dweller, a citizen of the United States, etc. Each of these integrities of Mr. Jones involves his location in different orders, and each order enters into his gross integrity. Should Mr. Jones move to a house, or give up his U.S. citizenship, or divorce his wife, some of his former integrities will cease to prevail, new actualities and possibilities will prevail in their stead. Mr. Jones' contour is the fluid expansion, contraction, or redirection of the totality of his integrities as they form a continuous interrelationship, in the order which is his gross integrity.

The category of "contour," of the interrelationship of the integrities of a complex as these integrities are given by the complex's location in many orders, is what gives depth to the notion of various perspectives or ways of "taking" a given complex. As located within a particular order the complex has ramifications which "belong" to that complex, although they may not be evident when the complex is considered in another of its integrities, viewed from a different perspective, located in another order. *All* its integrities enter into the determination of the contour of a complex: no integrity is, by itself, the "real" complex. All integrities are equally "real," all are constituents of the gross integrity.

III

Although the preceding section obviously does not do justice to the complete range of either the Buchlerian or Buddhistic metaphysical systems, those categories which have been explored provide sufficient background for the development and comparison of the concept of identity in the two approaches.

Buchler defines identity directly in terms of the categories already discussed: "The identity of a complex is the continuous relation that obtains between the contour of a complex and any of its integrities." (MNC 22)

In attempting to draw out the meaning and significance of this definition, the following features should be noted. First, *what* we are identifying is simply "a complex." That is to say, Buchler's definition of identity is broad enough to accommodate any and every discriminandum which we may frame or encounter. In this definition there is no hidden implication that the only "things" which have "true" identities are "substances," or individuals, or beings, or actualities, or any other such limiting notion. Thus whatever subject we may choose to investigate, Buchler's metaphysical system will help us to understand the limits of what is meant by *that* subject (as opposed to some other), and in so doing open avenues of exploration, rather than blocking access by *a priori* consideration which reduce some complexes to other kinds of complexes, said to be of a somehow more identifiable kind.

Second, the definition utilizes "the *continuous* relation" between contour and integrities. In so doing the definition immediately stresses the ongoingness, the continuity which can incorporate change, the nonstatic nature of complexes to be identified. The definition of identity here put forward does not require us to "freeze" or "entify" some "thing" in order to identify it. We can grasp it on the run, as it were, identifying the complex in the full movement of its existence. This is not to say that Buchler's view is a "process" system *requiring* constant change: the "continuous relation" in question *may* be a stable, relatively fixed, or even permanent one. The question is not pre-judged, not to be answered in advance of further investigation of the particular complex in question. The important point to be noted, however, is that the "continuous relation" does not *require* any fixity, any permanence, in order to assert or investigate identity. The very definition of identity incorporates the possibility of actual and possible change, change is not viewed as inimical to identity.

Third, by stressing the contour, the gross integrity of a complex as one of the relevant terms in the relation which determines identity, Buchler's definition emphasizes the multiordinal nature of the identity of a complex. Thus, to illustrate by an example: the table before me is identified by its integrities in many orders. Its identity includes its integrity as a sentimental object in the order of my emotional history, its integrity in a utilitarian order functioning as a firm and level surface to support writing materials, dining utensils or other equipment; its integrity in an aesthetic order as an object having pleasing proportions and quality of design; its integrity in the order of physical objects composed of molecules and atoms of certain kinds; etc. The table's sentimental and aesthetic integrities are as much a part of its identity as its physical integrity. Although some of its integrities are more comprehensive or pervasive than others, none is more "real" or more ontologically fundamental than any other. Each integrity is a matter of locating the table in some order, of viewing it from some perspective, but "the table," *qua* complex, involves the contour of all the perspectives within which it may appear. Further, it is always open to being located in yet another perspective (as the table in my example has now been located in the order of examples used in this paper), and these possible perspectives are also part of what is meant by the complex, part of the complex's identity.

Fourth, the definition concerns the continuous relation between the contour of a complex and *any* of its integrities. Thus as we locate a complex in an order, frame an integrity, we identify it by approaching it *through* that order and exploring that integrity's relationship to a broader view of the complex, an imaginative or recollective exploration of other possible integrities which may be associated with the given one and which form the complex's gross integrity. The significant point here is that it is not necessary to know all of the integrities of a complex in order to identify it. On the contrary, for any integrity in question it will be possible to explore that integrity's continuous relation to the broader configuration which is the contour of the complex. The gross integrity is never closed, never absolutely complete; but it has suggestive limits and directions which are knowable just because it is a *contour*—a complex which is given breadth and depth by the continuous relationship between the contour and any of its integrities. Each integrity will actualize some possibilities of the complex and, in so doing, crystallize new possibilities for the complex and cancel others. While all possibilities and actualities of the complex may never be known with absolute finality, the contour—as broad outline—is knowable sufficiently for identification of the complex as *that* complex.

In turning to the Buddhist view of identity, analysis is made considerably more difficult by the lack of a single sentence which conclusively defines the term for Buddhism, as Buchler's sentence defines the term for us within the context of his system. The concept of *svabhava* (own-being, self-nature, self-identity), as with all concepts, is one of a pair of opposites: *svabhava* and *asvabhava* (non-own-being, non-self-identity). As with all such pairs in the Madhyamika and following schools, it is the crystallization of a one-sided position, and thus from an ultimate epistemological perspective its assertion or denial is a falsification of the reality of *sunya*. As Nâgârjunâ points out in the section of the *Mûlamadhyamakakârikâ* entitled "Svabhava parîksâ" (examination of self-nature):

> Those who see (i.e., try to understand) the concepts of self–nature, extended nature, existence, or nonexistence do not perceive the real truth in the Buddha's teaching.[30]

To concern oneself with *svabhava*, or identity, is to focus on the separated, individuated aspects of what is. As the discussion on categories indicated, this is deemed the least useful, least productive mode of approaching reality within the Buddhist framework. If one were to pursue the concept of *svabhava* as such, the most adequate drawing out of this category would be found in Stcherbatsky's work[31] which deals with the Sautrantikayogacara school of Buddhism. While the description and elaboration of this category is indeed of significance, it seems to me that a more general notion of the Buddhist concept of identity may be garnered from a discussion which deals with other schools as well, and which, in so doing, gives proper weight to perspectives of reality broader than the one on which Stcherbatsky focusses. In order to develop this broader conception of identity I would like to reconsider each of the four points raised with regard to Buchler's definition and to explore relevant correspondences and contrasts with elements of the Buddhist system.

The first feature noted with regard to Buchler's definition was that the definition refers simply to "a complex"; the categories utilized in the definition apply equally to any and every complex which may be discriminated; no complex or type of complex is inherently more "identifiable" than any other. While we have no explicit Buddhistic definition before us for analysis, the general tone of Buddhist treatment is such as to encourage the view that on the level of categorial clarification every and any subject which we might wish to consider is equally amenable to treatment in terms of the Buddhist categories discussed. That is, there is no distinction maintained, in terms of levels of "fundamentality"—identifiability—between "things" and their relations, substances and their attributes, objects, fantasies, dreams, contrivances, states, or movements.

While characteristics such as *anâtman* and *duhkha* are essentially anthropomorphic in their derivation and primary application, they are expandable—as metaphysical categories—to all subjects for identification. No-separate-self, hindrance-riddenness, and nonpermanence are characteristics which apply to all that may be isolated as a subject for investigation. They apply to any "this" we may "point" to, whether it be object, state, dream, work of nature or of man, of material or mental creation.

The same may be said for the categories of *dharma* and *pratîtyasamudpâda* as they were discussed earlier. Every discriminandum may be "factored," explored in terms of the factors which compose it. No factors are "ultimate" or "primary" or more "real" than others: all are further avenues and directions for exploring what is never "finally" explored. Every discriminandum, in addition, is part of the network of "conditioned arising" or relational origination. Again, neither mountain nor dream, neither saint nor sin is an isolated "object" or event. Objects and events, subjects and traits are all equally relationally connected: part of a conditional network which sees neither nexus nor line of connection as metaphysically prior.

Further, as the process of definition, definitions as formulations, and categories themselves are natural complexes for Buchler; and as the definition of identity is thus identifiable by its own criteria within Buchler's system; so, in the Buddhist system the characteristics which have been described as applying to all which may be identified are themselves subject to the very same categorization. Thus the very categories themselves are without self-being, hindrance-ridden, impermanent, factorable, and enmeshed in the network of relational origination.

While the self-reflexive nature of Buchler's definition of identity simply gives us further material for analysis, i.e., the identity of the complex "the definition of identity," the self-reflexive nature of the Buddhist view ultimately leads to the transcending of the category of identity itself, along with the kind of metaphysical speculation which such a category promotes. The significance of this point will emerge more clearly as the comparison of the two views continues.

The second feature of Buchler's definition discussed above was the utilization of the "continuous relation" between contour and integrities. It was noted that this formulation is an attempt to avoid the necessity, present in other Western metaphysical systems,[32] of "freezing" discriminanda in order to identify them. It is obvious from the discussions in the first two parts of this paper that Buddhism also denies that it is necessary for there to be "entities," unchanging beings, or Forms for identification to take place.

It is also obvious, however, that again the Buddhist view goes further than the Buchlerian on this issue. That is, Buchler's system leaves open the possibilities for change, endurance and permanence: it is only after investigation that the relative duration, the perviousness or imperviousness of a complex to change may be determined. On the contrary, the Buddhist position stresses the necessary impermanence, even evanescence of any complex to the considered: continual change is *a priori* asserted to be of the nature of every complex whatsoever.

But if we return to the self-reflexive nature of the view of identity mentioned earlier, we find that once again the position contains within it the springboard which pushes towards its own transcendence. That is, as the categories themselves are subject to their own categorization, impermanence itself is impermanent—change itself is changing. The implied dichotomy between change and permanence is transcended in the self-reflexiveness of the category. Once again the situation becomes fluid, incapable of being grasped in onesided doctrine. The openness which is present in the precise Buchlerian formulation is maintained not in the specifics of the Buddhist categorial formulation, but is maintained in the fluidity of the transcendent view created by its self-reflexion.

The third feature of Buchler's definition discussed above was the multi–ordinal nature of identity as stressed in the relation of an integrity to the contour, the gross integrity of a complex. While Buchler's category of ordinality is not strictly isomorphic to the Buddhist notion of perspective, or standpoint, or levels of knowing which was discussed in the course of the examination of Buddhist categories, it does bear an important functional resemblance to this notion, with particular significance for the problem of identity.

That is, for the Buddhist there are the perspectives of *samsara* and *Nirvana*; of ignorance, sophistication, and enlightenment; of economic effectiveness, householder's functioning, or monk's spiritual progress. All of these, while yielding different discriminations, are yet no more than perspectives on the *one* reality. As was pointed out earlier, some perspectives are more spiritually productive than others, some are morally preferable to others, some are termed epistemologically more fundamental than others, but no one perspective yields a discrimination which is the exclusive presentation of reality. All the discriminations are equally perspectives, all are equally real.

As in Buchler's system we must not mistake *an* integrity—the discriminandum of *an* order—for the identity of the complex. As within his system the complex must be broadened and deepened by recognition of its multiple locations in order to be identified, so in the Buddhist framework the identification of a complex requires the recognition that it may be discriminated in many pespectives, but that no perspective is—by itself—the identity of the complex.

If we return once more to the example of the table before me: in Buddhist terms the table against which I bump my elbow is a real object having relations, causes, and conditions which are relevant to it as an object in the world—but, that is only the table from the *samsaric* perspective. To *take* that table, with its beginnings in the cabinetmaker's shop and its probable end in a town incinerator, as *the* table would be to miss the reality (the identity) of the table entirely. If we analyze the table into its *dharmaic* factors, its mental and physical constituents, we note the evanescent character of its existence: the changes and degenerations which are occurring minute-by-minute, the lack of solidity, the uselessness of depending upon it, the uncertainty of its continuation, etc. We are viewing the table from within a more sophisticated perspective, but, again, to *take* this discrimination as *the* table would be to distort it. We may further be capable of viewing the table as *sunya*: with neither constituents nor characteristics to distinguish it from the One Mind which is its original nature. But, once again, to take this nondiscrimination as *the* table would be to miss the possibilities for its use as a dining surface, to run the risk of bumping my nose on its non-existence should I try to bend through it! This nondiscrimination no more captures the "true" identity of the table than any of the other perspectives considered.

Thus the concept of identity in the Buddhist system requires the same kind of appreciation for the possibilities of multi-ordinal location as does the concept in the Buchlerian formulation. Rather than replacing an "appearance" with a "reality," ultimately the Buddhist notion of perspectives serves, as does "gross integrity" for Buchler, to broaden and deepen the one reality of the complex.

The fourth and final point raised in the discussion of Buchler's definition concerned the stress given to the relation of the contour of a complex to *any* of its integrities. It was pointed out during that discussion that Buchler's formulation here provides access to the identity of a complex through any one of the orders in which it is located: just as the third feature above noted that no identity was determinable without consideration of the multi-ordinal nature of a complex, this feature provides that while no single integrity offers privileged access to the identity of the complex, its identity may be determined with reference to any given integrity—any given order which we may discriminate.

As this feature of Buchler's system allows access to the identity of a complex without requiring that the complex be "closed" or fully determinate, without requiring an exhaustive inventory of every integrity of the complex, the Buddhist view also encourages the suggestiveness of a complex's identity to enrich our concept of its identity as grasped through any given perspective. Any given perspective of a complex, when properly understood as only one of the possible perspectives in which the complex may appear, and when seen against the background of the range of possible perspectives within which the complex may be perceived, allows access to the suggestive richness of the broader sense of the complex's identity. When perspective is adequately understood, the contention that some perspectives are primary is finally transcended in the realization that access may be had *through* whatever perspective is currently discriminated.

Again, however, the self-reflexiveness of the Buddhist notion changes the ultimate evaluation: for perspectives themselves, rather than being co-equal spheres of or for relatedness, are transcended in that form of being-in-the-world which does not *take* at all: which finally has no need to *identify*, which does not delimit or separate-out, which is no longer concerned with the nature of "this."

It is this final transcendence, this perspective-of-perspectives, which makes the Buchlerian and Buddhist views of identity ultimately incompatible. For Buchler, precise identification is a tool leading to ever more fruitful metaphysical investigation; for the Buddhist, the very similarly conceived process of identification is ultimately counterproductive in the achievement of the ideal spiritual mode of human being-in-the-world. Metaphysics itself is ultimately transcended; in the enlightened state it is finally irrelevant.

Notes

1. MNC esp. pp. 31–51. See "List of Abbreviations" for Buchler's works, p. xiii–xiv.

2. Cf. Ibid., ch. 1, esp. pp. 1–17.

3. Cf. Kenneth Inada, *Nâgârjunâ, A Translation of his Mûlamadhyamakakârikâ* (Tokyo: Hokuseido Press, 1970), esp. ch. 25 "Nirvana parîksa." And see also Frederick Streng, *Emptiness: A Study in Meaning* (Nashville: Abingdon Press, 1967); for example: "From the standpoint of highest truth there were neither many particulars nor an absolute single reality: all was empty of such ontological determinations." (p. 34)

4. *Saddharma-Pundarîka*, trans. H. Kern, in *Sacred Books of the East*, F. Max Muller (ed.) (Oxford: Clarendon Press, 1909), 21, p. 129.

5. Richard Robinson, *The Buddhist Religion* (Belmont, CA: Dickinson Publishing Co., 1970), p. 51.

6. Ibid.

7. When dealing with Buddhist ideas in academic formats, it is always necessary to utilize language, but in so doing one is inevitably distorting the position one tries to communicate. The term "transforming" suggests change from one state to another, different state. The Buddhist view, however, is that it is the change which is no–change. Nothing new is added, nothing is lost in enlightenment—nevertheless the enlightened one "takes" his experience differently, is integrated with his world in a way which ignorance bars the unenlightened from recognizing.

8. Chang Chung-Yuan, *Original Teachings of Ch'an Buddhism* (New York: Vintage Books, 1971), p. 130.

9. Cf. Streng, op. cit.

10. Inada, op. cit.,p. 24.

11. I am following Inada in translating this term as relational origination. It has been rendered in many other ways: usually as codependent arising (cf. Conze [note 15 below]). A deviant but important version is Stcherbatsky's use of "relativity" and his specialized notion of "synergy."

12. See material in the "Introductory Essay," in Inada, op. cit..

13. See F. Th. Stcherbatsky, *Buddhist Logic* (New York: Dover, 1962)

14. Cf. the work of Nâgârjunâ, in Streng, op. cit. and Inada, op. cit.

15. Cf. Edward Conze, *Buddhism: Its Essence and Development* (New York: Harper, 1959).

16. Cf. Streng, op. cit.

17. Inada, op. cit, p. 24.

18. Streng, op. cit., p. 30.

19. Inada, op. cit., pp. 7–9.

20. Cf. Stcherbatsky, *The Central Conception of Buddhism and the Meaning of Dharma* (Calcutta: S. Gupta, 1961).

21. Stcherbatsky, *Buddhist Logic*, Vol. 1, particularly p. 106 ff.

22. Inada, op. cit, p. 9.

23. This category will be examined in some detail below, when Buchler's categories are outlined.

24. Cf. Robinson, op. cit., p. 22.

25. Ibid., also cf. Conze, op. cit.

26. Esp. Conze, op. cit.

27. Stcherbatsky, op. cit.

28. Inada, op. cit., p. 17.

29. Cf. MNC 105–108.

30. Nâgârjunâ, in Inada, op. cit., p. 99.

31. Cf. esp. the two volume *Buddhist Logic*. In this school identity is defined with reference to objects as compact series of moments, showing directional development and exhibiting functional dependence upon their own past moments, and interdependence with the moments which condition the arising of each moment in the compact series, and which are in turn conditioned by the moments in the series.

32. Plato and Aristotle are prime examples of the sort of positions Buchler here attacks.

The Nature of Categorial Theory

Abraham Edel

The aim of this paper is threefold. First, I want to propose a fresh approach to Aristotle's *Categories*. Second, I want to reflect, in the light of the outcome, on the expectations we can have for categories in metaphysics. Third, I want to comment on Justus Buchler's view of categories in the light of the outcome of the two preceding parts.

No apology is needed for starting with Aristotle's *Categories*. Ever since the *Categories* was placed at the head of the Corpus, the foundational character of categorial theory has been explicit. That is why a fresh way of looking at the *Categories* is at the same time a fresh way of looking at Aristotle's metaphysics, and suggests a mode of reckoning with categorial theory generally.

I

Let us put before us the full list of the ten categories, as given in *Categories*, ch. 4 and *Topics*, Book I, ch. 9, with their familiar English names:

Substance *(ousia)*. The associated notion of Essence (what-it-is, here *ti esti*) is said to signify *ousia* in *Topics* (103b31).

Quantity *(poson)*, how-large.

Quality *(poion)*, what-sort.

Relation *(pros ti)*, with-relation-to-what.

Place *(pou)*, where.

Time *(pote)*, when.

Situation *(keisthai)*, also referred to as Position, Posture, literally, to be laid or to lie, more generally to be in a position.

State or Condition *(echein)*, literally to have or hold, and in intransitive, to hold oneself or be or keep in a certain state.

Action *(poiein)*, to do or make.

Passion *(paschein)*, to suffer, be affected.

There are many technical and textual problems about the categories. For example, it is not clear whether Aristotle intended the list to be complete, exclusive, exhaustive. There are variations in which category large blocs of material seem to fall. There are variations in the list itself; most notable, Movement *(kinēsis)* appears in a few partial lists to be standing in place of all or some of the last four categories (e.g., *Eudemian Ethics* 1217b30; *Metaphysics* Z 1029b24–25, I 1054a5 ff., L 1069a23 and b9 f.). This seems to conflict with Aristotle's procedure in determining types of movement *(kinēsis* is often used broadly to cover change as well, though *metabolē* becomes his technical term for the broader sense) in that the types are determined by the categories in which change takes place. A further, and we shall see a very important, question is the status of Situation and State. They are rarely listed and have to be presumed as included in the "etc." that is found in many of the passages.

A few points in relation to these problems will be relevant for initial clarity and for the development of my thesis:

(1) As to distinctness and scope of the categories, Aristotle tries to keep them apart and he gives them collectively almost unlimited scope. His central illustration in the *Categories* shows how a man may be talked of under all ten categories—in one answering what it is, in another what sort, and so on. Further, Aristotle's non-reductive conception of the sciences, which sharply distinguishes them as running, so to speak, in different tracks (arithmetic has its field and geometry another) would suggest that the highest genera, as the categories are often called by him, would have comparable sharpness. Again, the frequent denial that the categories are species of a higher genus ("being" and "one" are denied the status of a unitary genus) suggests ultimate plurality and distinctness.

The domain of entities to be characterized is pretty limitless, if we can judge by Aristotle's description of the categories as categories of things that are *(tōn ontōn)*. In short, anything that can in any sense be said *to be* whether in the sense of simple existence or of being such-and-such a character, whether predication is essential or accidental, is a fit candidate for categorization. In linguistic terms, even most prepositions—the likeliest candidates for exclusion—could be taken as designating relations or with different objects assigned as phrases to different categories.

(2) In spite of Aristotle's scrupulous attention to the differences of respect in which the apparently same material can come under one category in one way and under another category in another way (e.g., *Categories*

9a16 ff.), there is considerable raiding as between categories. Quality is particularly swollen. It covers habit *(hexis)* and disposition *(diathesis)*, natural capacities or incapacities, passive qualities and affections *(pathētikai poiotētes kai pathē)*, and the forms and figures or shape of things *(schēma* and *morphē)*. Now habits might seem to belong to the category of State or Condition *(echein*—to which indeed *hexis* is related etymologically), passive qualities to that of Passion *(paschein),* and even form and shape to Place, if we took the *where* which generated the category to be answerable by place *(topos)* and recalled that Aristotle's refined analysis of place in *Physics* IV defines it by limits, as the innermost boundary of the container. Aristotle is not unaware of such possibilities. In *Categories* 9a16 ff. he is careful to point out that a natural capacity is assigned not because a person is in a certain state or condition (not by *diakeisthai pōs)* but because of the inherent power to do or to suffer something. Aristotle seems to be guided by the fact that we call people healthy or good runners when they are of a *certain sort.* Now this may be a conclusive argument against the claims of Situation *(keisthai)* but does not touch State *(echein).* Indeed the first kind of quality (habit) is not even defended against State, although the very term for habit *(hexis)* is, as noted above, related to *echein.* Aristotle does defend passive qualities and affections against the claim that they fit under Action and Passion by pointing out that, for example, honey is not called sweet because it has been affected but because it can produce an affection of the senses. He would, presumably, not deny that causal processes of action and passion might underlie this quality, but they are not to be identified with it.

In spite of Aristotle's sensitivity to the problem of the relation of categories, we are left with the feeling that Quality has been making serious inroads on the last four categories. Such raiding to carry off large blocs of material would help explain why the last four are treated so briefly in the *Categories.* The particular patterns of raiding are a separate inquiry. One can easily conceive of the category of Time being wholly carried off to Quantity, for time is on Aristotle's view a measure of change, or to Relation, since the measuring is done by relating changes. But Aristotle does not do this.

(3) There seems to be a widespread opinion that Situation *(keisthai)* and State *(echein)* are relatively unimportant, that they have a very limited use, were abandoned by Aristotle, or do not have to be made sense of in any general interpretation of the categories. This starts from the very limited illustrations Aristotle gives of them in the original list of *Categories* 4—of Situation, lying and sitting; of State, shod, armed. The neglect is exacerbated by the fact that no exposition seems to be given of these categories in the *Categories* as there is of Substance, Quantity, Relation, Quality; and Place and Time in the *Physics,* and Action and Passion in *On*

Coming-to-be and Passing-away. And it is strengthened even more by the fact that in the numerous listings they rarely appear and have to be presumed in the "etc." Ross in his *Aristotle* and Tredennick in his translation of the *Metaphysics* both conclude that Aristotle abandoned these two categories.[1] It is no wonder that Moravcsik, when he offers an interpretation of Aristotle's categories which might stumble over these two categories feels that they can be ignored.[2] We shall come back to the problem of these two categories later on, but only after considering traditional and changing interpretations of the categories as a whole. To this we now turn.

Traditional controversy in interpreting Aristotle's categorial theory has centered on whether he was doing a linguistic analysis or providing an ontological theory. The first is suggested by the fact that the categories are, or serve as, *predicates* in asking questions about individuals. If we asked a great many questions about Socrates we could answer in sentences of the form "Socrates is X" where X could be replaced by the terms that appear as Aristotle's paradigmatic illustration in *Categories* 4: "a man," "five-foot," "larger," "white," "in the market-place," "yesterday" (not alone, together with some of the other terms), "sitting," "shod" or "armed," "cutting," "being cut." On the other hand, Aristotle typically calls the categories *genera of what is*, which suggests the second interpretation.

There is no need here to recapitulate this traditional struggle, and good reason in the light of Aristotle's own procedure not to pose this picture of contrasting paths. Aristotle himself rarely makes us choose between a linguistic and a physical investigation—on the one side examining a question *logikōs*, what people say, the questions asked, the definitions of terms involved, and so on; and on the other side examining a question *phusikōs*, gathering the facts of experience. The *endoxa* or initial beliefs with which a typical Aristotelian inquiry begins, will include a melange of facts, opinions, use of terms, theories, etc. And when an inquiry is completed and we have an answer, Aristotle does not expect the logical-linguistic and the factual to differ. In physical matters, to know the essence and so have an account *(logos)* of what a thing is, is also to know its nature *(phusis)* and so how it will typically behave. To make the logical versus ontological the central issue is to press a later formulation, not to ask for Aristotle's aim.

In the process of inquiry, however, Aristotle does recognize an occasional obstacle coming from too great a reliance on what we say as against what the facts are. For example, in *Metaphysics* H 1045a20ff., he says in exploring the problem of substance: "It is clear that if people go on in their customary way of defining and speaking it is not possible to answer and resolve the difficulty." And in *On Sophistical Refutations* he points out that we may place something in the wrong category if we simply follow verbal form: for example, "to flourish" has the same verbal form as "to cut" or "to build," but the first denotes a quality while the others denote actions (166b17f.).

It is refreshing to note that recent studies move away from formulations of what Aristotle is trying to do in simplistic dichotomous ways. Moravcsik takes "the constitutive principle of the list of categories" to be "that they constitute those classes of items to each of which any sensible particular—substantial or otherwise—must be related." And Ackrill in his notes to his translation of the *Categories* suggests that the list was arrived at by convergence of two different paths—one by observing what types of answers are appropriate to different questions, and the other by pressing the question "What is it?" to any thing whatsoever till we come to some very high genera.[3]

If the doors are opened by such studies to fresh approaches, it is only natural to look in wholly new directions. My proposal here is to track down more systematically the uses of the categories in the various parts of the Corpus. This is a kind of inner functional approach. Indeed Aristotle's own theory of the causes *(aitia)* itself would suggest such an approach, for he took his distinctive contribution to the theory of explanation to be the discovery of the final cause, how a thing functions and what it brings about. Why should not this mode, so central to the biological works and to the humanistic fields, be applied also to help solve the problem about the nature of the categories?

A distinction can be drawn between the uses to which Aristotle puts the categories as a set, and the specific uses of individual categories. Among the first we find: (1) Logical use—appeal to the categories to help clarify terms, furnish definitions, and detect fallacies of ambiguity. For example, "white" cannot be the genus of "snow" and "swan" because they are Substance while it is Quality (*Topics* 120b37ff.). (2) Use in physics— appeal to the categories directly to classify types of movement or change: coming-to-be and passing-away as change in Substance, alteration in Quality, growth and diminution in Quantity, and locomotion in Place (e.g., *Physics* III 200b33ff.). Aristotle patiently explains why there cannot be change in some of the remaining categories (*Metaphysics* K, 12; cf. N 1088a33ff.). (3) Use in metaphysics—Aristotle appeals to the categories as ultimate genera of being in a frequent attempt to head off any treatment of Being itself or of the One as ultimate substance.

As for specific use of individual categories, let us here take only the first step in such an inquiry—to locate the parts of the Corpus and the problems within which each category has a base of operations. The high status categories pose no problem. Substance applies to the whole field of natural bodies, whether inorganic or organic; its problem (highlighted in

Metaphysics Z-H) is to determine the criteria for identifying essence, that is, for understanding and explaining things and their operations. Quantity has a firm base in arithmetic and geometry; there are, of course, theoretical problems (e.g., incommensurables and the analysis of the infinite) and applied problems in physics (e.g., the existence of atoms). Quality is less easily discernible. But a little reflection will show that this category arises from and is oriented to the systematic treatment of a large class of changes (alteration) and is involved in the whole theory of contraries and the idea of change as passage within a definite track from one to another extreme within a given genus. There is perhaps a greater unity in the effort than a modern separation of the logical and the empirical might notice in Aristotle's arguments about the logic of contrariety (in *Metaphysics* I), the general theory of change (in *Physics* I), the detailed study of qualitative processes (in *Meteorologica* IV), the systematization of qualities in the chemical theory underlying physical motions of natural elements (*On Coming-to-be and Passing-away* II), and the specific contexts of physiological explanation of sensory phenomena (in *On the Soul* and *On Sense and Sensible Objects*). Perhaps taking all this together we have the problem matrix in which the category of Quality as a general concept takes its rise and builds up its hope of categorial rule.

Relation is a complex notion, especially since it operates on both the object level and the language level. Among the first, Aristotle's examples of the master-slave relation points to a concern with institutional forms and interactions, and again—even more centrally—his example of the bird-winged relation with a functional treatment of the working of different organs in the body. The whole theory of the mean in medicine and in ethics, and of balance in politics is through and through relational. On the logical level, especially in the *Topics,* Aristotle is sensitive to fallacies that arise from treating a relational term as if it were a simple unqualified term—treating *haplōs* what is *pros ti.* Finally, on the metaphysical level, a relational approach to interaction in the case of agent and patient (*Physics* III, 3) yields the formulation that the actuality *(energeia)* of the agent and that of the patient are one and the same. This goes beyond simply recognizing that that which is active (since it acts on something) is relative to that which is passive (*Metaphysics* D 1020b31). There has been much concern about the unevenness of Aristotle's treatment of Relation. His attention to it on the logical level came early, but never bloomed (obviously) into a logic of relations. His metaphysical treatment of Relation came late, and might have supplanted his whole idea of substance on the basis of his identification of actuality *(energeia)* with substance. But that is another story.

Place and Time have their limited but important provinces to rule. Place is analyzed in *Physics* IV, but it also enters intimately into the theory of *On the Heavens* and the determination of the character of the physical bodies (in the theory of natural places). It is fairly clear that Place as a category has won out over a number of rivals in the development of Greek science and philosophy—over the idea of the empty, of extension, of non-being. It unifies concepts of position and direction. In the long run it was to be replaced by the idea of space as extension (in the Euclidean, Lucretian and Newtonian manner). Time has its central base in the theory of change, and Aristotle develops this with fullness. It has a secondary place in the theory of truth (as in the naval battle tomorrow, of *On Interpretation* 9), and the overtones of determinism versus development. Contemporary logicians have only recently begun to give this serious attention.[4] It has also some fairly limited uses in the study of qualitative changes where attention is on the changing quality rather than the temporal aspects. A significant point here in the light of later developments is the treatment of the question of the velocity of light and the relation of small scale instantaneous to large distance changes (*On Sense and Sensible Objects* 6).

Let us skip over Situation and State for the moment and turn to Action and Passion. Certainly charges of triviality against the last four categories do not hold for Action and Passion since a great part of the Corpus is the home of these categories. In one direction, the *Poetics* is the study of *poiēsis* in one domain: here Aristotle goes about analyzing the nature of tragedy through the effect of a successful tragedy on the hearer—in short, the *pathēsis* or what he suffers. (Cf. also the study of the emotions in the *Rhetoric*.) In another direction lies the whole of chemical interaction: this is analyzed in Book I of *On Coming-to-be and Passing-away* in terms of the conflict of preceding theories about what goes on in what we would call chemical transformations. Much of the treatment of sensory experience in *On the Soul* is cast as an inquiry into the kind of action and passion that is taking place. On a vast scene, *poiēsis* as making emerges as one of the three great divisions of human activity, alongside of *praxis* (doing) and *theōria* (contemplation). It is quite an imperial sweep for a ''little'' category.

There remain the tasks of applying this functional approach to Situation and State, as well as of trying to solve the general problem of their meaning and nature. But perhaps we ought to state more definitely at this point that what is emerging in this survey of the other eight categories is a quite untraditional, but nevertheless very Aristotelian way of looking at Aristotle's categories. They are concepts that grew out of a variety of problems in a variety of domains of Aristotelian (and general earlier philosophic and scientific) inquiry and take on a key role in the formulation of questions and in guiding the mode of resolution. In this sense they set the whole direction of questions and answers in the philosophy. It follows as a secondary matter in the Aristotelian way of doing things that they will be regarded as the appropriate classification of terms or as designating the forms of being.

How are such concepts derived? Since they serve as principles *(archai)* or starting points they are reached in a sweeping inductive way. Aristotle's derivation of the principles of change in *Physics* I is the clearest example. He generalizes the principles of change by an inductive study of changes, boldly putting together changes in the physical world and changes on the nonphysical level (from blushing to learning). The categories are on a much more general level, but their emergence does not have to be different.

Why, if this is so—it may be objected—do the categories not include other concepts that play a comparable role—nature *(phusis)*, element *(stoicheion)*, cause *(aition)*, potentiality *(dunamis)*, actuality *(energeia)*, and so on? The best source of candidates for the position of category is of course *Metaphysics* D with its thirty concepts briefly and tersely analyzed as a philosophical dictionary. Now there is no shortcut to answering the question by reckoning with each and every one of these concepts (and others not included), but a few basic reasons for excluding them from the categories can be listed, with illustrations (putting aside those which are in fact in the category list):

(1) Some are special cases of a category on the list—for example, disposition *(diathesis)* and habit *(hexis)* fall under Quality, as we have seen.

(2) Some are analyzable into the terms of a category, as the "nature" *(phusis)* of something is simply the analogue in the physical context of "essence," and to have an account of the essence is to know the nature. Similarly, to be *per se* is equivalent to being essential.

(3) Some are clearly dependent rather than primary—for example, the false *(pseudon)* is posterior to what it is.

(4) Some are much too broad and abstract to be the categories of things. A Platonist might use Being and Accident, but for Aristotle, explaining things in this world requires the specific form of being in specific domains. Similarly, a modern systems theorist might operate with Part and Whole as categories, but for Aristotle these terms would be used only analogically for different domains.

(5) There is one class of terms we might have expected to be represented in the categories—potentiality *(dunamis)* which appears in *Metaphysics* D, and actuality *(energeia)* and movement *(kinēsis)*,

both of which are strangely absent from *Metaphysics* D as chapters (the terms of course do occur, but only in an ordinary everyday sense). As we have seen above, *kinēsis* does appear in some category lists, and this will have to be explained. It is possible too that since the *Categories* is an earlier work, the theory of the categories cannot be expected to include a concept like *energeia* whose technical use emerges in a later period of Aristotle's thought. But these concepts as a class are so central that their absence from a category list is puzzling on the thesis I am expounding. And it is this apparent gap which suggests that Situation and State are really the representatives of this concept family. It is time to turn directly to the problem of these two remaining categories.

In reassessing these two categories I should like to consider: (1) Aristotle's examples and where they lead; (2) correcting the balance with the other categories, particularly Quality and Relation; (3) relevant "dictionary" evidence; (4) their possibly broader and more fundamental meaning as categories; (5) their functional tasks, including first the problem of *kinēsis* among the categories, and second, their relation to concepts later developed by Aristotle.

(1) Aristotle's initial examples for these two categories—lying or sitting for Situation *(keisthai)* and shod or armed for State *(echein)*—had an unfortunately narrowing effect. The customary translation for the former, of "posture" or "position" and for the latter, of "state" or "condition," enshrines the almost sedentary effect. But it need not be so. Think, for example, of the role that "posture" plays in contemporary discussion of political attitude; it can betoken the "stance" of a country in a very active international goings-on—much more dynamic than the rather passive "image" it may desire to project.

There is ample evidence in Aristotle that these were not meant to be sedentary categories. There are passages in other contexts in which walking is associated with sitting and lying, so that walking would be an instance of *keisthai* (e.g., *Metaphysics* Z 1028a21, where "to walk", "to be healthy", "to sit" are taken together). Moreover, Aristotle does regard the two kinds of examples as in the same boat in his works. Motion and rest are treated together, having the same principles. And, most revealing, in *Metaphysics* Th. (1047a21–30) he puts into general form the character of potentiality for opposites, using walking, sitting, and standing as examples and includes becoming and being. He then goes on to explain how the concept of actuality *(energeia)* was extended from movement *(kinēsis)* to become a technical term. And he regards as *energeia* not only doing something in a narrow activist sense, but also being something: the statue of Apollo when complete is as much an instance of *energeia* as is seeing or knowing or the working of a craftsman insofar as he is fully energizing his skill. I am suggesting that the same was true of *keisthai*.

That State *(echein)* has a similarly dynamic aspect is suggested by Aristotle's general treatment of states of character *(hexeis)* as established potentialities for action. This is clear enough in the *Nicomachean Ethics* in the treatment of virtues. It is also clear in his remarks, noted above, about powers underlying states. But even on the surface, what is entailed by being shod or armed if not a readiness for walking or fighting? The difference between *echein* and *keisthai* would thus be between possession and exercise, for example of sensory power (cf. *Topics* 129b34f.; in 125b17f. he contrasts sensation, *aisthēsis*, as a state with movement, *kinēsis*, as an *energeia*).

(2) The above reference to *hexeis*, as evidence for the dynamic character of *echein*, holds of course only if *hexeis* is taken to be an instance of *echein*. This means correcting the balance of State and Quality as categories either by removing *hexeis* from the latter and restoring them to the former, or at least recognizing the connection, even if we leave states of character in the swollen territory of Quality. Similar jurisdictional disputes would have to be settled with respect to Action and Passion to ensure their separation from Relation, though I think Aristotle is himself careful about that. In the case of *echein*, serious reasons come from linguistic considerations.

(3) The "dictionary" evidence on *echein* is extraordinarily liberating. A broad term, with a central sense of to "have" or "hold," it has in its intransitive usage the sense of "to hold oneself," "to be or keep" in a certain state. And in addition, it has the proprietary sense of "have" as "possess" as well as to have power to do something. *Kalōs echei* and *kakōs echei* mean "it's going well" and "it's going badly" respectively, and *pōs echeis* is standard for "how are you?" One might, by the way, conjecture that if some of the categories take their rise from interrogative expressions like "how big," "what sort," "where," "when," the categories of *echein* and *keisthai* would have a similar relation to *pōs* which is "how" or as an indefinite adverb "in some way" or "somehow." Certainly *pōs* is an important interrogative adverb not exploited in the categories unless we assign it to our present couple under investigation.

It is worth glancing at the derivatives of *echein* and its second aorist infinitive *schein*. These are the sources of *hexis* (plural, *hexeis*), "a being in a certain state, permanent condition or habit" and *schēma*, "form," "shape," which goes on into "manner," and "the state, nature, constitution" of a thing. It looks as if the root idea of both *hexis* and *schēma* is a continued keeping, holding or getting in a certain state, a kind of stable identity.

If the difference between *echein* and *keisthai* is between the state in which one can do something and the exercise of that state, then *keisthai* will have to be given the same breadth of meaning and scope of use as *echein*.

(4) The suggestions so far open the way to a broader and more fundamental meaning for our two categories. But what is the evidence that it is more than a logical possibility, linguistically permissible? Why did not Aristotle cite the categories more frequently, as he did the others?

There is a dilemma in the situation. If we take the narrow meaning of the categories we find fewer references in the texts, but if we take the broader meaning there is plenty of evidence and numerous reference. The least we can do is to restore the balance and put the broader and narrower sense on an equal footing for research and interpretation, neither having the burden of proof on it alone. My own conviction is that the evidence is sufficient to adopt the broader interpretation.

This is not the place for a technical marshalling of the full evidence. Let me simply indicate the kinds of evidence there would be. First, there are several passages, beyond the two lists of the full ten categories, in which our two categories are quite clearly referred to. Second, there are complex expressions or compound uses which can be appealed to in order to throw light on our problem. And third, there are contexts which indirectly suggest the two categories have not been forgotten.

A casual inclusion of *echein* in what is obviously a partial listing of categories is found in *Metaphysics* 1016b7ff. where Aristotle is discussing the conditions under which things are said to be one. But by far the most impressive evidence comes in *Metaphysics* H when Aristotle is beginning to give his solution of the problem of what is substance. Some things, he tells us, are defined by their position (1042b19ff.) such as threshold and lintel, for these differ by *being situated in a particular way*. The exact words are *keisthai pōs*. And he goes on to other things that differ by time (breakfast and dinner), by place, by sensible qualities. He repeats (line 26ff.) that a thing is a threshold because it is disposed so *(houtōs keitai)* and that to be a threshold means to be situated in this particular way *(keisthai* again). In the passage beginning 1043a6 he tells us that as in substance the *energeia* or actuality is predicated of the matter, so in the case of a threshold we speak of it as wood or brick placed in a given way *(hōdi keimenon)* and similarly for a house. It would appear then that *keisthai* as a category, so far from being abandoned, is alive and well and preparing the ground for the critical identification of substance and *energeia*. It is not surprising, to find "sitting," the early example of *keisthai*, treated as an *energeia* (1047a25ff.) just before Aristotle explains how the term *"energeia"* was extended from movement *(kinēsis)*.

Once we are alerted to the broader meaning, complex expressions begin to be of interest. Not merely *keisthai*, but expressions like *diakeisthai
pōs*, to be disposed in some manner, appear to be applying the category
(cf. *Categories* 9a17–20; *Metaphysics* 1022b11f.) The same holds for
echein. When Aristotle says in a crucial passage that we should pay attention not only to how we should talk about things but how things actually are
(*Metaphysics* 1030a27ff.), the latter is expressed by *pōs echei* (cf. *Metaphysics* 1008b6–7, *pōs echoi an ta onta*). Similarly, the common expression
for something being otherwise is *allōs echei*, which enters into the almost
technical term for what is necessary—what does not admit of being otherwise.

Contexts that indirectly suggest the two categories are of different
sorts. For example, the opening of *Metaphysics* Z has a direct reference to
the categories commonly listed and ends with an "etc." But the very next
sentence (1028a20f.), while concerned with the contrast of infinitives and
substantives, uses precisely the same examples—walking, being healthy,
and sitting—that attach to the two categories we are concerned with.
Again, in 1029a13ff., a reference to affections, products, and potencies
sounds like a reference to the last four of the categories, in which case
"potencies" would be covering our two. Indeed, the many inclusions of
movement *(kinēsis)* in categorial lists may very well embrace *echein* and
keisthai as I have interpreted them (e.g., 1029b25, 1054a7; *Physics*
200b30ff.). In another direction, the possibility suggested earlier that *pōs*
(how, in a manner) might serve as the interrogative introducing the two
categories just as "what is it?" introduces substance and essence and
"when" introduces time, could lead us to attend to passages in which it
appears. For example, in *On Sophistical Refutations* 178b37ff. we find Aristotle saying that every generic term denotes not an individual substance
but a quality or relation or mode *(pōs)* or something of the kind; here *pōs* is
ensconced among the categorial terms (cf. 180a23).

(5) If the evidence here sampled is supported by a broader and more
thorough investigation, and if the wider sense is restored to *echein* and
keisthai, their field of operation in the Corpus would seem to be very extensive. *Echein*, through *hexis*, becomes fundamental to the whole of the
theory of virtue in the ethical writings and the theory of institutions in
the political writings. *Keisthai* has a broader metaphysical role. It is doing the
job in the earlier Aristotelian analysis that is taken over by *energeia* in the
later. The difference between *keisthai* and *echein*, between an actual dynamic situation and the state which can issue in one, is more than the broad
distinction between actuality and potentiality. It is rather like the more precise distinction of Aristotle's later development in the psychological writings between a *second entelechy* and a *first entelechy*. His paradigm is the

distinction between using a language and knowing a language. Neither is identical with learning a language. In sum, I suggest that *echein* and *keisthai* are to be regarded as precursors in the earlier Aristotelian work of the later family of concepts centering around *energeia,* and in particular *first and second entelechy.* Such an understanding also makes sense of the occasional appearance of *kinēsis* in the lists. Since it precedes the sharp separation of *energeia* and *kinēsis* it can be used generally to cover the last four categories (possibly, *Eudemian Ethics* 1217b28–30, *Metaphysics* 1029b23ff.) and sometimes in particular for a part of them (possibly *Metaphysics* 1054a5ff.; cf. 1032b10f. where a particular kind of *kinēsis* is called *poiēsis*).

In the light of the revised interpretation of the categories what shall we take categories in general to be? I suggested they are the philosophical concepts that emerged from the various problems to which Aristotle addressed himself—concepts that turn out to play a key role in the way questions are formulated and that set the directions for modes of resolution. Aristotle, like every other philosopher, operates with a conceptual network—basic concepts loosely related in different ways, responsive to the state of development of different areas and the organizing purposes and aims of the philosopher. Such concepts rarely exhaust the full inventory of his basic ideas; they are usually set in a background of other concepts, but the spotlight or focus is on them because they *are* the functioning network in terms of which proposed answers to philosophic questions are formulated and answers sought. Some suggestion of the relation of focus and background was given above in the winnowing of *Metaphysics* D to show why other important ideas were not taken into the categorial family.

The categories of a Cartesian philosopher would surely have included *life* or *mind,* because he would work in a dualist spirit.[5] But Aristotle does not need them as separate because he sees the unity of the natural and the human world. His initial concern is rather with the central philosophic issue inherited from the whole development of Greek philosophy—the relation and respective "reality" of the eternal and the changing. His initial inventory of the categories can be looked at along the joints of this problem. Substance designates what "really" is. Quantity comes next; it embodies the traditional sciences of the eternal—arithmetic and geometry—to be reduced in due course by Aristotle to sciences of what can be studied in abstraction from movement. (When this happens the eternal is taken over by the general background features of all determinate being, that is being-something: the laws of logic.) Relation is the clearest category of the accidental, in the Aristotelian inventory. It spawns the multiple and conflicting descriptions of the same thing that Plato had worried about (how the same thing can be both larger and smaller), as well as reflects the changes in things by their altered interrelations. Relation thus reflects in the domain of thought the world of the changing. Quality, which comes next, straddles the domains. Its primary meaning, according to *Metaphysics* D 14, is "the differentia of the essence." It should have had the post of honor next to Substance, differentia coming next to essence. But sensible qualities and their place in the scheme of contraries have made it important for analyzing changes. And so it is on the border. Place and Time are already over the border: they are clearly the static and dynamic aspects of change. And the last four categories are, if the interpretation offered above is correct, first attempts to fix aspects and ideas for identifying and understanding change itself.

What changes can be seen in the Corpus that affect the early picture of the categories? The last four give way to the richer development of the concepts of *energeia* and *dunamis* for major philosophical purposes. These are strengthened by their refinement and application in the analysis of psychological phenomena. They become so important that there is practically an assimilation of *substance* and *energeia*. In addition, the types of change have themselves been stabilized by use of the scheme of the categories. Note the interactive character of the scheme and the phenomena in this respect. A priori, Aristotle in going through the categories to locate types of change could have used *poiēsis*. What would be wrong with saying that one type of change is *purposive* change? Nothing, in a different conceptual framework in which the purposive and the non-purposive were as sharply separated as the Cartesian mind and matter. But for Aristotle all nature works like the artist. The stabilization of types of change according to four of the earlier categories gave these four a prestigious status. The last four dissolved into the general metaphysical inquiry, or became taken up in divisions along different philosophic interests, as *poiēsis* becomes aligned with *praxis* and *theōria*.

I have given a partly speculative but not implausible picture as to why the categories, though used for some purposes where a classification of types (genera) of being or a linguistic classification of predicates was needed, lose their vigorous role in the developed philosophy of Aristotle. They are merged with the tasks, problems, enterprises, purposes, that go on; they are not repudiated. A scenario of Aristotle's development is not vouched for in detail, since it would involve many uncertain historical assumptions about the order in which the doctrines developed. But there is one suggestion about major shifts in philosophical purpose in Aristotle which does, I think, stand out clearly in his *Metaphysics*.

The initial category list belongs quite definitely to a stage in Aristotle's thought when he is focusing on the problem of essence and accident. It is not Plato's problem of the relation of universal and particular, but the determination among the properties of a thing which constitute its essence and which are accidental. Most of this is being carried on in logical-linguistic terms. The quest is the central theme of the *Topics*, but it is also the recurring question of the *Metaphysics*, especially in Book Z: why do the properties of rational or biped and animal constitute an essential unity, while white or cultured and man do not? The question is already explicit in *On Interpretation* 17a12–15 (cf. 20b31–21a30). To provide an answer is not our present task. But the pervasive role of this question shows that Aristotle's concern with the essence-accident issue is not just an early matter.

We may note as an aside that it may not help us to see Aristotle's philosophical shift in terms of a relation to Plato. At least, it can be seen as internal to the Corpus. I think Aristotle himself gives us a clue in *Metaphysics* E when he discusses the different senses of Being. It is very much like the question which generated the categories, but it is a different interest. He answers with three senses. One is in terms of the essential and the accidental; a second in terms of the true and the false; a third in terms of the potential and the actual. In chapters two and three of E he goes on to consider the accidental, in chapter four Being as truth, and of course Book Th. is the central exposition of the potential and the actual. In the passage that initiates the discussion (E 1026a36ff.) the categories appear to be lined up as an additional sense. But clearly they belong to the first, with Substance giving the essence and the rest the properties and accidents (though in some contexts properties are a subclass of accidents). Now Aristotle's exploration of essence and accident, while pervasive, constitutes his basic formulation in the logical works—especially in the *Topics*, though it also inspires his whole analysis of the philosophy of science in *Posterior Analytics*. The treatment of Being as truth and falsity never reaches the same proportions since Aristotle points out that these are secondary to Being in its ontological sense—the truth depends on what is, not the reverse. The third (Being as potential and actual) becomes the center of his later metaphysical and scientific thought. Forged in the analysis of change in *Physics* III, it is utilized as a matter of course at critical points in *On the Soul* and it plays the crucial role of solving the problem of substance in *Metaphysics* H by aligning the matter-form distinction with the potentiality-actuality distinction. The conclusion would seem to be that Aristotle's categories belong to the first exploration, that a part of his categorial scheme was further developed in the third exploration, and that with this philosophical broadening the list was no longer of special separate importance. Put in Aristotelian terms, the first exploration which involved the categories was giving a formal cause, but the exploration in terms of potentiality and actuality was giving a final cause and so was superior in bringing understanding.

On this hypothesis it would be a mistake to treat a theory of the categories as if it were a distinctly separate part of a philosophy—as if it could constitute a closed and independent classification, whether of things that are or of terms. We know well enough by this time that much goes into any classification. It is guided by purposes, whether practical or theoretical; it is theory-laden, taking its direction from the outcome of previous inquiry while setting the terms for subsequent inquiry; properly, it should react to the growth of knowledge and the refinement of purpose—as indeed the conceptual network of any philosophy can be seen to do, and especially the comparison of differences in networks makes clear. Aristotle's categories cannot therefore be understood in an isolated fashion but are part and parcel of the whole development of philosophical concepts in his Corpus.

II

In this part I want briefly to draw the lessons of this inquiry for the nature of metaphysical inquiry in general, at least for that part of it which consists in categorial theory. Without leaving Aristotle let us move into considerations which involve contemporary modes of interpretation, and contemporary comparisons.

In the first place, the picture given above of the functions and development of the categories fits readily into a contemporary pragmatic interpretation of philosophical categories. Please note that I have not imposed this interpretation within the previous study. Our concept of function came directly from Aristotle's notion of final cause. We studied the work *(ergon)* of the categories in the Corpus just as Aristotle studies the functioning of the four causes throughout the Corpus: for example, the *Parts of Animals* gives the material cause of animals and man; the *Generation of Animals* the efficient cause; *On the Soul* the formal cause; the ethical and political writings the final cause. We have thus simply been applying Aristotelian methods to Aristotelian ideas. But of course for Aristotle the basic concepts enter into truths about the ultimate character of what is; in that sense he is a metaphysical "realist." They are not simply conceptual instruments to be stablized and perpetuated or reduced and rejected on the basis of their success or failure.

Viewed in this latter way, the essence-accident analysis was Aristotle's first great metaphysical experiment. It spawned the categories. It sent him into the logical inquiries, clarified large areas, formalized others, and got still others underway. We cannot begin at this point a general reckoning with "essentialism," whether to correct subsequent caricatures in the name of historical justice, or to complement the one-sidedness that sees Aristotle in terms of the formal structure of the *Posterior Analytics* by looking at the process of inquiry (whether logical as in the *Topics* or scientific as in *Physics* and *On the Soul*). But even in his own thinking, the experiment was not wholly satisfactory. In spite of the successes in logic, and in the biology of classification, it had rough edges, it failed to produce a coherent theory of natural movement in physics, and it came to an impasse in metaphysics in the central problem of the nature of substance. Aristotle, therefore, without abandoning the framework of his results, shifted to his second great experiment—to see the world in the focus of potentiality and actuality. It brought successes precisely at the points where the earlier experiment had come to an impasse—especially in psychology and metaphysics. It became the basis for revisions in physics, not completed and not precise enough for him to judge. But at any rate it helped avoid determinism in a deeper way than the mere assumption that there are accidents had done. (It did confirm a solution, even if a dogmatic commonsensical one, to the problem of the sea battle tomorrow.) And it could help out against the Democritean atomism and solve the problem of the infinite. And so on.

Aristotle never tried out—for reasons given earlier—the great experiment of epistemological categories. That remained for post-Cartesian philosophy. It has still to draw the lessons of how far describing the world in terms drawn from knowledge and its processes—rather than in ontological terms—is helpful, whether the numerous impasses come from mixing categories instead of following either the one set or the other through consistently, and so on. Contemporary naturalisms often have not quite made up their mind which to do.

If we treat categorial sets as great conceptual experiments, then our attitude to them is quite transformed. We no longer, for example, have a philosophical puzzle of the relation of the one and the many, the eternal and the changing, the human and the divine, the universal and the particular, the body and the mind, the sensory and the intellectual, and so on, for when a dichotomy leads us into an impasse it is the dichotomy that goes on trial. It is subjected to intensive search for its grounds in human purposes and interests, for its relation to the stage of knowledge and the development of theory in the varied fields of human inquiry. After that we have the evaluative task of reckoning how successful these dichotomies have been in solving the problems to which they were addressed or which they helped open up. And then we have the perennial task of conceptual reconstruction and innovation as knowledge and methods develop and purposes and interests are refined. It is rarely an all-or-none matter. For example, a Cartesian dualism of mind and matter helped isolate a growing physical science from all sorts of interference from religious and cultural beliefs. The havoc it created was in psychology, and it was the growth and problems of psychology that exerted pressure for reconstructing the dichotomous concepts.

The core problem in such a conception of metaphysics as conceptual experimentation—including experiment in principles as well as concepts (the latter have been central because the inquiry has been into categories)—is, of course, to furnish criteria for success. It is not a problem for philosophy alone but for science as well when it deals not with low-level laws that admit of ready falsification but with complex theoretical concepts where questions of fruitfulness predominate and even aesthetic considerations are admitted. It is the difficulty of this problem that tempts an occasional historian of science to offer sociological categories for understanding scientific change rather than philosophy-of-science categories.[6] But such sociological categories) would have to be evaluated in the long run for their own successes and failures, and not on sociological grounds alone. So in a sense a normative reckoning is unavoidable and the problem of criteria philosophically pressing.

I do not think the problem is inherently insoluble—it *is* difficult. But the view that we simply adopt categories by arbitrary commitment seems to me incorrect historically. We can, of course, play category games if we wish, in a purely mathematical or model building spirit. But in metaphysics, as in science, we are in some sense *trying out* categories, we are *experimenting*. And there is some sense of success or failure. The great problem is to clarify this. I do not think it can be advanced too far by general concepts of "fruitfulness" nor even at this point by general analyses of "simplicity," "range of application," although such analysis furnishes clues to be pursued. I suspect that the meaning of "greater adequacy" for categorial sets will have to be worked out by case studies in a variety of fields, scientific and humanistic and philosophical, which spell out in detail what has been gained, what jeopardized, what lost, what facilitated, what hindered, by formulations in one as against another categorial set. Aristotle is a very happy hunting ground for this kind of a study, both in a cross-sectional inquiry and where he shifts experiments on a developmental inquiry. The great and most difficult hunting grounds are, of course, the turning points in science.

If this analysis is not off the mark, then the treatment of categories in relation to fields of application is not a mere afterthought when the analysis of the categories is finished. It is part of the essence of their exploration, even of their construction. Hence metaphysics as a field of philosophy has to be carried out in intimate relation to the diversity of areas in which metaphysical concepts are being tried out. Such I take to be the lessons of Aristotle's categories when studied in depth.

III

Among recent experiments in categorial theory, Justus Buchler's stands out as offering a wholly fresh set to replace traditional sets.[7] This is not often attempted. Whitehead obviously comes to mind, but there are not many others. The usual procedure is to worry about present categories, to gnaw them and find a soft spot to chew away at till a crack spreads. Sometimes present categories are criticized directly, and patched up by alterations here and there. But to propose a wholly new set is a bold and revolutionary procedure. I cannot here undertake an examination of the one that Buchler offers, since my concern is rather with categorial theory in general—the whole categorial enterprise and the way in which proposed sets might be evaluated. It would be very worthwhile, however, to consider Buchler's procedures in comparison with the lessons elicited from the treatment of Aristotle's categories.

Buchler does not tell us too much about how he proceeds. He plunges into the work itself. He gives us the finished products of his reflection, illustrates them, touches some of the philosophical problems on which they help out, and leaves the rest presumably to our own insight and reflection. There is a great emphasis on generality and getting concepts that in some way rise above the particular philosophical struggles that were waged about their less general embodiments. It is reminiscent of Aristotle in *Physics* I developing a theory of *change* which will cover not only locomotion but qualitative alteration and the rest, so that change can be illustrated by everything from movement to learning to blushing. The effect was to set aside the particular problems of locomotion and let the general concept furnish the invariant essentials. In a similar way Buchler constantly juxtaposes illustrations deliberately from a variety of fields. He couples "a yawn, an exclamation, a crumpled piece of paper, a philosophic concept, and a madrigal" as human products (TGT 134) in indicating what *query* consists in, and he lines up a star, the economy, a proof, a poem (MNC 68) as illustrating situations that *arose*. This almost casual but far-flung juxtaposition appears to be an important procedure in communicating categorial ideas. And yet he insists that an adequate category is "to provide a just basis for distinctions, and not to blanket or transcend them." (MNC 9)

We do get some explicit statements about what categories are taken to be and what philosophical writing on categories is up to. It is "an attempt to discover fundamental traits in the process of experiencing" (NJ vii). More explicitly, "The philosopher, then, in formulating his categories and principles, represents a world that is always to some extent available to other perspectives. But inevitably he goes further than this. In shaping his structure he presumes to represent other perspectives than his own." (TGT 132) He thus incorporates a principle of criticism in framing his philosophic structure. Others can correct and amplify. "The minimal requirement of achievement in a philosophy is that it compel imaginative assent and arouse the sense of encompassment even where it fails of cognitive acceptance." (TGT 134) In such a view Buchler is not on the whole departing far from Aristotle as traditionally conceived. Categories and principles seem to be grasped in a kind of vision and their philosophic expression is a kind of invitation to other philosophers to try the vision. His actual categories, of course, are quite different. They can be seen from the topics of the first two books: proception, communication, compulsion, convention, perspective, validation, judgment, query, experience, meaning.

Why is a new set of categories required? The attempt to offer one clearly presupposes some inadequacy in current categories. It implies some understanding of what is wrong with them, what shortcomings, obscurities, provincialisms they have, what distortions of experience they produce, what contradictions and paradoxes they get us into. Or else it presupposes some vision of the categorial job performed better than it is being done. Do old categories simply wear out, become too loose to fit? In discussing "experience" and "experiencing" Buchler proposes to subordinate or lay these terms aside. "For the terms are so laden with a burden of contrary and confused differentia, so encumbered by the hoary banalities which cognate terms like 'empiricism' and 'empirical' suggest, that a fresh start with superior conceptual equipment is necessary. After reformulation and delineation of essential traits we may presumably return to the older language with greater control of the usage." (NJ 107)

Another course might have been taken. The history of the philosophic use of "experience" might have been studied to bring out the lessons for a reconstructed meaning. For example, in Aristotle's account, experience already involves repetition and memory. Later in a Lockean usage it is a stream of atomic sensations. What changes in psychological theory might account for this, or what use of new models, or what purposes and value attitudes in dealing with men? Again, in ancient usage, and even in recent medical usage, "empirical" is contrasted with "theoretical" as *merely empirical*. What scientific and social battles of "empiricism" led away from this to make "empirical" in modern usage be almost the equivalent of being scientific? Conceptual history is not the same as conceptual analysis, but at least it might provide causes and cures for banality, as well as set a proper path for a straying category.

Buchler is not attempting to fix a permanent terminology. He recognizes that novelty will have to be embodied either by stretching meanings or introducing new terms. (NJ 108) He calls for a *responsible* introduction or extension. But he does not work out systematic criteria for responsibility, nor a systematic mode of testing the new categories, nor even the various dimensions of a process of justification. It looks as if he thinks no other way is possible but the extension of experience and reflection and the mutual philosophic invitations to try out categories.

Let me pose the problem I have in mind with a simplified illustration. In the psychological literature of perception one occasionally finds use of a concept of *registration*. The human being *registers* an experience. (Compare Buchler's remarks on "record" in NJ 23). What is accomplished by speaking of registration rather than perception or memory or using the physiological language of traces?

The obvious advantage is that the term conveniently fails to specify which mode is taking place or which mechanism is operating. It can therefore be used where we are uncertain. For example, to choose one of physicalist or mentalist language—say in considering subliminal perception or repressed desires—would get us into trouble with the other. Is subliminal perception really perceiving or a physical trace whose effects intrude in consciousness? Is the notion of repressed desires equivalent to an unconscious consciousness? And so on. Of course *registration* is not a completely blank or open concept. It is something more than being affected and at least being affected in a way which allows of some subsequent repetition or some consequent effect in thought or behavior of what was registered.

The general philosophical advantage of *registration* is thus, that it bypasses the mind-body problem and directs inquiry into research which may produce wholly fresh directions, cutting the material in different ways from the ones dictated by apportioning all experience to mind or body. Of course there are additional related concepts that have to be readjusted. For example, it could be asked *where* the registration takes place, and one would have to deny that it is an appropriate question since the term is not given either a physical or a mental context to begin with; or one might answer, side-stepping again, that it takes place in a human being's *life*. Or again, it could be asked *who* or *what* does the registering, hinting once more at a mind-or-body answer. But the reply could be, as Woodbridge in philosophy and Woodworth in psychology dealt with thinking, that *man* registers. Thus the concept of *registering* experience becomes tied in with the concepts of *man* and *life* in a network of new concepts, and a naturalistic type of metaphysics is in the making.

Nevertheless, it is not enough to show what the new category does in avoiding traditional impasse-problems. Dewey is always fighting against dualisms, even analyzing their intellectual and social history to show why a new slant should be given to an older philosophical term. If new categories are offered with only a negative justification, they may be merely running-away categories, or stopgap provisional categories, or above-the-battle categories in a metaphysical ivory tower. Greater generality too is not enough. It could be a bare, thin, abstract generality, as terms like "value" or "power" have had, giving rise to endless controversy as different interpretations or models for interpretation are tried out to make some sense of

them, while the problems from which they ascended are left blindly grop-
ing. The positive hope of a new category that by-passes an older struggle is
that in some way it makes sense of what has been going on in the domain
of problems, that it be not merely neutral to them, but replace them with a
fresh direction of research, that it suggest new ways of parcelling the field
with the promise that if our questions are asked in these terms they will
more readily admit of fruitful answers. The old problems are thus not
merely left stranded but understood as formulations along inadequate lines.
We understand why we ended up in a blind alley—what intellectual and
scientific, religious and social interests and stages of development of
thought, and what advantages (though they proved at best temporary),
tempted thought into these paths. The crucial question to be faced ultimately is how such a testing procedure can take place, whether categories
can prove themselves in a common investigation beyond simply an invitation to personal experience, or whether they are simply supplanted either in
a sociological shift or a personal conversion or an act of metaphysical
whimsey.

With the preliminary example of *registration* to suggest the tasks pertinent to categorial evaluation, let us take two examples from Buchler's own
set. I shall focus on the basic initial concept of *proception* and the fascinating later one of *alescence*.

Proception is the first new concept introduced, in the first chapter of
the first book: "The interplay of the human individual's activities and dimensions, their unitary direction, constitutes a process which I shall call
proception. The term is designed to suggest a moving union of seeking and
receiving, of forward propulsion and patient absorption. Proception is the
composite, directed activity of the individual." (TGT 4) We are told that
any event in an individual's history enters into the proceptive direction, and
the way an individual will act at any time as well as modification of his
intellectual and moral character depends on his proceptive direction. A
man's whole self is summed up as represented in proception. The content
of the summed-up-self-in-process is the proceptive domain. (TGT 6) Three
distinctions are made concerning the domain—the gross domain (all his
interrelated procepts), the floating proceptive domain (the summed-up self
or proceiver within a given situation), the imminent proceptive domain (all
that is available for the proceiver at a given moment). (TGT 8–9) And two
fundamental and correlative dimensions are introduced in the proceptive direction—manipulation and assimilation. (TGT 17)

This brief characterization will suffice for our present purpose—to
ask what reforms this categorial candidate has promised that we should
elect him on his platform. The topic is vast but can perhaps be indicated in
a few comments.

(1) In one sense this category is a field indicator: it gathers the phenomena clustering around a given human individual. But it is not a neutral indicator of the phenomena themselves, for it cuts the field by introducing the idea of an individual. What then is an individual, clearly presupposed by the concept of proception? In the second book we are told that, "For us it will be sufficient to say that *a* human individual is whatever is identified or denominated as such." (NJ 106) In short, Buchler has no intention of explicating "individual" in other terms—we are certainly familiar enough with what is intended. There is nothing unusual in such a procedure; it is like dealing with the implicit definition of, say, "Euclidean point" and taking anything to be a Euclidean point which satisfies the Euclidean axioms in which the term appears. And it is certainly true that a set of categorial terms behaves often in such a manner, each being explained with reference to the rest and how they shape up into a network. But strictly, then, *individual* has to be included in the network. Perhaps also the concept of *activity* is involved in a similar fashion in Buchler's notion of *proception*.

(2) The point of the first comment is that the field is already being conceptually cut in a given way by thinking in terms of *proception*. For there are, as Buchler's discussion recognizes, alternative ways. One could think of *experience* and construct the individual out of experiences, or of *transactions* as unified goings-on from whose crossings we could frame the idea of an individual. The two main dimensions Buchler specifies—*manipulation* and *assimilation*—are quite definitely also a particular way of cutting the field. They generalize the older concepts of *action* and *passion*—the doing of the agent and the suffering of the patient—which played a large role in Aristotle. In *On the Soul* Aristotle had his eye directly on the processes of nutrition out of which he constructed a framework for analyzing interaction and then made emendations in the model as he moved up to the analysis of perception and thought. Buchler generalizes the dimensions till they become practically equivalent to perseverance and acceptance.

The variety of aspects that can be stressed in a concept of action is clearest perhaps in the historical vicissitudes of *motion* which went from an actualization of a potentiality to an activity of a body to a changed relation of position. Similarly, human action has been assigned different meanings: some have stressed the masterful expansive character, as if acting were a kind of dominating, others the ascriptive character in judgments of action ("he *did* it"), others the goal seeking or purposive character, others the relational character of man-environment interaction and so on. The question therefore persists as to why one aspect should be given priority in a categorial way.

(3) A distinctive characteristic of *proception* is that it is at home in both metaphysical and epistemological inquiries. In this respect it is like

what Dewey tried to do with *experience,* which in one sense takes us to experiencing, in another to the ultimate natural events in which a human being participates. So too *proception* is set among natural complexes, and a *procept* is itself a natural complex that has entered into a proceptive domain. (cf. NJ 122) Clearly, one of the chief reasons—if not the very chief—for the construction of the concept of *proception* is to exhibit the natural status of all, including mental, human processes, to suggest the continuities of human and prehuman ways, and to point to a full man-in-nature psychology.

Once again, it is worth noting that there are quite different ways in which philosophers have gone at this. For example, materialist philosophies have treated man as a complex of matter-in-motion, with powers more varied and complex so that behavior and consciousness are qualities on a distinctive level. Here the concepts of *matter, motion, qualitative level,* do the job of grounding epistemology in a metaphysical setting as the study of natural-psychological functions.

(4) The comparison of Buchler's naturalistic version and the materialist version raises the question how far the results of scientific knowledge enter into categorial formation. The naturalism of the materialists in epistemology rests on the outline of scientific conclusions that every so-called psychic act has an underlying material basis and the hope that fuller material *explanations* will be forthcoming. Roughly, the categories reflect the scientific results and are thought justified by the trend of advancing results. At times, Buchler's naturalism, because it appeals to ordinary examples and common experience, has an almost phenomenological character. Whichever source underlies the naturalism, however, both are set (like Aristotle) against primacy for an epistemological analysis, and the picture of *what is,* then, being cast in categories derived from the analysis of knowledge. For this is the mode that leads to subjectivism and phenomenalism and that renders the Deweyan use of *experience* also occasionally ambiguous.

(5) It may be questioned, in conclusion, whether the concept of *proception* can bear the weight of such objectives, whether it may not implant on philosophical analysis of nature and men a selected slant, whether it might not be more profitable to carry out the same discussions in a variety of traditional categorial frameworks and let the lessons emerge from them all. A categorial openness, with a kind of contextual relativism that shows how different structures can do the same philosophical job might be more appropriate for our time than a proposed new category. I shall come back to this later on, for it involves going more fully into the bases of categorial selection in general.

The concept of *alescence,* interestingly and richly developed in *Metaphysics of Natural Complexes,* raises the same kind of issues. I find it a fascinating object to reflect on. Derived by Buchler from a truncated "coalescence," (MNC 55–56) it stimulates the etymological imagination. Presumably, if "coalescence" is a kind of growing together, will "alescence" be a growing *simpliciter* or will it be a growing apart? It also stirs the constructional imagination. If we go in for such truncated words, can hair be "hevelled" as well as dishevelled? Certainly gasoline has become flammable, when in the old days it was highly inflammable, but probably this is to avoid a confusion of "in" as negative and "in" as intensive (especially for a car pressing too close to a gasoline truck). That "alescence" is not simply growth, however, can be settled by a substitutional test, so dear to Quinean logicians—I cannot revise the poet's "Grow old with me, the best is yet to come" and say "Alesce old with me. . . . "

I do not intend here to derogate verbal considerations. They have often practical as well as theoretical potency. For example, in impeachment hearings held by the House Judiciary Committee, the vast TV audience heard Chairman Rodino say "the gentlelady from New York." By this subtlety, I presume, he avoided offending the feminist vote which might have found the "gentleman-lady" contrast too blatant, but also avoided offending the antifeminist vote which would have objected to "gentleperson" as leaning too far to the other side. Categorial novelty needs at least the same subtlety as to what it is accomplishing.

Why did Buchler think a new concept was needed in this metaphysical area? Why, when the categorial supermarket was already displaying everything from Aristotle's *change (metabolē)*, and Hobbes's *matter-in-motion*, to Santayana's *flux* and at least three kinds of *events*—Russell's, Whitehead's, Dewey's—did Buchler turn private craftsman and engage in a fresh do-it-yourself? I think I can surmise the reasons, though Buchler may not agree with the analysis. Simply, he may have felt that the advertised categories incorporated outworn slants or lacked necessary ingredients. Aristotle's *change* is too teleological, Hobbes's *matter-in-motion* too physical and mechanical, Santayana's *flux* too indeterminate, and the very diversity of *events* too confusing. In any case, the events concept is usually set in a reductive effort so that complexes have to be constructed out of events. Where it is not, as in Dewey, it does little more than point to the flow of experience. Buchler would be most sympathetic perhaps to Aristotle. I interpret his concept of *alescence* (of course with its companion *prevalence*) to be carrying on the same kind of attempt as Aristotle did, but in a more generalized way and in a more modernized intellectual setting. Let me spell out this contrast and see what the alterations convey.

Aristotle's notion of *change* involves a subject-substance first lacking a given property and then ending up with it. The movement from this relative nonbeing to the terminal being has a dramatic-teleological character; even spatial motion has a kind of getting-there character (in natural motion it is almost getting-home). The four types of change, according to the categories involved, are *growth and diminution* (Quantity), *alteration* (Quality), *locomotion* (in Place), and *coming-to-be and passing-away* (Substance).

Buchler explains *alescence* as follows: "Now when a complex located in a given order is not prevalent in that order or ceases to be prevalent in that order, we shall say that it is *alescent,* or an *alescence.*" (MNC 55) Whereas Aristotle located the subject of change as an underlying substratum—in primary changes a substance—Buchler's continuity in change is a *natural complex.* Without attempting here an explication of this basic concept, it is clear that it incorporates the modern shift from an isolated subject-substance to a more or less structured field. This allows—as the concept of *proception* did in relation to experience—the incorporation of the environment with the individual *within* the subject of change. (Both Aristotle and Buchler are clearly opposed to Hume's formulation, in which the subject disappears into the succession of impressions, whether atomic as in Hume or field cross-sections as occasionally in theories of events.) But the shift from Aristotle involved in Buchler's concept of *alescence* is more than just a modernization of subject. It reverses the direction that allowed Aristotle to impose the teleology. Thus while Aristotle explicates *change* in terms of a subject going from absence of a property to the presence of the property, Buchler seems to go from the presence of a property to its absence. For example, if a light changes from green to red, Aristotle sees it as what-is-not-red issuing in red, while Buchler sees it as green going out of the field. This seems to me to parallel the metaphysical shift from a finalistic to a present-causal order that characterized the rise of modern science, while allowing change as so defined to be sometimes purposive, sometimes nonpurposive.

The differences become manifest also in the kinds of *alescence* compared to the forms of Aristotelian *change.* Buchler gives these as *augmentative, spoliative, coalescence, vagrant.* Now the first two clearly can be seen as combining Aristotle's growth and diminution with his coming-into-being and passing-away. This leaves the dramatic appearing and vanishing of substance out on a philosophical limb. But that aspect is apparently transferred to coalescence where "a complex arises from a junction or intersection or novel configuration of complexes." (MNC 57) Thus coalescence incorporates modern recognition of novelty and the emergence of fresh structures. Vagrant *alescence* seems to refer to isolated variation which does not involve deviation from any prevalence in particular. (MNC 65) I take this to mean isolated variation that (roughly) does not upset an order or create a new order. (An interestingly analogy would be chance variations that do not create new species.) The startling absence in Buchler's *alescence* of Aristotle's alteration or qualitative change is less significant when we realize that the latter has been promoted, as part, into the very concept of *alescence* itself; the emphasis on variation and deviation suggests it strongly. And the absence of locomotion suggests how easily spatial movement can be taken for granted as a special case of qualitative relational rearrangement.

This untangling and recombination of Aristotelian strands to interpret Buchler's concept of *alescence* may suggest what I meant by saying it was a modernization as well as a generalization. Indeed, I am not sure that it is more generalized than Aristotle's. It is rather that the abandonment of teleology and of the isolated subject-substance and the recognition of emergence (solidified by evolutionary theory) force a revision of the presuppositions of the concept of change and so a revision of the concept itself. But in the latter there seems to me to be a considerable variety of options. Other features might have been stressed to produce a different pattern. The very differences of *alescence* from *matter-in-motion, flux* and *events*, noted above, suggest some different patterns. Dewey's events lay primary stress on the processive, while Whitehead's early use of the concept, as well as Russell's, embodies the Einsteinian unification of space and time. Matter-in-motion in the earlier mechanist philosophies embodied the scientific promise of finding a physical executive basis for all allegedly nonphysical qualities and events, while later Marxian and many post-Darwinian materialisms add the emergence of qualitative levels of consciousness and social action. Santayana's flux looks like a fusion of mechanical motion and personal consciousness. If all the thematic differences were spread out fully before us, the temptation might be overwhelming to play with them matrix fashion and generate diverse sets of possible categories on the same philosophical level as Aristotle's *change* and Buchler's *prevalence* and *alescence*.

Two paths would then lie open to us, as we saw in discussing *procep-tion*. One would be to make comparisons, reveal problems and presuppositions, pinpoint relevant changing knowledge, and prepare the way self-consciously for some future categorial synthesis, probably more complex than simply getting a fresh technical term embodying a novel selection, and more directly attuned to the pinpointed growth of knowledge desired. The other would be the path Buchler has followed, to propose a new set of categories and invite us to see how it does the job in our own canvas of our experience.

This brings us to the last and most serious question indicated earlier—the bases of categorial preference. Here it is worth looking back to what other propounders of categorial sets did with them. Aristotle—if I have correctly analyzed his procedure—both derived his categories from the vital concepts that did the heavy work of analyzing and formulating questions in different scientific and humanistic disciplines, and returned the categories to these and other fields to continue the analyses and investigation. The traditional materialists either exported their categories from the physics of the day to other fields such as psychology and social inquiry or at least exported models that developed in the physical use of their categories; later materialists broadened the fields from which their categories were derived. Dewey applied his concepts of change and experience to field after field, from education and politics to law and morals. Whitehead was less systematic in this respect but developed particularly the concern with the growth of ideas in western science and general thought. Even Santayana put his categories to work in his *Life of Reason* to assess society and religion, art and science.

Buchler has not carried through this kind of task as yet. We have not seen his categories at work in area after area. Buchler's manner of philosophizing is much like Santayana's—a gentlemanly presentation of his reflections for the reflective reader's consideration. There is no attempt at a systematic mode of proof, justification or establishment.

My point is not simply that the categories have to be put to work to earn their keep, but the more significant hypothesis outlined in Section II above, that the testing and refinement and comparison of categorial sets lies in the arena of the history of thought, that categories arise and gain their energy from different fields and that their successes and failures in advancing concrete work in these fields is the measure of their adequacy.

Perhaps there is here some basic difference in the conception of metaphysics, for Buchler would seem to keep its development independent of its applications and in some sense prior to them. In that case, I do not see how his method as practiced in the four books, broadening as it is, will carry us far beyond the limits of an expanded ordinary consciousness. It will yield the expression of a personal outlook, the refined products of a civilized consciousness for others to compare. In this, fine slants and sensitive tunings will be of the essence—and Buchler is eminently sensitive in this—but it will not, for example, tap the sciences both in their established results and in their probing frontier efforts.

The problem I am raising is inherent in traditional metaphysics. It is not Buchler's own. Metaphysics has been the queenly science in the sense that her principles (sometimes her whims) were taken to be validated by her own processes, not by the fruitfulness of her constructions in the diversity of human inquiries. Metaphysical revelation had thus an ultimate character, whatever shape it took in particular theories. It is the idea of metaphysics as categorial experimentation for the full scope of human inquiry in all its provinces of experience—humanistic as well as scientific—that is a contemporary novelty, not the traditional isolation. In that case, perhaps the central significance of Buchler's metaphysical work—apart from its ramified sensitive insights—may lie less in the new technical categorial set he offers than in the indictment of the old, less in the specific revolution carried out than in the very act of calling for a revolution.

Notes

1. W. D. Ross, *Aristotle*, 5th edition (Meridian Books), p. 27; Hugh Tredennick, *Aristotle, The Metaphysics* (Cambridge: Harvard University Press, 1935), Loeb edition, vol. 2, p. 112, note b.

2. J. M. E. Moravcsik, "Aristotle's Theory of Categories," in his edition of *Aristotle: A Collection of Critical Essays* (Garden City, NJ: Doubleday Anchor Books, 1967), p. 144.

3. Moravcsik, op. cit., p. 143. J. L. Ackrill, *Aristotle's Categories and De Interpretatione* (Oxford: Clarendon Press, 1963), p. 79.

4. Cf. Jaakko Hintikka, *Time and Necessity* (Oxford: Clarendon Press, 1973).

5. I am indebted to Professor Elizabeth Flower for calling my attention to a passage in an early eighteenth century text which admirably illustrated this point, and incidentally takes for granted precisely the kind of interpretation of Aristotle's categories I am here proposing. It is William Brattle's *Compendium Logicae Secundum Principia D. Renati Cartesii*, used for a long stretch as a textbook at Harvard. In the 1707 edition, Brattle argues that neither the loci nor the categories of Aristotle are sufficient guides for finding out all the relevant aspects of the phenomena under study. Brattle proposes instead the categories of matter, measure, rest, motion, position, figure, and mind. This clearly shows the influence of Descartes and the new science, and probably Locke as well. Particularly significant are the substitution of matter for the Aristotelian substance, the mathematical emphasis in measure, and the similarity of the remaining categories to Locke's primary qualities. Aristotle's category of quality is explicitly reduced to the effects of figure and motion, but mind is regarded as irreducible, a category distinct from all material ideas.

6. Thomas Kuhn's *The Structure of Scientific Revolutions* is a recent example. But there have been many who, like Mannheim in his earlier work, were ready to offer this for the social sciences alone.

7. See Justus Buchler, TGT, NJ, CM, MNC. See "List of Abbreviations" for Buchler's works, p. xiii–xiv.

It is important to note that the present paper, written in 1974, was of necessity limited in its interpretations of Buchler's thought to the books that had then appeared. These works present a well-defined position which is interesting in its own right, even though his subsequent writings may invite reinterpretations. Future historians will have to decide whether to differentiate a late Buchler from an early Buchler.

Possibility: Three Recent Ontologies

Phil Weiss

The ontological status of possibilities has, historically, been a rather knotty problem. Are unactualized possibilities real? Or is only the actual real? Are there *real* possibilities, which have a higher ontological status than merely *logical* possibilities, since the former might just be actualized, while the latter will surely not? Are things which are possible *possible things*? If so, do possible things exist? Are they realized, perhaps, in other, merely possible, worlds? If so, are these worlds real? Do they exist? The language of being, existing and being real seems to lack the requisite precision for sorting out the difficulties involved in deciding whether and what possibilities are.

In this paper, I will consider and compare three recent theories about the ontology of possibility. Each of these theories presents an outlook markedly distinct from the other two. The first is the radically *realistic* account of David Lewis; second is Nicholas Rescher's *constructivistic* and *conceptualistic* account; third is Justus Buchler's *naturalism*. Throughout, the discussion will have a threefold focus. I will be primarily concerned with the notions of (1) *possible entities* (individuals or worlds or states of affairs), (2) *logical possibility* (as distinct from physical or nomic possibility), and (3) *natural possibility* (as correlative with actuality, not opposed to it). The initial motivation for this triple focus was my unease at the elimination of (1) and (2) in Buchler's work, which elimination is accompanied by eye-opening insight into (3) generated by the principle of ontological parity and the ordinal metaphysics central to Buchler's naturalism. I hoped that by examining philosophical perspectives in which (1) and (2) dominated the concern with possibility, I would be able to find the valuable inner core of these conceptions in order to locate that core, if possible, within the perspective of a metaphysics of natural complexes.

I. Lewis' Theory

David Lewis takes the apparatus of modal logic as the starting point for his speculation about possibility. This involves interpretation of two modal operators, a necessity operator $\Box$ and a possibility operator $\Diamond$. As is traditional with necessity and possibility, these operators are formally interdefinable: "$\Diamond\phi$=df $\sim\Box\sim\phi$, or $\Box\phi$=df$\sim\Diamond\sim\phi$."[1] The interpretation of these operators involves a hybrid of Leibnizian and modern logical language: "a *necessity operator*, in general, is an operator that acts like a restricted universal quantifier over possible worlds. . . . A *possibility operator*, likewise, is an operator that acts like a restricted existential quantifier over worlds." (pp. 4–5). The restrictions placed upon the operation of these quantifiers are called "accessibility restrictions." These function to determine the *sort* of modality being invoked on any given occasion. Each world which satisfies a given set of requirements relative to a given world is said to be accessible from that world, and the set of all worlds so accessible is said to constitute a "sphere of accessibility" around that world. (pp. 5–7) Given these interpretations of the modal operators, and the notion of accessibility, Lewis is in a position to offer the following metaphysical definitions of necessity and possibility:

> Necessity is truth at all accessible worlds, and different sorts of necessity correspond to different accessibility restrictions. (p. 5)

> Possibility is truth at some accessible world, and the accessibility restriction imposed depends on the sort of possibility under consideration. (p. 5)

Clearly, our concerns about possible entities (worlds) and logical possibility are shared by Lewis. For, in the first place, the general concepts of necessity and possibility are defined by him in terms of possible worlds. And, in the second place, he feels the need to indicate from the start that there are several different sorts of possibility and necessity, chief among which are the logical and physical sorts. Our first task is to clarify the subsidiary notion of sorts of possibility. Afterwards, we will examine Lewis' surprising theory concerning possible worlds.

As already indicated, different sorts of necessity and possibility are correlated with different accessibility restrictions, and thus with different spheres of accessibility. We have, then, the following accessibility requirements for logical and physical necessity respectively:

> Corresponding to *logical necessity* . . . we assign to each world *i* as its sphere of accessibility *Si* the set of *all* possible worlds. (p. 7)

> Corresponding to *physical necessity* . . . we assign to each world *i* as its sphere of accessibility *Si* the set of all worlds where the laws of nature prevailing at *i* hold . . . (p. 7)

The idea of different sorts of necessity and possibility, then, is just the idea of necessity or possibility relative to different *samplings* of possible worlds. It is a matter of wider or narrower bounds we set on items to be considered. If we are looking for physical possibilities, we will restrict our search more severely than if we seek logical possibilities. In the latter case all possible worlds are open to us.

What, then, are these possible worlds in which we are to find possibilities and in terms of which Lewis defines possibility? Lewis espouses a radical realism about possible worlds:

> I believe that there are possible worlds other than the one we happen to inhabit. If an argument is wanted, it is this. It is uncontroversially true that things might be otherwise than they are. . . . Ordinary language permits the paraphrase: there are many ways things could have been besides the way they actually are. On the face of it, this sentence is an existential quantification. It says that there exist many entities of a certain description, to wit, "ways things could have been". . . . I therefore believe in the existence of entities that might be called "ways things could have been." I prefer to call them "possible worlds." (p. 84)

This extraordinary piece of reasoning opens up to us a breathtaking metaphysical panorama. Possible worlds are just—well, *worlds*. All the things which could have been in our world but are not, are not lost; they are just located in other worlds. And these other worlds are just as real as the world we live in:

> Our actual world is only one world among others. We call it alone actual not because it differs in kind from all the rest but because it is the world we inhabit. The inhabitants of the other worlds may truly call their own worlds actual, if they mean by "actual" what we do; for the meaning we give to "actual" is such that it refers at any world *i* to that world *i* itself. "Actual" is indexical, like "I" or "here" or "now": it depends for its reference on the circumstances of utterance, to wit the world where the utterance is located. (pp. 85–86)

The universe is a superworld, teeming with worlds. Each world is actual relative to itself and possible relative to all worlds from which it is accessible on the sort of possibility in question. The situation is reminiscent of Borges' "Garden of Forking Paths," in which all possibilities are realized in different worlds, so that every alternative gives rise to a splitting into alternate actualities which could not all be simultaneously realized within one world, but which are realized in an expanding universe of many worlds. It is important, before we take a critical stance, to have a sense of the attractiveness of this theory. It is both expansive and ontologically tolerant. In opposition to narrow perspectives which want to eliminate all but bare actualities, Lewis wants to affirm the ontological parity of possibility and actuality.

He does not, however, succeed in this project. Lewis wants to understand what sort of being possibilities have. Things, as he says, might be otherwise than they are. Or rather, more accurately, things might have been otherwise than they are. The possibility existed that things be one of several different ways, but they turned out to be only this one way. Lewis fastens on the "ways," but in doing so, he loses all the possibilities. He claims that these "ways" have just the same sort of being as this one way things turned out. But if this one way is actual, then all the other ways must be actual. The universe on this picture is a superworld of *pure actuality.* To say that a possibility exists is just to say that somewhere an actuality exists. This is clear from the definition of possibility as *truth* in a world. On this view of worlds, the only way to be true in a world is to actually obtain there. On this theory, then, possibility reduces to actuality—somewhere else.

There is another aspect of this theory which makes it peculiar as a theory of possibility. If I say that it was possible for this (yellow) paper on which I am writing to have been white, then I mean it was possible for just *this* paper. On Lewis' theory, however, what I seem to mean is that there is white paper situated similarly to this yellow paper in another world. Rather than engage in disputes as to how to determine the identity of this yellow paper and that white paper, Lewis chooses "to escape the problem of transworld identity by insisting that there is nothing that inhabits more than one world." (p. 39) It thus turns out that "what something *might* have done (or might have been) is what it does (or is) vicariously." (p. 40) The *possibility* for *this* paper is identified by Lewis with the *actuality* of *that* paper. This clearly conflicts with the ordinary conceptions of the possibilities for a thing, and so casts doubt on the cogency of Lewis' initial understanding of the ordinary conception of possibility.

This move on Lewis' part is motivated by his understanding of possible worlds as worlds of pure actuality completely independent of one another. If these worlds have such strong independence, then there is no relation across worlds similar to the relations of causality and continuity which allow us to affirm identity within a world.[2] This understanding of possible worlds comes from trying to identify the being of possibilities in this world with the actuality of things and states of affairs in other worlds. And this in turn follows from the confusion of possibilities as possibilities of the actual with possibilities as "ways" of being actual. My suspicion is that this confusion is itself motivated by Lewis' participation in a tradition which strongly identifies the real with the actual, so that the only way to answer the question what sort of being something has is either to say what sort of actuality it is or to deny that it is at all. What this tradition seems to require is that the universe as a whole be completely determinate and that every element of the universe itself be completely determinate at every instant. That is, the universe as a whole must be a block, through which we can cut cross-sectional slices, however thin we like, for analysis. These sections are assumed to lose nothing in being separated out from the others. However, a great mystery ensues as to just how the sections are glued together and how the present grows out of the past. Lewis, in trying to make some headway in understanding possibility, falls back into an indefinitely ramified block universe. Ramification, however, ought not to be confused with movement. It will not account for process or change or causation.

We have seen that Lewis fails to develop an adequate theory of possibility because he confuses possibilities of the actual with ways of being actual. Thus, the central notion of the *actualization* of a possibility is lost to Lewis. There is no actualization, no process, only bare actuality. What have we learned from Lewis about possible worlds and logical possibility? Possible worlds seem to correspond to different "ways of being actual." Different sorts of possibility, then, correspond to different limitations on a search for alternative ways of being actual. If we are to clearly distinguish possibilities from ways of being actual, we must determine whether any such limitations are relevant to possibilities. If such can be found, they will determine different sorts of possibility. However, we must recognize that Lewis' realistic theory of possible worlds is unacceptable. It does not function adequately as an explanation of possibility. Moreover, the arguments given to support it are spurious. Despite his claims, Lewis does not really take seriously the implications of ordinary language for a conception of possibility. We are left with the task of understanding what these (so-called) possible worlds, these ways of being actual, are, if they are not possibilities, and how such worlds might be related to possibility. Consideration of Nicholas Rescher's theory of possibility will, I think, take us a step closer to that goal.

II. Rescher's Theory

Whereas Lewis begins with notions from modal logic and explicates them in terms of realistically construed possible worlds, Rescher begins with conventional logic and proceeds to show how possible worlds can be constructed. The theory of the conceptual construction of possible individuals, possible states of affairs and possible worlds is meant to be an exhaustive theory of unactualized possibilities. For Rescher, unactualized and never-to-be-actualized possibilities, what he calls "hard-core possibilities," are paradigmatic of the possible in general.[3] However, since Rescher views actuality as the whole of reality, he construes these hard-core possibilities as nonexistent. The ontological problem he tries to solve is: "just exactly what can the existential status of a possible-but-unrealized state of affairs be?" (OP 215) The conceptualist-constructivist solution to this problem is as follows:

> It is my central thesis that by the very nature of hypothetical possibilities they cannot exist as such, but must be thought of: They must be hypothesized, or imagined, or assumed, or something of this sort. (OP 214)

or, alternatively: ". . . possible worlds and possible individuals [are] most properly viewed as actual or potential conceptual artifacts."[4] Possibility, according to Rescher, is paradigmatically "mind-dependent" (OP 215), thus, "actuality is prior to possibility." (OP 221)

The point of claiming the ontological dependence of possibilities upon actualities is to counter a Platonic realism in regard to possibilities. Rescher wants to argue that "the world does not have two existential compartments" (OP 215), "that there is no Platonic realm where possible worlds are graven on crystalline tablets." (TP 3) He wants to eliminate this "Platonism" by insisting on the ontological priority of the actual. "By definition, only the *actual* will ever exist in the world, never the unactualized possible." (OP 215) It is by starting with the actual as given that intelligent beings construct the possible:

> actual individuals and the sundry properties they actually have are epistemically and ontologically basic, in that "merely possible" individuals (and states of affairs and worlds) are *intellectual constructions (entia rationis)* developed from a strictly actually-pertaining starting-point. (TP 2)

The initial actualistic materials from which possibilities are constructed are "(1) *a population census* or *item-inventory* of real individuals," and "(2) a *feature inventory* for these individuals." (TP 6)

From the very beginning, there is an ambivalence in Rescher's characterization of the actual, which threatens either to force him into dualism or to lead him into an admission of the correlativity of actuality with possibility. This ambivalence is rooted in the categorial division of actuality into individuals and properties. Rescher takes it as unproblematic that "the starting point is provided by a survey of *actual individuals and their properties*." (TP 6) But, in the first place, the notion of an "actual individual" is left completely unanalyzed. What is an individual as distinct from its properties? Are individual properties themselves individuals? If so, then the distinction between properties and individuals breaks down. If not, are individuals to be construed as spatial combinations of properties? If individuals are so construed, do they change in time? If so, what makes an individual the same individual once it has changed? If not, how do we know there are actual individuals at all, given that items in our experience which we identify as spatio-temporal individuals change? Is change then, an illusion produced by our stance within time? If so, we have returned to a dualism of a real world of actuality, which we don't experience, opposed to an illusory world of change, which we do experience. And this, the separating-off of a world of pure actuality from our experienced world, is the viciously threatening "Platonic" dualism. Problems like this in the notion of pure actuality initially gave rise to the conception of natural possibility or potentiality in Aristotle. To revert to a world of purely actual individuals is to return to the problems. Rescher at no point recognizes these difficulties.

In the second place, and Rescher seems to recognize this, the inclusion of properties in the realm of the actual seems to require trespassing on the bounds of pure actuality. Difficulties arise here primarily in relation to (1) unexemplified properties, and (2) dispositional properties. On the first count, Rescher's "starting-point" in the actual admittedly goes "beyond" an "actualistic basis" by permitting "properties, perfectly genuine and 'real' properties, that are not actually exemplified in nature." (TP 6) That is, by "theoretical systematization" we determine what other properties things might have had, but in fact don't, and these properties are to be included in the feature inventory of our survey of the real. "Properties must admit of exemplification, but they need not be exemplified." (TP 6) Rescher doesn't seem to realize that this interpretation of properties is just an invocation of a realm of pure possibilities which may or may not be actualized (exemplified). Though he ostensibly wants to overcome a dual–compartment ontology, Rescher is forced into just such an ontology by his metaphysics of purely actual individuals and properties which may or may not be exemplified.

On the second count, Rescher incorporates more than bare actuality into his starting point by allowing dispositions as properties. A disposition connects two "atomic" properties in the following way: (for atomic properties ϕ and ψ, an individual may have the disposition from ψ to ϕ : ϕ/ψ) "the individual may not just have ϕ and ψ, but may have ϕ *because* it has

ψ, if it does have ψ—or, if it lacks ψ, then be such that it would have to
have φ as a result of its possession of ψ, if this possession of ψ were
hypothetically the case." (TP 10) Rescher himself says of dispositions
that they "are amphibious in character; they have one foot in the realm of
the actual, another in that of the possible." (TP 132) However, he mistakenly understands the reference to the possible to be explicable solely as a
reference to the hypothetical. In this, he fails to observe that the notion of
causal connection is fundamental to dispositions. And the notion of cause
is inextricably linked with the notion of natural possibilities, for causation
involves the actualization and elimination of possibilities. But Rescher,
implying that all dispositions are conceptually dependent upon hypotheses,
subsumes them under his constructivist approach. He is thus ambiva-
lent about the "reality" of dispositions. We will come to see this ambivalence as symptomatic of an underlying ambiguity in Rescher's analysis of
possibility.

　　Let us put these problems aside for the time being in order to consider the mechanisms by which Rescher constructs possible individuals,
given actual individuals and their properties. We are first introduced to the
modality of property attribution through the question of the essentiality of a
property to an individual. A property may actually characterize an individual (φx, for an individual x and a property φ), it may be essential to an
individual (φ !x), or it may be a possible (accidental, if actual) property of
an individual (φ?x). A property will be a possible property of an individual
if and only if its lack is not essential to the individual. (TP 10) The determination of whether an atomic (nondispositional, nonrelational) property
actually characterizes an individual is supposed to be a rather straightforward observational affair. Determination of essentiality is not so easy.

　　Rescher "adopts," in regard to essentialism, "the posture of a pragmatic pluralism," maintaining "that there are various different and alternative bases upon which the essential/accidental distinction can be placed,"
and refusing to view any one of them as "uniquely and universally *correct*," but seeing each as "functionally suitable" in particular contexts.
(TP 22) In fact, Rescher sets out five such variable approaches to basic
essential properties:

(i) A property is essential to an individual if it is implied by a *canonical description* of the individual. (TP 23)

(ii) A property is essential if it is needed to maintain the *descriptive
differentiation* of an individual from all others. (TP 27)

(iii) A property is essential if its presence *maintains* the *uniformity of*
a *type* to which the individual belongs. (TP 28)

(iv) A property is essential if it characterizes an individual throughout its entire temporal existence *(Temporal Invariance)*. (TP 30)

(v) A property is essential if it would characterize an individual though it endured a "certain family of specified transformations other than temporal change" *(Invariance Under Transformations)*. (TP 32)

Notice that all of these are naturalistic criteria. However, only essentiality determinations of types (ii)–(iv) can be made by observation of atomic properties actually possessed by actual individuals. Determinations of type (i) depend upon which true descriptions are to be selected as canonical. It is not clear what will determine policy on canonization of descriptions. Likely, considerations such as determine types (ii)–(v) will be central here, besides contextual interests. But what is most important is that essentiality determinations of type (v) require all the apparatus of theoretical science, including the theoretical imputations of dispositions, and so, already bring us into the realm of possibility.

If we assume that we have been given, by the examination of the actual, a listing of properties, a listing of individuals, and for each individual a listing of its actual properties, its essential properties, its (merely) possible properties (that is, properties not actual and whose lack is not essential), and its dispositional properties, we are ready to begin the construction of possible individuals. If we take our initial listing of properties, we can theoretically set out a charting of all possible descriptions. Each description could be complete in the sense that every property was either categorically affirmed or categorically denied in each description. Moreover, we are (theoretically) in a position to set out for every actual individual a description complete not only in this sense, but in the stronger sense that each affirmation or denial of a property in the description could be specified as essential or accidental. Rescher calls a complete descriptive specification of the former (weak) sort a *c.d.s.*, and an essentialistically complete descriptive specification a *C.D.S.* We now have a *C.D.S.* for every actual individual and an array of *c.d.s.*es determined by the set of all properties.

For example, suppose an actual world with three properties: F, G, and H, and two individuals: x_1 and x_2, for which the following canonical descriptions are given: 'x_1 is the H which does not have G' and 'x_2 is the H which does have G.' (Such worlds are called by Rescher "micro-worlds.") Let the *C.D.S.* for x_1 be $(F, [\overline{G}], [H])$ (where $\overline{G}$ indicates the lack of G and brackets indicate essentiality), and let the *C.D.S.* for x_2 be $(F, [G], [H])$. Note that essentiality here is determined relative to the given canonical descriptions. An individual could be described canonically as 'the H which does not have G' and yet have $\overline{F}$ as part of its *C.D.S.* Such a description would differ from that of x_1 only in nonessential respects. Rescher calls such descriptions *variant descriptions* of actual individuals. (TP 46) Thus, we can set out the following table of *c.d.s.*es for the properties of our micro-world and locate on that table those descriptions corresponding to actual individuals and variant descriptions of actual individuals:

	F	G	H	x_1	x_2
1.	+	+	+		@
2.	+	+	−		
3.	+	−	+	@	
4.	+	−	−		
5.	−	+	+		#
6.	−	+	−		
7.	−	−	+	#	
8.	−	−	−		

Note: @ indicates *c.d.s.*, # indicates variant *c.d.s.*, for the indicated individuals.

It can be clearly seen from the chart that the available properties determine *c.d.s.*es which describe neither actual individuals nor essentialistically permitted variations on actual individuals. These may be taken as describing "supernumeraries" or *merely* possible individuals. This, then, is the mechanism by which possible individuals are constructed from the apparatus used in the description of the actual world. Rescher generalizes the domain of the possible:

> The *possible* will be construed broadly as a genus embracing three species: the *actual*, the realm of *actual-variant possibility*, . . . and the merely possible (or supernumerary). The latter two categories, taken together, comprise the realm of *unactualized* possibility. . . . The actual together with its actual-variant possibilities may be said to comprise the range of the proximately possible. (TP 51)

In regard to our world of experience, of course, we cannot specify individuals by giving a *C.D.S.*, but we can specify individuals ostensively.

Thus a fully individuating characterization *(fic)* of an individual can be given by an incomplete description and an ostensive indicator: $<d, i>$. (TP 45) We cannot ostensively specify an actual-variant, but we can name the actual individual of which it is taken to be a possible variant. The *fic* of an actual–variant, then, is given by $<C.D.S., x>$, where x indicates the actual prototype. Similarly, the *fic* of a supernumerary is given by $<C.D.S., ☆>$, where ☆ indicates the null prototype. (TP 63) Since we can never (except in theory) give the *C.D.S.* of possible individuals, we must recognize that we at best actually deal with incomplete descriptive schemata. (TP 57) There is thus always an ambiguity in the description of nonexistent possible individuals. This ambiguity is not to be taken as ontologically characterizing the individuals themselves; it is a purely epistemic ambiguity. Nonexistent possible individuals are, in principle, fully determinate.

What is the ontological status of such individuals?

An altogether nonexistent (that is, supernumerary) individual is to be construed as the product of an *hypothesis of incarnation,* postulating the actualization of a descriptive specification that is intrinsically (or "merely logically") possible. . . . The assumptive factor introduced by the "incarnation hypothesis" of this discussion is important, the descriptive specification of an individual must be distinguished from the individual itself; its description is a linguistic conceptual artifact, the individual itself presumably not. The individual is the *thing* that supposedly answers to its descriptive specification. And when nothing *in fact* does so, because a "nonexistent individual" is at issue, then this individual is, at best, the product of an assumption (supposition, hypothesis) that something does so. (TP 62–63)

It is of central importance to recognize that these possible individuals, like Lewis' possible worlds or "ways of being actual," are not the same as possibilities of the actual. They are rather assumptive or *hypothetical actualities.* They share with the actual a supposed characterization as fully determinate. Natural possibilities have thus far been passed over in silence, masked behind the acceptance of dispositional properties and essentiality of type (v). We will shortly consider in detail Rescher's metaphysics of possibilia. For the time being, we pass on to a brief consideration of the construction of possible worlds.

Just as the actual world is, for Rescher, a collection of related individuals, so "possible worlds simply *are* collections of possible individuals duly combined with one another" (TP 78). To be sure, we may not just take any possible individuals and throw them together to make a world. Restrictions of 'compossibility' must be met by sets of individuals, if they are to qualify as possible worlds. *Logical* 'compossibility' requires that "requirements of presence or absence" built into the descriptions of all its individuals be met. (TP 79) *Metaphysical* 'compossibility' requires (1) that the principle of Identity of Indiscernibles hold within all (merely) possible worlds, and (2) that possible worlds not contain "distinct versions of the same prototype." (TP 81) *Nomic* 'compossibility' requires the preservation in possible worlds subject to it of at least some of the laws of nature of the actual world. Thus, we will obtain sets of nomically possible worlds or metaphysically possible worlds depending on whether all three or only the first two compossibility requirements are followed in their construction:

> The theory thus develops a relativistic conception of possibility. Logical possibility is fundamental; other modes of possibility are elaborated in terms of logical possibility relative to certain presuppositions. (TP 84)

Possible individuals are constructed by logically (that is, formally) permitted permutation of the descriptions of actualia. Possible worlds are constructed by logically and metaphysically permitted combination of possible individuals. Nomically possible worlds are constructed by observing actual laws of nature as well as logical and metaphysical restraints upon combinations of individuals. (Note that in permitting laws of nature, Rescher may be once again covertly importing potentiality or possibility into his characterization of the actual.) Possibility, on this theory, comes down to lack of logical restraint against combinations of descriptive terms. Possibilities are just permitted combinations. Actuality is fundamental, for it provides all the basic material for combination.

If this is taken as constituting a conceptual analysis of possibility, then we can see that possibility is conceptually dependent upon language and thus upon the general realm of mind. We turn now to an intriguing *ambivalence* in Rescher's characterization of the ontological status of these mind-dependent possibilities. This ambivalence was in evidence in the pair of quotations given above (see p. 150) as expressions of the conceptualist solution to the problem of the existential status of nonexistent possibles. In the first, Rescher claims that such possibles, in order to exist "must be thought of." In the second, the claim is that possibles are "actual *or potential* conceptual artifacts" (emphasis mine). (Note that in the recent long quotation about the incarnation hypothesis, Rescher explicitly denies that possible individuals are conceptual artifacts.) On the one hand, Rescher wants to claim that "For such a possibility, to be *(esse)* is to be conceived *(concipi)*." (OP 218) On the other hand, he wants to demur: "We are not saying that to be a possible (but unactualized) state of affairs requires that

this state must *actually* be conceived. . . . Rather . . . possible, albeit un-
realized, states of affairs or things obtain an ontological footing . . . only
insofar as it lies within the generic province of minds to conceive them."
(OP 216–17)

In part, this ambivalence stems from Rescher's wanting both to deny
the objectivity of possibles and to affirm it. Thus we have both: "the hypothetically possible cannot just 'objectively be' the case; it must be hypothesized . . ." (OP 220) and: "independence of any specific mind
establishes the *objectivity* of nonexistent possibles." (OP 221) Clearly there
are two different versions of conceptualism operative here, and the two are
not compatible. Perhaps we can call one the "Berkelian" theory and the
other the "Kantian." On the Berkelian theory, the possibility must be *conceived* and thus can *be* only relative to individual conceiving minds. On the
Kantian theory, a possibility must be *conceivable,* and thus *is* relative to the
capacities of mind in general as evidenced in language. On the former theory, then, the possibility is subjective. It does not exist unless conceived by
particular subjects. On the latter theory, the possibility is objective in that it
exists even if nobody ever conceives it, if only it is conceivable.

The motivation for the Berkelian conception is to retain absolutely the
ontological primacy of actuality. All that exists is actual. When an actuality
is actually thought about we can distinguish "(1) The actually existing
thing or state of affairs" from "(2) The thought or entertainment of this
state of affairs." Both the thing and the thought are actual. (OP 215) But if
for nonactualized possibilities we distinguish (i) the thought of the possibility from (ii) the possibility thought of, "item (i) . . . exists unproblemati-
cally in the manner of thoughts in general," while "item (ii) does not
'exist' in reality," but only "*as the object* of the thought." (OP 216) Only
the actual thought (which somehow contains its object) exists; thus, only
actuality exists.

What, then, is the motivation for the Kantian conception? It is just
that we treat possibilities as objective and not as dependent upon being
conceived by individuals. Rescher wants to be able to accept such locutions
as: "The possibility existed . . . only nobody thought of it at the time."
(OP 221) Similarly, it would be strange to say: "The possibility of Paul's
going to the park exists only because I have conceived it" (when I have
thought of it, but Paul has not). Thus Rescher is attracted to the Kantian
conception, though a repeated thrust of his argument (from "hypothetical
possibilities" to "there must be an actual hypothesis") follows the Berkelian conception.

The possibilities of the Berkelian model are just what we have called
"hypothetical actualities." They are actually hypothesized alternate actualities. They are human products, and as such are causally dependent upon

human beings. They may be called conceptually dependent upon human beings as well. But they are not ontologically dependent upon human beings in any sense stronger than causal dependency (which they share alike with such other products as existing tables and spoons). Neither are they the sort of things we ordinarily call possibilities. For we want to say that in casting about us we discover and disclose possibilities which would have existed had we not discovered them, and that the possibility of there being minds antedates minds. Rescher senses this, although unclearly, for he never realizes that he espouses two mutually incompatible theories of possibility.

Perhaps he is kept from this realization by some of the consequences of the Kantian conception which threaten to undermine the entire project of a conceptualistic approach to possibility. In the face of the spectre of naturalistic realism in regard to possibilities, which would destroy his actualistic conception of reality, Rescher takes refuge in rigid idealism. Yet, his honesty before a sense of natural possibility leads Rescher out of this rigid Berkelian idealism into the moderate Kantian idealism. He wants to argue not for the causal mind-dependence of the possible, but only for conceptual mind-dependence, and this in a generic and not a specific fashion. But, in doing so, he lands in an apparently vicious circularity. Possibility on the Kantian conception is conceivability. But that is to say that the existence of a possibility is just the existence of the possibility of its being conceived. Now, either there is here a vicious circle with possibility depending upon possibility, or we have two distinct senses of possibility, one conceptually dependent upon the other—*and the other left unanalyzed* by the conceptualist approach. Rescher opts against circularity:

> Is not the qualification of possibility in terms of possibilities a nonproductive circumambulation? Not really. What we are saying is that the "reality" of certain possible states of affairs and things . . . resides in the reality of possibility-involving processes. . . . (OP 221)

This appears to be a recognition of two distinct sorts of possibility: the possibility of possible states of affairs and things and the possibility involved in possibility-involving processes. These are alternatively characterized by Rescher as "entity possibility" as opposed to "conceptual possibility" (OP 221), (in which case the latter seems to mean 'possibility of being conceived'), and "substantive possibility" as opposed to "functional possibility." (OP 222)

Rescher clearly indicates that functional possibilities are basic. Yet he does not seem to realize that he has not analyzed functional possibility but only substantive possibility. He seems to mistakenly believe that he can somehow limit functional possibilities to the realm of mind and that he can recognize functional possibilities as basic and still claim the primacy of the actual, which has hitherto only been argued against substantive possibilities:

> Our position is that . . . all the variant forms of possibility are, in the final analysis, inherent in the functional potentialities of the real through the mediation of the dispositional capabilities of minds. Thus *reduction* is the key. There is not and cannot be any ''objective,'' mind-independent mode of *iffiness* in nature: objective states of concrete affairs must be categorical, they cannot be hypothetical. . . . The introduction of the hypothetical mode requires—i.e., *conceptually* requires—reference to mentalistic capabilities of assuming, supposing or the like. Any careful analysis of possibility inevitably carries one back to the common theme that only the actual can objectively be real. (TP 203)

However, this return to the identity of the real with the actual is not motivated by Rescher's more careful analysis. It is carelessness of analysis which leads him this way. His more careful thinking leads, as we have seen, right to the doorstep of admitting functional potentialities of the real. In his analysis, functional potentialities and dispositions are basic to and *conceptually precede* the construction of substantive or hypothetical possibilities. They cannot be subsumed under the rubric of the hypothetical without vicious circularity.

We find that two radically distinct concepts of possibility emerge from Rescher's analysis. Substantive possibility, or entity possibility, is constructed (or constructable) possibility, or, more accurately, conceptually constructed (constructable) or hypothesized *reality*. Possible worlds and possible entities are possibilities of this sort: they are hypothesized realities. Functional possibility, or possibility of process, is unconstructed possibility. It is conceptually, causally and ontologically mind-independent, for it is involved in the reality of mind's having the capabilities (the possibilities) that it does have. Rescher glimpses the need for such a conception of possibility underlying the substantive model, but his being possessed by a prejudice in favor of actuality makes him unable to conceive of functional possibility except as hypothetical actuality. The resulting subsumption of functional under substantive possibility leads Rescher, against his will and despite his disclaimers, in a vicious circle.

Perhaps we have been overly hasty in concluding that Rescher argues in a circle. We said earlier (p. 156) that constructed possibilities fundamentally are based in logical possibility. We said that this possibility amounted to lack of logical constraint against combinations of descriptive terms.

Possibility in this sense requires language, which permits and rejects combinations of descriptive terms. Perhaps, then, we need not interpret functional possibilities or conceivability as natural potentialities of the real. Perhaps they are only the logical possibilities resident in language. But what are the logical possibilities resident in language if not natural capacities of terms to combine or resist combination? The terms of a language are not blank actualities completely determinate in themselves. They give themselves to combination and they resist other combinations. Thus even the bare, formal possibilities of logic, when filled out by a natural language show a character as natural potentialities of terms. If we are then to try to reduce these to the actuality of mind, we find that they reside not only in the actuality of mind, but in the potentialities of mind as well: in its capacity to name and describe and invent, in its capacities to create language and to use language. And there is no reason to deny possibilities for inorganic nature if we accept them for mind.

What *are* mind-dependent, in something like Rescher's sense, are hypotheses, hypothetical individuals and hypothetical "worlds." These are products of the human imagination. But if natural possibilities inform the actual, the natural possibilities also inform the hypothetically actual, the imagined and projected actual. Given Rescher's metaphysics of determinateness and naked actuality, it is hard to characterize accurately those products he calls merely logical or nonexistent possibilities.

III. Buchler's Theory

What have we learned about the distinction between logical possibilities and physical or nomic possibilities (different sorts or degrees of possibility) and about possible entities (individuals or worlds or states of affairs) from our consideration of the theories of Lewis and Rescher? The question of sorts or degrees of possibility, we have seen to be a question of the *scope* of our search among possibilities. That is, the issue is not one of inherently different sorts of possibility, some more "really possible" than others, but one of *varying perspectives* on possibilities, with some possibilities appearing in one perspective which do not appear in another and some perspectives generally wider than others. Logical possibility is usually taken to indicate the possibilities which would appear in the (theoretically) widest and most inclusive perspective, the one with the fewest restrictions; physical possibility indicates a more restricted perspective.

We have, further, come to see so-called possible entities as hypothetical or suppositional realities. The assumption that reality "really" consists just in bare, determinate actuality has severely distorted the accounts of both Lewis and Rescher. They have been unable to satisfactorily characterize possible entities, because they understood them as actualities divorced from possibility. Both of them lack a developed conception of natural possibility which is coordinate with natural actuality. Thus, although Lewis wants to assert the parity of actuality and possibility, he can only do so in terms of actuality, and so the coordination of actuality with possibility, indeed, possibility itself, is lost to him. And although Rescher approaches the recognition of a fundamental sense of possibility as functionally resident in and coordinate with actuality, he loses the scent and falls into a vicious circularity of hypothetical orders conceptually dependent upon themselves, because of his assumption that reality is a realm of pure actuality.

We turn now to Justus Buchler's theory, which preeminently contains just what is missing in the preceding analyses, in order to progress to a more adequate characterization of both sorts of possibility (as varying perspectives on possibilities) and possible entities (as hypothetical or suppositional realities).

The central claim of Buchler's treatment of possibility and actuality is that these are two co-ordinate modes (or categories) of being, that all being is pervaded through and through by actuality and possibility. The actual and the possible do not inhabit separate realms, but all the innumerable orders of nature possess traits of possibility and traits of actuality. In short, "a possibility is to be regarded basically in the same way as an actuality. Neither is 'prior' to the other—'logically,' 'metaphysically,' 'epistemically'."[5]

This way of viewing actuality and possibility is a rather straightforward extension of the fundamental stance of the metaphysics of natural complexes: "Whatever is, in whatever way, is a natural complex." (MNC 1) Since there are no levels of being, actualities and possibilities cannot occupy different levels of being. Actualities are natural complexes; possibilities are natural complexes. Since all being is complex, both actualities and possibilities are complex. Relations are included as constituent traits of the complexes related. Thus natural complexes overlap. Every complex constitutes an order of traits. The traits of a complex are themselves complexes, orders subaltern to the given complex. And every natural complex enters into superaltern orders as a constituent trait of those orders.

Every actuality has its possibilities and is an actualization of a prior possibility. These possibilities are constituent traits of that actuality. Every possibility is a possibility of or for an actuality and it may be realized in an actuality. These actualities are constituents of the complex identifiable as that possibility. All these actualities and possibilities are in turn subaltern traits of more comprehensive complexes. Thus all complexes, all orders involve traits of actuality and traits of possibility. The two, though distinguishable are inseparable.

The ruler which was situated in the desk drawer could have been removed and placed upon the surface of the desk or it could have remained where it was. These possibilities for the ruler were intimately related to its actual physical structure and location. The ruler's present situation resting upon the desktop is the actualization of one of the enumerated possibilities and the eradication of the other. Moreover, the current actual state of affairs involves further possibilities, such as the possibility that the ruler be accidentally knocked to the floor, or the possibility that it be returned to the drawer. Additionally, certain (actual) structural features of the ruler give it its characteristic possibilities of use in measuring and drawing lines. All these actualities and possibilities are relevant to the ruler in the course of its life history. They obtain on the same level. They are intertwined and inseparable. The example is mundane, even banal. But such mundane considerations serve best to show the artificiality of considering either actualities or possibilities as residing in separate compartments or different "worlds."

If actuality and possibility are inseparable and not located on different ontological levels, how are they distinguished? Actuality can be distinguished from possibility by its intolerance of contradictory traits. "Actualities are exclusive and restrictive in a way that possibilities are not," insofar as:

> The principal consideration with respect to actuality is that if mutually contradictory complexes are actual, they never prevail in the same order; if mutually contradictory complexes prevail in the same order, they are not actualities. (MNC 156)

Thus, actualities, not possibilities, observe a limitation imposed by, or, more accurately, reflect the logical law of non-contradiction. An order may tolerate possibilities whose actualizations would be mutually contradictory, but it cannot tolerate mutually contradictory actualities. The dog might possibly bark and it might possibly keep silent for the next minute, but it cannot actually both bark and keep silent for the next minute.

Possibilities may be characterized in a somewhat more systematic way, and thus may be distinguished from actualities in a way which clarifies the systematic standing of the previous point about actuality:

> The possibilities of a natural complex are those traits which define its contour (or any of its integrities) in so far as this contour is to continue or be extended. . . . In generalized terms, the traits of a complex define its contour (or, delineate a contour), and those [subaltern] traits which define or chart the "prospect before it" are its possibilities. (MNC 161–62)

Natural complexes are defined, insofar as they have already become what they are, by their traits of actuality. They are defined, insofar as they are moving into the future, by their traits of possibility. The actualization of a possibility of a complex is one sort of definition or delimitation of a complex. Only one of a set of possibilities whose actualizations would be mutually incompatible may be realized. But every trait of actuality involves projection into the future and limitation upon projection. These projections of a complex are its possibilities. They define the complex differently than do its actualities. This mode of definition, Buchler calls *prefinition*:

A possibility *is* an extension of a complex—an extension prefined. A possibility is that prevalent extension or continuation of the contour of a natural complex, whereby certain traits that are related (or, not related) to certain other traits will be related (or, not related) to the other traits. By contrast, an actuality is that prevalence of a natural complex whereby certain traits are related (or, not related) to certain other traits. (MNC 165)

This prefinition, however, is not prediction. The future is not, so to speak, *given* in the possibilities of a complex. What are given are the various projections towards the future of the complex, as they are limited by the traits of actuality with which they are correlated and from which they project. Thus, mutually contradictory futures may be projected, may be prefined by the traits of a complex. These mutually contradictory futures are relevant to the complex. They are its possibilities. One and the same order may thus contain possibilities whose actualizations would be mutually contradictory, though it can never contain mutually contradictory actualities.

Recognizing possibilities as prefining complexes, recognizing that complexes, so to speak, reach out in various directions, allows Buchler to escape from the stultifying image of a block universe. When the universe is dissected into microscopic temporal cross sections of pure actuality in the traditional way, possibilities are lopped off, and with them the connections between the sectional slices. Much of the mystery surrounding change, identity and causation is an artifact of such disruptive analysis. Restoration of possibilities to their rightful place, penetrating, connecting, and advancing actualities, returns to our analysis of the world the fluid, cohering character which the world itself presents in our experience.

What follows from this perspective in regard to different sorts of possibility (logical as opposed to nomic) and possible entities (or worlds or states of affairs)? Buchler perceives a threat to the ordinal conception of possibility from logical possibilities, conceived as "pure" or "free" or "abstract." On the ordinal conception, there are no degrees of possibility. If something is a possibility, it just is a possibility. A "logical possibility" cannot be conceived as more purely possible, as having no relation to any actualities. Thus, his defense is to claim that " 'purely logical' possibilities are not different from any other." (MNC 134)

We have hitherto found that, as used by Lewis, the conception of different sorts of possibility did not refer to inherent differences between possibilities *as possibilities,* but rather to different accessibility requirements placed on the scope of possibilities to be considered. In Rescher, again, this conception appeared in the consideration of different sorts of compossibility requirements for individuals in worlds. However, in Rescher there was a second conception of logical possibilities, for combination of descriptive terms, as simply given. Similarly, in Lewis there was the conception of the totality of possible worlds as simply given. We have critiqued these latter conceptions and found them untenable because they either argue circularly or deny possibility. Yet, the initial conception of logical possibilities as the possibilities which appear (or would appear) in the widest–ranging investigation, and other sorts of possibilities as those which would appear in investigations limited in different degrees and in different respects, still seems to indicate a useful distinction.

This conception of logical possibility is to be found, *in nuce,* in Buchler's writings: "The principle of non-contradiction itself might be regarded as a possibility characteristic of an order more pervasive than any other, or of an order overlapping all other orders." (MNC 139) Similarly, it stands to reason that laws of nature are possibilities characteristic of orders more limited. We might say, then, that logical possibilities are found in orders characterized by having the principle of noncontradiction as a constituent trait, and that nomic possibilities are possibilities found in orders characterized by having (all or some of) the laws of nature as constituent traits.

In arguing against the conception of purely logical possibility, Buchler follows a line of thought which seems arbitrary in that it appears to contradict other tendencies of the metaphysics of natural complexes. I think that by utilization of a distinction of the sort just indicated, this line of argumentation can be avoided without harm to the ordinal conception of possibility. The difficulty arises in consideration of the following objection:

Does not "logical possibility" generically include all other kinds, and are not purely logical possibilities present indifferently, regardless of specific orders of complexes? And is it not, then, true that it is "logically possible" to reject all the sacraments and still accept Catholicism? And is it not logically possible for a batter to hit a baseball so hard that it flies into orbit . . . ? Neither of these suppositions "entails a contradiction." Consequently, must not these and infinite other possibilities be acknowledged to belong to any of the complexes heretofore mentioned? (MNC 137)

The line of response Buchler develops is as follows:

> If Catholicism without sacraments and the batting of a ball into astro-
> nomic orbit were genuinely possibilities and did not involve contra-
> diction, they would be possibilities within orders quite different from
> the orders known as Catholicism and baseball. Such different orders
> would be much wider than the two familiar orders . . . the orders in
> which they are thought to be located . . . are tacitly stripped of vari-
> ous traits which would exclude them. In other words, the orders are
> covertly abandoned, although their social names . . . are retained,
> along with a number of superficially identifying traits. (MNC 139)

This argument seems to invoke a principle to the effect that, if one
wants to speak openly and clearly, one must change the name used for a
subaltern complex whenever one changes the ordinal location considered.
Otherwise, if one "covertly" abandons the order while retaining the name,
one is either covering-up or just confusing matters. Clearly, the issue here
is: when are we justified in saying that one and the same complex pertains
to two (or more) distinct orders? Now, the metaphysics of natural complexes is by no means committed to a principle that one cannot call a complex by the same name when considering it in its different ordinal locations.
Every complex enters into different orders, and its possibilities and actualities differ with respect to the order in which it is considered. Thus:

> It is necessary for us only to understand that although every discrim-
> inandum is as real as every other, not every one belongs to the same
> order as every other. The desert mirage belongs to a visual order, not
> to an order in which thirst is quenched. The pond may belong to both
> orders of being. The stick bent in the water is really bent—in water,
> and as seen in water, not as touched. The railroad tracks do meet—
> but in the order of vision, not in the order of public space.[6]

What is crucial to our point is that there is no dishonesty in referring
to *the railroad tracks* as *they* enter into different orders, the order of vision
and the order of public space. The actualities and possibilities of the tracks
differ in the different orders, but we can legitimately refer to *the tracks* as a
discriminable complex with a gross integrity and an identity function relating each of its ordinal integrities to the gross integrity.[7] Consistency, then,
demands that baseball still remains baseball, whether it is baseball on earth
in the twentieth century subject to determinate rules and the prevailing laws
of nature, or it is baseball in a literary or imaginative order subject to fewer
restrictions (or different ones, though never so few or so different as to
destroy the identity of the complex *as* baseball). It is not at all clear that

the traits retained in moving from the "current physical" possibilities for baseball to the "logical" possibilities for baseball are fairly characterized as "superficial identifying traits." They are identifying traits, and that is enough.

Buchler appears to have confused "consideration of baseball as located in a different order from that normally considered" with "consideration of a different order, not baseball." This is analogous to the confusion of those who want to say: "*The tracks* only obtain in public space and *they* do not meet. Something else (an image of the tracks?) must obtain in the visual order." We must reject the former confusion, just as we reject the latter. The mechanism of distinguishing sorts of possibilities can be understood as a way of directing us towards the general vicinity of the orders in which specified possibilities will be seen to be relevant to specified complexes. Often (not always) the designation of a possibility as a logical possibility will be an invitation to form a schema of an imaginary order in which the complex prevails with the specified possibility as relevant. Never will such a designation refer to a possibility not relevant to any actualities, or to one not ordinally locable.

Perhaps Buchler's unwillingness to admit such possibilities does not stem from the confusion indicated in the last paragraph, but rather from an uncharacteristic narrowness in the way he considers public and physical traits to limit the constituents of imaginary orders. Recently,[8] Buchler has indicated that he recognizes designations of logical possibilities to be invitations to form schemata of imaginary orders, and he reaffirmed his position that the original complex could not be located in such orders. In question is the logical possibility of insects talking. Buchler remarks:

> the so-called logical . . . possibility turns out not to be about insects at all. The alleged . . . possibility . . . *is* in fact determined in and by an order of complexes . . . in this case, an order of envisioned images. . . . For behold, we envision "insects talking." And indeed there are creatures plainly doing so in this visual order. But they are not insects. Insects, of course, may belong also to an order of reverie. But the integrity determined by this order must be reconcilable with the integrities determined by their other ordinal locations, otherwise we are thinking only of animals arbitrarily given the same name.[9]

This last sentence nicely puts the point at issue. Is the integrity of the (so-called) talking insects, determined by imaginary orders in which these little animals possess and realize startling possibilities, *not reconcilable* with the integrities determined for insects by their (other) ordinal locations? Buchler clearly thinks not, but I disagree. It seems to me that this reconciliation is not only possible but commonplace. Pogo, for instance, is a talking opossum. Recognition and acceptance of this fact, that it is possible for a cartoonstrip opossum to talk, does not cause us alarm or cognitive dissonance. It also does not lead us to expect the opossum in the woods behind the house to sing an inane Christmas carol. We have come to recognize that complexes obtain peculiar traits of both possibility and actuality when they enter into various orders of imagination and supposition.[10] This recognition is parallel to the recognition that physical objects have different traits of actuality and possibility in visual space than they have in public space. Still other traits might prevail for these same complexes when they enter the idiosyncratic aesthetic space of a painting by Van Gogh, Picasso or Dali.

In characterizing logical possibilities as those possibilities which would emerge in the widest ranging investigation of orders, we do not, as Buchler might fear, say that "anything goes." There are limitations in the framing of orders. Some identifying traits of importance must stay with a complex in any order (though not necessarily the same one in every order). Not anything goes; but it seems to me that things can go quite far. The notion of different sorts of possibility, like the notion of ordinality itself, allows us to map out the terrain into various regions of one or another variety of isomorphy or limitation.

The tendency of claims of logical possibility to have their ground and point in imaginary or hypothetical orders is relevant to the question of possible entities. Of these, Buchler has astutely remarked:

> Philosophers are wary of what some of them have called "possible entities." It is worth observing that we can hardly do without speaking of possibilities, but can very easily do without speaking of "entities." (MNC 40)

From which follows: "There are no 'possible entities' which wear the character of actuality without being actual." (MNC 129) There are no entities, only natural complexes, which, we have seen, all involve traits of actuality and traits of possibility.

In following Rescher, we found what he called possible entities to be hypothetical realities. We now can interpret them as suppositional orders of actuality and possibility. It was an unfortunate confusion on Rescher's part to consider them possibilities. Thus, what Rescher termed "substantive possibility" we see not to be possibility at all, but to be a product of imagination. He was forced into this confused posture by his banishment of possibilities from reality. He made only small and ill-fated progress away from it with the notion of functional possibility.

What relation have these hypothetical or imaginatively constructed orders got to possibility that might have misled Rescher and others like him?

Very often our encounter with possibilities is an imaginative encounter. I have climbed a tree. I meet the possibility of my falling in imagining myself falling from the tree. I produce an imaginary order in which I fall. I thus exhibitively judge[11] (before myself) that there is a possibility that I might fall from the tree. There is a temptation, from an epistemological and reductionistic starting point in ontology, to confuse the imagined object or state of affairs with the possibility, and thus to turn the possibility into a possible entity (or, as in this case, a possible state of affairs), a peculiar sort of actuality. This is easily avoided when it is realized that the imagined order is one in which I actually fall and in which there are the further possibilities of my landing smoothly, of my getting hurt, etc. That is, just as in public space and time there are actualities and possibilities, there are actualities and possibilities in imaginative orders through which we often encounter possibilities and in the hypothetical orders we often utilize in reasoning about possibilities. The imaginative and hypothetical status of these orders in no way affects the ontological analysis of possibility.

We may summarize the conclusions of this investigation as follows. Internal criticism of Lewis and Rescher shows that a conception of possibility as correlative with actuality (not identical with actuality or dependent on it) is necessary to an adequate ontology of possibility. Buchler provides just such an analysis. Possible entities (or worlds or states of affairs), while seen to be inappropriately identified with possibilities, seem to correspond with imaginative orders often associated epistemically with possibilities. Different sorts of possibilities correspond, even in Lewis and Rescher, to differently restricted orders in which possibilities may be located. Thus, this conception can be usefully located in a metaphysics of natural complexes, as long as it is consistently distinguished from a conception of *inherently* different sorts of possibility, which might involve gradations of possibilities more and less real, or more and less pure.

Notes

1. David Lewis, *Counterfactuals* (Cambridge: Harvard University Press, 1973), p. 4. All references for Lewis in the text simply cite the page numbers in this work.

2. A further problem, which escapes Lewis, is that without intraworld possibility there would be no relations of causality and continuity for identification of items within a world. Without possibility, change is incompatible with identity.

3. Nicholas Rescher, "The Ontology of the Possible," in Milton K. Munitz (ed.), *Logic and Ontology* (New York: New York University Press, 1973), p. 213. In the text, page references to this work are marked: OP.

4. Nicholas Rescher, *A Theory of Possibility* (Pittsburgh: University of Pittsburgh Press, 1975), p. xi. In the text, page references to this work are marked: TP.

5. MNC 130. See "List of Abbreviations" for Buchler's works, p. xiii–xiv.

6. ML 126.

7. See MNC 22.

8. OCW, 555–579, in MNC [1989] 224–259.

9. OCW, 576–577 in MNC [1989] 255–256. The indicated omissions delete references to pure possibilities, which are irrelevant to the understanding of logical possibility I am suggesting in this paper.

10. It is, of course, irrelevant to the point being made that there is no Pogo who is a particular opossum located in the order of public space and historical time. In political caricature, orders have been framed in which Gerald Ford could ski jump off Richard Nixon's nose. Who would argue with someone who saw such a cartoon and giggled: "Hey, that's Gerald Ford skiing off Nixon's nose!"?

11. See Justus Buchler, NJ Chapter 1, section iii.

Ordinal Possibility:
A Metaphysical Concept

Kathleen Wallace

The concept of possibility is one of the chief categories of Buchler's general ontology. Buchler's metaphysical system is shaped by three basic principles, the principle of ontological parity, the principle of ordinality and finally, the principle of commensurateness. (These are defined below, see section I.) The last is not explicitly identified by Buchler as such, but, as I have argued elsewhere,[1] it can be identified as a key systematic principle. Buchler's system is motivated by broader metaphysical concerns as well as by the goal of overcoming some of the difficulties recurrently encountered in contemporary analyses of possibility.[2] Weiss[3] has pointed to some of the latter and indicated how Buchler's general approach gives us a better handle on the concept of possibility. Given the scope of the reorientation advanced by Buchler, this paper will attempt to provide the reader with some sense of Buchler's system of categories as it pertains to possibility.

The paper is divided into two parts:

The first part focuses on the theoretical issue, namely, what the basic principles entail for the concept of possibility.

The second focuses on the implications of the ordinal[4] view for the notion of logical possibility.[5]

I

In this section I would like to lay a little groundwork to orient the terms of the discussion. In what follows I have included in the notes material (a) on technical terms in Buchler's system and (b) on systematic metaphysical issues. Because some of this material, while pertinent, might also digress from the focus on possibility, I have decided to flag such notes with an asterisk (*) as well as a number. Most of the material in these notes consists in quoted passages from Buchler where the emphasis is on clarifying or amplifying a term or the systematic stance in general rather than possibility per se. This is the best solution I could come up with to sustain, without interruption or digression, the analysis of the systematic principles and the arguments as they pertain to possibility and yet at the same time to anticipate unfamiliarity of Buchler's approach to many readers. My own advice to readers would be, wherever possible, to consult these notes (they are also cross-referenced to the page in the text) after having read the paper through, although, of course, the reader is ultimately the judge of what method best facilitates her/his understanding. On, then, to possibility.

Of the three principles I mentioned earlier, let's take ontological parity first. The principle of ontological parity is a commitment to the equal reality of all beings. For possibility this means that possibilities are as real as actualities. A distinction between "the real actual world" and "a merely possible one" is a distinction which Buchler would reject.[*6] This does not amount to a denial of remote possibilities as such, but rather, of their classification as "merely" possible and hence, "less real."

The classification of possibilities as less real than actualities is a result of habits of categorizing. For example, when existence is taken as the paradigm of having being or reality, then at least some possibilities, most conspicuously so-called logical possibilities, seem to have either no or lesser ontological status. "Possibilities exist" is a familiar locution. But if existence is also commonly associated with spatiotemporal location of some kind, then it would not capture the being of every possibility. In order to provide means by which to account for the equal status or reality of any *natural complex,* including a possibility, Buchler introduces the categories of prevalence and alescence.[7]

A possibility equally prevails, either as against any other possibility that might have prevailed instead, or as against the kind of world that would not have provided it or anything like it. The very concept of prevalence is introduced partly in order to permit recognition of possibility with categorial adequacy. (MNC 54)

Whatever is prevails, is real:[*8] individuals and societies, numbers, events (physical and mental), feelings, theories and facts, poems and paintings, possibilities and actualities, literally whatever. On Buchler's view, we don't have to wonder "where possibilities are." They are (prevail) in the ways and in the contexts in which they prevail. Fictional possibilities prevail in the story, drama or imagination; mathematical possibilities prevail in the *order* of mathematics; the possibility that it will rain tomorrow prevails in a spatial, temporal and meteorological order. No one of these possibilities is more or less real than another.

Prevalence and alescence, then, are categorial tools for formulating the [equal] reality or being of anything whatsoever. But no being merely "is," merely prevails or alesces. Rather, the being or reality of any being is always determinate and indeterminate, or in Buchler's terms, *ordinally* located. In order to fill out the meaning of prevalence and alescence we need to introduce the second systematic principle, the principle of ordinality.

The generic term of identification of any "being" for Buchler is *natural complex* or complex.[*9] Every complex prevails and alesces *in orders* or contexts. These locations constitute the "shape," the determinateness and indeterminateness or incompleteness of the complex.[*10] Numbers prevail in orders of mathematics. Human beings prevail in orders of kinship, employment, political and economic society, love relations, inquiry; they also prevail in orders of genetic, biochemical and physiological interactions, in their personal diaries and correspondence, and in their products, to name a few. To prevail in an order means to have a trait which excludes other traits, or other ordinal locations, from the trait structure of the complex (its contour).[*11] Possibilities, too, are complexes and, whether they "exist" or not, they prevail (or alesce) in some order, or context. Actualities and possibilities both prevail (and alesce), although in different ways. And both may have alescent traits or ordinal locations.

> All prevalences restrict and exclude, but not all in the same way. Actualities are exclusive and restrictive in a way that possibilities are not. In this "way," enunciated by the preceding paragraph, actualities always are exclusive, no matter what the order; whereas possibilities sometimes are and sometimes are not, depending on the order. (MNC 156)

The way enunciated is as follows:

> The principal consideration with respect to actuality is that if mutually contradictory complexes are actual, they never prevail in the same order; if mutually contradictory complexes prevail in the same order, they are not actualities. (MNC 156)

Every complex (and therefore every possibility) has actual traits, prevails as actual, in so far as it excludes having other contradictory ordinal locations (traits). So, for example, the dress worn by the woman walking in front of me cannot be both blue and not blue (green, pink, yellow, etc.) in the same respect (order) at the same time. If I put on sunglasses which block light rays in the blue range and I see the dress as green (a rather startling experience, I might add), the dress is not now in possession of contradictory traits. Rather, the dress is both blue and green at the same time, *but* in different respects. In relation to my friend not wearing the sunglasses (one ordinal location) the dress is blue, and in relation to me wearing the sunglasses (another context) the dress is green. By donning the sunglasses I and the dress I am looking at are in a new ordinal location; not an important or enduring location, but a location nonetheless.[*12] However, in relation to me simply as possessor of these dubiously useful sunglasses who may or may not don them, it is possible that the dress *qua* seen is green and possible that the dress *qua* seen is blue.[13] Both of these possibilities prevail in the order of my-field-of-vision-and-the-dress and *qua* possible neither excludes the other (they are both actualizable traits of the dress and of me in this mutually defined order), even if only one of them can be actualized at a given time.

The position Buchler is pushing here is that possibility means *actualizability*. What he is rejecting is the notion of an unlocated, "pure" possibility which would be actualizable in no respect.[*14]

A "pure" possibility independent of all complexes would be a complex unrelated and unlocated—an absurdity. (OCW, 566, in MNC [1989], 240)

If possibility means actualizability in at least some respect, then the concept of possibility cannot be disjoined from the concept of actuality. (Weiss has stressed the import of this, see Section III of his paper.)

So far, then, the ordinal principles of ontological parity and ordinality entail that there are no "pure" possibilities because minimally every possibility has *actual* traits. There are no unlocated possibilities because then they would have *no* traits and therefore, could not be at all. Possibilities are as real as actualities; they are not limited to spatiotemporal existence, but are complexes which prevail and alesce in orders.

In arguing that all possibilities are ordinally located Buchler is saying that all possibilities are "accessible." This does not require giving up those possibilities known as logical, but rather, if they are possibilities, requires defining their ordinal locations.[*15] To say that possibilities are accessible means that they are located, but not that they are necessarily spatially and temporally located.[16] Inferential possibilities of logic and mathematical possibilities are not necessarily defined (as either possible or actual) by spatial or temporal conditions. They are located in the orders of logic and mathematics respectively. (An individual is not the only kind of complex or even the paradigm of a complex or order.)

Now to the third systematic principle. The principle of commensurateness is not a merely formal principle of consistency, but is supposed to provide for the "hanging together" or "mediatability" (MNC 95–97) of the traits of a complex as *its* traits. It accounts for why complexes, while indeterminate and incomplete, are not merely free-floating collections of traits, infinitely modifiable and with no boundaries.[17]

So, to recall our earlier example of the dress: the traits of being seen as blue and green respectively, are reconcilable with one another and with other traits of the dress. This mediatability justifies being able to call them traits of the same thing. In this case mediated relatedness is possible between these traits insofar as the sunglasses provide an ordinal location for the dress which is commensurate with the other visual ordinal locations (traits) of the dress. Each trait of a complex is related to (continuous with) some other traits of the complex, although it may not have to be related to all. In the latter case, there would have to be mediating traits between them.[*18]

Some traits of a complex may also overlap with or be traits of another complex; distinctiveness does not preclude similarity, or sharing of traits. For example, the distinctiveness of a square from a circle does not preclude their sharing a trait, e.g., each has angles of 360°, albeit in different, distinctive senses.[*19]

What is at stake philosophically in this argument? In correlating possibility and actuality as commensurate, Buchler is arguing for a reconceptualizing of what a being is. A being (complex) is *what* it is in virtue of *both* its actualities and its possibilities. A being is as determined by its incompletenesses, *its* possibilities, as it is by its actualities. The identity and boundary of a complex are equally shaped by actuality and possibility.[20]

A possibility cannot be said to prevail or to arise if it is unrelated to any actualities, nor can an actuality be said to prevail or arise if it is unrelated to any possibility. Every complex that prevails as an actuality either arose under or is presently contingent upon limited, finite conditions. That is to say, it is an actualization. It derives from and reflects the possibilities of other actualities. It has its own finite boundaries, its own restricted connections. Its own possibilities are distinguishable from one another and from the possibilities resident in another complex. . . . A given trait (of actuality) is inevitably connected with various and numerous other traits (of possibility). Conversely, a given [trait of] possibility reflects (belongs to an order of traits containing) an innumerable train of actualities. (MNC 133)

Let me summarize the main features of the ordinal conception of possibility. First, possibilities are as real as actualities. Second, possibilities, whether they "exist" or not, prevail (and alesce) in order(s) or context(s). Therefore, there are no "pure" or unlocated possibilities. Third, every possibility is a complex and thus has *actual* (as well as possible) traits which distinguish it as *that* possibility and not some other (another reason why, on this view, there are no "pure" possibilities). Fourth, every possibility (like every complex) is also a trait of some complex(es) and therefore, must be commensurate with the actualities and other possibilities of that (superaltern) complex. The having of a possibility is an actuality. This entails that the *having* of one possibility may exclude the having of a contradictory possibility. Fifth, complexes do not all have the same possibilities. There are no eternal possibilities (although there may be persistent and pervasively recurrent ones) and there is no single order which defines every possibility *qua* possible.[21] For, if every possibility is a trait of some complex(es) or order(s), and no order overlaps with every other order, then the determining conditions of one possibility cannot be the same as those of every other possibility.

II

Let's look at logical possibility. When it comes to logical possibility Buchler seems to hold a view which is not only counterintuitive, but which, as Weiss argues, is contrary to his own principles. Buchler holds that logical or "pure" possibility—viz., possibility allegedly ascertained by ascertaining what is free from contradiction—is not *the* determining or defining condition of what is possible:[22]

> The trait of "not entailing contradiction" is a trait that belongs to all possibilities in so far as they are prospectively actualized. It is a trait that accompanies any recognition that "such and such is possible." But it makes no difference whether we say that what is possible is possible "because" it does not entail contradiction, or that what does not entail contradiction does not entail contradiction "because" it is possible. If we ask how we decide what is and is not possible, the answer is that we discover or calculate as best we can what are the limits and boundaries of an order of complexes. If we ask how we decide what does or does not entail contradiction, the answer is precisely the same. (MNC 137–138)

Buchler denies that the law of non-contradiction defines what is possible for an order of complexes independently of the relevant ordinal conditions. In order to amplify the kind of approach he takes to the concept of logical or "pure" possibility Buchler introduces the example of an insect talking:

In accordance with such an approach, we often hear something like this: "Insects don't talk, because that is biologically, empirically, impossible; but it is logically or abstractly possible that they could, for there is no contradiction involved." But a contradiction certainly is involved, a contradiction of the concept of "insect," an area of knowledge, and the conditions of linguistic meaning. That is, the so-called logical or pure possibility turns out not to be about insects at all. The alleged pure possibility free from all ordinal limitations *is* in fact determined in and by an order of complexes, but an order covertly introduced—in this case, an order of envisioned images. It is this order that serves as the guarantor of "non-contradiction." For behold, we envision "insects talking." And indeed there are creatures plainly doing so in this visual order. But they are not insects. Insects, of course, may belong also to an order of reverie. But the integrity determined by this order must be reconcilable with the integrities determined by their other ordinal locations, otherwise we are thinking only of animals arbitrarily given the same name. (OCW 576–577, in MNC [1989] 255–256)

But this seems to defy common sense. Why do we call the talking insect an insect if talking is not a possible trait in some respect of the insect, for example, in a cartoon? What does it mean to say that there is a contradiction involved in attributing talking to an insect as one of its possibilities in some ordinal location? Why can't we say that in one order it is possible for the insect to talk and in another it is not possible for the insect to talk? The orders of imagination, cartoons and physical relations are, after all, equally real. In a similar context Buchler admits, in fact insists, that the convergence of railroad tracks in the order of vision is just as much a trait *of the tracks* as is their nonconvergence in the order of physical space.[*23] Moreover, since the latter are actualities rather than possibilities, the conditions of mutual exclusion should be even stricter than in the case of possibility. (Buchler allows that an order may contain possibilities whose actualizations would be mutually contradictory, but which as possibilities may both prevail in the order.[24]) But with respect to the insect Buchler is making the even stronger claim that the *possibility* of the insect talking is not a trait of the insect; it is neither a trait *qua* possible nor in actuality.

Let us be clear about what Buchler is claiming. He is not saying that the talking "insect" is not a possibility (or an actuality for that matter) in some order. What he is saying is that it is not a possibility *of* the insect. In order to see the plausibility of what he is saying here consider, again, the railroad tracks. Suppose we say that it is possible to paint railroad tracks *not* converging as they recede into the distance (portrayed in the painting).

Is this visual nonconvergence a possibility *of* the railroad tracks, or is it, rather, a possibility of imagination or of painting? If it were a possibility of the tracks, then it would be possible for the tracks to converge and not possible for the tracks to converge in the same respect. This would seem to violate the law of non-contradiction. And, Buchler would say that the attribution of talking to the insect entails a like contradiction, viz., it would be possible for the insect to talk and not possible for the insect to talk in the same respect, i.e., communicative ability.

But why is this a contradiction? Because according to Buchler one has to suspend traits (or "integrities," i.e., strongly relevant traits) *of the complex* in order to get the alleged possibility. If one doesn't suspend them, there is, Buchler argues, a contradiction. If one does suspend them, it is not the same complex anymore.

But, Buchler also admits "that contradictory traits are sometimes both *found to prevail as possibilities* in an order." (MNC 157) So why aren't the nonconvergence of the painted tracks and talking possibilities *of,* that is, in the order of, the tracks and the insect respectively? The only answer in Buchler's system would be that they are not commensurate with what the beings (complexes) are, that is, with the constituent traits of the tracks and the biological insect.

> Behold, we envision "insects talking." And indeed there are creatures plainly doing so in this visual order. But they are not insects. Insects, of course, may belong also to an order of reverie. But the integrity determined by this order must be *reconcilable* with the integrities determined by their other ordinal locations . . . (OCW 576–577, in MNC [1989] 255–256. My emphasis.)

"Reconcilable" would be, I take it, another term for commensurate. If talking is not actualizable for the insect, then it is not a possibility of the insect. And, if divergence is not actualizable for the tracks, then it is not a possibility of the tracks. So, "logical possibility" may tell us when something is a possibility of the complex supposed if, in order to conceive the possibility, we do not have to tacitly suspend so many traits (specifically, "integrities") of the complex in order to avoid contradiction that we no longer have the same complex. "Logical possibilities" are possibilities of the complex supposed when they are reconciliable (commensurate) with the other traits/integrities of the complex.

What Buchler is getting at here with the notion of commensurateness has to do with how complexes are (self–)defined. We need to introduce, briefly, his concept of *natural definition* in order to make some sense of this. All complexes define themselves. This is not a conscious or deliberate process, but rather the limitation and boundary setting that is a function of the traits of a complex:

Defining is "by" the complex. . . . It is constitutionally basic. . . . On this conception of what may be called natural definition, every trait defines, and a possibility is one kind of defining. (MNC 162)

Buchler goes on to argue that if by definition is meant "the marking out of bounds and limits," then it is not only a human accomplishment, but "a more pervasive process which should be recognized as natural definition." (MNC 163)[*25] On this conception of natural definition every trait defines and a possibility (being a trait) is one way of defining. (MNC 162) With its possibilities a natural complex defines a prospect for itself. This way of defining through possibility Buchler calls *prefinition*:

A possibility is a *prefinition* of the relevant traits in the contour of a natural complex. (MNC 165)[26]

A possibility *is* an extension of a complex—an extension prefined. A possibility is that prevalent extension or continuation of the contour of a natural complex, whereby certain traits that are related (or, not related) to certain other traits will be related (or, not related) to the other traits. By contrast, an actuality is that prevalence of a natural complex whereby certain traits are related (or, not related) to certain other traits. (MNC 165)

A possibility then is a continuation or extension of a complex; it prefines not the future as such. Rather, it prevails in the present (assuming the relevance of time to its prevalence) as a possibility, as a certain kind of relative limit. If it were identified with the future that would define possibility as "the not yet" and actuality as what is. But, Buchler wants to argue that possibility *is,* prevails now; *qua* possible it *is.* What is not (yet) actualized is not the same as what is not yet.[27] A possibility, as a prefined extension of a complex or order, is that which is *actualizable* for the complex. This is a constituent, a trait, of the complex. (This, of course, is not fixed; the boundaries of a complex are not fixed since they admit of alescence and of extension or contraction, however minor, with each actualization.)

Thus, to return to the examples of the tracks and the insect, Buchler's argument is that talking is not an actualizable trait, not a prefined extension or possibility, of the biological complex, insect. To assert that it is ("logically possible") would violate the law of non-contradiction when it violates the commensurateness of the complex in question: we can only get the

possibility by suspending traits which are constitutive of (define and prefine) what the complex is.[28] Similarly, nonconvergence as tracks recede
into visual distance would not be an actualizable trait, not a prefined extension or possibility, of the tracks.

This is not a denial of the nonconvergence as a possibility of painted
railroad tracks or of talking insects in the order of human imagination, cartoons, and the like. It is only a denial that these are traits (possibilities) *of*
tracks which are running in the Northeast Corridor between Boston and
Washington, or a trait of some cockroach lurking in the basement of a
building in New York.

This is not a matter of having to "change the name used for a subaltern complex whenever one changes the ordinal location considered."[29]
Weiss suggests that Buchler's unwillingness to admit "logical possibilities"[30] stems "from an uncharacteristic narrowness in the way he considers public and physical traits to limit the constituents of imaginary
orders."[31] This seems to miss the thrust of what Buchler is trying to argue.
It is not that public or physical traits are more determining than others. The
cartoon talking insect is public; the painting is both physical and public.
Rather, the key here lies in the ideas of ordinality and commensurateness.

As sharp as his analysis and assessment of the positive contribution of
Buchler's view is, it seems to me that Weiss's analysis got sidetracked on
the question of logical possibility. But this is at least partly Buchler's own
fault. His formulations are, I think, unfortunate. For in stressing his rejection of logical possibility *as it is usually conceived* he makes it sound as if
he is rejecting logical possibilities altogether as unreal; as if imaginary and
fictional possibilities are not complexes at all, which is how Weiss interprets him. I think that what he is rejecting is a set of assumptions about
what kind of complexes those alleged logical possibilities are and what
their locations are. He asks, are they possibilities *in the sense supposed?*
He does not say they are not complexes, not possibilities.

But does Buchler's view then revert back to a view like Lewis's where
possibilities are not located in the world *qua* possible, are not actualizable
traits of the complexes in the world, but rather are just other actualities
located somewhere else?[32] As Weiss points out, the central notion of *actualization* of a possibility is lost to Lewis and would be to Buchler if this
were his view. It seems to me that the force of a principle of commensurateness strengthens the reconceptualization of possibility as actualizability
and preserves the notion of actualization. What Buchler's view does is force
us to examine whether what we imagine or conceive is a possibility of (is
actualizable for) what we think it is or not. His argument is that the law of
non-contradiction does not by itself abstractly or in principle tell us that.

Nor does this view force us into a naive essentialism—namely, that a complex cannot have possibilities which contradict its "essence." For Buchler, complexes do not have essential and accidental traits. A complex has strongly and weakly relevant traits; it *is* all its traits and it can lose some traits of either kind and still be the same complex. Its sameness, its identity, is a function of cumulative continuity, not unalterability in or of certain "essential" traits.[33] Buchler's argument is that if a possibility is a possibility *of* the complex supposed then it has to be reconciliable with what the complex is—otherwise, one would indeed lose the notion of actualization as Lewis does. If an alleged logical possibility is based on a pervasive tacit suspension of traits, then it may not be the same complex and the possibility would be an actualizable trait of some other (presumably similar) complex.

The rejection of the law of non-contradiction as the defining condition of possibility as such is based, I think, on a systematic commitment to the principle of commensurateness. The issue has to do with what a complex is. If its possibilities are part of what it is, then not just anything is possible for (a trait of) it. Its possible (actualizable) ordinal locations are not unlimited. Where the law of non-contradiction can be helpful in determining what is possible, it cannot do so independently of the traits of the complex itself. What turns out to be possible for a complex or in an order may be much more or other than we imagine. But what determines this is not solely what we can (and cannot) imagine, but the ordinal locations, the traits of the complex itself. To deny this would be a denial of the independent determinateness of the world, of natural complexes.

Notes

1. Sidney Gelber and Kathleen Wallace, "Justus Buchler: Nature, Power and Prospect," *Process Studies* 15:2 (Summer 1986), pp. 106–119, reprinted here, pp. 49–63.

2. For a review of some of the broader metaphysical issues which motivate Buchler's systematic reorientation see MNC, Chapter 1. (See "List of Abbreviations" for Buchler's works, here, p. xiii) See also Sidney Gelber, "Toward A Radical Naturalism," *The Journal of Philosophy* 61:5 (February 1959), pp. 193–199, reprinted here, pp. 21–27, Gelber & Wallace, *op.cit.,* and my Introduction to MNC [1989]. For a more detailed analysis from "inside" Buchler's view, so to speak, see Beth J. Singer, "Introduction: The Philosophy of Justus Buchler," *The Southern Journal of Philosophy* 14:1 (Spring 1976), pp. 3–30 and Beth J. Singer, *Ordinal Naturalism: An Introduction to the Philosophy of Justus Buchler* (Lewisburg: Bucknell University Press, 1983).

3. Phil Weiss, ''Possibility: Three Recent Ontologies,'' *International Philosophical Quarterly* 20:2 (June 1980), pp. 199–219, reprinted here, pp. 145–169.

4. Buchler's view has been aptly characterized as ordinal metaphysics by himself and his commentators, as for example, the title of Singer's book, *Ordinal Naturalism: An Introduction to the Philosophy of Justus Buchler.*

5. This issue is both a comment on the critique of Buchler's view of logical possibility advanced by Weiss in the preceding article and a development of the principles of ordinality as they bear on the concept of logical possibility. (Weiss, *op.cit.*)

6. (p. 172) The ordinal view of possibility and actuality which Buchler has developed is designed to acknowledge, among other things, the *equal* reality of fictional possibilities and actualities as well as those which are spatiotemporally located. In a discussion of the alleged contrast between the ''actual world'' and ''nonactualities'' Buchler says:

> Accordingly, a traditional source of puzzlement is the status of creatures like Apollo or unicorns or Hamlet. Surely unicorns are not actual in the ''true'' sense of the term? Not, of course, in the way that horses on my neighbor's farm are actual—just as horses on that farm are not actual in the way that contracts or inferences or sorrows are, and just as these are not actual in the way that intellectual trends or numerical relations or economic traditions are. Apollo, Hamlet, and unicorns are human products. Specifically, they are contrivances, or products of art. Products of any kind, like complexes that are not products, have traits of both actuality and possibility. Once the order which contains unicorns is produced, it has its distinctive possibilities and actualities: unicorns are actually white; it is not possible for unicorns to talk. Literature is more perplexing to philosophers, even to the aestheticians among them, than any other of the socially established arts. Its products, after being conceded a spatio–temporal term in the form of paper, ink, and furrowed brows, are supposed to vanish into the ''imagination,'' with no metaphysical nonsense permitted. Sculpture and painting somehow fare better. No one refers to their products in the way that literary products are referred to—as works of ''fiction.'' Strangely, a sculptured Apollo is more acceptably actual than the creature of literature that bears the same name. (MNC 154)

7. MNC Chapter 2, ''Prevalence and Alescence.'' Alescence allows us to identify the being of ''things'' like dying (its arising as an event or process), a class of deviant happenings, a cancer regressing, a growth of anxiety. (MNC 63–64. See also MNC 90 and Gelber and Wallace, *op.cit.*, p. 110, reprinted here, p. 54.)

8. (p. 172) Buchler eschews the term ''reality'' as distinguishing anything discriminable. If any complex, fictional, existential, universal or particular, idea or fact, individual or event, if any complex is real, then ''reality'' does not have a meaningful opposite as a philosophical concept.

9. (p. 173) In Buchler's system, the terms "complex" and "order" are logically interchangeable. Every complex is an order and vice versa. Complex can be used to identify a complex both when it is located by (is subaltern to) another complex (order) and when it locates or "orders" (is superaltern to) another complex. "Order" tends to be confined to the latter, that is, when a complex locates or is superaltern to other complexes. Every complex both locates complexes (is an order), including its own subaltern traits, and is located by other complexes. (See Gelber and Wallace, *op.cit.*, and MNC 13, 93–97.) The same complex can in one respect be an order (superaltern) and in another respect a trait-complex (subaltern). (See also my Introduction to MNC [1989] xviii.)

10. (p. 173) Nor, we should add, is there wholly determinate being. See MNC 48–51, 81–90. From the latter section:

No complex can be said to be indeterminate in all respects. It would not be a complex, and we would be contradicting ourselves by assuming that a discrimination has taken place. The latter assumption implies that traits have been made to be or found to be located in an order. A complex indeterminate in all respects would have no traits. For each trait is a determination, implying the exclusion of some other trait and the imposition of limits—implying a prevalence.

Can a complex be determinate in all respects? Determinateness in all respects implies that all traits attributable to a complex are exhausted, and that the complex cannot belong to any more or fewer orders than it does. Now whether there are complexes of which this can ever be said is a moot question. That it should be said exclusively of actualities is hard to understand. If any natural complexes at all are subject to alteration or modification or environmental relocation, actualities are. The number of orders in which an actuality is located, and the number and kind of relations into which it may enter, are exhausted or closed only when the actuality ceases to be that actuality. (MNC 82–83)

11. (p. 173) See MNC 21–22, 56; and OCW 564, in MNC [1989] 237. In his "Notes on the Contour of a Natural Complex" Buchler adds, " 'A contour' means: a complex in so far as it is manifested by many integrities, a complex which in and through its multiplicity retains an identity." (in MNC [1989], Appendix 2, p. 217. Hereafter, "Notes." See also MNC 22 on identity.)

12. (p. 174) This would be a trait of the dress, but probably not an integrity (a strongly relevant trait) of the dress. The dress seen as green might be categorized as a "vagrant alescence" in the order of the dress. (MNC 61–66)

13. Note that possession of these sunglasses is an *actual* trait of at least one of the possibilities here and is an actual trait of there being these alternative visual possibilities in this context.

14. (p. 174) A "pure" possibility would have to mean traitless complex or complex having non–ordinal traits or non–ordinal determinateness. Both of these

would be absurd on this view. It is, of course, logically or formally possible to state the negation of all possible traits. But even the logical negation is a determinate complex, just not in the sense usually supposed. It is a determinate complex of the rules and possibilities of formal logic or of language. The rules of logic constitute an order; in one respect, a superaltern complex to its own entailments, and in another respect, a subaltern complex exhibited as a trait of any one of its entailments. (For passages related to this point see MNC, Chap. 1, esp. 30–32, and Chap. 3, esp. 97–98)

15. (p. 174) "To speak of possibilities as complexes is itself an abstraction from the fuller consideration that every complex is also a sub-complex; so that a possibility is a sub-complex, and no complexes lack the kind of sub-complexes called possibilities." (OCW 566, in MNC [1989] 240)

One important way to see what the proposed conception implies is to understand its impact on the concepts of possibility and actuality. In denying "free-floating" status to any natural complex, we are, first, identifying any possibility as a complex and hence a subcomplex; and second, denying that any is a so-called pure possibility, one undetermined, unaffected by conditions both of actuality and related possibility. If ordinality is ubiquitous, then possibilities must be ordinally located. What is possible is possible only under given conditions. The conditions may be broad or narrow, constant and perpetual, or fleeting. They may be temporal or nontemporal, contingent or mathematical. When allegedly pure possibilities are thought of, they are in fact thought of ordinally, but the relevant conditions which are latently implied are unwittingly suppressed or overlooked. If a possibility were wholly independent of all other complexes, we surely could not conceive or envisage it, nor could we describe or formulate it. . . . We certainly can think of new possibilities, but not in complete discontinuity and isolation from all else. The complexes which we choose to talk and think about are partly but necessarily determining factors of the way we talk about them. A nonlocated possibility could not be identified. An integrity could not be framed for it. By contrast, to acknowledge that possibilities are traits and have subaltern traits is to acknowledge that each is bounded, limited. Perforce we ask: possibility of what, possibility in what respect, what direction? (PIN 165–166, in MNC [1989] 277)

16. Some would classify spatio–temporal possibilities as "material" (or "existential"). Such "material" possibilities are alleged to be a subset of the set of all, alleged "logical possibilities." Santayana seemed to hold such a view in his theory of essences, although he argued against applying the term possibility to essences. (George Santayana, *The Realm of Essence: Book I of Realms of Being* (Scribner's 1927). See also David Weissman, *Eternal Possibilities: A Neutral Ground for Meaning and Existence* (Carbondale & Evansville: Southern Illinois University Press, 1977).

17. See also, "Notes," in MNC [1989] 222.

18. (p. 175) So, for example, the fact that I am a granddaughter of Judge Wallace is a trait of me which may not be related to me in so far as I am a professor

of philosophy and a professor at a particular institution (although there would have to be other mediating traits to justify their all being traits of me). There may, of course, be other complexes for whom kinship and career or employment are closely related traits. It is an empirical matter which traits are directly and which mediately related to one another. The example I chose is only meant to illustrate the theoretical point that every trait of a complex may not need to be related to every other in order to be traits or constituents of the same complex. (It would depend on an analysis of reflexiveness.) Another way of putting it would be to say that commensurateness does not mean "internal" or "organic" relatedness of traits. On the ordinal view the distinction between internal/external relations is not an ontological one. (OCW 563, in MNC [1989] 236. See also "Notes," in MNC [1989] 220–221.)

19. (p.175) Similarly, I share the trait of "granddaughter of Judge Wallace" with my sisters and female first cousins even while I (and each of us) also have it in my own distinct way. The distinctness comes from how this trait contributes to and enters into my unique interrelation of traits or integrities.

20. I have not gone into a discussion of the distinctions between possibility, potentiality and power which Buchler develops (MNC 170–175). These are important for fleshing out the different kinds of possibilities complexes can have and are, as well as the differences in their modes of actualization. I have omitted such a discussion because I am more interested in developing the implications for the notion of logical possibility of Buchler's general reorientation to the concept of possibility.

21. While the locatedness of possibilities entails finiteness, it does not necessitate finiteness in every respect: "When a possibility is interpreted as a prefined extension of a complex, and as being therefore the natural definition of a relative limit, this does not imply that all complexes are in all respects finite. An infinite sequential order of numbers has limited and limiting traits, but this does not mean that it must have a final term. The possibilities inherent in the complex known as an infinite series are the natural definition of *its* relative limits, which are such, for example, as to allow any number to be succeeded by another." (MNC 170)

22. OCW 576, and in MNC [1989] 255. "Pure" and logical possibility are not necessarily equivalent, but we will not try to clarify the difference here. The point Buchler is probably trying to emphasize is that his conception of ordinal possibility treats both "pure" and logical possibility as suspect for the same reason, viz., both ignore that possibility is determined by the ordinal conditions or locations of a complex. The law of non-contradiction as it is traditionally used in arguments concerning logical possibility is exemplified no less by actualities. Therefore, it could not be the distinguishing feature of the possible *qua* possible. Moreover, on Buchler's view, the law of non-contradiction might be said to be more strongly exemplified by actuality than by possibility. (See above p. 173 and MNC 156)

23. (p. 177) Buchler takes this to be the commitment of ordinality:

The first note of ordinal metaphysics was struck in 1951, when I suggested that a house may fluctuate in its actual size, just as it may fluctuate in its monetary worth. Many philosophers who would agree that when we stand before a house it is the house we see, not an image or sense-datum or appearance of the house, would balk at the ordinal consequences. As we move away from the house, it becomes smaller. I am not saying, in the manner of certain epistemologies earlier in this century, that the house appears smaller, each appearance being just as much a reality as the house itself. I am saying that if what is called the "house itself" appears smaller, it is because it *gets* smaller. It is in the order of vision that it gets smaller. That is one of its ordinal locations, as much an ordinal location as its geometrical or financial location. As we move away from the house, it actually occupies a progressively smaller space in the visual order. This can be predicted and measured. The house is the same house, but in a different order. The different order yields a different integrity, another integrity of the same complex. What we should call the "nature" of the house is its network of integrities, its contour of ordinal locations. (PIN 167, in MNC [1989] 279)

The 1951 reference is to *Toward A General Theory of Human Judgment* (pp. 54–56, esp. 56).

24. See MNC 165 ff. and Weiss, *op.cit.*

25. (p. 179) He gives examples: an image is defined upon the retina, a course of events which has defined options available for action (MNC 163), the way an animal's sense organs define the immediate environmental prospect before it. (MNC 162)

26. "The specification 'relevant traits' underscores the truth that not all complexes have the same possibilities, that not all possibilities 'always were.' But [it] also allows complexes to have a possibility or various possibilities in common. They may all prefine the same relevant traits . . . " (MNC 165).

27. Relative to the possibility what is not yet may be the persistence of the possibility, its actualization (and hence, an actuality and another possibility), both or its expiration without actualization.

28. On this view, one would not affirm that the talking insect *is* the physical or biological specimen just now located in the order of imagination. Rather, if we do say something like that, it is probably elliptical for a complicated process of abstracting and transposing certain traits of the insect into the order of imagination and constructing a new complex which obviously is in some respects similar to the physical and biological specimen. The similarity is itself a universal, *another* possibility which both the talking insect and the biological insect may also have in common. In exemplifying the same possibility, or universal, the two different insects may in this respect occupy another, and the same for each, order. What this means is that distinct complexes can have overlapping or shared traits, without thereby losing their distinctness, which may also justify a common linguistic identification or name.

29. Weiss, *op.cit.,* 216 and here 165. Weiss realizes what the issue really is, for he goes on to say: "Clearly, the issue here is: when are we justified in saying that one and the same complex pertains to two (or more) distinct orders? Now, the metaphysics of natural complexes is by no means committed to a principle that one cannot call a complex by the same name when considering it in its different ordinal locations. Every complex enters into different orders, and its possibilities and actualities differ with respect to the order in which it is considered."

30. Buchler does not *not* admit that such possibilities prevail. What he argues is that they are not necessarily possibilities (traits) of the complexes supposed. His argument is two-fold: one, it is an attack on the law of contradiction as *the* defining condition of possibility; two, it is an argument for the conception of possibility as ordinally located.

31. Weiss, *op.cit.,* 217, and here 166.

32. See David Lewis, *Counterfactuals* (Cambridge: Harvard University Press, 1973) and Weiss, *op.cit.,* p. 202 and here 148.

33. See Marjorie Miller, "The Concept of Identity in Justus Buchler and Mahayana Buddhism," *International Philosophical Quarterly* 16:1 (March 1976), pp. 87–107, reprinted here, pp. 93–113.

Weiss/Wallace Discussion: Possibility and Metaphysics

Weiss, Possibility: Temperament and Argument

Kathleen Wallace has presented, in her paper "Ordinal Possibility: A Metaphysical Concept,"[1] a valuable exposition of Justus Buchler's metaphysical system and of the place of possibility in that system. I am quite sure that she represents, clearly and forcefully Buchler's response to my little criticism of his theory of possibility.[2] Nevertheless, just as Buchler's and Wallace's opinions were not changed by my article, my opinion is not changed by what Wallace has written. In this brief essay, I would like to indicate why my mind isn't changed and why I'm not sure any arguments I can muster would change every mind.

I

Part of what is going on here has to do with philosophical temperament and feeling-tone. When I studied Buchler's works, "ordinality" did not excite me and "commensurateness" did not occur to me. Ontological parity excited me, and natural complexity excited me. Ordinality just seemed useful as a way of explicating parity and complexity. The natural complexity of all that is was exciting as a way of moving beyond analysis in terms of relatively static, perfectly self-identical substances. Ontological parity was exciting as a way of moving beyond any analysis which sees some kind of privileged "hard stuff" as really real, relegating other items to a more shadowy and lower ontological status, viewing them as not quite real, as requiring reductive explanation in terms of the really real stuff. The virtues which attracted me to the world as envisioned in Buchler's system were its ontological fluidity (complexity) and tolerance (parity).

Specifically, in relation to possibility, the parity of actuality and possibility was a way to get out of the prejudice in favor of the determinate (the unfuzzily fixed, the really *there*), which turns the world into a reality wholly actual, in which possibility remains a mystery to be explained away (and therefore in which everything which depends upon possibility—identity over time, causality, change, induction, etc.—remains mysterious, requires reductive explanation). This explaining away of possibility seems always to result in explaining possibility in terms of actuality—actuality somewhere else or actualities of mind. This does not work.[3] Buchler's system works on possibility because actuality and possibility are given equal and correlative status. Accepting the reality of possibility is accepting a kind of indeterminateness within nature. This is not absolute indeterminateness, but it is indeterminateness in contrast to the kind of determinateness which actuality has. (Loosely, contradictories can't both be actual, they can both be possible.) This is why I am taken aback when suddenly Buchler and Wallace begin hardening the boundaries and insisting upon a more strict sense of identity, so that, according to them, talking insects are not *really* insects, painted tracks are not *really* tracks, and the possibilities for things actualized in imaginative or literary or painted orders are not *real* possibilities. The sudden invoking of what Wallace has termed "the principle of commensurateness" feels to me to be an uncharacteristic insistence on determinate self-identity of a more traditional kind, the very determinateness from which Buchler's system, as I experience it, can liberate us.

My presumption is that Buchler's and Wallace's insistence upon a more determinate principle of identity than I would invoke, comes from wanting to avoid an anything-goes type of relativism in a completely relativistic metaphysics. Clearly, complexes must have integrity and contour. Everything cannot be the same thing, not every thing can be identified with something else. There is a limit to tolerance! My sense is that where this limit is drawn may be more a matter of temperament than of principle.

To this point, I haven't been engaging in philosophical argument. I've been trying to explain why I don't think philosophical argument is going to change minds on this matter. We are at a temperamental sensitivity point. My *feeling* is that Wallace and Buchler are arbitrarily limiting the wonderful looseness (ontological fluidity and tolerance) of the system. Their *feeling* (I think) is that opening this hole I want to open will so loosen the fabric of the system that it will cease to hold together—anything will be possible for anything, if only we could conceivably imagine it!

II

Now let me restate my objection in a more argumentative form, admitting that I don't think my argument will convince Wallace any more than her argument has convinced me.

I will try to make my point by putting together two illustrations: the parallel tracks and the funny glasses.[4] In the order of interpersonally objective space the tracks don't converge into the distance, but in the order of visual space the tracks do converge. Now we consider the possibility of the tracks actually diverging in some order.[5] I exhibit this possibility in a painting. What does Wallace say about this painting? She says it is not about the tracks. But I thought I was painting the tracks in order to exhibit, by way of construction, the possibility of an order in which the tracks diverge into the distance. I would say "in my painting the tracks diverge." I would not simply say (as Buchler and Wallace might require) "in my painting some lines representing tracks diverge" because the (two dimensional) lines in the painting are not identical with (not doing the same things as) the (three dimensional) tracks in my painting.

Let's follow this out further. An optician comes along and views my painting. She says "Wow! I never thought of that. Tracks could diverge into the distance, instead of converging." What does she do? She constructs a set of reverse telescopic lenses which make what is near seem far away and what is far away seem near. You put them on and what do you see? Voila! The tracks diverge into the distance in your visual field. Now what would traditional philosophers have wanted to tell us about this? "The tracks are not diverging in our visual field; images representing the tracks are diverging. After all, the tracks are parallel; they don't diverge, and they cannot both diverge and not diverge (let alone diverging, converging, and running parallel all at once!). You destroy the integrity of that set of objects we call "the tracks" if you claim contradictory things about them. Thus, however much you are tempted, naively, to talk about the tracks diverging, if you were really careful, you would talk about something else [superficially similar to the tracks]."

Now the metaphysician of natural complexes would try (probably without much success) to convince the traditional philosopher that one needn't worry. Buchler is not destroying the integrity of the tracks, and he is not contradicting himself. The tracks diverge in one order, and they remain parallel in another. No need to panic. It's not that the tracks can do contradictory things at the same time. They do these things in different respects (in different orders). These different ordinal locations are perfectly commensurate, we can move among them without confusion or contradiction. The tracks in the interpersonally objective spatial order are parallel; the tracks in the ordinary (to us) visual order converge; the tracks in the visual order determined by these special lenses diverge. No problem!

All *I* do is add: the tracks in the order of this painting of mine diverge too, and there is no problem here either. I know perfectly well that I can find objects doing things in paintings that they do neither in physical space nor in ordinary visual space, nor perhaps in any possible alternative visual space not privileged with the unique possibilities of painted space.

Two things are important here. First, my painting does not merely exhibit possibilities of painting (as Wallace seems to want to say); it exhibits possibilities of painting the tracks. This is a relational order (all orders are relational) into which the tracks enter. If the tracks didn't enter into this order, it would not be the order of painting the tracks, but the order of painting something else, and its reference to the tracks would be incomprehensible. (It is not, for example, an order of painting things similar to the tracks. That would involve painting ladders and such.) So one possibility of the tracks (a possibility actualized in my painting) is that they diverge into the distance in painted orders.

Second, the possibility of the optical opening up of a visual field revealing the tracks as diverging was suggested by my painting, precisely because the painting was a painting of tracks. It was an exhibition that this was possible for the tracks in some orders. This led the optician to look for other orders in which it was possible. We often begin the investigation of possibilities of complexes located in physical or communal or visual or painted orders by constructing imaginative orders into which those complexes enter, in the relevant respects. (Before I painted the tracks diverging, I imagined the tracks diverging. Before the optician constructed the funny glasses which would make the tracks diverge, she imagined them.)

This is the exploration of "logical possibility." I may be able to construct imaginal orders in which possibilities of complexes are actualized and in which possibilities prevail as such, which cannot be extended to other, more "hard-headed" orders.[6] In doing so, I explore the logical possibilities of these complexes regardless of the biological, physical, ordinary visual, or peculiar visual orders in which they may also be located. I may be concerned just with the imaginal or conceptual orders in which they may be located. This is fun (talking insects) and it may also turn out to be useful to other people (diverging tracks, people employing flying machines and submarines before they've been invented, etc.). I see no incommensurateness with other ordinal locations in this. We expect things to have traits in one order that they don't have in others.

Wallace and Buchler do feel some incommensurateness here. Other philosophers feel incommensurateness in considering the same thing to have mutually exclusive traits in different orders. It *feels* to me that I am taking Buchler's system where it wants to go. I don't, philosophically, understand Buchler's or Wallace's resistance to this move. Thus it seems as arbitrary as the resistance Buchler's system meets from more traditional philosophers, whose sense of the commensurate and of the determinate leads them to speak of perceiving images and leads them to deny possibility parity with actuality.

As I indicated before, I would be surprised if these arguments made a difference in Buchler's or Wallace's opinion on the subject. I suspect that this has something to do with differences in how we need to feel the shape of the world.

Notes

1. In the present volume, pp. 171–187.

2. Phil Weiss, "Possibility: Three Recent Ontologies," *International Philosophical Quarterly* 20:2 (June 1980), pp. 199–219. Reprinted here, pp. 145-169. See section III of the paper.

3. Ibid., sections I and II.

4. See Wallace, Loc. Cit. text at notes 12 and 23.

5. Ibid., as the text continues in the paragraphs beyond note 23.

6. Wallace is quite right in criticizing my use of "public" and "physical" in this context, and I don't know quite how to name the prejudice I sense in the rejection of the legitimacy of this mode of exploration of the possibilities of a complex. But it strikes me as prejudice against complexes from some "ontologically privileged" orders entering into orders which are, relative to these complexes, relegated to an ontological "second class." See Ibid., text following note 29.

Wallace, Skeptical Openness

Ontological parity is an exciting and radical idea in the history of philosophy, and it may well turn out to be both the most accessible and the most influential of Buchler's contributions to philosophical thought. For it does affirm that the world is a "rich and multifarious place," plurally constituted. And, it affirms a radical openness to the equal *reality* of possibilities and does so in a way that no other philosophical approach has been able to even remotely accomplish. One of the strengths of Weiss's paper, "Possibility: Three Recent Ontologies," which I did not emphasize in my own, but which I can here take the opportunity to acknowledge, is to exhibit the contribution which Buchler makes by contrasting the very limited conceptions of possibility advanced by Lewis and Rescher with the philosophical aptness of Buchler's view which captures the full ontological reality of possibility.

In addition to the openness captured by ontological parity, I feel that there is another side to Buchler's thought which for me is captured by Santayana's epigram, "Naturalism, Sad."[1] In Santayana this epigram is an emotional formulation of the sobriety and tolerance of a naturalistic attitude, an attitude which renounces excessive optimism, idealism and anthropomorphism. And for Santayana, naturalism is the unrelenting awareness of the "helplessness of spirit" when faced with and conditioned by the intractable "nature of things," whether that be brute material forces or feeble human nature itself.

Unlike Santayana, Buchler does not think of human beings as by any means helpless, but there is a streak in Buchler which recognizes the finiteness of human beings and the recalcitrance of complexes. Complexes have their own determinateness and limits which may constrain our ability to manipulate them, imaginatively or otherwise.

There is this tension in Buchler's thought between, on the one hand, the exciting categorial breadth and richness which ontological parity opens up and on the other, an unrelenting sobriety and ontological acceptance of, even if not moral tolerance for, whatever is part of nature, whether it favors us as human or not. This tension is exemplified in the system he has created. The genius of his categories, at least as I see it, is that they provide for both the openness which is so attractive to Weiss (and to myself, I should add) *and* the independent integrity of complexes. I think the tension itself is exciting. It poses in philosophical terms the recurrent challenge to push the limits of what is and may become possible, because there are limits (changeable and not), not because there are none. Openness is not unqualified, parity is not without ordinality (and commensurateness). If it were, there would be no mark or measure by which to distinguish it from closure. And lacking that, what would openness mean?

The principles of ordinality and commensurateness[2] entail that possibility means actualizability in at least some order(s). I can see why some of my formulations might seem to suggest that this restricts the openness and incompleteness of complexes, and I stand corrected for some infelicitous formulations. I don't think, though, that commensurateness compromises either openness or incompleteness, and I'll address that below. But I also don't see, as Weiss suggests, how it compromises ontological parity as such. Ontological parity affirms only the equal reality of every complex, every order, every ordinal location, whatever it happens to be, not that a complex can occupy any order. Our imaginative actualities and possibilities are no less real than those of any other non-human or non-mental complex. So, I do not assert that talking insects are not really talking insects or that talking insects are not real complexes in the order of, say, cartoons. What I assert is that the talking insect is not the same being as the biological specimen. And, I do not assert that "the possibilities for things actualized in imaginative or literary or painted orders are not *real* possibilities." On the contrary; they are real whether fictional or not, and no less so than fictional or nonfictional actualities. My argument was not directed against their (equal) reality, but concerned their location. I do not doubt their reality, but ask, what are they possibilities of?

The real issue has to do with whether what I have called a principle of commensurateness undermines or compromises the fluidity and indeterminateness of complexes, which I think Weiss is right in emphasizing as a clear commitment of the system.

Weiss's counterexample forces me to admit that in the railroad tracks example I may be wrong and may have arbitrarily set the boundary for the tracks too narrowly. On the other hand, I wonder if divergence would be a possibility *of the tracks* if the optician had *not* constructed or been able to construct the reverse telescopic lenses or until she had done so. To recall the funny glasses example, the greeness of the dress is a possibility of it because there is another complex, the glasses, which mediates between the two otherwise incompatible traits, the dress *qua* blue and the dress *qua* green. In one sense, the glasses provide the condition of actualizability for the dress of being both green and blue at the same time.

Now, it may be that sometimes our imagination or imaginative products are the mediating complex(es), the condition for a complex having an actualizable trait in some respect. Weiss may be right in the case of the painted, diverging tracks and it may be that the painting is a new order into which the tracks have entered. I may have to concede that I set the boundary too narrowly. But, it is also an empirical problem where the boundary is. Where the boundary of a complex is in any given case may be indeterminate, or as Weiss would put it, fluid. But, boundaries there are. Whether something is logically possible or not for a given complex has to do with whether traits, and more specifically, the *integrities* (strongly relevant traits), of the complex have been retained or tacitly suspended. So, if Weiss is right about the tracks, it's because we don't have to tacitly suspend integrities of the tracks in order to get the divergence. I am not sure, empirically, whether we do or don't have to suspend them, even though I find Weiss's counterexample persuasive that in this instance we may not suspend them. But, I'm not yet persuaded that the cartoon insect is the biological insect, now located in the order of cartoon images. Rather, it seems to me that someone has abstracted and transposed some traits of the insect (and suspended many others) into the order of imagination and constructed a new complex which is similar in some respects to the originally inspiring insect.[3]

I have no problem with saying that our imagination can create possibilities for other complexes. What I balk at—and whether this is just stubbornness on my part or not, only further query will tell—is the implication that every imaginable trait is a trait of what we think it is a trait of. I am skeptical of such a conclusion. Can't we be wrong? Couldn't we be wrong that what we can imagine as a possibility of some complex, or could imagine becoming a possibility of some complex (like, for example, the parent imagining his child becoming the renowned cellist of her generation) is a possibility of that complex? The issue is not whether what one imagines is real or not. Of course, it's real. Rather, the question is, what is it a possibility of? Is it the child located in the parent's imagination and possessing the imagined possibility? I would not deny that it might be the same complex, but whether it is or not depends on whether it retains its integrities. I dream something about a friend. What is the location of that possibility? Is it therefore a possibility *of my friend?* Is it my friend now located in a new order, i.e., my dream, and therefore, possessing a new trait which I have dreamt? Maybe, but maybe I have constructed a new complex, as the projection of a wish or desire or the expression of a fear, which is similar in certain respects to my friend, as the talking cartoon insect is similar in certain respects to the biological specimen. Or, depending on the case, maybe it's both: that my friend is located in my dream, *and* that what I dream about my friend is the projection of a wish. It would depend on the dream, the friend, the wish, etc.

Of course, there has to be some relation between me and my friend such that it is even possible for me to have such a dream, just as there has to be some relation between us and insects for it to be possible that we can imagine or draw talking insects. But I don't see how that entails that the traits of the complexes which spin off from those relations have to also be traits of their progenitors. Why isn't the multifariousness of the world still preserved by admitting that we can also create new complexes (talking insects, dreamt-of-friends, diverging railroad tracks) which are similar to, and therefore, in some sense continuous with, insects, friends, and railroad tracks, but which have distinctive traits and integrities which do not belong to the latter? Reverse telescopic lenses are a new complex, albeit continuous with, say, the painting and other optical possibilities and complexes. Why can't a cartoon insect, too, be a new complex? My dreamt-of-friend and the talking insect are complexes and possibilities of, or in the world, just as much as historical, biological and physical individuals are. Where else would they be?

I'm not sure that Weiss and I do disagree or if the examples have led us to think that we do, for I grant Weiss's point about the railroad tracks example. It's precarious to base a theoretical point on examples because in their specificity they are rarely unadulterated instances of the point being illustrated (which is probably why a metaphysician shouldn't rely too much on examples). Where empirically we would draw the lines, whether I think that talking is a possibility of the insect (just now located in the order of cartoon images) or not, and who is right may be metaphysically indeterminate. If I am skeptical of where the boundary should be drawn, it's not just because the boundary is indefinite, but because each complex, not I, defines its boundary.

Maybe the world just doesn't feel as malleable to me as it does to Weiss. Maybe I just feel the recalcitrance of things; that I am struck by my experiences that what I thought or imagined were possibilities aren't. But, then what we each notice is a matter, as Weiss pointed out, of psychology and temperament. Our temperaments, too, are complexes, subaltern complexes of each of us. What is compelling to me is that Buchler's system has the categorial means with which to interpret each of our feelings about how the world needs to be shaped.

Notes

1. George Santayana, *The Life of Reason; or The Phases of Human Progress,* vol. I, *Reason in Common Sense,* ch. 8 (1905).

2. The latter, commensurateness, is a principle which I should take responsibility for elevating to the status of a systematic principle. Buchler does not identify it as such, and he might not have agreed with my articulation of it. It is my feeling, however, that such a principle is the reason why the system does not degenerate into a sort of "anything–goes–relativism" whereby beings would have no discriminable identity.

3. And, as I said in my paper, the similarity may itself be a universal, *another* possibility which both the talking insect and the biological insect may also have in common. In exemplifying that same possibility, or universal, the two different insects may in this respect occupy another, and the same for each, order. What this means is that distinct complexes can have overlapping or shared traits, without thereby losing their distinctness, and which may also justify a common linguistic identification or name.

Ordinality and Materialism

John Ryder

It is a common practice to view materialism in terms of its traditional versions.[1] Materialism has tended to be reductionistic and mechanistic, and it is often assumed that these are among its definitive characteristics. In their book *Philosophy: An Introduction,* Justus Buchler and John Herman Randall, Jr. discuss materialism in this way. Materialism, which they describe as a "narrow" version of naturalism, is contrasted with critical naturalism, the perspective both authors endorse. They describe materialism as the view which identifies nature with the physical world, and which further holds that whatever exists is physical, which is to say that everything is "composed of" material constituents. Buchler and Randall also ascribe to materialism the view that the universe is mechanical, which implies that it is lawful and that phenomena are ultimately explainable by the science of mechanics. They say, in fact, that "these are the two main theses of materialism: that all realities are material, and that the functioning of the material universe is machinelike [mechanistic], devoid of genuine novelty."[2]

Materialism, they point out, has claimed several advantages. It avoids any necessity to appeal to mysterious principles or "non–natural" phenomena as explanatory devices. It is a simple and economic view. It is faithful to experience in that we know that "mind" and society can only exist if material things exist, while matter can exist without consciousness and society, and it is more faithful to science in that mechanism can account for science's ability to predict. These alleged advantages of materialism are illusory, Buchler and Randall argue, for several reasons. While mind and society do indeed require matter, it does not follow that they must therefore be material. Furthermore, experience is characterized not only by the recognition of the dependence of consciousness on matter, but also by the fact that human life is infused with values and purposes, phenomena for which materialism cannot account. And materialism is no more consistent with science than it is with experience since science no longer interprets the world mechanically; mechanistic determinism is too simple an account of nature.

If this account of materialism were adequate, there would be no doubt that an ordinal ontology is inconsistent with a materialist world view. Ordinality involves the explicit rejection of atomism and reductionism in favor of a categorial structure which is able to account for the full range of natural phenomena and which is not forced to deny the reality of novelty in nature. However, though traditional materialism has indeed been atomistic, reductionist and mechanistic, contemporary materialism is not committed to ascribing these traits to nature. While Buchler and Randall are correct in their description of the "two main theses" of traditional materialism, contemporary materialism can avoid both the view that all realities are physical and the insistence that nature is mechanistic. Contemporary materialism understands nature, natural phenomena, consciousness, experience, and human activity in ways much more like those of the critical naturalism for which Buchler and Randall were arguing.[3] The fact that materialism has overcome its atomistic and reductionist past is precisely why it is pertinent to explore the possibility of an ordinal materialism.

The argument to be developed here is that ordinality is not only an appropriate categorial structure of a materialist ontology, but further that an ordinal materialism can resolve fruitfully issues which raise serious problems for a materialism which attempts to utilize more traditional categories. The discussion will proceed in three stages. It is first necessary to describe at least the general characteristics of contemporary materialism. The second task is to clarify the several aspects of ordinality by which it contributes to an adequate materialism most clearly. The third concern is to discuss those aspects of ordinality which require revision in light of a materialist perspective.[4]

As R. W. Sellars has pointed out, modern materialism differs "profoundly from the materialism of Democritus, Hobbes and Moleschott."[5] The most general characteristic of modern materialism is its insistence on the objectivity of nature. Whatever general traits nature has, it has them independently of our knowledge and experience. This position alone does not define materialism, however, since other perspectives also incorporate objectivity. Plato's Forms, for example, were independent of knowledge and experience. For materialism, then, not only are the traits of nature objective, but nature in general is not contingent on anything non–natural. More specifically, matter is fundamental among the phenomena of nature. This is the sense of the claim that matter is primary. While it can be true that a given material object is affected in one way or another by non–material phenomena, it is primarily the material order which provides the framework of, which locates, the nonmaterial. Matter, therefore, is primary. Our knowledge of the specific traits of material phenomena, however, is not to be determined by philosophic reflection, but rather by the sciences. This is why materialism is not by definition committed to atomism and mechanism. If the results of the inquiry of the sciences indicate that neither atomism nor mechanism adequately account for the behavior of material objects, which is in fact the case, then materialism's conception of the specific characteristics of matter is altered accordingly.

A second general trait of modern materialism is its rejection of reductionism. Though matter is primary, the many and varied traits of natural phenomena cannot be explained by the principles and laws of material objects alone. Matter functions at a variety of levels of complexity, and at each level natural phenomena exhibit new traits not reducible to those of other levels. For example, organic matter is not "simply" molecules in certain interactions, let alone "nothing but" atoms in the void. Matter functioning organically exhibits new traits, for example organic growth, which differ in kind from those of inert matter. Inert matter may undergo additive or diminutive changes, but it does not grow in the way organic matter does. Consequently, the principles of organic growth and decay are different from those which determine the processes undergone by inert matter. Another example of the significance of the concept of levels of material functioning is afforded by the diversity in the characteristics of animal species. The traits which characterize increasingly complex animal forms are not reducible to those of other forms. The sociality of certain species, for example, is a trait peculiar to them, and it is an aspect of their lives which cannot be accounted for by appeal either to the more general principles of organic matter, or the still more general principles of inert matter. Sociality, though it is a characteristic of natural, indeed material, phenomena which are subject to the general principles of inert and organic matter, introduces principles of its own, the specific nature of which are revealed by biological, anthropological and sociological study. A final example is in the nature of human being and its many more or less distinctive characteristics. The phenomenon of consciousness, for example, is an aspect of complex material beings yet at the same time is sufficiently distinctive that it cannot fully be understood on more general material principles alone. Consciousness introduces new phenomena and consequently new principles in nature. Materialism attempts to understand consciousness without appeal to a radically distinct ideal substance, but also without positing the identity of consciousness and matter.

Implicit in the concept of levels of material functioning is the recognition of novelty. The activity of matter is a dynamic process which issues in qualitatively distinct phenomena, the understanding of which requires both an appreciation of their relation to general principles of matter as well as an awareness of their distinctive characteristics. Also implicit is the recognition of the existence of nonmaterial phenomena. Ideas, purposes, some human products and a host of other natural phenomena are consequences of material processes but are not themselves material objects. Materialism, then, is committed to the view that matter is primary, and not to the view that it is exhaustive.

A final definitive characteristic of modern materialism is its conception of knowledge. Contrary to a prevalent tendency in pragmatist epistemology, the materialist holds that knowledge is not a form of world making, but is rather a reflection of the objective traits of nature. To know a subject matter is to understand *its* traits and *its* principles. Furthermore, knowledge includes an understanding of the lawful regularities of the activity of natural phenomena at all levels, including the social and the ideal. This is one of the respects in which materialism differs from several forms of philosophic naturalism. Many philosophic naturalists tend to recognize lawfulness at the inorganic and biological levels, but are inclined to reject the lawful activity of social and ideal phenomena. To insist on the lawfulness of all levels of natural phenomena is not to imply a strict determinism or the inefficacy of human activity. Rather it is to acknowledge the fact that fruitful human activity requires methodic inquiry, which in turn requires cognizance of the objective traits and laws of its subject matter. Human activity does affect nature, for better or worse, but the systematic fulfillment of human purposes and plans requires as full as possible an understanding of that with which we interact. If we wish to build, we must understand the nature of the materials we use and the processes they undergo. If we wish to promote social progress, we need to understand the characteristics of historical and social processes. On the materialist view, the lawfulness of natural phenomena and an understanding of it does not preclude human creativity, but in fact enables it. Science, the materialist holds, is the most valuable, though not the only, method by which to acquire this sort of knowledge, and whatever else science is, it is at least the search for the regularities of nature.

There are several characteristics of an ordinal ontology which enable a materialist interpretation. An initial necessary condition of a materialist approach to nature is the view that its traits are objective. With respect to the question of the natural status of human beings, the materialist argues that human beings are natural phenomena and are to be understood at least in part within the context of more general natural principles and categories rather than reading nature through categories more specifically human. The latter approach has had adherents throughout the history of philosophy, and continues to be advocated in more recent years. Whitehead's elevation of feeling into the ontological category of prehension is an example, as is Dewey's inclination to read nature in terms of experience. Approaches such as these may well have the admirable motivation of attempting to avoid an unduly deterministic and mechanistic conception of nature. Their shortcoming, however, is that they "may well result," as Buchler has said, "in a human world writ large."[6] An ordinal ontology has the decided advantage of explicitly avoiding this inclination. "Any complex is determinate," Buchler argues, "whether it is related or unrelated to mind. Its gross integrity cannot be obliterated by decision, or deemed non-prevalent if it falls outside the range of finite intellectual machinery. It is determined by and determines other complexes." (MNC 87) The traits of the complexes of nature are determined not by our interaction with them, but by their own processes and relations, their own actualities and possibilities. It is consequently inappropriate to apply explicitly human categories to complexes generally. This perspective does not, however, ignore the fact that some complexes do interact with human beings. The categorial structure of an ordinal ontology makes it possible to understand how even those complexes which *are* related to mind, for example as complexes known, are nonetheless not "essentially constituted" by the knower. Being located in the order of knowledge, i.e. being an object of knowledge, does not exhaust the ordinal locations of a complex, and thus its prevalence in any number of orders, its contour, is not necessarily a function of its being known.[7] A complex may enter human experience as a problem for scientific investigation, for example, and this would make the complex determinate in a respect in which it had not been previously. Buchler points out, however, that this does not mean that the relation to inquiry is the exclusive or even primary source of the complex's determinateness:

> The solution of the problem by investigation would make the complex determinate in yet another respect. But not in *all* respects. For its relations within the order of investigation would not exhaust all of its possibilities, any more than its relations within another order would. And its traits within the human order may be far less pervasive than its other traits. (MNC 88)

Ordinal categories acknowledge the objective determinateness of not only those complexes which enter human experience, but also those which emerge from human activity. A work of art, for example, though it is a human product, obtains and may well be efficacious in any number of ordinal locations, and thus be an aspect or trait of objective processes. It may become determinate in respects wholly unrelated to its producer or her intentions.

The concept of natural definition further indicates the extent to which an ordinal ontology endorses the objectivity of natural complexes. Though the term "definition" may appear to be strictly appropriate to human activity, specifically linguistic definition, Buchler utilizes its more general meaning as "the setting of bounds or limits." Every complex of nature is determinate in some respects, and thus both includes and excludes any number of actualities and possibilities. The "bounds" or "limits" of any complex are established by its actualities and related possibilities, by its traits. The traits of a complex "define" its character and its future. "This *defining*," Buchler says, "is 'by' the complex. It is inherent in the complex. It is constitutionally basic." (MNC 162) A complex is objectively "defined" by its traits and the "spheres of relatedness," the orders, of which it is itself a trait.

An ordinal ontology acknowledges and categorially accounts for the reality of lawful regularity among natural complexes. Specifically, Buchler interprets a law of nature, whether it be a law of motion, a law of capitalist development, or the law of non-contradiction, as "a possibility with continuous or recurrent actualization." (MNC 176) The unique and distinctly valuable treatment of the character of objective lawfulness in an ordinal ontology derives from its approach to the categories of actuality and possibility. An ordinal ontology rejects both poles of the traditional debate between realism and nominalism. Realists have argued that universals exist and constitute a "realm of possibilities," or a set of "eternal possibilities," while nominalists have rejected the existence of universals and insist only on the reality of particulars. The former view posits an eternal reality distinct from nature, and the latter eliminates the possibility of objective law. Materialism cannot accept either position. A "supernatural" realm of universals is antithetical to materialism, as is the positivistic rejection of lawful regularity. An adequate materialism requires a conception of law which affirms its significance and understands it as fully a trait of natural processes. The ordinal treatment of possibility and actuality provides precisely such a conception. A possibility is no less a natural complex than is an actuality, and on the principle of ontological parity it makes no sense to say that one is "more real" than another. Possibilities and actualities both obtain, though as different kinds of complexes. As "a possibility with continuous or recurrent actualization," a law is a natural complex which contributes to the natural definition of the complexes to which it is related. It is a factor in the further determination of the actualities and possibilities of a complex. From an ordinal perspective, law is natural, objective, and efficacious.

In its rejection of reductionism the concept of ordinality would contribute further to the development of an adequate materialist ontology. With the abandonment of the concept of ontological simples, an ordinal ontology overcomes the predilection for reductionism characteristic of a "building block" ontology. If one presumes, as many philosophers from Leibniz to

Russell and the early Wittgenstein did, that complexes must be constituted by simples, it is then a quick step to the view that the characteristics of complexes are but accumulated sets of the characteristics of their simple constituents. This in turn leads directly to the view that to understand the character of a given complex it is necessary and sufficient to understand the nature of its simple constituents. A reductionism such as this is incompatible with materialism's emphasis on the novelty which emerges in the levels of development of material complexes. In an ordinal ontology, all complexes prevail in some order or orders, in some sphere or spheres of relatedness. Each complex of nature, then, has its integrity, its contour, its identity. The specific traits and ordinal locations of a complex distinguish it from others, and complexes with sufficiently similar traits and ordinal relations form a class which itself is distinct from other classes. The characteristics of a particular class (or order) of complexes, for example a species, are to some degree distinctive. The specific traits involved, and their unique relations, contribute to the integrity of the species. A species, then, is not reducible to another, nor to the more general order of biological complexes. It is, however, related to them. The order of social animals, for example, has characteristics which render it distinct from and discriminable among other complexes of nature. At the same time, however, the order of social animals is itself a complex ordinally located and in relation to other complexes as traits of a more encompassing order. Sociality is a distinctive order which locates its constituent complexes, and is in turn a constituent complex of, for example, the more pervasive order of biological complexes. The category of "order" makes it possible to understand a complex in its own right, and thus avoid reductionism, while categorially acknowledging its relations with other complexes.

In addition to its rejection of ontological simples, an ordinal ontology also excludes the traditional ontological category of substance and the related distinction between substance and attribute. The category of substance has been used in a variety of ways. It has meant a totality, as for Spinoza, and it has meant individuality, as in Cartesian mental and material substances. Buchler suggests that the many manifestations of the concept of substance have in common the view that the substantial is "less dependent" than the non-substantial. (MNC 47) This lesser dependence, he continues, is sometimes expressed by substance as the unanalyzable bearer of traits, sometimes as the subject of predicates which itself is never predicated of something else, and sometimes as that which is "in itself." Materialism requires none of these three senses of lesser ontological dependence. Each of the conceptions Buchler mentions involves the relation between that which has traits and the traits which it has. In general this is a useful and defensible distinction. That which has traits is not identical to any one of its traits, nor is it identical simply to the set of its traits. Even in an ordinal ontology a complex is not simply its traits, but rather its traits in certain specific relations. The category of order, of a "sphere of related-ness," is crucial to an adequate ontology of complexes. The problem, then, is not with the mere distinction between traits and that which possesses them. The problem, rather, is with the view that the distinction requires that the possessor of traits and the traits it possesses must be ontologically distinct kinds of being, that they must be different kinds of phenomena. The latter view is unacceptable to both an ordinal ontology and materialism.

The conceptions of substance Buchler mentions all imply that sub-stance is not capable of analysis and development. To say of substance that it is unanalyzable, for example, is to suggest either the impossibility of access or that it is an ontological simple. To presume that some natural phenomena are in principle unavailable to inquiry is to commit oneself to a skepticism which is directly contrary to the spirit of materialism. If, on the other hand, substance is incapable of analysis because it consists of nothing which analysis could reveal, then it is an ontological simple, which in turn leads directly to a reductionism which is antithetical to a materialist view of nature. Not only does a traditional conception of substance raise the specter of reductionism, but it also implies that natural phenomena are incapable of development. If nature consists of substance in one of these traditional senses, then the emergence of novel phenomena would be impossible. Natural change would be restricted to a mechanical reshuffling of traits. Such a view is inconsistent with the materialist acknowledgment of novelty and the processes of natural development from which novelty arises.

Materialism, then, rejects any conception of substance as an unana-lyzable subject, or as that which is "in itself." It does, however, require some sense of matter as "less dependent" than other natural phenomena. The question whether an adherence to the primacy of matter is consistent with an ordinal ontology indicates one of the several areas in which mate-rialism and ordinality are less obviously compatible than in the respects already discussed. The categories and principles of ordinality exclude a number of respects in which one might be tempted to say that matter is primary. If no complex is "more real" than another, then it is not possible to say that matter is "more real" than ideal phenomena. Buchler also con-siders the claim sometimes made that matter is primary in the sense that it is exclusively efficacious, that "the only complexes with efficacy are 'material' . . . " He rejects this view, claiming that it "belongs in a rather naive metaphysics." (MNC 146) Complexes which are not material may be efficacious no less than material complexes. There are, then, at least three specific senses in which matter is not primary. It is not an unanalyzable substance, it is not more real than other complexes, and it is not exclusively efficacious.

Naturalists have not been averse to flirting with materialism. Sellars argued that a materialist ontology is the only one adequate for naturalism, as long as it overcomes its mechanistic and atomistic past. Edel has explicitly acknowledged the primacy of matter, and Dewey, Nagel and Hook have collectively agreed that naturalists are materialists, given certain specific revisions of the traditional materialist view.[8] Buchler himself incorporates the fundamental significance of matter into his early conception of critical naturalism. His objection to philosophical materialism was that it necessarily includes, he thought, the denial of the existence of nonmaterial phenomena and that it is necessarily committed to a universal mechanism. He does not, however, oppose the view that matter is fundamental in the sense that nonmaterial phenomena depend on matter in ways in which matter does not depend on the nonmaterial:

> The error of materialism is that it confuses the *dependence* of biological, social, and psychological phenomena on physical phenomena with the *unreality* of such phenomena. To say that they cannot exist unless physical conditions exist and that yet the latter may exist independently, does not mean that they are "nothing but" physical . . . The physical may be a *basis* of all else, but it does not *exhaust* all.[9]

Buchler, at least in this early work, objects not to the claim that matter is less dependent than anything else, but to what he correctly describes as the fallacious inference that matter is therefore exhaustive. Naturalism, then, has room for, and I wish to argue requires, the primacy of matter in the sense that it is the "basis of all else," though the meaning of this needs to be clarified.

The question is still open, then, how this view is to be expressed with the categorial structure of an ordinal ontology. Once materialism acknowledges the reality of nonmaterial complexes, the issue of the primacy of matter becomes the question of the relation between the material and the ideal. Both are equally real, both are efficacious, and neither is an unanalyzable substance, yet matter is the basis of the ideal. The ordinal categories of prevalence and relevance enable us to capture and refine this sense of the primacy of matter. Every complex prevails in some order or orders. This is a categorial formulation of the point that all complexes are constituted relationally. The material order is primary in the sense that it is the condition of the prevalence of nonmaterial complexes. Nonmaterial complexes, of any kind, are not conditions of the *prevalence* of material complexes. This is the sense in which matter is "less dependent" than the ideal. That ideal complexes obtain at all means that material complexes have enabled it. Ideal complexes, whether they be human products, natural laws, or the possibilities of a given complex, are rendered possible by material complexes.

That matter is primary, that it is the condition of the prevalence of nonmaterial complexes, does not mean that matter is "more real" than other complexes. Thus it is possible to reconcile the primacy of matter with the important principle of ontological parity. Nor does it imply that matter alone is efficacious. The ordinal concept of strong relevance makes it possible to clarify the point that nonmaterial complexes are efficacious in any number of significant ways. The identity of any complex involves the relation of its contour, its gross integrity, and any of its integrities, its specific ordinal locations. If complex A is a condition of the integrity of complex B, that is if A is strongly relevant to B, then A is a factor in the identity of B, it contributes to B being the complex that it is. The efficacy of both material and nonmaterial complexes can be expressed categorially in that both material and nonmaterial complexes can be strongly relevant to other complexes. That a work of art, for example, is a work of *art* involves other than material complexes. Art is conditioned by a range of factors including social history, aesthetic style, expectations, intentions and others. In varying degrees these are all conditions of a work of art being *a* work of art and *the* work of art that it is. Among the many factors which contribute to the nature and identity of work of art are nonmaterial complexes. Similarly, the plans, purposes and decisions of a builder are among the conditions of the integrity of her product.

The materialist, then, must emphasize the efficacy of material and nonmaterial complexes within the context of the broader point that matter is a condition of the prevalence of all complexes. That matter is primary does not, however, imply that it is a substratum or unanalyzable foundation of all else. Material complexes are as fully ordinal as all others. They too are constituted relationally, prevail and are alescent in various respects, and have whatever possibilities they have. It is important to see that the ordinality of material complexes does not imply that matter cannot be primary in the sense specified any more than does the principle of ontological parity. The possibilities of material complexes, for example, are not themselves material complexes. They are, nevertheless, possibilities *of* material complexes, they prevail and are alescent in material ordinal locations, and though they contribute to the integrity of the complexes of which they are possibilities, their prevalence as possibilities is conditioned materially.

Still, there is a temptation to say that if all complexes are equally real, and if all complexes are ordinal, which is to say are constituted relationally, then it is incorrect to claim that any sort of complex is "primary" in nature. Buchler has said, for example, that "No order has absolute priority over any other. . . . Priorities of all kinds there surely are—causal, logical, explanatory, ethical, literary—but all are conditional." (OCW 577–578, in MNC [1989] 257) Since no order can be prior in *all* respects, since no order is exhaustive of nature, since no order is independent in the sense that it is unrelated to all other orders, the inclination has been to deny that any order can be primary "in general." This is the reason ordinality, and some other versions of philosophic naturalism, have been said to overcome the dichotomy between materialism and idealism. Neither the material nor the ideal orders can be absolutely primary, therefore materialism and idealism are both inappropriate.[10] This way of putting the matter, however, both presumes too much and leaves too much unsettled.

The primacy attributed to the material order does not require the claims that matter is primary in all respects, that matter is exhaustive of nature, or that matter is unrelated to other orders. A person, for example, is not exclusively a material complex, nor is the material order prior to all others in all respects relevant to a human life. It remains the case, however, that the material order is primary with respect to a person in that it establishes the most fundamental parameters of what a person may do, or achieve, or undergo. We engage the world in a variety of ways, and are subject to a number of forces, including the social, the psychological, and others. But all of this occurs within a framework established by material processes. Social and psychological factors interact with the material, and may even alter events which might otherwise take place, but they do so within the parameters established by the material order. Even if it is true of a particular person that she "lives on" through the consequences of her actions, this does not deny the primacy of the material order in human life. It rather extends its range.

The alternative which seems to be suggested by denying the priority of the material order is a "nominalism" antithetical both to ontological generalization and the possibility of scientific inquiry. To say simply that a person is a complex located in multiple orders, and to leave it at that, is surreptitiously, if unintentionally, to preclude sufficient generalization concerning the nature of human being. It would certainly be possible to generalize further, and fruitfully, as Buchler's own works, specifically *Nature and Judgment* and *Toward a General Theory of Human Judgment,* demonstrate. But I would argue that a metaphysics of the human process needs to incorporate the general relations among the traits of that process. It needs to account for the material grounding of human beings, and it needs to do so at the most general level. The contribution of ordinality to materialism is that it enables an understanding of the relational character of natural phenomena and thereby makes it possible to overcome the insufficient categories of traditional philosophic inquiry. And since the primacy of matter can be endorsed without insisting that it is exhaustive, independent, or determinate "in itself," ordinality does not require the view that no order is primary "in general."

The distinction between absolute primacy and primacy in general is crucial. Matter is primary in general in that it is the condition, mediately or immediately, of the prevalence of all complexes. Matter's general primacy is to be contrasted with an "absolute primacy" which might be ascribed, for example, to a realm of eternal possibilities, or an unmoved mover, or a Spinozistic substance. Unlike most traditional metaphysical views, ordinal materialism is not forced to posit an independent foundation or principle which is ultimately an exception to the categories and principles applicable to everything else. Eternal possibilities or an unmoved mover are ontologically independent of that which they enable, and are in that sense primary "absolutely." But this is not the case with the primacy here attributed to matter. Material phenomena are fully natural and ordinal, and in addition they are that which enables, which is to say they are conditions of the prevalence of, other phenomena.

Related to the question whether an order can be primary, not absolutely but generally, is the issue of pluralism. One of the admirable features of Buchler's philosophical work has been his recognition of diversity and variety, and his consequent refusal to limit the complexes of nature to a minimal number of kinds. The picture of the human process painted by the theory of judgment, for example, celebrates the richness of human being. The more general category of ordinality reflects the insight that by virtue of their relational character, the complexes of nature each have a plurality of traits and prevail in a variety of ordinal locations. The oft invoked chair, in addition to being an object on which to sit, is as much an example for the clarification of a philosophical theory. Both are equally integrities of the complex, neither more "essentially" than the other. The ordinal understanding of identity, as the relation between the contour of a complex and any of its integrities, requires this view. This acknowledgment of the plural character of complexes has, however, been extended by commentators, and perhaps by Buchler himself, in ways which materialism cannot abide, and which in any case are not required by the principle of ordinality or the theory of judgment.

Buchler has taken pains to argue that there is no World or Nature which is a totality or order of orders.[11] The reason for this is fairly clear, and follows directly from the principle of ordinality. An order is by definition a complex, and a complex by definition has ordinal location, it prevails in some order or orders. Ordinal location provides the integrity of a complex, and the multiple integrities of a complex in ongoing relation to one another are the identity of the complex. A complex without ordinal location could not be *a* complex at all. A totality or order of orders could have no ordinal location, since if it did it would not be a totality or order of orders. Since it could not be ordinally located, it could not be a complex. But if it is not a complex, then it is not an order, since an order is a complex in so far as it locates traits. Thus there can be no World or Nature as an overarching order in which all complexes are located. What precisely is there, then, if there is no totality? The answer is that there are complexes and orders, innumerable and varied. If there is no totality or "whole" of nature, then there is no sense in asking for the "system of nature" or the "world order."

This much is fair enough, but what else can be said about these innumerable and varied orders? Buchler says that:

On the basis of the unrestricted view as stated thus far, science would be said to be concerned not with nature in an unqualified sense but with a given world or worlds—the physical world, the social world, the psychological world. These worlds are pervasive orders of nature, for we no longer can make sense of "the" order of nature. . . . A tenable conception of nature recognizes many orders occupied by man among the innumerable orders not occupied by man and many orders devised by man. . . . Nothing is implied about a totality or whole or collectivity, no embarrassing commitment made to an ultimate integration which lacks integrity. (PIN 163–164, in MNC [1989] 273–274)

In my view Buchler has moved here from the denial of a totality to a rejection of inquiry into the "integration" of the innumerable orders. Perhaps he would deny that he has rejected the pursuit of the integration of orders, and claim only that he rejects an insistence on an "ultimate" integration. It is not clear what the difference would be, but even if we grant that there is a meaningful difference, this line of reasoning has led some to the conclusion that if there is no totality, then there is no sense to a suggestion that there is priority or primacy of one order to another. Thus Singer, for example, concludes that "The physical universe, great as it is, is but one world. The social world, the universe of discourse, the literary world are also natural orders and have their own natural locations."[12] There are, in other words, various orders which may or may not be related to one another in any given situation.

This, however, is precisely the detrimental "nominalism" alluded to earlier. We are left with no alternative but to pursue the relations of natural orders piecemeal, prevented from asking what otherwise appears to be the perfectly reasonable question, ''But how are the orders of nature related *in general?*'' A metaphysical pluralism which precludes this question is unacceptable because the possible answers to it matter for our understanding of the varied orders of nature. It is not enough to say that in some respects the literary world is dependent on the universe of discourse and in some respects it is not. Nor is it enough to say that the social world is in some respects dependent on the psychological world and in some respects it is not. It is important to know whether the processes of social and historical development are *in general* the result of our ways of thinking about them, or whether *in general* our social ideas reflect more objectively determinate processes. Without an answer to that sort of question, adequate social and historical theory is impossible because the systematic relation of events and phenomena could not be accurately discerned, and if social and historical theory is impossible, so is social and historical inquiry. The same is true of the relation of the general material order to the biological, and of the biological and material orders to the social and psychological. Knowledge of the complexes and orders of nature requires that we understand their general relations to one another. To elucidate those relations does not, however, mean that any given complexes located in those orders must be related in the same way. If objective social processes, for example, are in general the conditions of our ways of thinking about society, it does not necessarily follow that every idea we have is mechanically traceable to some social complex. The important point here, however, is that though complexes in different orders may be related to one another in different ways in different respects, it does not follow that there is no general relation among the orders.

Metaphysical pluralism, then, is an untenable position, and it should be noted that such a pluralism is not a necessary aspect of an ordinal ontology.[13] The principle of ordinality precludes a totality, or finished whole of nature; it precludes Buchler's *ultimate* integration of the orders of nature. It does now, however, preclude the general integration of orders. Thus when materialism asserts the primacy of matter, it does not imply an eternally complete whole or immutable order within which natural processes occur. Nature understood by the materialist is nature in process, open-ended, and capable of generating unpredictable novelty. It is nonetheless a nature which is characterized by discriminable processes, relations, and integration among its varied phenomena, one of which is the primacy of the material order.

In addition to metaphysical pluralism, some have inferred from the principle of ordinality a methodological pluralism. Kathleen Wallace, for example, points out that on the principle of ordinality, complexes have their traits perspectivally, which is to say by virtue of ordinal locations.[14] She infers from this that by describing a complex in different respects it is quite

possible to say very different things about it. Thus, she points out, it is true
that "a length of wood is *really* 1 meter *and* 39.37 inches." Similarly,
Buchler has said that in the order of physical complexes railroad tracks do
not converge, but in the order of vision they do. Neither trait is more true
of the complex than the other, and they differ simply because complexes are
located in different orders. If complexes are plural in this sense, then our
description or knowledge of them can be equally plural or perspectival.
Thus by analogy with different systems of measurement, each of which may
be equally "valid," different ontological claims, indeed differing ontological systems, may be equally "valid," albeit in different respects. On this
approach, it is no more appropriate to say that the material order is primary
in nature than to say that the psychological order is primary.

Wallace proposes that we think of metaphysics, or general ontology,
"as the shaping of categories with which to orient ourselves to understanding the world at a very general level." Just as in some cases we might
choose to employ one standard of measurement while in other cases a different one, in some respects it is possible and reasonable to describe the
world one way while in other cases it is equally legitimate to describe it in
a different way. The point would be a reasonable one given the analogy, but
the analogy is inappropriate in crucial ways. First, different systems of
length are directly correlated with each other, so that a proposition using
one is translatable into a proposition using another. This is very often not
the case with differing ontological systems, and it is not the case precisely
at those points in which the differences matter the most. There is no way to
translate Plato's conception of Form into the categories of the materialism
being defended here, and if Plato were right that particulars require immutable universals, then materialism is wrong. Second, and more importantly, methodological pluralism is tenable only if general ontology, and by
extension science and other modes of inquiry, are to be evaluated prag-
matically.[15] But by "pragmatizing" ontology, the enterprise loses its cognitive capacity. Ontological claims are claims with truth value, and they are
claims about some aspect of natural phenomena. They must be evaluated by
determining as fully as possible whether they are true, not simply whether
they work. Of course they may or may not work, but that will depend in
large measure on their truth.[16]

The principle of ordinality, in any case, does not commit us to a pragmatic conception of knowledge. I take it, for example, that to claim as
Buchler does that "the categories of my general ontology . . . stand for
being of *any* kind, and they are *designed* to do so," means that the categories describe nature in ways which rule out alternative descriptions.[17] Thus,
if it is true that "whatever is, in whatever way, is a natural complex," then
different categorial descriptions, which in this case include virtually the

entire history of philosophy, are to some degree false. (MNC 1) General ontology is a descriptive enterprise, though it is also prescriptive in that ontological categories are the conceptual tools necessary for further inquiry. It is necessary though not sufficient for a general ontology that one develop a coherent system of categories. The enterprise of general ontology is, at least, a species of inquiry. It may also be exhibitive and functional, but in so far as it is assertive it seeks knowledge which, in relation to less general disciplines, can contribute to an accurate understanding of nature. Thus it is possible to claim both that an ontological proposition has truth value, that "categories stand for being of *any* kind," and that "the work the categories do is their justification."[18] Categories function successfully to the extent that they are true. Their "work" is their justification in that their success is evidence of their truth, not a criterion of it. Furthermore, the relationality of complexes no more implies methodological pluralism than it does metaphysical pluralism. Complexes have whatever relations they have, they are located in whatever orders they are located. Some categorial accounts of the general characteristics of nature capture those relations and ordinal locations more adequately, fully, sensitively and fruitfully than others. If the goal of inquiry is to understand nature as adequately, fully, sensitively and fruitfully as possible, then a methodological pluralism must be abandoned in favor of the view that some positions fulfill that goal better than others. I have been arguing throughout that an ordinal materialism is just such a position.

These considerations have not exhausted the relevant issues. A more thorough study would need to investigate several additional questions, two of which stand out. The first is explicitly ontological. One of the conceptual virtues of materialism is its recognition that natural phenomena undergo processes and development which under certain circumstances engender novel complexes and orders. An adequate ontology should be able to elucidate this general trait of natural complexes by virtue of its categorial structure. To the extent that it is currently articulated, ordinality is not yet able to do this. The categories of prevalence and alescence acknowledge both the continuity and modification of complexes, but they do not articulate the general character of complexes which accounts for development. If it is an aspect of the orders of nature that they produce qualitative novelty, then we need an understanding of this at the categorial level. For example, dialectical materialists argue that phenomena are constituted by contradictory traits, and the tension generated by such contradictions is what generates change and novelty. There remain conceptual difficulties with this view, but it is an example of an attempt to articulate, at a most general level, traits of natural phenomena which help us understand the general processes which characterize them.[19]

The second issue which most obviously demands further consideration concerns the character of knowledge. The ordinal conception of knowledge is an aspect of the theory of judgment, and the relation of this general perspective to a materialist understanding of knowledge needs to be considered. In so far as the theory of judgment presupposes the categories of the general ontology, it meets at least a minimal requirement of materialism, which is that our understanding of nature not be derived from our conception of human activity. The more detailed relations of a materialist view of knowledge as reflecting objective traits of nature and the view embedded in an ordinal theory of judgment, however, is yet to be explored.

It will be useful to conclude by way of a summary of the argument which has been developed here. The point has been to suggest that an ordinal materialism is not only possible but also desirable. The explication of this claim has taken two forms, the first indicating specific ways in which ordinality enriches the materialist perspective, and the second pursuing those respects in which materialism requires a redrawing of the implications of ordinality. With respect to the first stage, there are several aspects of ordinality which allow and enhance materialism. The first is that natural complexes are objectively determinate. Ordinality recognizes that the natural definition of complexes is not a function of their discrimination, but further it accounts for the fact that even those complexes which are related to human processes are objectively determinate as well. Location in the orders of knowledge, or perception, or invention does not exhaust the relational structure and integrities of a complex. Thus complexes which are objects of knowledge or human products are also related to other complexes and objective processes. Ordinality further accounts for the objectivity of lawful regularity through its approach to the ontological status and relations of possibility and actuality. The most significant advantage of ordinality for materialism, however, is its ability to avoid reductionism through the categorial alternatives to traditional conceptions of substance and ontological simples. An understanding of natural complexes as relational and ordinal opens the way for an understanding of natural development and qualitative novelty for which traditional materialist categories cannot account.

In other respects, however, materialism requires the revision of some conceptions which have been associated with ordinality. One of the definitive characteristics of materialism is the view that among the orders of nature, the material order is primary. This does not mean that matter is more real, exclusively efficacious, an unanalyzable substance, or exhaustive of natural complexes. It means, rather, that the material order is "less dependent" than other orders of nature in that it is a condition of their prevalence, and thus is primary not absolutely but generally. If we exclude the various forms of overt idealism, the only alternative to the view that the material order is primary is one or another form of pluralism. Metaphysical pluralism is the view that there is a plurality of natural orders, but no general hierarchy or priority among them. The primary problem with this view, however, is that without an understanding of the general character of the integration of orders, systematic inquiry and knowledge is impossible because adequate and sufficiently determinate theory would be impossible. Ordinality, however, does not necessarily imply metaphysical pluralism. Furthermore, the view that the relationality of complexes implies the appropriateness of any number of otherwise inconsistent ontological systems requires that ontology be given a pragmatist bent, which in the end conflates truth with utility. Since ontology is both descriptive and prescriptive, it cannot be "pragmatized" without sacrificing too much. But since ordinality does not require a methodological pluralism, it remains both possible and desirable to pursue an explicit ordinal materialism.

Notes

1. I would like to thank Kathleen Wallace, Armen Marsoobian and Robert S. Corrington for their helpful comments on an earlier version of this paper.

2. Justus Buchler and John Herman Randall, Jr., *Philosophy: An Introduction* (New York: Barnes and Noble Books, 1942) revised edition 1971, p. 244.

3. I use the term "contemporary materialism" here to cover a range of views. Several versions of materialism have emerged in the analytic tradition over the past thirty years. Representative works include J. J. C. Smart, *Philosophy and Scientific Realism* (London: Routledge & Kegan Paul, 1963); Paul Feyerabend, "Materialism and the Mind-Body Problem," *Review of Metaphysics* 17:1, (1963), pp. 49–66; Richard Rorty, "Mind-Body Identity, Privacy, and Categories," *Review of Metaphysics* 19:1, (1965), pp. 24–54; D. M. Armstrong, *A Materialist Theory of Mind* (London: Routledge & Kegan Paul, 1968). The various views represented by these works and others have all tended to embrace a reductionism of some kind. The materialism I wish to defend differs in important ways from these other recent materialisms. For a recent attempt to develop materialism in a way which explicitly avoids some of the traditional shortcomings, see Joseph Margolis, *Persons and Minds* (Boston: D. Reidel Publishing Co., 1978), and his "Constraints on the Metaphysics of Culture," *Review of Metaphysics* 39:4, (June 1986), pp. 655–673.

The most systematically developed form of contemporary materialism is the tradition of Dialectical Materialism. There is unfortunately very little material from this tradition in English, since Western European and American philosophers have tended to ignore it. This has not been the case, however, in much of the rest of the world. For representative works in translation, see M. E. Omelyanovsky, ed., *Lenin and Modern Natural Science* (Moscow: Progress Publishers, 1978), and Igor Naletov, *Alternatives to Positivism* (Moscow: Progress Publishers, 1984). For a provocative discussion of ontological issues concerning the relation between the material and the ideal see, in Russian, D. I. Dubrovsky, *Problema Idealnogo* (Moskva: Mysl Publishers, 1983). Dubrovsky comments, in English, on recent materialism in the West in "From 'Scientific Materialism' to 'Emergent Materialism'," *Soviet Studies in Philosophy* 27:1, (1988), pp. 51–76.

4. This last point means, of course, that I am not attempting to describe the views held by Buchler or any other advocate of an ordinal ontology. It will become clear, in fact, that ordinal materialism diverges from at least some of the perspectives of others, including Buchler. The point is to develop the insights of ordinality in ways which seem to me to be appropriate and fruitful.

5. Roy Wood Sellars, "Why Naturalism and Not Materialism," *Philosophical Review* 36, (1927), pp. 216–225, reprinted in W. Preston Warren, ed., *Principles of Emergent Realism* (St. Louis, Mo.: Warren H. Green, Inc., 1970), p. 132.

6. MNC 101. See "List of Abbreviations" for Buchler's works, p. xiii–xiv.

7. The term "contour," as it is used here, is a category of Buchler's ordinal ontology. It means the totality and interrelation of the ordinal locations of a complex. Other technical terms to which I will have recourse also require brief explanation. The first is the principle of ontological parity, by which Buchler means that no complex is more real in any sense than any other complex. Second are the pair of terms, prevalence and alescence. A complex prevails in that it maintains traits, that is, "it is restrictive and exclusive of other complexes." (MNC 53) If a complex is prevalent in so far as it excludes traits from its contour, then it is alescent in so far as it admits traits into its contour. (MNC 56) By the alescence of a complex Buchler means "the introduction of some different integrity within the contour of that complex." (MNC 72) An integrity is an ordinal location of the complex.

8. Roy Wood Sellars, "Is Naturalism Enough?" *Journal of Philosophy* 41, (1944), pp. 533–544, reprinted in Warren, ed., op. cit., pp. 140–150; Abraham Edel, "Naturalism and Ethical Theory," in Yervant Krikorian, ed., *Naturalism and the Human Spirit* (New York: Columbia University Press, 1944), pp. 65–95; John Dewey, Sidney Hook, and Ernest Nagel, "Are Naturalists Materialists?" in Sidney Morgenbesser, ed., *Dewey And His Critics* (New York: The Journal of Philosophy, Inc., 1977), pp. 385–400.

9. Buchler and Randall, op. cit., p. 210.

10. See, for example, Beth J. Singer, *Ordinal Naturalism* (Lewisburg, Pa.: Bucknell University Press, 1983), pp. 210–211.

11. See Justus Buchler, OCW 555–579, in MNC [1989] 224–259, and PIN 157–168, in MNC [1989] 260–281.

12. Singer, op. cit., p. 210.

13. For another discussion of ordinality and pluralism see, Robert S. Corrington, "Naturalism, Measure and the Ontological Difference," *Southern Journal of Philosophy* 23:1, (1985), pp. 19–32.

14. Kathleen Wallace, "Making Worlds or Making Categories," *Journal of Speculative Philosophy* 2:4, (1988), pp. 322–327.

15. While Wallace does not explicitly advocate a pragmatic understanding of general ontology, it seems to me that such an understanding is implicit in the methodological approach she does advocate. For an explicit formulation of a "pragmatic" understanding of ontology see, Sandra B. Rosenthal, *Speculative Pragmatism* (Amherst: The University of Massachusetts Press, 1986) and Rosenthal, "Third Alternative: Speculative Pragmatism," *The Journal of Speculative Philosophy* 2:4, (1988), pp. 312–317.

16. A detailed account of the shortcomings of a pragmatic approach would be too lengthy to develop here. I have attempted to sketch the problem in my "Pragmatism as Idealism," *Journal of Speculative Philosophy* 2:4, (1988), pp. 317–322.

17. Justus Buchler, "Reply to Anton: Against 'Proper' Ontology," *The Southern Journal of Philosophy* 14:1, (Spring 1976), p. 87.

18. Ibid., p. 85, in MNC [1989] 201.

19. For a recent discussion of issues concerning the nature of contradiction as an ontological category see Erwin Marquit, Philip Moran and Willis H. Truitt, eds., *Dialectical Contradictions: Contemporary Marxist Discussions* (Minneapolis, MN: Marxist Educational Press, 1982).

Part Three

Systematic Extensions and Applications

Introduction to Part Three

The nine essays in this section fruitfully explore some applications of ordinal metaphysics and expand upon Buchler's general categorial framework. In each case, an effort is made to show how the ordinal perspective enables us to transform some of the more recalcitrant or limited perspectives of the tradition. Ordinality is seen to provide illumination about the problems of relativism, the nature of art, dream material, the nature of community, and God (the divine natures). Such systematic extensions of ordinal metaphysics may argue or assume that some of the key concepts of ordinality need to become modified or altered to serve new interests, yet the commitment to ordinality remains central.

Lipman, in "Natural Obligation, Natural Appropriation," writes a meditative elaboration upon the Buchlerian claim that "Man is born in a state of natural debt." (NJ 3) He traces the implications of a deepened sense of naturalism upon a philosophic characterization of the nature of the human process. Unlike contemporary existentialist or pragmatist conceptions, the source of the human appropriation of nature does not solely lie within the human, whether it be in consciousness or transactional problem solving. For Lipman there are two co-equal modes of appropriation: production and extraction. Nature both acts upon and acts through the human. It has been the unfortunate tendency of most modern philosophy, even when claiming to be overtly naturalistic, to overemphasize the role of production in its characterization of the human process. Taking up Buchler's insight that " 'activity' is best regarded as drawn from the individual rather than contributed by him," (TGT 61) Lipman explores its implications for a theory of the human process. For such a theory to be truly naturalistic it must place equal emphasis upon the coercive and extractive character of the person *as* nature and *in* nature.

Cahoone, in "Relativism and Metaphysics: On Justus Buchler and Richard Rorty," argues that Rorty's various critiques of metaphysics as an enterprise do not hit the mark when applied to Buchler's ordinal metaphysics. Buchler envisions a metaphysics that is equally critical of foundationalisms and equally open to the novel and divergent. From this emerges a new definition of rationality and reason that moves beyond the paradigm of conversation toward a deepened sense of conceptual encompassment. Thus, Buchler's perspective is held to provide much wider contexts of intelligibility within which Rorty's discourse relativism can function in a more self-consciously provincial manner.

Richards, in a justly famous analysis of *The Main of Light,* "The Assertive, the Active, and the Exhibitive," carefully traces out the larger implications of ordinal metaphysics and the theory of judgment for our understanding of poetry. In particular, he draws attention to Buchler's correlation of judgment and utterance as they relate to the appreciation of poetry.

Garrett, in "Reading Poems with Buchler," takes issue with Richards on the status of general theories as they apply to poetry. In particular, he insists that the general concepts of "sense of prevalence" and "sense of parity" do not illuminate specific features of a poem such as meter, stress, cadence, and typography. He works through some of the same poetic material cited and analyzed by Buchler to show what he considers to be some of the difficulties entailed in applying a generic theory to given poems.

Marsoobian, in "Reference, Interpretation, and Articulation," uses Buchler's theory of communication to show the limitations both of Goodman's referential theory of the arts, which he holds to be dyadic in nature, and of Danto's interpretive view of the arts. He argues that semantically based theories of meaning privilege the mode of assertive judgment and thereby make it difficult to understand the more basic exhibitive dimension of works of art. In contrast to "interpretation," Marsoobian stresses the concept of the "articulation of a perspective."

Wachter, in "Exhibitive Judgment and Freud: Toward a New Interpretation of Dreams," uses Buchler's theory of exhibitive judgment to reconstruct Freud's theory of dream material. She argues that dreams are spontaneous exhibitive judgments and not, as Freud would argue, distortions of assertive judgments. She applies the concept of exhibitive judgment to Freud's own "R" dream to show how an exhibitive analysis brings us closer to the actual dream material. Dream analysis is seen as a form of query. She holds that Freud's approach is reductive and that it relies too much on the distinction between latent and manifest contents.

Campbell, in "Buchler's Conception of Community," contrasts the "honorific" and "eulogistic" communal theories of Royce and Dewey to the more "descriptive" theory of Buchler. He argues that Buchler's metaphysical framework makes it possible to develop a more generic account of communal life in that it avoids making normative distinctions, at least on the metaphysical level, between good and bad forms of community. Yet, such a generic analysis still leaves us with profound questions about the perennial human striving for normative communities and the means for their attainment, issues addressed with great insight by Royce and Dewey.

Hare and Ryder, in their joint article "Buchler's Ordinal Metaphysics and Process Theology," are concerned with showing ways in which ordinal metaphysics can shed light on the nature of God. Hare, in particular, wishes to show how the concept of "proception" can be applied to the divine life. Ryder takes issue with the traditional notion of *creatio ex nihilo* and argues that God, as a natural complex, cannot be the creator of the innumerable orders of nature.

Corrington, in "Ordinality and the Divine Natures," extends the ordinal perspective in order to develop a conception of the four divine dimensions. The first divine dimension pertains to God's sheer embeddedness within the orders of nature and is manifest in the fragmented powers of origin. The second divine dimension also pertains to God's locatedness within the world, that is, to God as a natural complex, but is manifest in the fragmented powers of expectation. In the third divine dimension, God is not a natural complex, but is akin to the "providingness" (*natura naturans*) that sustains all orders against non-being. In the fourth divine dimension, God is eternally self-surpassable in the face of the "encompassing." This analysis of the divine natures requires, among other things, some modification of the concepts of weak and strong relevance.

Together, these essays show the continuing growth of a distinctively ordinal perspective as it enters into more areas of profound interest to the human process. Further areas of query suggest themselves. Buchler, while not using the vocabulary of phenomenology, remains sensitive to the traits of experience (or, in his reconstruction "proception") and provides a larger conceptual setting within which experience can be located. A dialogue between ordinal metaphysics and phenomenology would make it possible to explore more fully just how the human process enters into intentional meaning horizons, and renders them available to the community of interpreters. There are striking parallels between some of Buchler's conceptions and those of Heidegger.[1] In particular, the commensurate concepts of "throwness" (Heidegger) and "natural debt" (Buchler) point to the sheer embeddedness of the human process within the innumerable orders of nature. Both Buchler and Heidegger attack what Heidegger calls the ontotheological conception of metaphysics in an effort to find a distinctive means for probing into the most pervasive traits of the world. Buchler's analysis of the concept of "the World" and his understanding of the basic ordinality of nature bear strong resemblance to Heidegger's understanding of world-hood.

Process metaphysics has long argued that its categories are the most fruitful for analyzing the divine natures and the divine life. Ordinal naturalism, while reticent to speak directly about God, can provide a much more compelling conceptual framework within which philosophical theology can be reconstructed to better illuminate the divine. Process theology needs to take heed of a perspective that contains the same longing for conceptual encompassment. The conceptual portrayal of God that can emerge from this dialogue may well be of value to the divine life itself.[2]

Finally, ordinal naturalism needs to be brought into intersection with postmodern perspectives that would challenge the status and role that Buchler gives to metaphysics and general ontology. The concepts of identity and difference need to be freed from their polemical contexts and refined in ways that will enhance our understanding of the more elusive traits of the world. This means that the concepts of textuality and interpretation need to be relocated in more pervasive orders of relevance and meaning thereby empowering hermeneutic theory for a more generic portrayal of the horizonal powers of the world.

—*RSC*

Notes

1. For an analysis of ordinal naturalism and its incorporation of Heidegger's understanding of the ontological difference, see "Naturalism, Measure, and the Ontological Difference," by Robert S. Corrington, *The Southern Journal of Philosophy*, 2:1, (1985), pp. 19–32.

2. For an attempt to challenge process thought from the ordinal perspective, see "Toward a Transformation of Neo-classical Theism," by Robert S. Corrington, *International Philosophical Quarterly*, 27:4, (1987), pp. 393–408.

Natural Obligation, Natural Appropriation

Matthew Lipman

> Man is born in a state of natural debt.
>
> —*Buchler*

Our earliest discoveries of nature reveal to us our natural obligations, obligations which possess a primordial and foundational character, for they antedate our births and accompany and direct us to our deaths. Alive, we are committed to courses of behavior or to the achievement of satisfactions which we have no choice but to pursue. Insistent and urgent demands press upon us, the goals and deadlines of innovative, as well as of routine existence. As these demands are inexorable and can never wholly be satisfied, incompleteness and unfulfillment come to be characteristic of man's natural condition. Far from being "unnatural," inadequacy, impotence, and failure are among the most natural things in the world.

When we say that nature obliges, we are being appropriately ambiguous. Nature is both compelling and compelled, subservient and coercive. Insofar as it can compel us to discharge our obligations, nature is sovereign. Such sovereignty, of course, is not a contingent matter, nor is natural obligation a contractual affair. Being obligated is intimately involved in being human, and since nature is in a position to enforce its mandates, being human involves susceptibility to natural coercion as well as to natural indebtedness and requiredness.

In different contexts, this requiredness takes on different forms. In one instance we see it as moral obligation; in a second, as esthetic obligation; in a third, as logical obligation. There is no need to search for a natural basis for these obligations: they are already natural, for they are simply exemplifications of natural obligations in general.

A metaphysical pathology might concern itself with the various types of inadequate responses to natural obligations. Discussions of the "inability to develop one's constructive potentialities," or the "failure to realize one's ideal self," may suggest that the recognition of indebtedness brings on feelings of guilt. At any rate, this implication is apparent in the writings of Heidegger and Fromm. But it would also be possible to follow up the concept of natural obligation by examining its consequences in terms of the ways in which indebtedness is met or discharged. And if we pursue this line of inquiry, we find that in whatever manner a debt is discharged, it is fundamentally an instance of appropriation. Thus, the same necessity which imposes obligations on man may appropriate from him what is situationally required.

It should be noted that indebtedness is a natural, rather than a specifically human characteristic. We speak of man the debtor, but even if we referred to him as creditor, the fact of indebtedness would remain. For instance, a paucity of opportunities may manifest itself in terms of a surplus of human abilities or energy. Such a situation is nevertheless experienced as incompleteness, unfulfillment, or lack, just as is the situation in which the human being is impotent in the face of unavoidable challenges or invitations. The fact of incompleteness or precariousness remains, although at different times different factors may be held responsible. Whether we call the feeling of incompleteness "void" or "emptiness" or "nothingness," it is clear that its stimulus can be human or non-human, that its intensity can rise to anguish of tragic proportions, and that the behavior consequent upon it may diminish but can hardly eliminate the incompleteness and need, the imbalance and precariousness of the human situation itself.

Natural appropriation consists of those modes by which one's world compels the discharging of natural obligations. Where indebtedness takes the form of man exigent and his world deficient, we may speak of human appropriation. The modes of natural appropriation are production and extraction, while those of human appropriation are assimilation and irruption. Obviously the former modes are issues or emanations; the latter are absorptions or engrossments.

We can roughly distinguish production from extraction by noting that, in production, nature acts coercively through man, while in extraction, it acts coercively upon him. Extraction is peremptory, imperative, and undisguised. But in production man is manipulated, for it occurs in a manner which persuades him that the initiative is his own; it is subtle and indirect, often revealing nature as artful and designing.

The varieties of appropriation are phases of the ebb and flow of natural activity. For example, a nursing mother is productive of milk, which the child assimilates after having extracted it or after having had it irrupt within him. Analogous processes are involved when a confession is extracted by logic, persuasion, or torture, or when a painting is commissioned.

Extraction is coerciveness which, acting upon an individual, forces him to act, to assert, or to arrange. Production is coerciveness which, acting through an individual, likewise forces him to carry out active, assertive, or ordering forms of behavior. As it is customary to refer to the result of production as a product, we may similarly designate the outcome of extraction as an extract. Both terms may of course be employed to refer to the same object. A servile gesture can be produced, as by an actor in a play, or extracted, as by a master. A sigh may well-up within us or be drawn out of us, and we may gasp because of overeating or because of a breathtaking sunset.

Once we recognize the significance of existential indebtedness, we can perhaps acknowledge that the concept of man as debtor is at least as fundamental as that of man as producer. Production and extraction stand on equal footing as dual modes of that natural appropriation by means of which our basic obligations are discharged. Modern philosophy has tended to exaggerate the role of production, by emphasizing such factors as "creativity," "originality," "initiative," and "expression." This tendency has been rightly criticized by Buchler:

> Activity which would ordinarily be ascribed to a positive impulse is often better interpreted as a response than as a drive, as a struggle to stand up rather than as a readiness to run. For the most part, 'activity' is best regarded as drawn from the individual rather than as contributed by him. (TGT 61)

This is not to imply that man, in the face of natural coercion, is completely docile and acquiescent. Better to say that he is yielding. He yields to nature, giving in and giving up, bowing to it and yet bringing forth, as yield or crop, some appropriate issue. Only in the most rudimentary cases is the issue necessitated by a purely internal drive or need. The brute, far from being "more natural" than any other being, is less involved in nature (insofar as his behavior is determined by his individual organism alone) than one who is also susceptible to more remote and pervasive influences.

It is interesting to observe the historical background of the conviction that what human beings make and say and do are products of drives and impulses, rather than the meeting of natural obligations or the response to natural imperatives. For the purpose of envisaging man primarily as a producer was originally honorific and polemical. An earlier view had been contemptuous of man, and had portrayed him as basically inert or lazy, driven to act only by urgent needs or appetites, or forced to produce by external coercion. Men did not naturally love to work or to invent: they did so only out of necessity. This apparent derogation of human dignity was subsequently subjected to bitter criticism. Men were now asserted to be productive by their very nature, instinctively workmanlike, although they could be corrupted by faulty social institutions. Laziness was not man's normal state but a consequence of the worker's alienation from participation in modern industrial life. The human organism was now described as a reservoir of energy, capable of being reduced to frustration or inertia by a stultifying environment, but fundamentally dynamic and active. Today we can see that productivity is dependent upon conditions which are highly complex and often obscure, and that it is usually more fitting to describe human behavior as responsive rather than initiative, as evoked by one's world rather than as expressed by one's self. We can also recognize more clearly now the significance of extraction as a process coordinate with production and frequently cooperative with it.

It is common to think of the productive individual as perhaps ill-adjusted to his society, but certainly well-adjusted in regard to nature itself. This belief is prevalent because it is related to the common belief that man is productive "by nature," or that he can have an efficient and balanced function in nature, characterized by spontaneity, fecundity, and absence of need. It is taken for granted that perpetual incompleteness does not have to be indigenous to the human situation. Yet incompleteness and precariousness may well be ineradicable factors of human existence (since civilization may multiply the obstacles to satisfaction at a faster rate than it diminishes them). Moreover, a man's natural obligation need not diminish proportionately to his productivity; on the contrary, it may well increase.

It would be incorrect to infer from what has been said that production and extraction, the two modes of natural appropriation, are categorized as evaluations rather than as descriptions. How these processes are appraised does not affect their status as natural issuances. At its worst, of course, extraction may disclose itself to be predatory and exploitative. In the face of such extortion or rapacity, man is victim, man is prey. But extraction similarly comprises processes which are subject to praise or condonation. Natural obligations arise in situations whose character may be esteemed or deplored, and our efforts to behave in a manner called for (i.e., appropriate to and appropriated by such situations) may be attended by consequences which we find harmful or beneficial. Thus acting, arranging, and asserting may be exacted from us by cooperative situations as well as competitive ones, and the need for retaliation can appear just as obliging as the need for justice.

Every extract, like every product, is a judgment. That is, it discloses an individual version of one's world, or of some aspect of it, and in so doing, discloses an aspect of oneself. It is a discovery of possibility and an invention of actuality. Every issue is a judgment by the individual and of the individual. By him, because through it he pronounces upon his significant involvements. Of him, because each issue throws open to the world a characteristic or symptom of the individual, so that it represents a judgment of oneself, and invites the judgment of others.

Extractive processes therefore fall into the same three classifications of judgment as those which, in Buchler's writings, are referred to as assertive, active and exhibitive. Consequently we can take note of assertive, active and exhibitive extraction.

Confessions, acknowledgments, admissions, all of these are assertive judgments in the form of verbal responses (either true or false) to demanding situations. It is clear that our utterances are solicited by countless environmental requisitions and invitations. If man is considered productive when, through inquiry, he puts questions to nature, then nature must be extractive when it demands responses of man. Assertive extraction is, in fact, a kind of natural interrogation. If many of our assertions seem to be made without duress, it is because circumstantial coercion has been transformed into personal compulsion, and utterance perseverates of its own inertia. Or we may become so perceptive of the structure of natural interrogation that we develop an acute prolepsis, anticipating demands before they are imposed upon us, arriving at decisions and assertions in advance of the development of obligations that would require them and call them forth. In any case, when nature holds us answerable, we are obliged to reply. Hence our responsibility does not rest on our natural responsiveness, but conversely, it is because nature holds us responsible to our obligations that we respond as we do.

It is customary to use the term "conduct" to refer to behavior that is susceptible to moral evaluation. The term seems to suggest the productive aspect of moral behavior: initiative and self-control are strongly implied. One conducts oneself, deports oneself, behaves oneself. But action can also be conductive in the sense that it represents the active carrying out or discharging of natural obligations. Does this mean that conductive extraction is immune to moral appraisal? Certainly not, since ethical judgment relates to the fittingness or appropriateness of actions, as well as to the investigation into the degree of initiative exercised by the agents of those actions. Moreover, the assignment of natural responsibility does not logically necessitate the assignment of moral responsibility, for it is possible to be naturally responsible without being morally responsible.

Extraction has perhaps been most overlooked in the area of exhibitive judgment. Artistry and production are frequently taken as synonymous. The most honorific categories are those such as "creativity," "originality," and "expression," which are presumed to reflect the artist's innerness, uniqueness, and initiative. (However, extractive processes are customarily acknowledged to be at work in the case of "interpretive" artistry: It is readily enough granted that a conductor evokes music from his instrumentalists, or that an actor elicits fear, pity, or applause from his audience.) We have tended to misjudge the extent to which the discoveries and inventions of art are responsive rather than initiative. Perhaps it may be said that the freedom of art lies not in any ability to construct *ex nihilo,* nor in a supposed absence from coercion, nor in the capacity to alter one's responses at will, but in the skill with which one recognizes the needs and requirements of a situation, organizes the sequence in which those obligations are to be faced and met, and controls the conditions under which artistic responses take place. Especially noteworthy is the degree to which artistic responses elicited by nature in turn demand responses to themselves, in a progressively evocative sequence which ultimately issues in a work of art at times utterly remote from and irrelevant to the natural complex whose coerciveness was first encountered. Moreover, artistic behavior involves the discharging of a multiple indebtedness, for if an artist is gripped by his subject matter, he is controlled even more by the quality and requiredness of the developing work of art, and by his need to conform to the stringencies of the medium in which he operates.

It may be thought that our admissions, our conduct, or our orderings are extracted from us only on the occasional development of existential problems. But this would be incorrect. There is a continuity to requiredness which is the foundation of the needfulness of individually problematic situations. Nature is subtly and persistently evocative, manifesting a quizzical, enigmatic reserve which often functions as a powerful heuristic to inquiry and other forms of discovery. And just as the human need to investigate and pronounce upon the world is not sporadic, neither is it an innate disposition which would manifest itself under any circumstances. It is rather the pervasive enigmaticity of nature which elicits our inquisitiveness and stimulates our curiosity, as it is the precariousness of nature which commands our doubt and our constructive responsiveness.

If nature functions extractively then, if it is inquisitorial and demanding, surely it must be an over-simplification to identify experience merely with production or productivity. Too frequently we have interpreted experience as a matter of individual initiative and enterprise. It has even been assumed that one organizes experiences as an entrepreneur organizes corporations. Life should not merely be lived; it should be promoted. The error here, once again, is the assignment of initiative to man and man alone. Extractive processes are exemplifications not of human initiative, but of human initiation: the initiation of man by nature and into nature. If the productive interpretation of experience tends to identify it with experiment, with problem-solving, or, more grossly, with "trial-and-error," it is likely that for man seen as natural debtor, to exist is to be tried. To have an experience is to have, to some extent, a trying experience, for man is always, himself, on trial. This is equally true of experimentation, for just as judgment is always reflexive, doubling back on oneself, so trying out alternative modes of behavior places in jeopardy the experimenter, and makes him subject to appraisal.

Man has been described by Buchler as an animal that cannot help judging in more than one mode. For the judgments man makes in any one mode are usually not exhaustive: the plurality of modes of judgment is a reflection of the fact that nature is susceptible to various types of appraisal and pronouncement. In short: nature is not univocal but equivocal—hence a plurality of modes of judgment is possible. And nature is not passive but coercive; hence judgment becomes necessary.

Notes

1. See "List of Abbreviations" for Buchler's works, p. xiii–xiv.

Relativism and Metaphysics:
On Justus Buchler and Richard Rorty

Lawrence E. Cahoone

A comparison of Justus Buchler's systematic philosophy and Richard Rorty's recent work might seem unnecessary. Buchler is a metaphysician; Rorty rejects the legitimacy of metaphysics. Buchler seeks the generic traits of existence; Rorty denies the cogency of that search. Buchler's system would seem a prime example of the foundational "Philosophy" (with a capital "P") that Rorty deconstructs in favor of the "informed dilettantism" and "frank ethnocentrism" of "philosophy" (with a lower case "p").[1] The Philosopher and the philosopher ought to have little in common.

This conclusion would be hasty. Buchler's system is an unusual one, at cross–purposes with the systems at which Rorty's critique is aimed, so that this critique strikes Buchler a glancing blow. Rorty is a relativist (his protestations to the contrary), but Buchler remarks that his own system supports an "objective relativism." Rorty's attack on the differentiation of higher, transcendental knowledge and reality from lower, empirical truth is answered by Buchler's own principle of ontological parity. The philosopher and the Philosopher may have more in common than first appears. And because both deal with crucial questions in a radical way, the comparison will be instructive, although only a few points of contact between the two can be explored here.

I

Rorty's critique is by now well-known.[2] He argues that much of that literary tradition called philosophy embodies an illegitimate intellectual project (Philosophy), which must be rejected, and a more modest, legitimate form of philosophy (philosophy). Without going into detail, I will summarize Rorty's attack on Philosophy as a rejection of foundationalism, metaphysics and epistemology.

(1) *Foundationalism.* Rorty rejects the notion of Philosophy as an autonomous discipline or activity which provides the necessary justification for the rest of culture by discovering an ahistorical, certain, universal, "neutral matrix for inquiry." For Rorty philosophy is *not* an autonomous discipline. It is not capable of providing epistemic justification for other cultural activities. We cannot discover an ahistorical matrix for inquiry, since there is no such thing. Philosophy does not "found" or "ground" anything. What is central to Rorty's anti-foundationalism *per se* is an attack on philosophy's vaunted position in culture. The *reasons that* philosophy's vaunted position is untenable have to do with the metaphysical and epistemological *content* of philosophy.

(2) *Metaphysics.* Rorty rejects the cogency of the search for ultimate things, categories, the "generic traits of existence," the inquiry into the nature of normative concepts, any claims regarding the ahistorical nature of reality. This includes any naturalistic metaphysics, which Rorty regards as falling into the same problems as any traditional idealistic or transcendental metaphysics. It does *not* include Sellars' attempt to "see how things, in the largest possible sense of the term, hang together, in the largest possible sense of the term," a project that is perfectly legitimate according to Rorty, however "bland."[3] This exclusion clarifies Rorty's critique: the search for what is universal, necessary or prior in the order of being, is metaphysics, while the Sellarsian inquiry into the hanging-together of whatever, is not.

(3) *Epistemology.* This is, as we will see, the heart of Rorty's position. He argues that all attempts to explain the nature of truth or knowledge as correspondence to reality, or to produce cases of certain, universal or ahistorical knowledge are doomed to failure. They are doomed because they ultimately hinge on trying to say how all saying, all language, relates to or "hooks onto" nonlinguistic reality, which would presume some nonlinguistic vantage point, "neutral" with respect to all competing theories, paradigms, languages and cultures. But there is no such vantage point, because any checking of a theory or the beliefs embedded in a language against reality presumes some theory or language in which the checking must be carried out. As a result, such attempts produce no useful results: the theory of truth and knowledge does not help us know true things about the world. Correspondence "works" for "small routine assertions"—we know what it means for the statement "the cup is in my hand" to correspond to reality. But with the "large debatable assertions" of Philosophy—like "All is One"—we can make no sense of correspondence.

Before proceeding with the discussion of these criticisms a related theme indicated in my title needs explication. That theme is relativism. What is it? And is Rorty a relativist? The answer will be yes, although the type of relativist he is needs to be specified.

II

In a paper published in 1979 Rorty denied that he or anyone else is a relativist. He did so by defining relativism quite narrowly as the view that "every belief on a certain topic, or perhaps about *any* topic, is as good as every other." (COP 166–67) He immediately refined this view to distinguish between "metaphilosophical" relativism, the view that competing philosophies are as good as each other, and "real theory" relativism, the view that any theory is as good as any other. It is the latter which can claim no adherents; Rorty accepts the terms of the former, and denies that metaphilosophical relativism affects our realistic and legitimate concern for the acceptability of scientific theories, political theories, and other "real" theories.

Rorty makes his position even more clear. Absent any way of checking the correspondence of the most basic beliefs embedded in any discourse to nonlinguistic reality, the criteria of warranted belief-acceptance are pragmatic, hence consensual, hence ethnocentric. "The pragmatists tell us," he tells us, "that the conversation which it is our moral duty to continue is *merely* our project, the European intellectual's form of life." (COP 172) Rorty encourages us to be "frankly ethnocentric," to admit that our criteria for inquiry and knowledge can never be justified outside of our intellectual tradition, a tradition defined by those same criteria. We should accept that "solidarity" or consensus within a tradition or community is the ultimate condition of knowledge, not "objectivity" or correspondence to reality.[4]

In order to decide whether this view is relativist, we first have to ask: What is relativism? Many types have been distinguished.[5] Literally, relativism is the view that something, or some aspect of something, is relational in nature, and so is what it is only given its relation to something else. Three broad types can be distinguished: moral, epistemological and metaphysical. The questions of this paper primarily concern epistemological relativism. The variety of types of epistemological relativism can be simplified, which does not imply that the various types are not importantly different. Two points aid this simplification.

First, beliefs, theories, concepts, perceptions or perspectives, and the "having" of them, are indeed "relative" to a great many things, but this is entirely different from the question of whether their *truth* is relative. It is the spector of a relativistic view of the *truth* of beliefs, not the existence or the *having of* beliefs, that is central to epistemological relativism. And it is this kind of relativism that is at issue for Rorty.

Second, our job will be greatly simplified if we lump perceptions, conceptions, beliefs, theories, perspectives and propositions together and consider the question of the relativistic character of their truth collectively. For my purposes, if 'truth' can be predicated of something, then it can be included in the same case. For convenience I will use only one of these items—beliefs—as representative for all, which is not to imply that the others are beliefs.

Given this, the issue of epistemological relativism is: is the truth of beliefs a relative or relational characteristic of those beliefs? This question obviously requires a further specification: relative or related to what?

That the truth or falsity of a belief is relative to reality, to the state of the world or to the state of affairs which the belief concerns, is not a problem. It is part of our notion of the truth that the truth of beliefs is relative to the states of affairs concerned, such that, if those states are not what our beliefs assert, then the beliefs are false.[6] Relativism is only an issue to the extent that the truth of beliefs is relative to *something about us*—to some characteristic, activity, state or history of those who assert, test, accept or deny the truth of beliefs—namely, human inquirers.[7]

What is it about us to which the truth of beliefs might be claimed to be relative? The most obvious factor is human nature, that is, the universal characteristics of the human species, to which could be added the general features and limitations of the environment that condition most human feeling, perceiving and knowing. The determination of the nature of these characteristics and features may be problematic and no doubt qualifies the extent and character of human knowledge.

That the truth of our beliefs is relative to human nature—a "species relativism," as it were—might prove to be the least refutable, most impregnable form of relativism. But it is by no means the most disturbing. A species relativism would place all human knowledge alongside the knowledges of other possible species of inquirers (the existence of which is yet unknown), thereby putting the adequacy of the former in question by making a cross-species comparison of validity difficult or impossible. But contemporary forms of relativism do more than impugn the validity of our beliefs relative to nonhuman inquirers we have not yet encountered: they impugn the validity of our beliefs relative to other human beings. This is a far more extensive brand of relativism, albeit no harder to contend with, than species relativism. Taking first things first, I will deal with only the former here, leaving the latter to another time and space.

Contemporary epistemological relativism focuses not on truth's relativity to universal human traits, but on its relativity to traits shared by indefinitely smaller subsets of humanity. These subsets are individuals or groups who have or share sets of beliefs, or use language in which such beliefs are embedded. Proponents of relativism, including Rorty, often equate the claims that truth is relative to a perspective, a conceptual scheme, a cultural tradition, a paradigm, or a language. This equation can create problems, since the feasibility of relativism might depend on which type of belief-set is claimed to be that-to-which truth is relative. So, for example, Davidson criticizes "conceptual scheme" relativism as nonsensical, while allowing that the truth of beliefs is relative to a language (and implying that this raises no serious relativistic problems.)[8] Rorty takes up this same issue.[9] Davidson's critical separation of conceptual and linguistic relativism is, however, beside the current point, which is to say what epistemological relativism is in general.

Ignoring for my purposes the differences between the items cited, I will refer to all of the candidates for that-about-us-to-which the truth of beliefs might be claimed to be relative with the term "discourse." A discourse may indifferently be an argument, theory, perspective, paradigm, cultural tradition or natural language. Among discourses, cultural traditions and/or natural languages (which cannot always be separated) are *"basic discourses,"* the widest, most comprehensive or most logically prior kinds of discourses. A theoretically constructed discourse—e.g. a logical argument, a scientific theory—must presuppose a natural language or cultural tradition, either because it uses terms of the latter or because its meaning is explicated within the latter. Natural languages and cultural traditions, however, presuppose no other kind of discourse for their explication or justification. The beliefs embedded in a basic discourse constitute the *"foundational set"* of beliefs for that basic discourse and for any discourse which presupposes the basic discourse.[10]

Now the position of the most important form of epistemological relativism—which I will call *"discourse relativism"*—can be stated: it is the view that the truth (or falsity) of a belief (or set of beliefs) is dependent on the relation of the belief(s) to some discourse (whatever else it is dependent on). Truth (or falsity) of belief(s) holds only with respect to, or in relation to some discourse, and need not hold with respect to other discourses (that is, there is nothing in the nature of its truth or falsity that necessitates its holding with respect to other discourses.) Under this definition, Rorty's anti-epistemological critique makes him an unrepentant relativist.

Armed with our definition of discourse relativism, we will turn in section six to the question of the validity of Rorty's argument for relativism. But first we must see whether Buchler can weather the Rortyan attack.

III

How does Buchler's system fare under Rorty's criticisms of foundationalism, metaphysics and epistemology? It is not possible to outline that system here, but the description of a few central notions will show that it evades much of the force of the attack.[11]

Buchler does not regard philosophy as providing a necessary foundation for other modes of cultural expression and investigation.

The philosophic viewpoint is not sacrosanct, and not by itself morally
better than any other form of query. It is simply a different mode of
encompassment. [12]

This view is buttressed by Buchler's refusal to make assertive judgment
more essential or important than active and exhibitive judgment to the human process and to the development of civilization.

Buchler's theory of judgment generates a profound shift in our perspective by making human acts, constructions and assertions equal as forms
of judgment. Philosophy, theory, and inquiry take their place alongside all
the arts, alongside moral action, manners, habits and every day behavior as
features of the human process. None of these elements are any more essential to the human process than any other. This means that philosophy is
continuous with the rest of culture, the rest of human judgment, indeed,
with the rest of human experiencing. Philosophy does not occupy a different
"level," although it does seek, for Buchler, the greatest possible generality,
sweep or range among forms of inquiry (to this we shall return).

The term "foundation" carries a powerful metaphor. It connotes the
basis or undergirding of a building. The philosophical significance of this
metaphor is that, while philosophy is not dependent on any other form of
inquiry and/or culture, all other forms of inquiry and/or culture are logically
and epistemologically dependent on philosophy. Philosophy alone seeks the
bedrock on which all other inquiries (or even all other forms of civilization)
are cognitively based. Five elements within this idea can be distinguished:

1. Philosophy is epistemically necessary for other inquiries; the latter would have no justification without the former.
2. Philosophy seeks to provide certainty, since foundations need,
   above all, to be stable. (If an empirical generalization in chemistry fails, we replace it. If a metaphysical or epistemological principle is faulty, all knowledge trembles.)
3. Since philosophy is prior, no other inquiry can guide philosophy
   or provide it with presuppositions.
4. Knowledge is arranged in a hierarchical system, such that some
   kinds of knowledge are fundamental, hence presupposed by other,
   subsidiary kinds (like a deductive system).
5. Philosophical inquiry and knowledge are qualitatively different
   from all other forms of inquiry (just as the foundation of a building differs from the structure it supports). It is the most general,
   or most comprehensive, or most fundamental, or most abstract

inquiry—and it seeks a different kind of knowledge, for example, knowledge of frameworks, structures, categories, or contexts that lack the particular content of subsequent, lower-level knowledge.

Rorty rejects all of these elements of the foundational metaphor. They characterize the Philosophy he subverts. Rorty denies that philosophy can do any of the things ascribed to it by the foundational metaphor.

Buchler also rejects the first four elements of the metaphor. For Buchler other forms of inquiry, query or culture do not depend on philosophic justification. There is no certainty for philosophy, or any other inquiry, to seek. Philosophy is not isolated from other forms of query, it often learns from them, for example, from poetry and literature. Knowledge is not a hierarchy proceeding from the presuppositionless to the presupposition-dependent. In short, Buchler rejects as fully as does Rorty the notion that cultural life is a hierarchic structure with philosophy providing the necessary foundation.

The last element of the foundational metaphor raises a question, however. Buchler remarks that philosophy is only a "different form of encompassment," not the truest or best form—but is it the most comprehensive? Does it seek a uniquely general form of knowledge or articulation? Is philosophy unique and, if so, in what way?

If Buchler conceives of philosophy in general, or metaphysics in particular as providing a "framework" of categories in terms of which all else is to be articulated, a framework which interprets everything else, but is not itself subject to interpretation from the standpoint of what it interprets, then he would seem to be a foundationalist in a limited but significant sense.[13] The conception of philosophy as providing the most general frameworks for inquiry or query would, for example, seem to fall prey to a version of what Davidson has called the "third dogma" of empiricism, the scheme-content distinction.[14] This would hold even if the framework is hypothetical. It is this limited but important sense of foundationalism that we must now examine.

IV

Philosophy is unique. It performs an activity not carried out by other forms of endeavor. It does seek to select features of reality, sets of ideas or categories in relation to which reality in an indefinitely wide sense can be claimed to be more fully understood or appreciated.

But an important distinction must be made. Every philosophy selects (explicitly and/or implicitly) traits of reality in terms of which or in relation to which other realities, or the rest of reality, ought to be interpreted or understood. The selected traits form the "categories" or "categorial traits" of the philosophy. The presence or absence of foundationalism hinges on this: whether the philosophy in question asserts that among all the various distinctions that obtain or could be drawn between any realities, the distinction between its chosen categorial traits and all other realities is intrinsically more significant than all other distinctions between all other realities. If a philosophy does assert this, then it is foundationalist. If it does not, then it is not.

For a nonfoundationalist philosophy, the categories, the framework, that in-relation-to-which reality gains intelligibility, on one hand, and everything else, on the other, is a purely *functional* distinction. Those features of reality which serve as categories are no more qualitatively different from the rest of reality than any set of things is from any other set. The chosen categorial features are distinct in the way that anything else may be distinct; but there is nothing in their distinction in itself that makes it in itself the most significant distinction of all. The chosen features serve a function: they are that in-relation-to-which an inquirer asserts that the widest and most significant set of things becomes most intelligible. They *function as* the scheme or framework. The terms "category," "framework," "scheme" have the unfortunate connotation of an abstract filing system, of slots into which the rest of reality is to be filed. For a nonfoundational philosophy categories are not slots; they refer to whatever functions as a point of reference.

Now, Buchler does not explicitly discuss or endorse this relativist-functionalist view. But it is a view that is inspired by, and, I would argue, is consistent with, his principles of ordinality and parity. For Buchler, "there is no final hierarchy of complexes," which implies not only that there is no final hierarchy of *all* complexes (e.g. a World-System), but that there is no final hierarchy of *any set* of complexes, where "final" means "not ordinally located and conditioned." This means that Buchler's own categories—natural complex, order, trait, prevalence, alescence, etc.— must also be considered as one set of discriminated factors of what is, a set which establishes a perspective and embodies a policy or stance in relation to which what is can be judged and articulated.

Philosophy in general and metaphysics in particular are special, but their speciality lies in their indefinitely wide range:

> Philosophy effects a distinctive realization: that the categorial struggle to emcompass structures of indefinitely greater breadth is both inevitable and valid. (TGT 81)

This indefiniteness of range does not entail the ascription of unique ontological significance to the features of reality in reference to which the philosopher seeks perspectivally to articulate what is. Simply put, systematic or comprehensive philosophy *need not* entail that categories or frameworks be treated as *foundations*. Rather, they may be treated as *functional reference points*. The result is that a philosophy, like Buchler's may be systematic in the sense of seeking a perspective from which everything can be addressed *without* being foundational. Rorty does not recognize this possibility, except insofar as he would regard it, with Sellars' definition of philosophy, trivial.

V

Buchler is a metaphysician, but an unusual one. Three features of his approach make it unusual.

The first is his principle of ontological parity, according to which nothing which is discriminated (no "natural complex"), "is more 'real,' more 'natural,' more 'genuine,' or more 'ultimate' than any other." (MNC 31) There are no higher realities, nothing more authentic than anything else, no primary substances which are more independently real than their characteristics.

The second principle, which some have called "ordinality," is that Buchler's is a *local* metaphysics. Buchler's perspective dictates that anything which is, any natural complex, stands in (is related to) a number of orders (relations among complexes). Nothing fails to be related to something such that the relations are integral to what the thing is. (This by no means implies that everything is related to everything else, or that things are just relations. Buchler emphasizes that continuity and relatedness are no more prevalent than discontinuity and unrelatedness.) Buchler gives us categories for articulating the context or locale of any thing; he does not give us an inventory of the universe, a vision of the whole. He rejects the cogency of any such vision, arguing that "the world" is not a complex, not a discriminable something. It is merely a name for the "innumerable complexes" there are. (OCW 574, in MNC [1989] 251)

The third principle is this: if things are ordinal, such that what they are is at least in some way relative to the orders in which they are located, then our experiences (for Buchler, "procepts") and judgments, which are "facts of nature" like anything else, are ordinal constituents of the things experienced and judged.

> . . . in every instance where a natural complex becomes a procept, a change takes place in the status both of the individual and the other existence involved. Two natural complexes each become modified in their total relations, and a full description of each would have to

record the role of each in a larger or newer complex of which it is an element. Thus "naive realism," "representationalism" . . . have no meaning here. On the other hand, the general approach sometimes called "objective relativism" is given support. (NJ 127–28)

A complex has an "integrity" in each order in which it is located, and all its integrities taken together are its "contour" or "gross integrity." A human individual's experience is an order (a proceptive domain), and so the procept of any experienced complex is located in that order. The procept and the complex may be either "strongly" or "weakly" related, and this may or may not be reciprocal. The proceived complex may be strongly relevant for me, hence part of my gross integrity (as part of my history of experience). If my procept of the complex is strongly relevant to the complex, then my procept is part of the complex's gross integrity.[15]

Buchler's metaphysics could legitimately be called a relativistic metaphysics. This does not mean a metaphysics which regards everything as relations. It means a metaphysics which regards every item as related to at least some other items in such a way that these relations are a constituent of it. It means a metaphysics which regards what things are as related—and since "the whole" could not be related to anything, "the whole" is not a something. Thus there is no final framework, no orders of orders, no hierarchy, no system of systems, no ultimate context for all things. And if there is no ultimate context for all things, there is no ultimate context for *any* thing.

Rorty would regard metaphysical relativism as a contradiction in terms. Buchler does seek the "generic traits of existence." This makes Buchler a metaphysician in Rorty's eyes. But Rorty does not imagine a metaphysics which is not foundationalist, does not invoke ontological priority or its own necessity, and which describes the "generic traits of existence" in purely ordinal terms. How then would Rorty factor a Buchler-like metaphysics into his categories? Rorty's options are to claim that any Buchler-like metaphysics is: a) trivial (as with Sellars); b) not a metaphysics at all, but a legitimate case of some other type of theory; or, c) a legitimate nontrivial metaphysics, thereby widening his notion of metaphysics in a Buchlerian direction, and making his critique of metaphysics *per se* into a critique of traditional or inadequate metaphysics. Which of these is reasonable?

Rorty's problem here is that the option he would presumably prefer is the least defensible. That is option a). For b) makes little sense, and c) is the capitulation he would want to avoid. But how to show that Buchler's kind of metaphysical project is trivial or "bland," as he says of Sellars? What are the criteria of triviality and nontriviality? It would seem that something can be judged trivial only from some perspective and in reference to some project. What project does Rorty have in mind, in relation to which Buchler's metaphysics would be (as Sellars is) discounted as trivial? It would seem to be the kind of metaphysics Rorty criticizes. And in a sense he is right: the Buchlerian project would probably fail to live up to whatever nontriviality criteria are implicit in the perspective of the kind of metaphysical project both Buchler and Rorty reject. But this only serves to point out that Rorty is assuming the perspective of the foundational and transcendental metaphysics he criticizes, in order to reject it. He is accepting its definition of what counts as metaphysics, and so of what is and is not trivial.

The choice for Rorty, and for us, comes to this: either we define a field of inquiry to be coextensive with the theories in that field that are invalid—thereby making the field *a priori* invalid—or we define the field more broadly to include theories that view themselves as critical responses to its traditional theories and whose validity has not been foreclosed. I will offer two reasons to prefer the latter. First, banishing Buchler-like metaphysical systems to the twilight of triviality is a blatant attempt to, as Peirce warns us, block the way of inquiry. For it is a decision *not* to inquire, a decision that theories need not be interpreted or tested. Second, this approach is historically naive. Traditions of inquiry change and progress, not only through reconception of the objects of inquiry, but through concomitant redefinition of the scope and nature of the inquiry itself. In all such changes fields of inquiry redefine continuity with their tradition: the aim of research is recast in a way that, under the new view, still captures what is now seen to be the core of the tradition. The attempt to exclude new metaphysical programs like Buchler's as trivial would deny metaphysical inquiry the right to redefine itself. Most of all, it would deny that there is any continuity between Buchler's project and that of the metaphysical tradition, which is clearly false. It would imply that by eliminating ontological priority and other notions Buchler had ceased doing ''real'' metaphysics and was in fact doing something else, whatever that might be. Such an attempt to deny continuity is reminiscent of the linguistic cure for split personality: give the patient two names and send them on their way.

VI

Rorty's most powerful and far-reaching attack on Philosophy comes in the form of his anti-epistemological argument endorsing a discourse-relativism, which claims that the truth of beliefs is relative to discourses and ultimately to foundational beliefs which cannot be justified. We must now see whether this claim is valid.

Rorty's argument for a discourse-relativism seems to be based on the following four claims:

1. The truth of any belief is relative to the truth of other beliefs (which is not to deny that it is also relative to reality).
2. For any belief, there is an ultimate, most comprehensive, logically prior set of beliefs, such that the truth of the former is relative to the truth of the latter, and there are no other beliefs to which the former's truth is relative. This set is the foundational set of beliefs embedded in the basic discourse to which justification of the belief must ultimately recur. It is the complete justificational (foundational) set of beliefs for the belief in question.
3. The truth of the foundational set of beliefs cannot be known or justified. This is because there are only three ways to attempt its justification: a) it could be shown to be derivable from a logically prior or more comprehensive set of beliefs; b) it could be justified by a different discourse, that is, one with a different foundational set of beliefs from which the foundational set of the discourse in question cannot be derived; c) its fitness or correspondence to nonlinguistic reality could be checked. The first is impossible by definition, there is no prior or more comprehensive set of beliefs from which a foundational set could be derived (if there were, then *that* set would be the foundational set). The second is impossible because a different discourse could only evaluate the original foundational set as meaningless, nonsensical or false. The third leads back to either of the first two, because the fitness of the foundational set could only be articulated in some discourse, one whose beliefs would depend for their justification on either the original foundational set (a) or a different set (b).
4. Therefore, if truth is correspondence to nonlinguistic reality, the truth of our beliefs cannot be known or justified.[16]

This argument is flawed in three ways. First, it is not true that every check of beliefs against reality presumes some discourse. Second, we know of no discrete basic discourses. Third, there are no identifiable foundational sets of beliefs in basic discourses. I will explain these in order.

First, it is not my intention, nor is it Buchler's, to defend an "intuitive realism" which claims for nonlinguistic judging a kind of validity not available to linguistic beliefs and not subject to relativistic criticism.[17] My point is not that nonlinguistic judging takes place outside of perspective; it is that perspective cannot be equated with discourse, language or cultural tradition. Perspective can be rudimentary, nonlinguistic, inarticulate—which is not to say inarticul*able*.

This point has significance. If reality is encountered and beliefs checked only within language, as the most basic kind of discourse, then that-to-which belief is relative is greatly simplified. There are not that many languages in the world. If reality is, alternately, judged in perspective and not necessarily in language, then that-to-which belief is relative is immeasurably complicated. For while most persons have but one language, they can occupy an indefinitely large number of shifting perspectives.

My second objection to Rorty's argument is that there are no discrete basic discourses on earth. We cannot make sharp distinctions between natural languages, nor between cultures. We can make rough distinctions. English is not French. But languages change and interact and adopt foreign terms. Languages overlap, as do cultural traditions. Given that languages and cultures are products of the interaction of members of a single species with similar physical environments, one would expect to find common beliefs among differing linguistic and cultural communities. And, of course, as far as we can tell, differing linguistic and cultural groups do share beliefs. This is no surprise, but it does affect Rorty's argument with respect to human beings.[18]

My third objection is the most far-reaching. It is that there are no identifiable foundational sets of beliefs in basic discourses. My claim is not that we cannot say that there are such sets because we could never recognize the existence or employment of an alternative set from the standpoint of our own. It is rather that we could never identify any foundational set, *including* one alleged to be *our own*. I say this for two reasons, one mundane, one more significant.

First the mundane. Natural languages are enormously complex and flexible. They continually change. They include in principle the possibility of norm-violating usages in metaphor, neologism and other departures. How could we ever identify a set of beliefs that is implicit in all, for example, English usage; or in all American-English, or even in all Brooklyn-American-English usage? To think that there is such a set of beliefs flies in the face of the flexibile, novelty producing and pluralistic nature of language use. And these points hold, I would argue, for cultural traditions as they do for languages.

The more significant reason for denying that there are identifiable foundational sets of beliefs is itself a relativistic one. First principles are first only in relation to those beliefs for which they are regarded as providing context or justification. There are no first principles, first beliefs, first premisses in an absolute sense: there is only the progressive articulation of sets of justifying beliefs, beliefs which serve to validate the belief(s) in question.

Rorty's discourse-relativism presumes that there are ultimate limiting contexts for justification such that the process of articulating the justifying or validating relations between beliefs must run up against a limit. His "frank ethnocentrism" requires that there be such limiting contexts which cannot themselves be justified, making all justification internal to such a context. These contexts, defined by foundational sets of beliefs, are presupposed by all other beliefs within the context, but themselves do not presuppose any other beliefs. The foundational, context defining beliefs are *independent*, not dependent on other beliefs for their justification (hence, for Rorty, unjustifiable), while all other beliefs are *dependent* for their justification on the former. In this sense, the attempt to distinguish between foundations, frameworks and ultimate contexts in a nonrelative sense is an epistemological version of the long-standing search for what is independent and nonrelational, a search characteristic of much of Western philosophy.[19]

My claim is not that we can step outside of these limiting contexts. It is that *there are no limiting contexts,* there are no ultimate stopping points for the process of giving reasons or seeking justifications for our beliefs, *there are no first principles* in an absolute sense.[20] If there is no foundational set of beliefs presupposed by all of a linguistic community's beliefs, then we can no more say that there is an unjustifiable foundational set than that there is a justifiable foundational set. The ultimate justifying context for our beliefs is not unwarranted or false, because it does not exist.

I take this to be a Peirceian and a Buchlerian point. It is Peirceian in the spirit of his denial of intuitions of "cognitions not determined by a preceding cognition." If we substitute "justifications" or "beliefs" for Peirce's "cognitions," then his denial would resemble my point.[21] It is Buchlerian in that there is no ultimate order of beliefs for all of my or my community's beliefs that is not itself located in an order. The distinction between foundation or framework and logically subsequent beliefs or content is purely relative or, in Buchler's terms, ordinally located; the distinction holds only with respect to something, like a perspective.

What lessons can be drawn from my, I hope, Buchlerian response to the question of discourse relativism?

No human individual, and certainly no community, is characterized by a single basic discourse, perspective, content or cultural tradition. Each of us stands at the intersection of many communities, languages and perspectives, whose influence on us constantly shifts. Further, we are not "in" discourses, so the question of whether we can "stand outside" of them never arises. They are not containers. They are orders in relation to which we experience, judge, assert and validate.

Lastly, there are no ultimate contexts or conceptual schemes or worlds or frameworks. There are only an indefinitely large number of complexes which can serve as reference points, items-in-relation-to-which we will articulate other items. When we change large theories or metaphysical systems we do not go outside the system to some other point. We shift our reference point to begin with some other sets of things.

VII

Even if the foregoing has successfully deflected the letter of Rorty's critique he would likely deny that it has defeated its spirit. In that spirit he might ask two well-taken questions: What is to be gained from legitimizing Buchler's kind of systematic metaphysics, and, how could Buchler's system be justified?

Regarding the first question, wider contexts of intelligibility, such as Buchler seeks to provide, affect our interpretations of more local and practical matters; philosophies concerned with what is, what is true and what is good have an impact on our cultural, political and scientific judgments. In properly denying that philosophy grounds culture, Rorty has also denied that philosophy is related to, is part of, culture. More accurately, Rorty merges philosophy into culture, which is where it belongs, but he utterly separates Philosophy from culture. In this he has no doubt been misled by Philosophy's own mistaken self-understanding.

Rorty's separation of the Sellarsian notion of philosophy, against which "no one" could object, and Philosophy, like his dichotomy of "large debatable assertions" and "small routine assertions," is entirely unjustifiable. Rorty indicts philosophers who regard the transcendental questions as having priority over everyday or "real theory" questions, but it is uncritical to regard the life of culture and society as represented solely by "small routine assertions." This is a simplistic view of culture; and I refer not to "high" culture, but to barroom, lunchcounter and kitchen culture.

The second question—how could Buchler's system be justified— leads us to two final issues: whether perspective is escapable, and whether consensus must replace objectivity as the arbiter of truth.

For Buchler every judgment is a potential vehicle of communication and, as such, stands "in need of a certain kind of actualization which . . . can never be wholly achieved; they [judgments] require to be validated." (TGT 140) Every judgment seeks to secure itself. This is a natural phenomenon for, "The primordial claim latent in human existence itself is the claim of valid continuance." (TGT 141) This security is always security "within a given perspective." For Buchler, "the flight from perspective is a dream." (TGT 127) Validation is progressive, demanding a widening or sharpening of perspective beyond the perspective of the original judgment. Rationality, says Buchler, "could be defined as the willingness to discover other perspectives, to attain community of perspective, and to reconcile community with conviction." (TGT 116) So, Buchler would agree with

Rorty that his own system is validated only within some perspective, that it does not constitute the final or ultimate perspective.

Rorty distinguishes between two ways of regarding the validation of judgments. (SO 3) One is to seek validity with respect to what is judged. This is the way of objectivity. The other is to seek validity in respect to shared perspective or community. Rorty rejects the former as a part of the Philosophical correspondence theory of truth, and endorses the latter, regarding it as Deweyan and pragmatic.

Buchler would reject Rorty's "solidarity," not because he seeks a metaphysical objectivity over a relativistic consensus, but because he denies the cogency of the distinction.

For Buchler, what I experience (proceive) and judge are the things themselves, natural existences, in their relation to me as an individual (as they affect, condition my history).

> A procept is the *existence itself . . . in so far* as it is relevant to an individual as individual. . . . The complexes of nature . . . *constitute* experience. (NJ 122–23)

Any set of related procepts constitutes a perspective. Each individual judges in relation to an indefinitely large number of perspectives. Each of us is a community of perspectives.

Consequently, *perspectives are the things judged, as they obtain in an order of relevance* established by those things. Perspectives are not something "subjective" through or by which we judge; they are complexes whose interrelation constitutes reference points, and when we judge we take a stand on such reference points, revealing traits of the things thereby judged and actualizing traits of the perspective, the order of reference. Just as, Rorty knows, mind is not a "mirror," perspective is not a lens, a medium (ocular or linguistic), or a tool.

What distinguishes Buchler and Rorty here is that Buchler has removed the question of the validity of judgments from the subject-object model that continues to inform Rorty's program. For the much maligned correspondence theory, the problem of valid belief took the form of the insoluble conundrum of relating subjective belief and objective thing. Rorty eliminates this conundrum by substituting consensus for correspondence. But this strategy presumes the opposition of correspondence-to-things ("objectivity") and correspondence-to-other-beliefs (consensus). In place of a Cartesian solipsism of the individual mind it leaves us with a Rortyan *communitarian solipsism*. In contrast, Buchler refuses to accept an absolute (nonordinal) distinction between proceptive orders and all other orders of natural complexes.

It is only in the unending process of revision of judgments, where no judgment has an absolute validity and all judgments achieve their validity only in perspective, that Buchler's system can itself lay claim to validation. Does this mean that Rorty is right, that the validity of Buchler's system can be established only in reference to some other perspective whose validity is neither necessary nor self-evident, leading inquiry on to other perspectives in search of validation, with no hope of an intrinsically prior or final perspective? The answer is yes. And does this mean that we can never know whether our perspectives have purchase on reality in itself, that we are confined within our cultural consensus, and that the comprehensive inquiries of philosophy are invalid, circular, trivial, or all three? The answer to this is no. It is, I believe, implicit in the profound shift of perspective to which Buchler invites us that we cease to see this "yes" and this "no" as inconsistent.

Notes

1. See p. xv of Richard Rorty, "Pragmatism and Philosophy," in *Consequences of Pragmatism* (Minneapolis: University of Minnesota Press, 1982), pp. xiii–xlvii (hereafter COP). Other works of Rorty's frequently cited herein are: "Dewey's Metaphysics," COP, pp. 72–89; "Pragmatism, Relativism, Irrationalism," COP, pp. 160–75; and "Solidarity and Objectivity," in *Post-Analytic Philosophy*, ed. John Rajchman and Cornel West (New York: Columbia University Press, 1985), pp. 3–19 (hereafter SO).

2. See Richard Rorty, *Philosophy and the Mirror of Nature* (Princeton: Princeton University Press, 1979).

3. Regarding the Sellars definition Rorty says, "No one could be dubious about philosophy, taken in this sense." (COP, pp. xiv–xv). See also COP, pp. 29–30.

4. See Rorty, "Solidarity or Objectivity."

5. Martin Hollis and Steven Lukes, *Rationality and Relativism* (Cambridge: MIT Press, 1982), pp. 5–13.

6. I am presuming some kind of correspondence theory of truth.

7. To be sure, if one adopts a naturalistic perspective then our traits are also traits of a part of the world.

8. Donald Davidson, "The Very Idea of a Conceptual Scheme" (1974), in *Inquiries into Truth and Interpretation* (Oxford: Clarendon Press, 1984), pp. 183–98.

9. Richard Rorty, "The World Well Lost" (1972), in COP, pp. 3–18. Rorty knew of Davidson's argument since 1970, before publication of the essay above.

252 *Cahoone*

10. This use of "foundational" does not prejudice the case against Rorty. As we will see, he aims to deny such foundational sets any possibility of justification, but does not question their existence as a cogent but false proposal.

11. Justus Buchler's system is articulated in five books: *Toward a General Theory of Human Judgment, Nature and Judgment, Metaphysics of Natural Complexes, The Concept of Method, The Main of Light: On the Concept of Poetry.* Buchler published an earlier (1939) work on Peirce, *Charles Peirce's Empiricism* (New York: Octagon, 1966). Also important is Buchler's essay, "On the Concept of 'the World'," *The Review of Metaphysics,* 31:4, (1978), pp. 555–79 reprinted in MNC [1989] Appendix Three, pp. 224–259, hereafter, OCW with first *The Review of Metaphysics* and then the MNC pagination. See "List of Abbreviations" for Buchler's works, p.xiii–xiv.

12. Buchler, NJ 8. Query is the methodical articulation of a judgment. Since there are three types of judgment (active, assertive and exhibitive) there are three types of query. Inquiry is assertive query, query as assertive judgment.

13. See Sidney Gelber and Kathleen Wallace, "Justus Buchler: Nature, Power and Prospect," *Process Studies* 15: 2, (Summer 1986), pp. 106–07 reprinted here, pp. 49–63.

14. Davidson, p. 189.

15. For a general discussion of these matters, see Buchler's MNC, ch. 1, and TGT, ch. 1.

16. For Rorty, correspondence "works" with "small routine assertions," but not with "large debatable ones." See COP, p. 164.

17. See Rorty's discussion of "intuitive realism" in COP, pp. xxix–xxxvii.

18. Which is why Rorty seeks to buttress the argument with nonhuman examples; see COP, pp. 8–11. This is not illegitimate, but it reveals the degree to which terrestrial basic discourses are insufficiently foreign to make discourse-relativism complete.

19. I discuss this point in a section on integrity and relation in *The Dilemma of Modernity: Philosophy, Culture and Anti-Culture* (Albany: SUNY Press, 1988), pp. 235–45.

20. The only ultimate limiting context is the world, understood as everything that is.

21. See Charles S. Peirce, "Questions Concerning Certain Faculties Claimed for Man" (1868), in *Writings of Charles S. Peirce*, ed. Edward Moore (Bloomington: Indiana University Press, 1984), vol. 2, pp. 193–211.

The Assertive, the Active, and the Exhibitive

I. A. Richards

Lecturing in the 1920s in England, T. S. Eliot found that the poem which went down best was T. E. Hulme's *Fantasia of a Fallen Gentleman on the Embankment*:

> Once, in finesse of fiddles found I ecstasy,
> In a flash of gold heels on the hard pavement
> Now see I
> That warmth's the very stuff of poesy.
> Oh, God, make small
> The old star-eaten blanket of the sky
> That I may wrap it round me and in comfort lie.

It is a poem which deserves to be better known; in any case it is a compact type-specimen through which to consider poetic imaginings. How securely it relies on indirect meanings needing, for that scene and period, no explication: that *fallen gentleman* of the title, those gold heels and the miracle-working *star-eaten!* Yet, for a reader for whom such implications do not work, how little any elucidations can do; and, for others, how easily they may merely smutch its delicacy.

None the less, for almost all its words and phrases questions arise about how much of their meaning must, in some measure, be perceived and explored and in what ways. Take the musical sense of *fantasia:* "an instrumental composition characterized by freedom of fancy unrestricted by set form." How much of that perfectly fitting description of the poem will, ordinarily, be openly or covertly active in a good reader? What other nouns that might follow *fallen* should add their flavour? How much should be recalled of the chill river airs that breathe on the occupants of those Thames-side benches, before *warmth* gets to work? Does the card-player's usage of *finesse* take a part? Does the unuttered *moth-eaten* connect with a

realization that clear nights are colder than cloudy ones? And is a thought
that Heaven might *peep through* at all in place?

The Main of Light has inevitably much to do with such questions, and
indeed in his chosen title Mr. Buchler challenges us to divine a good deal
that is scarcely more than touched on, if that, in his pages. It has infinitely
explorable mysteries.

> Nativity, once in the main of light
> Crawls to maturity, wherewith being crown'd
> Crooked eclipses 'gainst his glory fight.

This, from Sonnet Sixty is Shakespeare at *his* most provocative and
baffling, writing on the most provocative and baffling of all our problems.
How are we to read these lines, and what do they tell us of the book? What
is this *nativity*, which *once* had such place? And what may we look for,
with its warrant, in a work whose subtitle is ''On the Concept of Poetry?''

Once in the main of light: of what promise (and frustration or preven-
tion) may this remind us? Is *once*, here, more than *as soon as*? Can it be an
anticipation of the *Intimations* theme? But against that there is the force of
crawls, evoking the new-born's clumsiness. Or are we not rather to realize
anew with what a sunrise the creative drive comes up in us? Should we
perhaps compare the *nativity* of a Homer with the *maturity* of Sonnet Sixty,
and may the *crooked eclipses* be (among all else) the troubles poetry has
had to struggle with since? More specifically, are they those misconceptions of the nature and role of poetry which this most preveniently resource-
ful essay in metaphysics would correct?

In his first four chapters, Mr. Buchler attacks ''an unaccountably persistent . . . group of ideas, rendered sacrosanct by long tradition . . . hard-
ened into a sterile language'' which ''continues to talk about poetry in
terms of 'the imagination', 'reality', 'unity', 'inner experience', 'form and
content', and the like.'' After this considerably destructive engagement, ''a
just theory of poetry'' is constructed. This theory aims ''to be 'faithful';''
''Such fidelity ultimately lies in a theory's directive power, its ability . . .
to enhance the identifying grasp, the awareness of each manifestation.''
This aim is adequately ambitious and it will be found, I think, that it is
pursued with high success.

Fundamental to this is Mr. Buchler's division of ''utterance or judgment'' into three modes, assertive, active and exhibitive. This last covers
the arts, within which the poetries are a sub-class. This is, I think, the
moment to issue an alert to the reader: this division is inviting us to think
anew and to think deeply. An identification of *judgment* and *utterance* goes
with it. *Or* is here playing one of its tricks: *utterance* and *judgment* are two

names for the same thing, not for alternative, different things. A kick, e.g., is a judgment-utterance. I should perhaps add that *The Main of Light* manages to make itself unusually clear, exacting though its invitations are. On the delineation of these modes Mr. Buchler lavishes delicate and often exquisite care, seeing that their clarification requires the exposure of "a number of stiff philosophical bulwarks that doubtless will endure forever."

Among these erroneous notions are: that judging can be limited to "occasions of intention or voluntary choice;" that "judging is necessarily deliberate," that it is a *mental operation* in a man, rather than the man himself, that judges; and that judging "always takes the form of thinking something or saying something about something else." Through these misconceptions "still another unfortunate transition has taken place: 'utterance' has acquired a eulogistic import." But "utterance is manifested by concentration camps, bombs and child-beating along with agriculture, medicine and poetry." Here again, however, a misapprehension has been shown to be possible. Mr. Buchler has been taken as saying that all or most utterances praise. What he says is that utterance as such (i.e., human activity) has *by careless people* been supposed to be, in general, good.

The three modes of judgment-utterance are "to be understood in terms of the way in which human products (i.e., what you do) actually function," for, under varying conditions, a product may function in all three ways: thus a drawing of a dancer may either *state*, or *direct*, or *contrive-invent*, i.e., present a possibility. Each instance of judging is "at bottom an attitude or 'stance'." It may be an *affirming* (with a truth claim), an *acting* (morally assessable), or a *creating* (right or wrong), and—I think Mr. Buchler would allow—it may be all three of these together. There are many cases where what appears to have one function may actually have another. We should recognize all three functions as equally judicative and equally fundamental. The *assertive* only occupies first place because traditionally it has been given an illegitimate priority; the *active* and the *presenting-shaping-exhibiting* modes are just as much ways of judging. They all, to a radical degree, entail commitment.

Mr. Buchler is concerned in *The Main of Light* with exhibitive judgment as manifest in poetry. Others of his writings present the frame within which this liberating and illuminating conception has its place. What he does here is to provide us with an intelligible philosophic *articulation* of this useful and salutary meaning. "Exhibitive judgment . . . is that process whereby men shape *natural complexes* and communicate them for assimilation as so shaped." Two expressions I have italicized here call for explanations: *articulation* and *natural complexes*. I can best give them in Mr. Buchler's words: "The meaning of a judgment in any of the three modes is grasped only through articulation of that judgment, and there is no foreseeable termination to the process of articulation." We may see in this, I think, a favouring influence from C. S. Peirce (on whose empiricism Mr. Buchler wrote in 1939). Roman Jakobson, in *On Translation* (edited by R. A. Brower, Harvard University Press, 1959), thus alludes to Peirce's stress on what is, I think, very nearly Mr. Buchler's articulation:

> For us, both as linguists and as ordinary word-users, the meaning of any linguistic sign is its translation into some further, alternative sign, especially a sign "in which it is more fully developed," as Peirce, the deepest inquirer into the essence of signs, insistently stated.

Natural complex is the name Mr. Buchler gives to "whatever is, and therefore to whatever can be dealt with; to what is produced by men as well as to what is not." *Natural* warns us that "all complexes are aspects of nature;" that "no complex can be dismissed or exorcized." In spite of which, and very refreshingly, the term *complex* "eliminates the idea that there are, or that we may be concerned with 'simples'. . . . The simple, the seamless . . . is in effect the traitless. . . . A simple could not be."

So fine-spun a complex of philosophic distinctions might give a sampling reader a false impression: that *The Main of Light* is remote from minute and intimate explorations of actual poetry. Such a reader should therefore take note of the selection of poems with which Mr. Buchler exemplifies his positions. His choices are to me enviably apposite and discerning. He is as much at home when commenting on what a specific poem is doing, and how, as in discussing theoretical errors about poetry in general. As he gracefully remarks: "At certain points, I have dealt in a somewhat unceremonious way with positions or formulations put forth by writers whom I otherwise admire."

Among many others, these include Shelley, Coleridge, Valery, Santayana, Hegel, Whitehead, Eliot and Auden. The overall impression is that of highly discriminating fairness as well as of an acute concern with actualities. Thus:

> Cognitive gain may or may not be moral gain. There is a great deal of knowledge which has made men unhappy and that makes human woe possible. A major problem of man is the coordination and harmonization of judgments that arise in the different modes. (ML 152)

How to prevent the assertive, the active and the exhibitive functions of utterance from corrupting and bedeviling one another as they do, for example, so often and so typically, in advertising? It is very likely this, with its ever encroaching novelty and its protean guises, both political and cultural, which may prove the grimmest threat so far offered to the human effort.

Mr. Buchler's book essentially embodies a philosophic search for "a unique over-arching 'quality of wholeness in man'." My own feeling is that, although he sees that "in no philosopher is the scope of exhibitive judgment so great as it is in Plato," Mr. Buchler misses (as the key to his chief difficulties with Coleridge's "whole soul of man") the exhibitive of human wholeness offered in *The Republic*.

At the same time he achieves and secures his flexibilities of treatment through his metaphysical resources. He can speak of a complex "being rotated, so to speak, delineated successively in a number of perspectives." It is possible to miss the implications *rotated* here. It is a compact metaphoric way of indicating that *everything* whatever (i.e., every *natural complex*) can be looked at from many angles—as we may, to learn more about it, turn an object over in our hands. This applies *throughout*, though often, of course, great changes in our presuppositional scaffolding may be required. The resulting liberations may be immense, as we will realize if we recall that the aim of thought (as of persecution) has from age to age been to discredit and destroy, if possible, all but one single position. And in how many classrooms is that not still the case?

Any general account of modes of judgment, any deep contrast of fundamental positions, would seem to need to ask: what is this account itself—in which of the *modes of judgment* are we judging here *about* these judgments? And what is any such contrast itself *doing*? Which side of the quarrel is it itself exemplifying? I have the impression that these questions are seldom asked and even less answered, adequately or not.

And yet, surely, a comprehensive enough account, a calm enough contemplation of them, should not only include their exploration, but also find in this exploratory activity useful controls over all querying and all judgment. The Vedantist ruling of Yadnyawalknya that "you cannot see the seer of seeing . . . or know the knower of knowing" looks, from this position, itself partisan. I have above ventured the opinion that Mr. Buchler may allow some judgments to be assertive, active and exhibitive at once. In doubting Yadnyawalknya's declaration am I not, simultaneously, claiming-for-true, directing a moral effort and shaping a possibility, i.e., exercising the three modes together in coordination? Does not the doubt thus *rotate* our chief mystery?

Objection will, of course, claim that, in the assertive mode, *cannot* and *can* would destroy one another. "You can" and "you cannot" are contradictories. So, we may agree, they would be if the two propositions they deal with were in all other respects entirely the same in meaning. But though the words in them are the same we can ask, are *they*?, and in this perhaps come closer again to seeing (i.e., being?) the seer of our seeings. He is truth-seeking (and sometimes truth-claiming), but he is also responsibly directive and the shaper of that which is being shaped.

Yet what of the sense of guilt which may so often attach to such pursuits? In his recent book *Thieves of Fire*, Denis Donoghue rightly observes that when Lawrence speaks of the sun he is not talking physics; the scandal is doing so. The most poignant page of *Thieves of Fire* is about this trouble:

> Theft of the divine fire of knowledge made reflection possible and therefore necessary; it made men self-aware, self-conscious, it made the human race a multitude of reflexive animals.

And further: "The reflexiveness of mind, which is in one sense its glory, is in another a token of its criminality, its transgression at the source." How challenging is this ellipsis, this way we have of talking as though old stories were somehow History! The source here is a myth, a traditional story, itself reflecting . . . what? Both *re-* and *flect* (*flectere*), "back" and "bend," have their comments on this, fitting into those offered by the etymons of *straight*, *true* and of *right* and *wrong*. We may also reflect again, on the significance of taking *fire*, of all fearsome destroyers, as a symbol of knowledge. Recalling how Coleridge haunts all this with "The infinite I AM" and with "the whole soul of man," in those references to the analogy (so to speak) between poetic and divine creativity, he may again offer us light in Aphorism Nine of his *Aids to Reflection*, and the passage may serve as a further gloss on Mr. Buchler's title.

> "And man became a living soul." He did not merely possess it, he became it. It was his proper *being*, his truest self, *the* man *in* the man. . . . This *seeing* light, this enlightening eye, is Reflection. . . . This, too, is THOUGHT: and all thought is but unthinking that does not flow out of this, or tend towards it.

Reading Poems with Buchler

Roland Garrett

When Justus Buchler's book on the concept of poetry was published in 1974, it was welcomed with a full page review by I. A. Richards in the *Times Literary Supplement*. Richards, one of the great literary critics of the century, felt the power of Buchler's philosophy. He called attention to the "infinitely explorable mysteries" of the book, the ambition and success of Buchler's theory, the book's unusual clarity despite the exacting problems it deals with, the "delicate and often exquisite care" taken in some of its philosophical distinctions, its "liberating and illuminating" conception of exhibitive judgment in poetry, and its combination of a "highly discriminating fairness" to earlier theorists with "an acute concern" for "actualities"—actualities such as poems and the things that they do. Richards was satisfied with the conceptual resources and flexibilities of the metaphysics that Buchler brought to the analysis of poetry, and he gave a dramatic generality to the compliments he offered in the review. "Mr. Buchler's book," he said, "essentially embodies a philosophic search for "a unique overarching 'quality of wholeness in man'."[1]

Richards' commentary is surprising and troubling, however, in its generality. It avoids details in the logic of Buchler's theory and in the application of the theory to individual poems. As Richards was aware, Buchler had previously spent decades in the development of complex philosophical theories of nature, experience, knowledge, and meaning. These provide conceptual background for the analysis of poetry that Buchler offers. Specific technical categories from the previously published metaphysics are introduced into aesthetics in the definition of poetry that Buchler advances. The new concept thus provides poetry with a grand universal significance and intellectual content. Yet there is an historic risk in such an approach. Does a universal concept of poetry in fact apply to this and that individual poem? Buchler wants a theory of poetry that would not merely ascertain pattern in the various manifestations of poetry but that would also "enhance the identifying grasp, the awareness, of each manifestation." (ML 4) Does the universal definition he provides actually do this? Does it illuminate the internal dynamics of a poem, how the features of sound, rhythm, language, imagery, and meaning develop in the poem, and how they relate to or distinguish themselves from one another in the experience of reading the poem? Does a universal concept of poetry actually help to identify the mechanisms by which *this* poem has its effect on *me*?

Richards, although known for his attractions to abstract theory, was aware of this danger. After summarizing some of the ideas that Buchler imports from metaphysics into aesthetics, his review brings up precisely this concern and acquits Buchler with additional praise:

> So fine-spun a complex of philosophic distinctions might give a sampling reader a false impression: that *The Main of Light* is remote from minute and intimate explorations of actual poetry. Such a reader should therefore take note of the selection of poems with which Mr. Buchler exemplifies his positions. His choices are to me enviably apposite and discerning. He is as much at home when commenting on what a specific poem is doing, and how, as in discussing theoretical errors about poetry in general.[2]

Notice, however, that here Richards refers to no examples from Buchler's text. The theory may seem lucid and cogent in abstract analysis, but if we are interested in how it is supported by the reading of individual poems, Richards' enthusiasm provides no help.

What is even more surprising is that one who searches Buchler for analytical illustration finds little help too. Buchler's theory of poetry is rich in conceptual elaboration and articulated relations of conceptual structure to the experience of poetry. But the actual analysis of individual poems to illustrate or test the definition he puts forward is remarkable in its paucity of detail. Several poems are quoted, some in full, and connections to theory are asserted. But in not a single case is there an analysis of a poem that even attempts to explain or show how the features of the poem produce the effect that Buchler's general definition of poetry highlights. Thus there is an astonishing logical gap in the development of the definition. Nor is the difficulty simply that an obviously illuminating general definition needs more detail in its application or defense. The absence of detail in fact threatens the viability of the definition and therefore the larger aim of Buchler's account of poetry. As we have seen, Buchler recognized that a general definition should enhance the identifying grasp in each specific manifestation of poetry. The detail is needed in order to show that the definition can serve this function. Without it, a reader may wonder whether Buchler has after all captured in theory "what it means to be an instance of poetry." (ML 5) If there is such a logical gap, what reason is there for thinking that the proposed definition is a definition of poetry rather than simply a record of how one theorist has described, in a distinctive language drawn from metaphysics, his own unique responses to a few poems?

In the following pages we will explore this gap by illustrating in some detail the incompleteness which characterizes Buchler's use of quotations from poetry to reflect and support his theory. This, undertaken in section one below, will document the distance of theory from evidence in Buchler's account of poetry. But the incompleteness of the theory is only part of the story. It is hard to believe that a critic as insightful and experienced as Richards would be carried away by a metaphysics of poetry that cannot provide plausible detail on how poems work. We will therefore also consider, in section two, ways in which the analysis of a couple of individual poems might be undertaken to exemplify and buttress Buchler's theory. As we will see, there are interpretive possibilities that can extend and deepen the application of Buchler's metaphysics to poetry. I suspect that Richards' intuitive grasp of the possibilities of fruitful application contributed to his enthusiasm for a novel theory of poetry that came with so little evidence. Finally, in section three, we will stand back from the developed theory to look more broadly and skeptically at its adequacy. Is there reason to think that the theory, sympathetically applied, in fact illuminates what it means to be an instance of poetry? Is it clear enough to be productive and useful in thinking about what poems are and how they work?

I

It will be helpful as a preliminary to recall briefly the metaphysical categories that Buchler brings from his prior philosophy to the definition of poetry. Two are particularly important, "ontological parity" and "prevalence."

First, Buchler in his metaphysics systematically demolishes the distinction between appearance and reality, and he sees a similar function in poetry. "All appearances are realities for the poet," he writes. The poet "communicates a *sense* of ontological parity, a sense of the equal reality, though not necessarily the equal importance, of all the complexes he deals with." (ML 126)

Second, Buchler says that poetry provides "a sense of prevalence." For any complex, or anything of any sort identifiable through poetry, the diction, sound, pace, and other features of the poem combine to communicate "a sense of the complex as ineluctably what it is," a sense of *its* being instead of some other, a sense that "it is what it is in the way that it is with the scope that it has." Poetry thus provides a unique emphasis on "finality" in any complex, on its exclusion of "what is contrary to its integrity."

A poem shows: "here is a relation of traits sovereign unto itself and irreducible." (ML 137, 130–131, 136)

Standing behind this characterization of poetry is a comprehensive, systematic metaphysics which defines complexes, ontological parity, and prevalence. "Prevalence" is contrasted with the neologism "alescence," which expresses not what prevails but what arises or comes to be, the introduction of something or of some traits into some context. There are various forms of prevalence to which attention is directed in Buchler's metaphysics, including continuation, recurrence, invariance, constancy, endurance, completeness, structure, fact, the irreversibility of a terminated occurrence. In each of these there is a restrictive or exclusive aspect, an array of traits that is what it is (continuously, or recurrently, or etc.) and is not something else that might have been (or that it might have become) in its place.

In Buchler's book on poetry, these concepts are applied to poetry in a chapter entitled "Ontological Parity and the Sense of Prevalence." In the course of this chapter, Buchler describes the two attributes, the sense of ontological parity and the sense of prevalence, and he claims that it is these two attributes that distinguish poetry most sharply from nonpoetic forms of literary art. These attributes thus mark the conceptual essence with which I will deal in studying his definition of poetry. Let us look now at how specific poems are, or are not, used in this chapter to illustrate and support the definition of poetry based on these two attributes.

The first point to notice is that the presentation of ontological parity as a category of poetics includes no reference to individual poems and no quotation from poetry. (ML 120–129) Rather it argues generally that there is a unique intonational impulse in poetic speech which departs from the distinction between appearance and reality that dominates ordinary speech. This unique impulse is said to be manifested in the formality, solemnity, or controlled intensity found in oral reading of poetry, with its vocal stress or cadence, and has a written parallel in the physical form that typically distinguishes the printing of poetry from the printing of prose. But Buchler here offers no illustration whatsoever to help us grasp how meter, stress, cadence, or typography contribute to formality, solemnity, or controlled intensity. Presumably the controlled intensity in reading is motivated by the elements of the poem and its relation to these elements is what makes it important to the poem. Moreover, controlled intensity in reading does not always make speech poetic. A paragraph in a chemistry textbook does not call for the stylized reading that Buchler has in mind, and a stylized or solemn reading of the chemistry text would not transform it into poetry. Buchler's mode of reasoning thus does not show how the sense of parity is grounded either in individual poems or in the traditionally recognized features of poetry, such as meter.

Here we see how the distance of the theory from the evidence of particular poems threatens the viability of the theory. Is there really a controlled intensity, or a solemnity in the oral reading of poetry? If we are left in the dark about how the various elements of a poem, like meter or typography, contribute to the controlled intensity, we begin to wonder whether the controlled intensity is in fact an important condition of poetry. And we begin to wonder even what the controlled intensity or solemnity really is. A political speech, or a public announcement of danger, or an actor's soliloquy on stage, for example, can each, it seems, be characterized by a controlled intensity that does not render the utterance poetic. Why look on controlled intensity as a clue to anything distinctive or even clearly identified in the experience of poetry? And why therefore look on the sense of ontological parity as a defining feature of poetry rather than as an incidental psychological effect that may derive from various uses of language, both poetic and nonpoetic?

When he turns from ontological parity to the sense of prevalence in poetry, Buchler quotes several poems in their entirety or at length. (ML 129–140) But a similar problem arises due to the abstractness of his commentary. Let us look at what he says as he quotes specific poems to reflect this aspect of his theory.

How does a poem provide a sense of prevalence? Buchler quotes in full a brief poem by Saigyō Hōshi, as translated by Arthur Waley. In order to produce a sense of his method, I will give the text of this poem together with the sentences through which Buchler introduces it and a couple of sentences which follow. Buchler writes:

The poetic shaping of a complex discriminates the aspect of finality in that complex. It exhibits the complex as a finality. It conveys the sense of prevalence.

> Those ships which left
> Side by side
> The same harbor
> Towards an unknown destination
> Have rowed away from one another.

A prevalence is not always starkly delivered for grasp. The textures of poetic judgment submit to classification no more easily than do its themes. (ML 131–132)[3]

Although prevalence is not always "starkly delivered," there is at least, Buchler says, a "pattern of relatedness" in a poem. And then he goes on to the next illustration, a poem by William Carlos Williams.

The sentences which Buchler has here written to surround the Hōshi/
Waley poem have a strange quality of separation from it. Technically, they
do not commit Buchler to a claim that the shaping of this poem discriminates an aspect of finality in the poem or in its subject, or that in the instance of this poem the presentation of prevalence is distinctive in its being
"starkly delivered." The absence of a stipulated relation of the poem to its
theoretical context in Buchler's presentation leaves each, poem and context,
to exhibit itself to the reader in juxtaposition with the other. Such a procedure may on occasion be useful in the articulation of critical or philosophical theory, if the larger presentation of the theory were sufficient to enable
the reader to supply the needed connections. Here, however, the procedure
allows the poem little service as an illustration of what the "sense of prevalence" in poetry is. By pressing questions of detail regarding the possible
relation of the quoted poem to the conceptual context, we can see how the
absence of explicitness again threatens the viability of Buchler's definition
of poetry.
    Is there an aspect of "finality" in the Hōshi/Waley poem? If so, what
is it? If the aspect of finality were simply the fact that two or more ships
have parted, a prose description of the same phenomenon—for example, in
a letter from a passenger—would presumably have a similar finality. Perhaps the logic of Buchler's position on this poem is that certain characteristics such as, say, typography, lead to a poetic reading, which provides a
sense of finality. But it is not explained what qualities of, say, typography
generate a sense of finality, and how they do this; or why these characteristics of the poem manifest the particular form of prevalence that Buchler
calls "finality." How the spatial forms, grammar, imagery, rhythms,
sounds, style or even meanings of this poem reflect finality we are not told.
And if we were to rely on literal meanings in interpreting the poem, we
would have to face the fact that the poem seems to describe not only a
finality but an incomplete process toward an "unknown destination." Why
assume that the finality of the literal separation of the ships is more important than the uncompleted process of which the separation is literally one
element? If it is the whole process that is, in some respect, final, we would
have to retreat to Buchler's metaphysics to attempt to learn how that is, for
his commentary here provides no clue. The trouble with returning to general metaphysics for such an explanation is that the metaphysics explains
how everything is (in some context) a prevalence and yields no distinctive
role for poetry. To fulfill the promise of poetics, we are entitled to be in-
structed more on how *this* poem, with its specific features, produces in us
the sense of prevalence. In the absence of such detail, the reader is at a loss
to construe the notion of finality, to discern any relationship of finality to
the poem, or to understand, let alone accept, the larger principle that a

sense of finality, or a sense of prevalence, is important to the experience of
poetry. Thus the absence of detail undermines Buchler's central goals in the
development of his theory of poetry. In his handling of the poem by Hōshi/
Waley, he appears to be assuming the intuitive assent of a sympathetic
reader, such as Richards.

It is instructive at this point to look again at the conceptual structure
of Buchler's definition of poetry. The phrase "a sense of prevalence,"
which refers to a sense that poetry communicates or generates in the reader,
contains not one but two crucial components. "Prevalence," one of the
components, is defined and illustrated at length, going back to systematic
presentation in metaphysics. Obviously, however, the notion of "sense" is
equally in need of analysis. Buchler defines "a sense of" as "a grasp
within keenly focussed awareness." (ML 130) But this definition is left
quite abstract, causing the problems of interpretation and application we are
discovering. What is the nature of the "grasp" and the "focus" that characterize the poetic stance, as contrasted with the keen focus that can be
provided by literal description, scientific formulations, or prose? And what
is it in a poem, or in *this* poem, that produces certain psychological forms
or responses (viz., formality, controlled intensity, the "sense" of prevalence) rather than others? Since general metaphysics does not tell us, we
look for evidence in the commentary on poems.

In Buchler's comments on the poem "The Lion," by William Carlos
Williams, he points to an abruptly suggested kinship of traits whose depth
only emerges in the course of the poem. He quotes the first part of the
poem, then interrupts to note that the components grow into a "horrific
whole, the prevalence of which takes the form of irrevocability." (ML 132)
This brief statement is immediately followed by quotation of the second
part of the poem, and there is no further commentary to guide our application of the concepts of irrevocability and prevalence to the poem. What is it
in the poem, we may ask, that gives the impression of irrevocability? Does
this impression rest on the sounds of the words, the rapid and definite sequence of phrases, or the violence of the images? Does it rest on the repetition of pattern from the first part of the poem to the second part, or on
the literal reference at the conclusion of the poem to an event that occurs
"for the last time?" Presumably we can expect that there can be some
explanation as to why the form of prevalence this poem yields is irrevocability rather than one of the other forms, such as continuation, recurrence,
constancy, or finality. Not only is no explanation given or suggested, but
Buchler shies away from even identifying the whole which is prevalent.
"To name a prevalence, apart from the poem's way of naming;" he says,
"to pinpoint it by a phrase, is anticlimactic when plausible, but is implausible most of the time." (ML 133) Such interpretive, descriptive, and

pinpointing phrases, however, are essential to both the critical analysis of poetry and its use in the validation of poetic theory, despite the wisdom of Buchler's caution against prose summaries of poems (and against the association of prevalence in every case with some one datum in a poem). The evidential needs of criticism and theory are not met if poems are printed interspersed with a critical theory that does not analyze their theoretical relevance. Again, the paucity of detail threatens Buchler's central project. What, after all, is the "irrevocability" that Buchler claims to find in the poem? Does the poem really give a "sense" of it to any reader not already caught up in this metaphysical approach? Why should such a "sense" be thought fundamental to the experience of poetry?

Buchler's use of other poems is similarly brief and abstract. The poem "Young Poets" by Nicanor Parra, as translated by Miller Williams, is inserted without analysis in the middle of a general elaboration of the difficulty of trying to capture the sense of prevalence in words other than those of the poet. In Marianne Moore's poem "The Fish," the title is the grammatical subject of the first two lines, and Buchler, quoting most of the poem, notes the difficulty of readily identifying the major prevalence in the poem.[4] The title, he says, introduces a "concatenation" of elements which, however, does not collapse into a "miscellany" in part because there is a rhyme pattern that "firms the exhibitive structure." (ML 134–135) This reference to the function of rhyme comes closer than most of Buchler's other comments on poems to revealing the logic of his reasoning, for firmness of structure is implied in his metaphysics to be a form of prevalence. Yet, useful as this may be in explanation, it does not take us far in a theory of poetry which not only recognizes that rhyme is inessential to poetry in general but which provides no analysis of the nature and function of rhyme when it does occur, what it is about rhyme that yields firmness, or the combination of rhyme with other factors to produce in the reader a "sense" of prevalence. The restraint of Buchler's commentary even keeps him from being explicit on whether a sense of prevalence in reading of this poem derives in part from a sense of firmness in its exhibitive structure. So distant, once more, is the theory from the evidence needed to make it intelligible.

Buchler's use of other poems from Ezra Pound, the Bible, Henry King, and Charles Baudelaire follows the same abstract method, with brief comments mostly not explicitly linked to specific features of the poems—with phrasing, in fact, typically contrived in generalized form to avoid such a commitment: "a perception of incommensurables that prevail," "the coolness of such a delineation," "when the prevalence of a complex is seen in the form of irreversibility." (ML 138, 139) "When a condition in the universe is overwhelming in its hellishness, such as Decay, there are at least three ways of meeting it: emotional frenzy, retreat, or dissection of the condition. The last of these, in the form of poetic control, is the demarcation of a prevalence.'' (ML 140) There is a clue to the possibility of greater detail in a comment on the poetry of Psalm 137, which Buchler describes as passions vibrating side by side, not in process, with past and future combined in "the compresence that prevails." (ML 139) Yet this is narrowing and dramatically misleading in a way also, for, although timelessness is a kind of prevalence, there is a process and sequence to any poem that presumably contributes essentially to its fundamental effect, and this is exactly what the poetics of prevalence must explain. Why, in any specific poem, should we feel called on to recognize the sense of prevalence as fundamental to experience of the poem rather than, say, a sense of variation, or change, or development over time? Although the expressed compresence may combine past and future, the "sense" produced in the reader is a complex temporal phenomenon that alters and grows during the time that it takes to read the poem.

Thus there are grave shortcomings in the theory of poetry that Buchler advances which are pervasively revealed in the hesitation and distancing that characterize his quoted references to actual poems in the presentation of the theory. Throughout his quotations from poetry to illuminate the theory we see the theory dimmed by abstraction, which strikes at its pertinence to the experience of poetry and its very intelligibility.

II

Let us see now whether we can construct remedies to fill the gaps in his reasoning and give intelligible content to his definition of poetry. Do the "sense of ontological parity" and the "sense of prevalence" have a significance that is continuous with Buchler's metaphysics and demonstrably discernible in the experience of poetry? Are there conceptual resources in his metaphysics, in its scope or subtlety, to answer some of the questions we have raised? Is there any basis for the theoretical power that Richards felt as he read Buchler's account of poetry? If we probe the possibilities of Buchler's conceptual perspective in describing how poems work, I think we can discover some strengths in it. It can help to draw attention to features that are important in much poetry. Even a sympathetic construction will continue to show, however, deep difficulties in his definition. In order to exhibit both the strengths and the difficulties, let us read closely two of the poems that Buchler quotes in the exposition of his theory. In reading each of these two poems—the poems by Hōshi, as translated by Arthur Waley, and by Marianne Moore—we will first attempt an analytical reading that is adequate to the particulars of sound, structure, and meaning in the poem. Then we will explore the relevance of Buchler's definition to these details. Since Buchler's definition as we have seen remains abstract and distant from particulars, this latter effort involves some innovation in construing and applying the definition, in which I will attempt to be true to the aims of his project on poetry.

Consider first the poem by Hōshi/Waléy. The poem consists of five lines linked in a single sentence. The division of lines in the poem renders each of several grammatical units in the sentence a perceptibly discrete stage in the sequence of the whole. One line identifies the togetherness, one line the original location in the harbor, one line names the ships, the fourth notes the unknown destination, and the fifth the parting. The poetic function thus creates a distinctive sequential structure, each line presenting or focussing on, if not completing, a distinguishable image or idea. As one reads the poem, the line structure will affect the stresses and pauses, introducing a specific form of temporal regularity.

Moreover, the number of syllables and the natural stresses of the individual words used in the poem contribute to a larger pattern of emphasis. In the first three lines all but one word are monosyllabic. This fact, combined with the discrete line for each of three elements, spreads the emphasis relatively evenly over the words in these lines, many of which call for individual stress. Accordingly, the first three lines of the poem read slowly. The fourth line, however, "Towards an unknown destination," speeds up, due in part to the length of the individual words and the consequent spacing between accents (e.g., three unstressed syllables before the final stress in the line, which comes in the second last syllable). The fifth line of the poem then settles down once more to a pattern of stress and wording that recalls the opening three lines, yet with an echo in the last phrase ("from one another") of the speed of the fourth line, now regularized into a brief alternation of stressed and unstressed syllables. Thus in the rhythmic structure of the poem, the fourth line, which introduces the mystery of the unknown destination, is an unsettling and disruptive moment that is controlled in the conclusion. In ideas and images, we go from demonstrative identification of "those" ships in the "same" harbor side by side, to awareness of an ultimate unknown, to a joining of these two in the fact of separation or individuality: the ships are in fact distinct and go their separate ways, each of them thus a mystery to the others. In sounds, the definiteness that emerges in the concluding line is reflected also in the disappearance of the *s* and *sh* sounds which soften the divisions in the first four lines, from the beginning ("Those ships") to the unknown ("destination").

It is no surprise that the poetic form influences meaning. A prose rendering of Waley's translation of the poem in natural English would probably run like this: "Those ships which left the same harbor side by side have rowed away from one another towards an unknown destination." These are the same words that Waley uses, but the poetic version he gives reverses the order near the end and distinguishes different stages into different lines, thereby also drawing attention to word length, stress patterns, and sounds that in the prose rendering remain distant from the reader's attention and from the routine expectations of ordinary communication. Moreover, in the prose version, although the words are the same, different implications or associations seem relevant. While the framing of the poem in a distinct, contrived structure gives a sense of relative completeness, the logical and descriptive function of prose suggests the need for additional context or explanation of a different sort. Thus, in reading the prose translation, one is more likely to sense a relevance to questions such as the following: Which ships are you talking about? Which harbor? A destination unknown to whom?

We have enough detail on this poem now to see how Buchler's theory of prevalence and ontological parity can bear on interpretation. The distinctiveness of each line places an emphasis on the factor revealed in that line, so that each factor is recognized in its own right and all are equally real, none ontologically prior to the others, none "mere" appearances. The ships, for example, are not more real than the togetherness, the harbor, the destination, or the movement of the ships away from one another. The poem communicates a sense of ontological parity by giving each of these elements the recognition appropriate to its role in its context, the parity in recognition deriving from parity in the stress introduced by the line structure of the poem. Material objects, their traits, their relations, their goals, the events in their histories—all these have different functions and different types of contribution to make in the whole, but they do not denote different levels of reality.

Moreover, the details in the way the various elements of the poem combine with one another arguably create an impression of finality, or, in Buchler's language, exhibit the complex as a finality. The elaborate structuring of the poem by line, word length, stress, and sound mark it off as a distinct entity, join its elements in a regularizing pattern, and therefore give it a sense of completeness as this poem, these voyages, this parting of ships. It provides a "sense of prevalence" by distinguishing the poem as a recognizable collection of identifiable traits, these traits and not others, with the identifiable and felt relations that they have to one another. It is felt as this complex, with these traits, not replaceable by or reducible to something else which might have existed in its place. Each trait is given importance by the role it plays in the modulated but unifying rhythm of the whole, the rhythmic pattern thus creating "a sense of the complex as

ineluctably what it is," a sense that "it is what it is in the way that it is
with the scope that it has." A "sense of prevalence" thus comes not only
from the placement of the completed fact in the concluding line (the parting
took place, the voyagers have separate journeys) but in the metrical patterns
whereby this conclusion (individualization) is felt to emerge from undiffer-
entiated process. Accordingly, the psychology of prevalence in this poem
arguably derives in definable ways from the elements of the poem. It does
not emerge from a prose translation, despite the identity of words and the
similarity of literal content. In this fashion one might elaborate, apply, and
defend Buchler's theory of poetry in its application to the Hōshi/Waley
poem. Here, it seems, the defining criteria of "a sense of ontological parity" and "a sense of prevalence" do have an intelligible and deep bearing
on the distinctive nature of the poetic experience. Before we stand back to
evaluate the theory in this developed form, let us see also what might be
similarly done with the example of a second poem.

Marianne Moore's poem "The Fish" is marked by pattern in strik-
ingly different ways than those of the Hōshi/Waley poem. Beyond the
rhyme to which Buchler calls attention, the Moore poem has a rigidly defined visual and mathematical structure deriving from the distribution of
syllables. Each stanza consists of five lines, totaling twenty-seven syllables
per stanza, and the syllables are uniformly distributed so that the first line
of each stanza has one syllable, the second line three syllables, the third
line nine syllables, the fourth six syllables, and the fifth eight syllables.
The numerical sequence 1, 3, 9, 6, 8 suggests the geometrical structure of
a tropical fish from its nose to the tip of its tail, the nose a point (1), the
head wider (3), and the body the widest point (9), narrowing somewhat (6)
before widening again in the tail (8). It is common in critical commentary
on the poem to assume or conclude that it is not about the fish mentioned in
the title, but that is misleading, for structurally the fish-shape is everywhere
in it, frozen in mathematical form. Contrary to Buchler's comment, the
title does identify a central trait and does not merely lead us into the poem.
Moreover, the jagged indentation of lines also suggests the diagonal, back-
and-forth, darting motion of fish in water. The temporal motion is thus
translated into a fixed visual pattern, just as the form of the fish's body is
translated into the arithmetic of syllable count. There is a similar translation into fixity in the images: the fish do not flow smoothly but "wade,"
as if water were foreign to them; water is not soft, clear liquid but "black
jade," a "wedge / of iron," and barnacles "encrust" the water rather than
the adjacent rock; rays of sunlight assume the hardness of "spun / glass";
a living mussel is like an "injured fan," a broken machine; the sea is a
"sea / of bodies"; the details of the rock cliff are its "external" and
"physical" features.

In this stable context dominated by the cliff, the poet places a sequence of sentences each of which is syntactically correct and complete,
but to which, as Hugh Kenner pointed out,[5] the poem provides no audible
rhythmic form. The poem is thus an overlap of two independent systems
that are distinguishable but joined together: the system of linguistic meaning and the arbitrarily imposed structure of stanzas, lines, indentations, and
syllable counts, the accidental nature of which is subtly focussed on the fact
that the word "accident" is the one uncompounded word in the poem selected to be split in two pieces to conform to the mathematical and geometric structure. The overlap makes even the rhyme, a distinctly poetic
addition to language, seem in this poem to be forced and unpoetic. Hence
the contrast between sea and cliff is represented in the contrast between
sentence meaning and imposed structure. And, as we see in the last stanza,
also in the contrast between life and death. The accidental physical features
of the cliff, created by action of the sea, are interpreted in terms of living
intent and struggle: "abuse," "defiant," the "cornice" of architecture,
"dynamite," "burns" (the one function that water most obviously cannot
provide), and "hatchet" strokes. In one sense, the cliff is dead; but, given
its intersection with the sea, it undergoes changes like a living thing. The
sea creatures are alive, but in another sense they are captured in repeated,
changeless forms. The cliff and the arbitrarily imposed structures of the
poem perform limiting functions, like death, but they also thereby become
endowed with life, not in the sense of birth or youth, but at least in
the sense of aging, changing, assuming new variations, new words, new
meanings, startling images, unpredictable specificity, bright colors. The
flow of life and reading is a struggle against the arbitrarily imposed limitations, as one senses in reading the poem. But the limitations also enhance
the vitality. One critic, Donald Hall, said: "At no time do I feel Miss
Moore's presence more closely than when I am noticing the means she has
taken to preserve her syllable count."[6] The "Repeated / evidence" of
structure in the poem presents life and death in it as different aspects of the
same phenomenon.

    Let us test now how this poem by Marianne Moore might be taken to
reflect Buchler's definition of poetry based on "the sense of ontological
parity" and "the sense of prevalence."

    In this poem, as in the Hōshi/Waley poem, there is a regularity and
recurrence of form that allots a defined place to each element in a comprehensive structure. The mussel-shells, the water, the jelly-fish, the marks of
abuse, the cliff and its youth, the various other objects, traits, and relations—each has its own unique position in the mathematical structure of
the whole, although the character of the structure could not be more removed from the audible rhythm of the Hōshi/Waley poem. None of these

elements is therefore given any greater reality than the others, or any greater or lesser reality than the whole, for each has its place. The individual images are in fact unusually vivid and well-defined. No element is therefore insignificant or "unreal," none a "mere" appearance or unsubstantial reflection of other things more real than itself. Thus again there is a "sense of ontological parity" in the distinct, structured parity of recognition given to each element or trait in the poem, with no division of things into separate levels of reality.

Moreover, the structure that defines and limits the poem also formalizes and limits the whole range of traits found in the interaction between the sea and the cliff. Not only is each element given its place in the whole, but the whole is, through the same inclusive structure, given a distinct identity. It is this whole with these elements that function in these ways, with these movements, these colors, these physical features, these implications of meaning. The universality of limitation identifies this marine environment as what it is with these specified traits rather than other traits which (in a different poem, like Moore's earlier version of "The Fish"), it might have had instead. Hence this marine environment is given by the poem the finality, definiteness of traits, irreducibility, and constancy of form that create in the reader what Buchler calls "the sense of prevalence." As in the case of the movement of ships in the Hōshi/Waley poem, we are given here "a sense of the complex as ineluctably what it is," a sense of its being this complex instead of some other that might have prevailed in its place. The definiteness of individual traits and the definiteness of unifying structure combine to emphasize for the reader the distinctiveness of this poetic whole.

There are questions that might come to mind in the reading of a prose translation of this poem: In what respect are crabs really like green lilies? What is meant by the youth of the cliff? But these questions seem somewhat distant and intrusive in the poem itself precisely because they challenge the felt distinctiveness and completeness of the poetic whole. Critics may raise such questions usefully but only as an analytical preliminary before returning to the poem to see whether the questions have any bearing on the "sense of prevalence" created by the pattern of relatedness of words and meanings. For reasons such as these, the "sense of ontological parity" and the "sense of prevalence" would in this poem be arguably important to the poetic experience.

At one point in his account of prevalence in poetry, Buchler says: "The main point is that the specific characteristics of the poetic complex are ultimately what convey the sense of prevalence." (ML 142) The same might be said for the sense of ontological parity. A detailed analysis of the structure of these two poems, the first by Hōshi as translated by Arthur

Waley, the second by Marianne Moore, seem to give a plausible account of how the specific characteristics of a poem can do that.

III

Do these poems in fact make Buchler's account of poetry plausible? Let us now stand back from the interpretation of these two poems, looking more critically at what we have done—and at Buchler's definition of poetry.

Consider first the question of a sense of prevalence in the Hōshi/ Waley poem. In one respect, this poem does give a sense of finality, as we have seen. The parting of the ships is something that has happened to those ships in that context with the traits that they irrevocably have had. Let us press now the question: Why should the sense of prevalence be construed as fundamental to the reading of the poem? If it is there, it is not the only "sense" there and perhaps it is not more important than others. Consider, for example, that the poem reveals a parting, a variation or novelty in this context. Why view the sense of finality as more important to poetic character than the sense of novelty? In the carefully defined comprehensive structure of the poem, there are elements of sound and meaning that manifest the structure at particular moments. Is not the transition from one unique sound or image to another as important as the pattern of sound, rhythm, and meaning that unites them? In one respect, the entire poem is a stable, unified structure with the traits that it irrevocably has. In another respect, however, the entire poem is a novelty in the world or in my experience of the world. Why not say therefore that the poem gives a sense of novelty, variation, spontaneity, what Buchler calls in his metaphysics "alescence"?

Look again at the images in the Marianne Moore poem: the "crowblue mussel-shells," the "spotlight swiftness" of the rays of sunlight, the "pink / rice-grains" of the starfish, the "dynamite grooves" in the cliff wall. The poem does not simply combine these in an elaborate mathematical and geometric structure. The elaborate structure also embraces the variation from each startling, unique image to another. Syllables are elaborately counted, but in reading the poem there is a sense of variation from one syllable to the next. Why should poetic theory emphasize the constancy of structure anymore than the felt variation within the structure? If the experience of poetry is a multiplicity of different, perhaps contrasting or even conflicting "senses" of prevalence and alescence, what justification is there for building a concept of poetry around a sense of prevalence alone?

These reflections suggest that a "sense of prevalence" has no greater significance for the definition of poetry than a "sense of alescence." If these two poems are evidence, it seems that reading poetry may involve both of these senses, neither automatically assuming dominance. The reader grasps the sheer definiteness of traits, the presence of these traits rather than others that might have been there instead. But the reader also grasps the introduction of traits and the variation of traits over time, since reading is a process.

We can see now the seriousness of Buchler's failure to elaborate and illustrate in detail his notion of "sense." By "a sense of," as we have seen, he means "a grasp within keenly focussed awareness." (ML 130) However, in the keenly focussed reading of a poem there are not simply one or two aspects of the poem or its subject that are grasped. By this definition of "sense," each image is sensed, each line, each unit of meaning, each introduction of a new trait, each transition from one identifiable phase to another, omitting only those that pass unnoticed even if they are relevant in ways of which the reader is unaware. The number, variety, and interrelationships of the distinct elements that are sensed are such that a reading of the poem seems to give no priority to an umbrella "sense of prevalence" or to multiple senses of prevalence. The absence of detail in analysis of individual poems in Buchler's text can be viewed as an absence of phenomenological detail on the complexity of the "sense" or "senses" that inform reading: what the "senses" are in a particular poem, how they overlap or merge or become distinguished from one another, how they are informed or modified by information and currents of meaning from outside the poem, how the sense of the elements contributes to the ways in which one senses or grasps the whole, how one sense may come in the course of reading to dominate or be more fundamental than others.[7]

Paradoxically, it is the very metaphysical power, the generality, of the concepts of prevalence and alescence which makes it difficult to separate them in the "sense" that poetry creates, and to distinguish this sense from the grasp of prevalence and alescence through nonpoetic forms of language. Illustrations are easy to find or construct. For example, a history of a political conflict, or a novel about a political conflict, can give a sense of prevalence. One who reads the history attentively may come to grasp the conflict as this conflict, with the traits that it has instead of some other traits, with its own distinctive character instead of some other traits that it might have had instead; the reader gets "a sense of the complex as ineluctably what it is." Moreover, the same history can at the same time give a sense of alescence, as the reader grasps the transitions in its course, the introduction of new events and traits. When Buchler faces directly the discovery of a sense of prevalence in linguistic creations other than poetry (ML 142ff), he calls it poetic, assumes that the emphasis in poetry has been shown to be an emphasis on things as prevalences, and does not escape the abstractness that undermined his attempt to make this clear. To be sure, discursive prose, such as the history of a political conflict, may be more likely to suggest questions that lead readers beyond the language of the work they are reading. But this does not imply that the sense of prevalence is less pervasive or fundamental in the written history than in a poem, and it certainly does not justify such a conclusion comparing all prose histories to all poems.

I conclude that the sense of prevalence has no distinctive importance in the definition of poetry, both because it is not dominant in reading poetry and because it can be no less important in reading of other sorts, such as history, philosophy, scripture, journalism, and prose fiction. What Buchler identifies as distinguishing traits of poetry seem instead, insofar as they are discernible, to be widespread features of human experience, appropriate therefore to general metaphysics or philosophical psychology rather than to a definition of one form of literature.

In metaphysics, it will be pointed out that an alescence may also be, in some other respect or perspective (in some other order, as Buchler would put it) a prevalence. Thus the transitional or alescent character felt in a poem might also be viewed as prevalent and yield a "sense of prevalence." If so, would not the sense of prevalence retain priority? Without going into the deeper issues of metaphysics, it is clear that such an approach would continue to miss the point regarding the multiplicity and ambiguity of sense, awareness, and feeling in the experience of poetry. Prevalence is always prevalence in some order or context but Buchler carefully avoids saying that a sense of prevalence includes also a sense of some order in which the prevalence is located. For the psychology of "sense" in reading poetry is too variable and diffuse to make such a universal claim plausible. Accordingly, the sense of variation or alescence in a poem may or may not involve a sense of a context in which it might alternatively be or produce a sense of prevalence. Whether it does or not would have to be shown through a phenomenology of reading, to which the conclusions of metaphysical analysis, which is a different function of discursive consciousness, may be irrelevant. One is not necessarily aware of, and does not necessarily "sense," everything that is there. Thus the fact that an alescence can be a prevalence (in a different order) does not help Buchler's claim regarding the distinctive importance of a sense of prevalence in the nature of poetry. A sense of alescence is not automatically a sense of prevalence, any more than a concept of alescence would automatically be a concept of prevalence.

Difficulties no less telling apply to the notion of ontological parity in poetry. There may be a sense of parity, if the intellect is looking for comparisons in the ontological status of things discriminated and minimally accepts them all as discriminated, each with its identifiable function and status. But a particular poem, or phase of a poem (section, stanza, line, image, sentence), may prefer this element to that and may subordinate one to the other by representing one as less real than the other. The phenomenological fact that each element is given an assigned position in a comprehensive order does not mean that the assigned position is one of (or creates in the reader a sense of) equal reality. On the contrary, the historic systems of thought and art which seem built on the basis of, and give the reader a sense of, ontological priority—like the poetry of Dante—also often give each element a defined position in the whole. It seems to me that the sense one gets of parity or priority in reading poetry is relative to the complexities of the poem and its varied contexts of meaning. The same is true in science. Galileo, working in physics, looks on secondary qualities as unreal. But a modern psychology of perception may take a different stance, and Freud even attempted to construct a science of dreams. Poetry does not assert ontological parity, in Buchler's view. (ML 125) But whether it even gives the "sense" of ontological parity as he claims depends on the intent and function of the poem, or the part of a poem, we are talking about—as well as on what the mode of comprehension called "sense" is in the play of knowledge, meaning, and feeling that the poem produces in the reader.

To be sure, the prose translation of the Hōshi/Waley poem is open, as we have seen, to questions which introduce concerns that may be of practical importance to the reader. A difference in the status of various elements in the prose communication with respect to these practical goals may lead to relative judgments of reality and unreality of different elements. But prose does not necessarily lead that far, or else there could never be a prose metaphysics of ontological parity. Descriptive prose, whether in science or philosophy or in some other field, can give a sense of ontological parity, just as poetry such as that of Dante can give a sense of ontological priority. In Buchler's text, the lack of detail on the multiplicity of "senses" in reading means that there is no reason for thinking that one of these senses, at one level of generality, is dominant in the experience of poetry. The situation is the same here as in the case of the sense of prevalence, and for the same reason. Neither seems to have any special value for a definition of poetry.

Is there any larger merit to Buchler's theory of the nature of poetry? Although I believe his definition of poetry does not work as it is intended to work, I will conclude with some brief comments that limit and qualify this conclusion.

First, as will be evident to students of Buchler's philosophy, I have not dealt directly with his notion of exhibitive structure. This is important to the definition of poetry he offers, since poetry is embodied in exhibitive language, as are novels, folktales, and other nonpoetic forms of literary art. Buchler has much more to say about the nature of poetry than what is summarized in the twin senses of prevalence and ontological parity.

Second, an emphasis on exhibitive structure may help to explain why poetry seems to be more distant in some fashion from commitment to ontological priority. Perhaps poetry can exhibit ontological priority, and therefore generate a sense of ontological priority, as I have suggested above, but without committing the poet to acceptance of a metaphysics of ontological priority. A carefully applied distinction between exhibition and assertion may thus get Buchler something like what he wants in his theory of poetry—that the poet is committed to parity as a "working attitude" (ML 126), even if the poem does not necessarily or always give a sense of parity. As I see things, it would however remain difficult to locate in this way a distinctive feature of poetry, for the working attitude of the practicing scientist or philosopher may similarly be argued to be one of ontological parity, although the assertive conclusions of the scientist or philosopher may simultaneously reflect a conflicting commitment to ontological priority.

Third, Buchler's emphasis on prevalence rather than alescence in the phenomenology of poetry bears some similarity to the conceptual emphasis of many literary critics. Prevalence highlights the definiteness of traits, the presence of these traits rather than others that might have been there instead. It therefore suggests, as we noted in specific cases, the pattern or structure in which each of the elements has its place, whether it be a pattern of sounds, rhythm, line lengths, syllable counts, or meanings. Since literary criticism looks for patterns of various kinds, and at various levels of generality, the notion of a sense of prevalence may be a useful heuristic ideal in the advance of literary criticism. Even where the poet deliberately disrupts a pattern, as in much twentieth century poetry, and where new forms of linguistic transition are worked into the medium, there are other patterns that the insightful critic will discern. Perhaps, though, the notions of pattern and structure are inappropriate to some nontraditional poetry. The potential advantage of the notion of prevalence as a guide or ideal in literary criticism is its generality, its openness to different manifestations or types of prevalence—even going beyond those forms of prevalence that Buchler identifies—and its suggestion that it may be possible to devise a unifying background theory that can link into a single concept the various forms that literary criticism discovers. The focus in such a unifying effort would then be on the goals and the knowledge of the literary critic rather than on the phenomenology of reading poetry, although the development of such a theory of criticism would not easily avoid the problems we found in the direct application of Buchler's theory to the reading of poetry.

Notes

1. Buchler's book on poetry is entitled *The Main of Light: On the Concept of Poetry* (ML). Richards' review is entitled "The Assertive, the Active, and the Exhibitive," *Times Literary Supplement* (November 29, 1974), p. 1343, reprinted here, pp. 253–58. The primary statement of Buchler's metaphysics is his *Metaphysics of Natural Complexes* (MNC). See "List of Abbreviations" for Buchler's works, p. xiii.

2. See Richards, "The Assertive, the Active, and the Exhibitive," here p. 253.

3. See commentary and reference in Note 7 regarding Hōshi/Waley poem.

4. The poem is printed on pp. 279–80 and is analyzed subsequently in the text. Also see commentary in Note 7.

5. Hugh Kenner, "The Experience of the Eye," in *Modern Critical Views: Marianne Moore*, ed. Harold Bloom (NY: Chelsea House Publ., 1987), p. 17.

6. Donald Hall, *Marianne Moore: The Cage and the Animal* (New York: Pegasus 1970), p. 47.

7. It is perhaps worth noting that the sense of prevalence of any complex, whether in or out of poetry, depends in part on the act of discriminating the complex and therefore of recognizing it as "one." The perceived and studied unity (structure) of a poem thus depends on its being identified as one poem. The importance of such initial identification in the larger development of a phenomenology of poetry is dramatically illustrated by several of the poems Buchler quotes, which exist in different versions, each of which may generate some different sense or senses than other versions of the same poem, compounding the difficulties we have been studying. The Hōshi/Waley poem, for example, is originally in Japanese and then translated into English, and in Buchler's book the English is printed with two of Waley's lines transposed. Are the English versions (Waley and Buchler) two poems or one? (See Buchler's, p. 263 and Waley's, p. 279.) Marianne Moore's poem "The Fish" is a revision of a version previously published three times with the same words in the same word order but with a different stanzaic system (the third and fourth lines of each stanza in the earlier version being combined into the third line in the later version). Analyzing the impact of the change, Kenner writes: "One can nearly say, putting the first and second versions side by side, that we have a *new* poem, arrived at in public, without changing a word, by applying a system of transformations to an existing poem." (Kenner, op. cit., p. 18) There are variant versions also in the poems Buchler quotes from Williams, King, Pound, Parra, and the Bible, if we count such things as visual format, typography, line lengths, the inclusion of an epigram, spelling, punctuation, alternate translation, the alteration of words, and the omission of lines. Since the mere identification of a poem is not an easy matter, the complications of the phenomenology of reading are not surprising.

The two poems we have studied are found in the following books: Arthur Waley, *Japanese Poetry: The "Uta"*, new ed. (Honolulu: University Press of Hawaii, 1976), p. 103, which also includes a transliteration of the Japanese (to which Buchler's transposition of lines is closer than Waley's text is) as well as a footnote justifying an exclamation mark that Buchler omits; and Marianne Moore, *Collected Poems* (New York: The Macmillan Co., 1951), pp. 37–38 for the revised version of "The Fish" which Buchler and I have used.

Poem By Saigyō Hōshi (1118–1190 A.D.)

1	*Tomo ni narite*	3	Those ships which left
2	*Onaji-minato wo*	2	The same harbour
3	*Izuru fune no*	1	Side by side
4	*Yuku-ye mo shirazu*	4	Towards an unknown destination
5	*Kogi-wakare-nuru!*	5	Have rowed away from one another!

l. 4 lit. "destination being unknown."
no followed by the attributive *nuru* turns the sentence into an exclamation.

The Fish

wade
through black jade.
   Of the crow-blue mussel-shells, one keeps
   adjusting the ash-heaps;
      opening and shutting itself like

an
injured fan.
   The barnacles which encrust the side
   of the wave, cannot hide
      there for the submerged shafts of the

sun,
split like spun
   glass, move themselves with spotlight swiftness
   into the crevices—
      in and out, illuminating

the
turquoise sea
   of bodies. The water drives a wedge

of iron through the iron edge
of the cliff; whereupon the stars,

pink
rice-grains, ink-
  bespattered jelly-fish, crabs like green
  lilies, and submarine
    toadstools, slide each on the other.

All
external
  marks of abuse are present on this
  defiant edifice—
    all the physical features of

ac-
cident—lack
  of cornice, dynamite grooves, burns, and
  hatchet strokes, these things stand
    out on it; the chasm-side is

dead.
Repeated
  evidence has proved that it can live
  on what can not revive
    its youth. The sea grows old in it.

Reference, Interpretation, and Articulation: Rethinking Meaning in the Arts

Armen Marsoobian

The aim of this essay is to develop in a preliminary fashion the conceptual basis for a general theory of aesthetic meaning. I will begin by first exploring two approaches to meaning commonly found in contemporary discussions of art. These I call respectively the "referential"and the "interpretational" approaches. I will then argue for an alternative, more generic approach, which does not entail the rejection of either reference or interpretation, but will seek to demonstrate their limited purview. My approach is largely indebted to the philosophical work of Justus Buchler, in particular his theory of communication. I will argue that aesthetic meaning ultimately makes sense only within human communication broadly conceived.

While most contemporary approaches to aesthetic meaning recognize the role of both reference and interpretation, one or the other of these is conceptually dominant. Typical of these alternatives are the theories of Nelson Goodman and Arthur C. Danto. Though it is not my intention to examine the complexities of their respective philosophies of art, I must sketch some important contrasts in their positions as they pertain to our topic.

Let me begin by making the somewhat bald assertion that one way of reading Danto's philosophy of art is to see it as a search for alternatives to Goodman's referential theory. While Danto's dissatisfaction with Goodman focuses primarily upon the latter's inability to answer identity questions for artworks, that is, to provide the defining difference between "works of art" and "mere real things," its source lies in the concept of meaning. The multifarious kinds of reference identified by Goodman do not serve to mark off aesthetically meaningful artifacts from the other meaningful products of human endeavor. Danto by shifting the focus away from reference to that of interpretation poses a serious challenge to Goodman's approach to meaning.

I

In order to understand Danto's criticisms we must first sketch Goodman's approach to the "languages of art." For Goodman the notion of reference, which lies at the heart of representation, is a more complex affair than simple denotation. Denotation is only one of a number of species of reference, some important others being "exemplification" and "expression." Denotation itself also has a variety of subspecies. Reference is Goodman's most generic term for what he calls "all sorts of symbolizations, all cases of *standing for.*"[1] Denotation is reserved "for the application of a word or picture or other label to one or many things." (MM 55) In verbal denotation the word "cat" and in pictorial denotation the drawing 🐱 denote the many animals of the feline species. Among the many subspecies of denotation relevant to art, Goodman has identified three: 1) verbal denotation, both fictive and nonfictive (e.g., words, phrases, or predicates), 2) notation (e.g., musical scores, dance notation), and 3) pictoral denotation (e.g., depiction or representation by drawing, painting, sculpture, photography, film, etc.).

Goodman first enunciated this theory in his book *Languages of Art.* Much of the initial criticism directed against this work focused upon the third mentioned subspecies, pictorial denotation. Goodman had argued that for a symbol (i.e., a painting, drawing, sculpture) to represent or depict an object it must participate in a conventional symbol system similar to that of verbal language. The possible resemblance of the symbol to its object has nothing to do with it being a representation of that object. What determines the referential relationship is a matter of the conventions or rules within the symbol system. Symbol systems themselves vary, often greatly. The syntactic structures of these systems determine how the symbols are identified and distinguished from each other. The semantic structures do the same for the referents. These structures are largely determinative of how a symbol functions.

A detailed account of Goodman's general theory is not our primary concern. What does concern us is the primacy of reference. For Goodman some form of reference is always generic to an artwork if it is to have meaning. Diverse artforms all depend upon some primary referential relationship for the conveyance of meaning to spectators, audiences and readers. An instance of this can readily be seen in Goodman's handling of such traditionally nonrepresentational arts as abstract painting and nonprogram or absolute music. Goodman introduces the species of reference called exemplification to encompass these forms. Exemplification "runs in the opposite direction" from denotation:

Exemplification is selective, obtaining only between the symbol and some but not others of the labels denoting it or properties possessed by it. Exemplification is not mere possession of a feature but requires also reference to that feature. . . . Exemplification is thus a ceratin subrelation of the converse of denotation, distinguished through a return reference *to* denoter by denoted. (MM 59)

Goodman further claims that the properties (or labels) that a symbol (i.e., an artwork) possesses may be of two kinds: "literal" and "metaphorical." Metaphorically a symphony may be "tragic," a painting "powerful." Such metaphorical exemplification is called by Goodman "expression." Expression on this scheme is yet another subvariety of reference. Goodman rejects both traditional "viewer-centered" and "artist-centered" theories of expression. In his words:

A symphony that expresses feelings of tragic loss does not literally have those feelings; nor are the feelings expressed those of the composer or spectator; they are feelings that the work has metaphorically and refers to by exemplification. (MM 61)

Thus a symphony may express a variety of emotions but does not express its literal properties. Literal properties are exemplified by what Goodman calls "instantiation." He illustrates the latter species of reference by the example of a tailor's swatch instantiating certain physical properties of the cloth (e.g., texture and color but not size, shape, or "made in Hong Kong").

For Goodman both "expression" and "instantiation" are forms of selective reference:

Plainly not all the countless features of the work matter (not, for example, the painting's weighing four pounds) . . . but only those qualities and relationships of color or sound, those spatial and temporal patterns, and so on that the work exemplifies and thus selectively refers to . . . (MM 60)

The process of exemplification *is selective*. Not all the properties of the symbol are of equal relevance. The features that are selected in this self–referential process often vary for any given symbol. Just as we may have ambiguity of reference in a language system, so may we have ambiguity of exemplification in the arts. This can be as crude as the smudged handprint on the Warhol *Brillo Box* that a careless spectator left for future puzzled spectators or as complex as the expressive ambiguity of a major symphony. For example, when the Central Committee of the Communist Party interpreted the improvisational bassoon recitative of the fourth movement of Shostakovich's Symphony No. 9 as an expression of "bourgeois decadence," metaphorical exemplification was being judged univocally. This music's drollness was unappreciated, for it was a time (i.e., the defeat of Nazi Germany) which called for the portrayal of the heroism and nobility of the working man and woman. The ambiguity of expression (metaphorical exemplification) may have been lost on the Party in its confusion of the ironic with the trivial in Shostakovich's work. As Mozart taught us long ago, the comic may be a means to unmask the truth, not merely a celebration of the banal.

At this point we may ask what, if anything, controls the selection of the symbol properties (labels) that are exemplified? Symbols, in Goodman's scheme, require reference to be the symbols that they are; but what requires the reference to be the kind of reference that it is? Though there may be multiple and often complex chains of reference, I will argue that a crucial feature of symbolization is conceptually underemphasized in Goodman's analysis. Simply put, *meaning requires interpretation.* Goodman's theory lays stress upon the dyadic nature of symbols. "A symbol system consists of a symbol scheme correlated with a field of reference."[2] Critical practice among the practitioners of a symbol system ultimately determines this correlation. Such practice within music theory supposedly determines what "literal" vocabulary (e.g., pitch, tone, melody, etc.) is appropriate to the characterization or expression typical of music. If a bassoon recitative is "droll," it can be so only relative to some literal theoretical description in musical terms (i.e., the key, tempo, and rhythm). Yet it is *how* the key, tempo, and rhythm are *read* that ultimately determines the music's expression as droll. This *how* may be quite conventionalized and formulaic or novel and unprecedented. Determining how these elements work together is best understood, I will argue, not through the identification of metaphorically exemplified "labels" or properties, but through how the product as arrayed or shaped is discriminated in a communicative act. The minor key, quick tempo, the irregular rhythm of the bassoon melody have a relative finality of their own which is not captured in Goodman's notion of reference as "standing for." These features may "stand for" drollness but they do more than that.

Charles S. Peirce implicitly recognized the limitations of reference when he identified meaning not with the sign-referent relation but with the sign-interpretant relation.[3] Signs for Peirce are triadic. He claimed that a sign has meaning only if it is translatable by another sign, that is, only if it has an interpretant. Reference, on this view, is ultimately determined by interpretation. Aesthetic meaning is much more a matter of the continuing translatability of artworks by interpretants (other signs) than it is the identification of the appropriate objects of reference. We will need to come back to this notion of translatability and the central role it plays in communication when we examine Buchler's position. For the moment we will turn to Danto's theory.

II

In contrast to Goodman, Danto's analysis of aesthetic meaning can be seen as an extension of Peirce's insight into the centrality of the interpretant. In his treatment of this issue in *The Transfiguration of the Commonplace*, Danto is initially fascinated by Goodman's suggestion that metaphorical exemplification lies at the heart of aesthetic expression and thus may serve to answer the identity question.[4] But Danto soon finds exemplification unable to handle the burden of meaning. Danto claims that any strict distinction between literal and metaphorical properties cannot hold up under close examination. By citing examples of supposedly literal predicates which are *both* literally and metaphorically exemplified, Danto calls into question Goodman's classification by the varieties of reference.

It is Danto's contention that expressive predicates *can and often do* fall under the conventional extension of an artwork's alleged literal properties. If I cite his own example, the Beauvais Cathedral, unlike the tailor's swatch, expresses "verticality" (a so-called "literal property"), it does not merely instantiate it. (TC 192) According to Danto we have to know *how* a predicate is employed by a work before we can grasp its reference. It is not enough to know that certain properties are "ordinarily" or "conventionally" associated through critical practice with specific symbol systems while others are not. For instance, weight is normally associated with the literal (i.e., the nonaesthetic) properties in the symbol system of painting. But Danto challenges such easy associations. Much that we find in modern art can be marshalled in support of his challenge. The mere lack of conventional literalness is not an adequate basis upon which to identify metaphorical properties. More is needed to distinguish the *how* from the *what* than is provided for by denotation, inverse or otherwise. Danto concludes: "The philosophical point is that the concept of expression can be reduced to the concept of metaphor, when the *way* in which something is represented is taken in connection with the subject represented." (TC 197) The notion of "standing for" at the heart of most referential theories of meaning is simply inadequate for this task.

Danto's philosophy of art does take another direction. In a number of places he has argued quite persuasively that interpretation is constitutive of

art. To cite his strongest formulation: "An object is an artwork *at all* only
in relation to an interpretation."[5] Interpretation is the agency by which
quite commonplace objects can be raised or "transfigured" to the level of
art. (PDA 44,78) Even primarily referential works, for example, portraits,
are "never merely referential." (PDA 79) They have what Danto calls a
"semi-opacity":

> By a semi-opaque object, I mean one which presents a content, but
> where the mode of presentation—once more a fregean notion—must
> be compounded with the content to determine the meaning of the
> object. There is a rhetorical dimension to any work of art in conse-
> quence of this interplay between content and mode of presen-
> tation . . . it is internally connected with the psychology of artistic
> response, in which interpretation is coimplicated with appreciation.
> (PDA 79)

An object is meaningful as an artwork only when we see the interrelation
between the "what" (the content) and the "how" (the mode of presentation) of the work. Danto has recognized that artworks are *relational complexes* whose constituent traits go well beyond the status of being
surrogates—surrogates ultimately for objects falling under the extension of
a so-called "label." There is an incipient recognition that the artwork as
shaped and contrived is as primary as any role it may play in a system of
reference. As we will shortly see it is precisely this recognition that is systematically developed in Buchler's concept of exhibitive utterance.

In his emphasis upon interpretation Danto is striving to chart a middle course between two extremes in the theory of art. One extreme, deriving from semantical approaches to meaning, is labeled by Danto the
"Transparency Theory." On such a view artworks themselves begin to
"disappear" as they more adequately "mirror" what they are "about,"
what they "mean." On the other extreme we find current literary theory's
obsession with "intertextuality." A text, be it in language or some other
medium, is meaningful solely in terms of other texts. This approach, while
dismissing the semantical approach as committing what it calls the "Referential Fallacy," errs by narrowly identifying meaning with the "literary
culture" of the artist (e.g., the conscious or unconscious influence of other
texts upon the artist).

Danto contends that both of these approaches distance artworks from
their audiences. He writes that "if art [has] something important to do with
our lives . . . this is utterly unexplained if its meaning is a matter of its
reference, and its candidate referenda are as bizarre a menagerie of imag-
inabilia as the fancy of man has framed." (PDA 144) On the one hand,

semantical theory falls short, according to Danto, because the only kinds of connections it understands between symbols and the world are "reference, truth, instantiation, exemplification, satisfaction, and the like." This approach distorts the world "in order that it can *receive* literary representations . . ." (PDA 145) On the other hand, if artworks are simply Derridean "networks of reciprocal relationships," this puts them at an "intraversable" distance from their audience. As a consequence literary works "become simply artifacts made of words, with no reference save internal ones, or incidental external ones. And reading them becomes external, as though they had nothing to do with us, were merely there, intricately wrought composites of logical lacework, puzzling and pretty and pointless." (PDA 160)

The middle course that Danto proposes ties together three of the points we have already stressed: (1) the importance of interpretation for reference, (2) the emphasis upon the *way* in which something is represented, and (3) the notion that artworks have a kind of semi-opacity. In a number of recent essays Danto brings these points to bear upon an analysis of the differences and similarities between literature and philosophy. Though tentative in his claims, the implications of his approach are suggestive and worth pursuing.

Danto claims that a literary work is a metaphor for the reader—an admittedly vague claim. Reference is still operating but in a very unusual fashion:

> The universality of literary reference is only that it is about each individual that reads the text at the moment that individual reads it, . . . identifying himself not with the implied reader for whom the implied narrator writes, but with the actual subject of the text in such a way that each work becomes a metaphor for each reader: perhaps the same metaphor for each. (PDA 155)

Although "metaphoric identification" of the reader with the work is at first blush a rather startling notion, it does hint at an important aspect of the alternative theory of meaning I wish to propose. In anticipation, let me say, that this approach emphasizes the fact that meaning is an achievement of human communication. For something to "have" meaning it must *function* communicatively within some perspective. Meaning is a form of communicative efficacy. To understand meaning we must look toward the "effect" of the work and not merely at what it "stands for."

For Danto the effect in artistic communication is achieved in a manner different from that in philosophy or other non-literary forms. In art the idea is "embodied" or "incarnate" in the work; in nonartistic works there is a weaker sense of embodiment, a greater transparency, a lesser opacity. He writes: "What makes [Andy Warhol's] *Brillo Box* a work of art is that it incarnates, expresses, whatever idea it does express, hence is an idea and a mere thing at once, a box transfigured if only into the idea of a box." (PDA 178)

Admittedly embodiment is a vague notion. Citing Platonic dialogues as primary examples, Danto does recognize that certain philosophical texts do "embody" philosophical ideas. But the need to draw a stricter line between art and nonart forces him to set certain qualifications on the notion of embodiment. For the philosopher the character of the communication is essentially different from that of the artist. The assertive nature of language is paramount or to put it in Danto's terms, the ideas are more directly conveyed or "mainlined." He further qualifies the difference with a self-consciously banal remark concerning subject matter: "Literature cannot stray very far from the structures that define the life of those who read novels: love, jealousy, friendship, adventure, conflict and crisis . . . " (PDA 184) But in the end, even Danto himself admits that a restriction of subject matter is perhaps too arbitrary, yet he offers no alternatives.

While having rightly focused the discussion of artistic meaning on artistic communication, Danto's analysis is stymied by an inability to generalize the chief terms of his analysis. For in the end, he relies upon a semantically based conception of communication: Artworks express ideas, albeit in unique and unusual ways.

III

Justus Buchler's general theory of human utterance or judgment overcomes the difficulties of semantically based theories of meaning by broadening our understanding of communication while providing the conceptual basis for meaningful distinctions between different kinds of communication. If, following Buchler, we treat all human utterance broadly conceived (verbal as well as nonverbal) as falling under three general functional types, that is, as assertions, contrivances, and actions, we avoid the need to rely upon either of Danto's criteria of "directness" of communication or "appropriateness" of subject matter to distinguish art from nonart. The focus must shift to the issue of *how* human beings produce, that is, to the character of human production.

Buchler contends that "every product is a judgment." What he means is that every product is at bottom a stance adopted toward the world. Man naturally and continuously discriminates, selects from, and adds to the complexes that make up his world.[6] Judgment, in this sense, is inevitable, ubiquitous, and never fully isolatable into discrete events. And most importantly, judgment is never exclusively identified with mental activity or consciousness. Buchler writes:

> Man judges continuously, through what he includes and excludes, preserves and destroys, is inclined to and averse to; through what he makes and fails to make, through the ways he acts and refrains from acting, through what he believes and disavows. His attitudes, and hence his commitments, are his whether he is aware of them or not. (ML 93)

To fully appreciate this insight into the judicative nature of human production, it must be emphasized that judging is not primarily a discrete mental act preceding or subsequent to other forms of behavior. We do not necessarily judge first, in the sense of formulating a course of action, and then act. The action, the doing itself, is a form of judgment. Thus the artist in the act of making is judging, so too, albeit in a different sense, is the spectator in the act of appreciation. Neither activity is adequately translatable into a semantical model. The emphasis and ultimately the basis for distinguishing the three modes of judgment (i.e., active, assertive, and exhibitive) rests upon the way in which the judging occurs:

> To say that a man judges, for example, through what he makes, does not mean that he makes after he has discriminated and selected and become committed. It means that his making what he makes *is the way* he has discriminated and selected and become committed. (ML 93–4)

Active, exhibitive, and assertive judgment do not mark structural but rather functional differences. A given product may function in more than one mode. This is an important consideration for resolving some of the difficulties raised in Danto's analysis, in particular his proposal for distinguishing borderline cases between literature and philosophy. Summarizing the important functional differences between these modes Buchler writes:

> (1) When we can be said to predicate, state, or affirm, by the use of words or by any other means; when the underlying direction is to achieve or support belief; when it is relevant to cite evidence in behalf of our product, we produce in the mode of assertive judgment, we judge assertively. (2) When we can be said to do or to act; when the underlying direction is toward effecting a result; when "bringing about" is the central trait attributable to our product, we produce in the mode of active judgment, we judge actively. (3) When we

contrive or make, in so far as the contrivance rather than its role in action is what dominates and is of underlying concern; when the process of shaping and the product as shaped is central, we produce in the mode of exhibitive judgment, we judge exhibitively. On the methodic level, where (minimally) purposiveness and intention belong to judgments, assertive judgment is exemplified by science, or more generally, inquiry . . . ; active judgment, by deliberate conduct morally accessable; exhibitive judgment, by art. (ML 97–8)

   This functional approach to judgment can clarify the difficulties we encountered earlier with literary and non-literary exemplification. No product is intrinsically active, assertive, or exhibitive. The judicative function is determined by the communicative context. For a literary work the communicative context typically does not call for interpretation in terms of truth and falsity. The artwork does not primarily aim to compel or support belief, although this does not rule out its possible role in the expression or inculcation of beliefs. For example, Harriet Beecher Stowe's *Uncle Tom's Cabin* may support certain beliefs about abolition, but in the artistic context the latter is incidental to exhibitive confrontation. Thus, Danto's earlier notion regarding the "semi-opacity" of artworks has more to do with their mode of utterance than with the fact that content is presented. In the literary context the artwork offers itself to interpretation and appraisal as an arrangement or constellation of qualities or traits; in literature it may do so through the use of either conventional or devised linguistic signs and through the use of such signs in conventional or nonconventional ways.[7] As an exhibitive judgment its communicative effect, contrary to Danto, is neither more nor less direct than that of language used assertively.
   On the other hand, the exhibitive dimension of philosophic writing, or for that matter even of mathematics, subserves and even extends the role of assertion. In a philosophical work assertions may be arrayed in a particular exhibitive manner in order to communicate univocally and compel greater unanimity of belief. Spinoza's choice of the order of geometrical demonstration in his *Ethics* is a case in point. Yet in this case the showing ultimately subserves the saying.
   The modes of judgment do not privilege one form of communication over another. Semantically based theories of meaning, while recognizing the role of the active and exhibitive dimensions of communication, tend to subordinate their judicative and cognitive value to that of the assertive. This leads, as Buchler says, "[to] the false implication . . . that the work of art always conforms to the model of dumb-show pointing to one-knows-not-what [representational theories], or to the model of total sensory-affective involvement [expression theories]—both wholly noncommittal."

(ML 100) In either case art functions primarily to "convey" ideas whether of the "internal world of the imagination" or the "external world of reality." When such ideas are not easily located in recognizable or conventional orders of semantic meaning, the prejudice that art is a "lesser" or "more unreliable" form of assertion is perpetuated.

If we turn directly to the issue of meaning, we may say that in its most generic sense a product or any existent related to man (Buchler's term "procept") functions meaningfully if it *initiates the articulation of some perspective* within which it is located. A perspective is an order of human existence or functioning.[8] A product is located in innumerable orders, some of which include human traits while others do not. The specific gravity of a painting would normally belong to a nonhuman order of existence while the same painting's monetary worth would be locatable in the perspective of the art market. The scope of a particular perspective may be wide or narrow. In the usage I am adopting from Buchler, a perspective is not an unsharable psychological or historical point of view. It is not a window on the world—a world somehow set apart from man. Such locutions as "in my perspective" or "the medieval perspective" when used to imply totally unique and nonoverlapping orders of relatedness are specifically denied. As such, perspectives are not arbitrary conventions of or for relatedness, whether language based or not.

It is important to note that for Buchler the phrase "articulation of perspective" is more generic than interpretation. Contrary to some associations of common usage, articulation is not limited to verbal language and assertion. Articulation may take place in any of three modes of judgment. The molding of clay in the sculptor's hands as well as the reading of a book are articulations of perspective. For Buchler articulation is a bringing out, a deliverance—a deliverance from what is given.[9]

The perspective that is articulated is the communicative context broadly conceived. This context may vary in scope for each particular instance of communication. There are an indeterminate number of perspectives in which an artwork may meaningfully function. Though varying in importance, Buchler contends that: "There is no ultimate mode of articulation." (NJ 89) This permits us to claim that an artwork has meaning in nonartistic orders of judgment. For instance, a Freudian interpretation, or any "deep interpretation," to use Danto's phrase, would be meaningful, but not in the same manner as that found in the exhibitive order of artworks.[10] Freud's interpretation of Leonardo da Vinci's *Virgin and Child with St. Anne,* is meaningful primarily in the perspective of psycho-biography, though it may contribute in a secondary way to the aesthetic (or even the art-historical) appreciation of the work by drawing our attention to the similarities in physical appearance between the two female figures in the painting.

David Hockney
"A Visit with Christopher and Don, Santa Monica Canyon" 1984
Oil on two canvases   72 × 240"
© David Hockney, 1984

In the exhibitive order of art, articulation takes the form of either the *production* of or the *discovery* of, by means of subsequent utterance, other elements within the perspective. Judgments are thus ramified and ramifiable.

Ramification is not merely the expansion of the identifiable traits of the perspective (i.e., the communicative context). Articulation may take place by the elimination or attenuation as well as by the addition or expansion of traits within the perspective. Often both occur at the same time. For example, the painter David Hockney, by consciously jettisoning single-point perspective in many of his later works, is thus able to capture an element of temporality and motion often missing in this medium. In his paintings of the interiors of California homes (e.g., *A Visit with Christopher and Don, Santa Monica Canyon 1984*) the eye is not drawn to a single focus but is drawn across the canvas as if one were entering and exiting a room. As spectators we are forced to give up a long ingrained habit of viewing paintings.[11] The painting is meaningful in just such a way. This is more than merely saying that the painting is "about" the lack of perspective. Of course this is not to deny that we often make such assertions when asked "What does the painting mean?" Yet such assertions may only identify one of the many forms in which the "meaning" of the painting is made available—frequently its least efficacious form.

According to this general theory of meaning, the ramification of judgment is what we mean by the phrase "the articulation of perspective." Accordingly, it is synonymous with the further availability of the product for assimilation and manipulation.[12] Within the order of artworks, ramified judgment may take the form of the artistic influence of one artwork upon another, or one school or style of artistic invention upon other schools, styles or individual artists. For example, the perspective that Beethoven is articulating in his piano sonatas includes the conventional sonata form as developed by Haydn and others. Beethoven's sonatas, especially the late sonatas, are an extension of this conventional form by means of both assimilation and manipulation. Taking the specific instance of the Opus 106 Sonata in B flat major *(Hammerklavier),* we can see that the communicative context (i.e., the perspective) includes the artist's creative assimilation and manipulation of both the musical conventions of his day and those of prior generations. What Beethoven leaves us with is not a sonata in any easily recognizable sense. For example, in the fourth movement of Opus 106, Beethoven writes a fugue whose counterpoint taxes the imagination, let alone the fingers, of those raised on the fugues of Cherubini, Kirnberger, or even Bach. It is in this sense that the meaning of the Fourth movement is more than merely referential. While it is "about" the art of the fugue, it is much more than that. What we have is Beethoven's brilliantly unique exhibitive articulation of counterpoint. Our realization, as an audience, of what is going on in the Fourth movement is itself a ramified judgment. We are judging exhibitively in our recognition of Beethoven's assimilation and manipulation of counterpoint. *The articulation of perspective is what we mean when we say that an artwork has meaning for a viewer, a reader, or an audience.*

The insight that articulation of perspective may be in any of the three modes of judgment, either singly or in combination, generalizes the notion of interpretation. The meaning of an artwork is not primarily or solely a function of reference. On this view meaning in the arts is no longer limited to a model of "messages" or "themes," whether in the form of a predicate or a property, to be conveyed or denoted by the artwork. Meaning is not fixed—either by the artist or the critic. Yet this does not mean that any meaning at all is possible. There is no denying the determinate traits of the Fourth movement, it is a fugue.[13] The artwork has determinate traits which enter into, that is, communicate with viewers, other artworks, and even whole artistic movements. These communicative contexts become the meaning*s* of an artwork. The need to encompass the multitude of articulations that an artwork engenders challenges us to fundamentally rethink our standard conceptions of meaning. My remarks have been intended to serve as a prolegomenon to such a rethinking.

Notes

1. Nelson Goodman, *Of Mind and Other Matters* (Cambridge, Mass: Harvard University Press, 1984), p. 55. Hereafter cited in the text as MM. In all of Goodman's works the terms "predicate," "label," and "property" are used in a synonymous fashion.

2. Nelson Goodman, *Languages of Art: An Approach to a Theory of Symbols* (Indianapolis: Bobbs–Merrill Co., 1968), p. 143. Hereafter cited in the text as LA.

3. Unlike Goodman, for Charles Sanders Peirce "sign" is the generic term and "symbol" is a type of sign. Peirce maintained that every sign involves a triadic relation between a physical object or quality (the material thing taken as a sign), something which it denotes or refers to (its object), and another sign which it is said to "mean" or "connote" (its interpretant). Though many of the details of Peirce's general theory of signs are open to dispute, it is clear that "sign" is a relational and functional notion. The sign relation requires not a particular class of things but an object functioning significatively. To function significatively, that is, to have meaning, a sign must be translatable, be interpretable by another sign, its interpretant. The sign-object relation (reference) is conditioned upon the sign-interpretant relation (interpretation). The sign-interpretant relation, to use Peirce's language, provides the "ground of representation." This determining relation is a rule of interpretation. Rules needn't be formal or presented in propositional form. They are sign conventions which take the form of habits, varying in strength and alterability. They pro-

vide the standpoint, the perspective for interpretation. All interpretation is thus selective or abstractive. Features of the sign (or to use Goodman's terms, labels of the symbol) are necessarily included or excluded in relation to this standpoint. All representation involves the selection and discrimination of specific properties by means of an interpretation. The object (referent) is thus related to a sign by the interpretant. For a fuller discussion of these issues see my essay "Art and Interpretation: Peirce and Buchler on Aesthetic Meaning," forthcoming *Peirce Studies*, ed. Ken Ketner, (Indianapolis: Indiana University Press).

4. Arthur C. Danto, *The Transfiguration of the Commonplace: A Philosophy of Art* (Cambridge, Mass: Harvard University Press, 1981), pp. 188–201. Hereafter cited in the text as TC.

5. Arthur C. Danto, *The Philosophical Disenfranchisement of Art* (New York: Columbia University Press, 1986), p. 44. Hereafter cited in the text as PDA.

6. "Complex" or "natural complex" is the most generic form of identification for Buchler. "The expression 'natural complex' . . . applies to whatever is, and therefore to whatever can be dealt with; to what is produced by men as well as to what is not. It is the expression we have been using for whatever we wish to include in our range of reference without having to specify a mode of being." (ML 103) See also MNC 1ff. See "List of Abbreviations" for Buchler's works, p. xiii–xiv.

7. See in particular Buchler's interpretations of the poems of Browning, Donne, Blake, and Pope. (ML 101–116)

8. See MNC ch. 3, passim.

9. Buchler's naturalism in this regard is both pervasive and radical. The opening words of his book *Nature and Judgment,* in which he sets out his theory of meaning, highlight this fact: "Man is born in a state of natural debt, being antecedently committed to the execution or the furtherance of acts that will largely determine his individual existence. (NJ 1)

10. Marking out such differences is a task beyond the scope of this essay, but clearly there is a growing recognition in current literary theory of the importance of non-reductionistic approaches to interpretation. Buchler's theory provides the philosophical basis to support such insights.

11. David Hockney discussed what he was trying to accomplish in this painting in an interview: ". . . I was trying to create a painting where the viewer's eye could be made to move in certain ways, stop in certain places, move on, and in so doing, reconstruct the space across time for itself. I was combining lessons from both the Chinese scrolls and my study of Cubism. I mean, unlike the scrolls these were going to be large images meant to be seen all at once, but the thing was what I was aiming for was that in another sense they wouldn't be able to be seen all at once after all. They were filled with incident, but whenever you focused on any single detail everything else blurred into a sort of complex abstraction of shapes and colors, and the image as a whole was always primarily abstraction. This sense of

multiple simultaneous perspectives was something I'd, of course, honed during my work on the photocollages.'' Specifically leading the viewer through the painting Hockney continues: "You see, it's meant to be read from left to right unlike the Chinese scrolls, although there's a kind of tribute to the scrolls in a sort of pro-logue, the yellow strip at the top of the canvas, moving from right to left, which represents Adelaide Drive in Santa Monica. When I drive up there, I always know when to stop because of the big palm tree, and then there, at the number 145, there's the little driveway where they park their two cars. . . . From that position you look out over Santa Monica Canyon, which is painted in reverse perspective, so it clearly places you up there looking down. You then come down the steps, and they're painted that way because it's not you looking at the steps from afar, you are actually moving down them as you approach the entryway. You come into the living room, and there are those two wicker chairs. . . . Anyway, from the living room you can look out the window and you see the view of the canyon again, which means you've moved, you have to be seeing it. We then make a little detour here to the left into Don's studio, and there's Don drawing. You can go upstairs and down-stairs; you see the same view again from two different windows. Then coming back across the living room, moving rightward, you walk down a corridor, past the bed-room. If you notice, the television set, everything, is actually in reverse perspective, meaning you're moving past it, seeing first the front and then the back. And then you walk right to the end, into Christopher's studio and even past him, to the very end, at which point you're looking back because he's looking out through his win-dow, and its the same view of the canyon. So there, you've reconstructed the space, and now your eye is free to roam about from room to room, taking in more details." Quoted in an article by Lawrence Weschler, "A Visit with David and Stanley, Hol-lywood Hills 1987," in *David Hockney: A Retrospective* (Los Angeles: Los Angeles County Museum of Art, 1988), pp. 93–94.

12. For a discussion of the assimilative and manipulative dimensions of hu-man experience see NJ 131–142. Also TGT passim.

13. The complex issue of identity, especially with regard to artworks, can't be dealt with in this essay but Buchler's metaphysics can shed some fruitful light on this matter. For a discussion of the concept of identity see Majorie Cantor Miller, "The Concept of Identity in Justus Buchler and Mahayana Buddhism," reprinted here, pp. 93–113.

Exhibitive Judgment and Freud:
Toward a New Interpretation of Dreams

Ann-Mari Wallen Wachter

In this paper I will apply Buchler's concept of exhibitive utterance, not to art or general epistemology, but to Freud's theory of dreams and dream interpretation. I will hold that dreams are exhibitive utterances or judgments rather than distortions or disguises of suppressed assertive judgments or "dream-thoughts."

I begin with a brief, selective summary of Buchler's theory of human utterance or judgment, with emphasis on his concept of exhibitive utterance or judgment. I then make some critical remarks on the reductionism of Freud's approach, and its impact on his theory of dreams and dream interpretation. Buchler's theory of human utterance, especially his concept of exhibitive utterance, provides the basis for this criticism and for the alternative theory of dreams and dream interpretation which I offer.

In his theory of human utterance Justus Buchler speaks of "utterance" as more inclusive and more basic than the concept of "language."[1] Human utterance falls into three general modes of utterance: (1) *Assertive,* that is, predicating, stating or affirming, by the use of words or by any other means, when the underlying concern is to achieve or support belief, (2) *Active,* that is, doing or acting; when the underlying concern is toward effecting a result, (3) *Exhibitive,* that is, showing, contriving or making, when the shaping or arranging of materials in order to display the resulting exhibitive product as a completion or finality is the underlying concern. (ML 97) The three modes of utterance are also modes of judgment according to Buchler. Whatever human beings do, make or say involves appraisal. In judging one must select from options. Judgments are *cognitive* in this sense. "Cognitive" then is not restricted to assertive-logical cognition alone.

Every act, assertion or contrivance reveals something about the subject—the doer, sayer or maker. This is what Freud has made us all aware of. "Utterance" expresses adequately the revelatory aspect of what we do, say or make. But Buchler wants to say that in addition to the revelatory aspect of human products there is what he calls a "substantive" function of utterances that warrants naming them "judgments." While seeing every utterance as revelatory—seeing all human products as reflections of the self—accords all modes of utterance equal communicative status with that of "saying," it obscures their other aspect as pronouncements or judgments.

"Saying," "doing" and "showing" may be used as convenient tags for memorizing these concepts, but it is the *function* rather than the form of the utterance that labels it as "assertive," "exhibitive" or "active." A nod may function as a nonlinguistic *assertive* utterance. A command, such as "halt!" functions as an *active* utterance. A poem is an example of an *exhibitive* utterance presented by linguistic means. "Exhibitive," then, need not always mean "visual." A musical composition is another example of nonvisual exhibitive utterance. The products of exhibitive judgment may yield knowledge just as much as any other mode of judgment may. Their mode of showing allows a proceiver[2] to visualize and sense imagine in new ways that is exhibited by the judgment. I will suggest that dreams can be fruitfully understood as spontaneous or autonomic exhibitive utterances or judgments that uncover and reveal knowledge which may be unavailable to our ordinary wakeful means of inquiry.

The three modes of utterance or judgment are irreducible in the sense that no utterance in one mode is fully translatable into any other mode. But every utterance in one mode is somewhat translatable into the other modes of utterance and can be explicated or extended by articulation in another mode. (ML 101) By *showing* us, a play, painting or poem communicates exhibitively what could not be as effectively said by assertive utterance alone. We need not be consciously aware of what is exhibitively communicated. We can, though, reflect on the play, painting or poem and articulate, assertively or actively or exhibitively, some of the knowledge communicated by the exhibitive utterance or judgment (of the play, painting or poem).

The utterance in one mode, though not reducible into an utterance in another mode, or fully translatable into an utterance in another mode, is thus, nevertheless somehow relatable to utterances in other modes in that it can be accented and augmented by articulation in other modes. (NJ 39) It is therefore accurate to say that the meaning of the utterance or judgment is *achieved* by articulation. (ML 102)

Buchler defined "articulation" broadly as "effective interpretation in any mode of utterance." Assertive articulation, such as linguistic-logical rendering of a state of affairs, elucidates by "expressing clearly" or "uttering distinctly." This kind of elucidation is what is traditionally meant by "articulation." Active or exhibitive "articulation" in Buchler's broadened sense of the word elucidates differently than assertive articulation, but not less effectively. The Eiffel Tower and modern steel bridges can be presented as examples of active and exhibitive articulation of scientific assertions in that the actively supporting metal beams of the constructs are made to accord with mathematically derived theoretical lines of force. Being visible, the steel beams also *show* us the lines of force.

Exhibitive articulation is best exemplified by art. Art in general has served the function of bringing out or uttering effectively what may have been strongly but indistinctly present in experience. In the "blues" African-American musicians uttered effectively through music, just as the poet may have uttered in words, the "spiritual needs of the community." In both cases there is an articulation of experience in Buchler's broad sense of effective uttering in a distinct mode of utterance. Faulkner's short story "That Evening Sun" draws on the jazz composition the "St. Louis Blues" and could be said to articulate the musical piece. Both the story and the music articulate the black experience in the American South. The story rasps through one's soul as the jazz dissonances had the power to do when they were still felt to be disturbingly deconstructive musically. The active utterance of a battle can be articulated in a ballad or in a painting such as Picasso's *Guernica*. The painting again can be articulated by verbal statements of interpretation. Modern medical practices articulate medical theories.

Buchler uses "query" in a broader sense than "inquiry." "Inquiry" is *assertive* query. But there is also *exhibitive* query and *active* query. Explorers such as Columbus and Vasco da Gama engaged in active query. Any methodical physical search is active query. All query is methodical. Art in all its forms—not only those society chooses to designate as art—is exhibitive query, that is, art is a methodical form of exhibitive utterance. Common contemporary belief holds that only assertive and active query contribute to knowledge—or rightfully constitute query—but our general human query employs all three modes of judgment and each mode's way of contributing to human knowledge is equally important.

It is clear that active and assertive utterances and judgments are intertwined in query, that acts and verbal reasoning work hand in hand as exemplified in scientific inquiry where experiment and logically drawn conclusions interact towards the furthering of knowledge. It is less immediately evident that exhibitive utterance or judgment is as centrally involved in that general quest for knowledge which constitutes human query, and that it continuously interacts with the other modes in the general pursuit of knowledge.

All query is methodical, but the method of exhibitive query differs from that of inquiry. Exhibitive query does not attempt to substantiate truth claims; it does not aim at negating other views. It does not aim at terminating wonder. The interrogativeness of exhibitive query like the interrogativeness of inquiry lies in its seeking. But in exhibitive query the seeking and finding are less separable than in inquiry. (ML 111) Science attempts to solidify our knowledge into an univocal order of "facts" that fit within a framework or "theory," making for a fixed system of knowledge. Inquiry attempts to resolve wonder, it aims at coming to the end of query or at least delimiting query. Exhibitive query opens up ways of seeing for us by departing from hierarchical systems of ordering. Exhibitive query is not bound by the priorities of inquiry, for its desire is for exploration rather than final answers. This is why art is often claimed to provide no knowledge. Like Socrates it concocts questions rather than formulates answers. This was what vexed Plato. The mathematician in Plato wanted final and absolute, fixed answers. The dialectic method Socrates and Plato borrowed from sophism used the "power of the negative" to delimit query. But the informal oral format that Socrates favored allowed a free dialogue that was active as well as assertive and to a high degree exhibitive in function. Buchler points out that the turn of interrogative temper that directs the artist also in some respects directs the philosopher. Philosophic query may be variously informed by both the kind of wonder that seeks to be appeased (the assertive dimension of philosophy) and by the kind of wonder that perpetuates itself (the exhibitive dimension of philosophy). (ML 144) This was the case with Plato. "The relation we are entitled to expect among constituent aspects of a philosophic outlook," says Buchler, "is that of mutual enhancement and complementation, not that of formal consistency." (ML 146) Consistency is a norm that belongs to *assertive* utterance or judgment. When a philosophic outlook is predominantly *exhibitive,* as Plato's is, we should not simply demand consistency but rather ask whether the different modes of philosophical query enhance one another, whether the presence of each sharpens the awareness of the integrity and value of the other. Plato deploys inquiry and exhibitive query skillfully, but the final impact of Plato's method lies in its effectiveness as exhibitive query.

    Exhibitive query uses its own kind of analysis. A Henry Moore exhibition represents a concrete and recent example of artistic analysis.[3] All the sculptures exhibited had "Mother and Child" as their motif. Most of Moore's artistic life was devoted to what amounts to an analysis of the mother-child relational complex. The analysis varies the depiction around that theme: In some of the sculptures the infant is fetal in shape, in some a fairly fully formed child is seated on the mother's knee, standing beside her or playing near her. The child figure is always somewhat undeveloped, dependent, and secondary to the mother figure which is always of strength and comfort and much content; she is not only flesh as women often appear to be in artist's eyes; Moore's woman figure is of fleshed bone. The bones are of varied strong, molded pelvic shapes—emphasizing the pelvic bones in woman as one of nature's central, important structures—a construct of engineering that must support and hold the future of humans. In some of the variations she contains cavities—caves or openings to the daylight— holes one could emerge through as in birth or in leaving the shielding, primeval darkness of Plato's cave, caves one could withdraw into for protection and comfort. The chest is often softly concave rather than protruding. This seems artistically "right." It takes a moment's effort to articulate (in words) what the gently concave chest of a mother depicts: The slight concave shows the ease with which one can lean on her breast. A protruding breast is depicted in the instances where the child's mouth reaches for a nipple. Even then the other breast may be hollowed out.

There were a few family groupings, too, in the exhibition. In one of them the father figure was hollow—somewhat in the manner of the Eiffel Tower or a construction crane where only the necessary structural supports exist and all else is emptiness. This emptiness of content and emphasis on the outward or barest mechanical functionality set a stark contrast to the highly "overdetermined" concave and convex structures of the mother-body. There was one circular family grouping where the father figure was not an empty construct but contributed to help form a family whole. The individual sculptures and the collection as analysis articulated the mother-child relational complex. In such an exhibition variations of constellations are shifted about and arranged around a theme. In this case the theme was the mother-child relational complex. Within the guidance of the theme each individual sculpture or product of art in the exhibition is a product of artistic query, a shaped or formed finality, and the collection as exhibited also is a product of artistic shaping or artistic query resulting in a finality.

Ordinarily knowledge is obtained through a cooperative interaction of the three modes in query. Buchler points out that reflection or thinking as *assertive* utterance moves dialectically, and that the dialectic involves a recurrent change of positions or perspectives, and that this change itself is an act, that is, an *active* utterance. Furthermore, there is always an *exhbitive* element in thought; constellations of signs are arranged and shifted about until at a point one order is accepted as the order to be consummated in thought. The exhibitive query may be of fleeting duration but it nevertheless occurs. Buchler thus holds that thought as reflective assertion cannot be dissociated from acting and making. There is also a converse dependency: Acts and contrivances require assertion for their cognitive augmentation or even for their cognitive consummation (NJ 38) which would indicate that assertion has a special function within cognition, that it augments or even consummates cognition of acts or contrivances. As assertion is assuredly human, this makes for one cognitive advantage of human utterances. But human acts and contrivances are cognitive without assertive augmentation or consummation of their cognitive content. And language can diminish the cognitive content of acts and contrivances as well as augment or consummate it.

According to Buchler, mutual intimacy and proximity of judgments of the different modes is the rule rather than the exception. The spontaneously occurring junctions of thinking, contriving-composing and acting may or may not further knowledge. These unpredictable junctions or associative jumps between modes of judgment may inform by permitting insights unavailable to an orderly and restricted query, or they may merely cause confusion. In the former case they may incite or rekindle query. Francis Bacon contrasts "the promiscuous liberty of the search, and the severity of inquiry," whereas Locke says that "all reasoning is search and casting about." Buchler points out that "the severity of inquiry" actually presupposes "the promiscuous liberty of search." There would then be something akin to a dialectic between the modes.

The modes blend in human query but are separable in theory and relatively separable in practice. The methodical separation of the modes is as important as the cooperation between the modes. Without the deliberate ascesis of using a mode in its greatest possible purity we would not have achieved as much as we have achieved in science or in art. Mathematics and abstract art are examples of such ascesis, that is, of cases when a mode of utterance or judgment, *assertive* in the case of mathematics and *exhibitive* in the case of abstract art, is methodically applied and given priority over the other modes.

Buchler stresses that none of the three modes of judgment is to be seen as preeminent or as more foundational than any of the others. (ML 100) The modes interact in general human query, but in some circumstances one mode is preferable to the others, that is, "better"—as is, for instance, the assertive mode when verification is our concern. The ascesis of the assertive mode demands a formal consistency, while the exhibitive mode of query allows mutual enhancement and complementarity of contradictions.

In his psychoanalytical method Freud attempted assertive articulation of nonassertive utterances such as dreams and parapraxes (slips of the tongue or pen, revelatory "errors" of behavior) that comprise "unconscious" utterances. Psychoanalysis is a "talking cure" that gives us at least some indirect assertive control over the unconscious—precisely by exposing these mental acts to verbal analysis. The exhibitive utterances of dreams may require assertion for the cognitive consummation, but the road to the unconscious is not via assertion but via exhibitive means. Free association provides the bridge between the exhibitive utterance and its conscious, assertive, cognitive consummation. The associative "field-logic" of dreams and of free association replaces linguistic logic when we seek to communicate with the unconscious. Assertive judgment is applied only afterwards and conflicting assertive interpretations are acceptable and even welcomed. I will argue that in allowing, and even demanding, several, often contradictory, assertive interpretations or judgments, the dream analysis as a judgment retains a definite *exhibitive* element. It is an exhibitive-assertive cooperative discipline or query. Dreaming itself does not constitute query, in the Buchlerian sense of methodical activity, although dream interpretation does.

One question which immediately arises is, the question to what extent Freud's own approach to dream interpretation was enhanced by *and* limited by his theoretical framework? Freud wanted the libido to be seen as the basic force beneath all human acts. He demanded full reducibility of all desire to libido. The reason for this demand was that he wanted to create a science.[4] The libidinal theory comprises the organizing core for the reductive assertive-active or (pseudo) scientific aspect of Freudianism.[5] Jung quotes Freud's demand that, "the sexual theory must be taken as dogma."[6] Narrow angles, such as Freud's way of seeing man, can assuredly be sharper and more penetrating than wider ones. They focus in on truth aspects that are not so visible from a more generalized perspective. Focusing on one aspect in this way causes us to lose other aspects altogether, as did Freud in the "Dora" case.

Freud's move to label all desire as sexual was startling in more than one way. It had shock value, which made Freud's theory noticed, but that was not its only value. That Freud did just what he did was useful on several accounts: First, it worked well in psychoanalysis on the whole, although not in every case, as indicated by the "Dora" case.[7] Secondly, it necessarily widened our concept of sexuality. Freud's reduction of all desire, of all appetites, to libido, brought out not only the kinship but also the surprising convertibility of forms of desire, in other words, their near reducibility to libido. Freud aimed for more than showing the libido to be a more basic force than it had been taken to be. He wanted the libido to be seen as the basic force beneath all human acts. Freud demanded full reducibility of all desire to the libido.

Freud of course expands his own theory by formulating three models or ways of seeing the *psyche*. First we have the "topological" model in which "areas" of the *psyche* are mapped out as the "conscious," the "unconscious" and the "pre-conscious".[8] This is our *psycho-spatial* metaphor. Secondly, we have psychic *time* represented in the "historical ego" model: The genealogy of developmental stages—all seen as sexual, each with its own sexual preoccupation—oral, anal, phallic and genital. The developmental stages form the ego historically and are retained in it. Thirdly, we are given the *psycho-dynamic* model of the "ego," the "id" and the "superego" where the id represents the urges of the organism—all of them sexual—and the ego is a dynamic-relationship-ego arising in the interaction between id and environment or superego. The latter entity stands for the internalization of certain parental and social demands. The id functions according to the "pleasure principle" and the superego is the seat of our conscience. Due to its function as a link between the organism and the external world as perceived through the senses, that is, the "real," empirical or perceptual world, the ego stands for the "reality principle" or the "rational principle".[9]

I see Freud's division of the *psyche* into three personae as a dramatic means to display the interplay of forces within the *psyche*. This is a dynamic view or scenario where the "play of forces" gives us a selected perspective on the energetics of the human *psyche*. Freud's other tripartite division—the charting of the *psyche* into the conscious, preconscious and unconscious—and the developmental stages also have an exhibitive function. Freud's three models or "theories" of the *psyche* function differentially, each displaying an aspect or angle of it.

Does Freud's giving us three theories then comprise a departure from the assertive method? Are these models to be seen as mere heuristic aids, that is, metaphors that "show" us aspects of the *psyche,* rather than as scientific theories about real or even about properly theoretical entities? Are we not right in saying that the "id" is no entity but only a representation of the various separate instincts and drives, and that the "superego" merely stands for certain pressures and rules imposed on the individual? Is what we call the "ego" actually just the organization of the interaction between instincts and external reality for the good of the organism as an ongoing act or process?

Insofar as the drama played out by the personae of the id, the ego and the superego is metaphorical in function it serves as a vivifying heuristic device. What does not easily lend itself to assertive explication is often quite effectively explicated by exhibitive means—or what has been called the "mute analogy" of the metaphor. It is "mute," one assumes, because it does not "say," it simply "shows." In giving us these personae of the id, the ego and the superego, Freud intended more than metaphor. He intended them also to be theoretical entities that could be said to exist within the view of a depth psychology such as Freudianism. When internalized, various pressures of the culture, in themselves unconnected, form the superego. Only as internalized do they function as an entity or personae within the larger *psyche*. What matters in psychology is this inside reality. That depth view, or inside view, is what Freud attempts to make a science of the soul about. According to the theoretical framework of that science there exists an id and a superego within the formed person. But they "exist" in a different sense than material objects.

If the function of these personae is primarily exhibitive—that is, they "exist" as constructs which exhibit interrelated but distinct processes of the psyche—then they would have to be seen as exhibitive representations of these processes and their relations, that is, either as representative in the manner of metaphors or mythical entities or representative in the manner of charts or models. As mere metaphors they would not have any degree of objective existence and they are clearly not scientific models in the usual sense. Perhaps we should agree that Freud saw them as metaphorical representations of real, existing "powers," or organized biological energies. The topographical and historical ways of organizing the ego function not in terms of entities or personae, but as chartings of ego functions into realms. They are models, albeit not quantifiable scientific models. Metaphors are exhibitive or active-exhibitive means of judgment while models are exhibitive or assertive-exhibitive means of judgment. Freud's several ways of organizing the psyche then assist query by primarily exhibitive means.

Freud saw our dreams as private, custom–made myths, and our myths as the waking dreams of peoples.[10] This was one of Freud's great insights. But Freud wanted to translate such exhibitive utterances or judgments into assertive ones—or as Freud himself saw it—he wanted to bring out the unconscious or "latent" (repressed) assertion behind the conscious or "manifest" (censor approved) nonsense version given in the dream-as-remembered or in the myth as worded. That was what the "talking cure" of psychoanalysis was designed for.

As Freud showed us by his use of free association in the practice of psychoanalysis, the associative "field-logic" of dreams and of free association must replace linguistic logic if we are to communicate with the unconscious. But the Freudian interpretation of dreams into assertive judgments may not be the best articulation available. A strict univocal assertive utterance cannot accurately express the meanings of the exhibitive utterance of the dream. Diverse assertive interpretations or articulations of the exhibitive utterances should rightly be allotted ontological parity. This entails a double description through two modes—assertive and exhibitive—which then yields a dynamic view of our relationships that can enrich our self-understanding.

Dreams can be seen as giving us a fresh, that is a second, perspective on what our linguistic-assertive thinking monopolizes in our waking hours. This approach rejects Freud's theory of a "latent" dream "text" cleverly hidden beneath a methodologically distorted, "manifest" dream-as-remembered. Dreams reveal rather than hide or disguise prevalences in

our experience. The so-called "manifest" dreams show, they are themselves exhibitive utterances. The configurations they show differ essentially
from the configurations given through assertion. Psychoanalysis is a "talking cure," it is a linguistic method. Freud's belief that the manifest content
of dreams hid the "real" latent text was based on a view that required
seeing dreams as systematic distortions that served the purpose of disguis-
ing an original (or "real") assertion. Dreams told the truth, but in a coded
way, in which the literal assertion of the manifest dream was a "lie" or
distortion of the asserted truth of the latent dream-thought. We could analyze the dream, unravel its lie and reassemble or unmask the truth behind
it. This theory fits readily with psychoanalysis for the very reason that psychoanalysis is a "talking cure".[11] From an assertive, linear-logical perspective, the dream-utterance appears distorted, its objects displaced, its logical
connections broken. But from the perspective of the exhibitive mode of
dreams or art, the assertive presentation is a truncated and distorted view;
its focus is displaced (because it focuses on things as abstracted from their
relations), its connections are limiting (because assertion limits us to linear-
logical connections and leaves out a multitude of associative connections).
The dream utterance articulates relational complexes of personal experience
exhibitively. The dream interpretation in turn articulates the dream-
utterance by assertive means. The latter articulation clarifies and simplifies
the dream-utterance for the dreamer, but any one assertive interpretation
also reduces and therefore distorts its exhibitively conferred content. Making the set of interpretive readings an open set combines assertive and exhibitive methods by providing the clarifying aspect of assertion, without
denying us the richness of content of the exhibitive utterance. We do, of
course, not get the richness all at once as it is given us in the exhibitive
utterance of the dream, but we can continue unravelling the content via
differing interpretations.

If the Freudian theory were indeed correct and a dream were only a
distortion of a linguistic-logical assertion—the original dream-thought—it
would follow that the latent content could be expressed clearly and univocally and with finality. On one hand, Freud tended to point to the sexual
explanation as a full and satisfactory one, but on the other hand, he did
state that the dream utterance is "overdetermined"—the dream allows for
more than one interpretation.[12] Freud cites ways in which dreams show the
feature he calls "overdetermination": A particular manifest dream can assume a form that stands for a cluster of wishes or a serial wish developing
through stages and dating back to an early childhood wish,[13] or several
separate dream thoughts may "converge" into one image.[14]

Manifest dreams also often contain compressed or collective images;
a persona seen in the dream may represent several people from one's life

experience. On the other hand, the dream can do the opposite and picture one person as imaged through several people in the dream. Freud tells of a dream in which he saw his friend R take on features of his late Uncle Joseph. Freud had been recommended for an appointment to a professorship.[15] Shortly thereafter he had a visit from his friend R, who had been a candidate for a professorship for some time but who had nevertheless not been granted that rank. R had found out that the denial was because of his denomination—he was Jewish. The night after R's visit Freud had a dream in which he saw his friend's face as changed: "It was as if it had been pulled lengthways," until it resembled Freud's Uncle Joseph's elongated face. R's black beard had also changed to yellow. Freud's uncle's beard was fair. During R's visit Freud had noted that his friend's beard, like Freud's own beard, was turning from a rich black to a mixed color of yellows and browns—the color a black beard takes on when it loses its splendor, according to Freud, and before it turns grey. At first Freud was reluctant to analyze the dream and told himself that the dream had been nonsensical. His professional judgment told him that this was a sign of resistance to what was contained in the dream; therefore he forced himself to analyze it as he would a dream of one of his patients. He remembered that his Uncle Joseph had come to disgrace and misfortune, and that Freud's own father—who turned gray in a short time upon hearing that his brother had been jailed—had said the whole occurrence was accountable to Freud's uncle being a "simpleton," rather than to any real misdeeds by the unfortunate man. Freud read the dream to say that his friend R was a "simpleton" for judging as bad Freud's prospects of getting the professorship. Freud also remembered having been aware, during the dream, of a feeling of affection towards the combined person in the dream. As he had never known his uncle enough for such affection, he assumed the affection to be directed to the friend R. This also was not likely as their terms of friendship did not go that deep. Freud therefore explains the feeling as a "making up" for accusing a man who was never a simpleton for being just that.

I would contest Freud's interpretation of this dream on several points. First: What the dream revealed, and Freud did not want to think, was that both the uncle and the friend were treated ungenerously because of their Jewishness. Secondly: Freud's own face was elongated and bearded too. The face in the dream represented the long face of several losers. One of them was the dreamer himself. Thirdly: The feeling of sudden affection was for the uncle with whom Freud now was able to empathize and identify, at least unconsciously. It was a shared situation which Freud identified in the dream, though not in his daytime mode of cognition. Freud's father had said about Freud as a boy that "he will amount to nothing." Freud himself was the "simpleton" of the dream, for like his uncle, he was not

sharp-witted enough to accurately judge his precarious position in that society. Freud's father had also had to contend with these same difficulties of
being an outcast of sorts in the Germano-Christian society. But Freud never
wanted to face up to the facts of prejudicial treatment of Jews and of women
in the society that he lived and worked in. Having been his mother's favor-
ite, prejudices had once been easy to accept and tempting to see in the
flattering light that we sometimes choose to see them in, when the prejudices are in our favor. Freud's dream uttered what Freud's conscious
thoughts stubbornly denied: that he was an unfavored child of that society.
Freud's conscious (assertive) mode showed a remarkable recalcitrance to
accept the prevalence the dream so clearly revealed to him exhibitively.
    Freud recognized symbolization in dreams and hysterical symptoms.
Symbols were symptoms to Freud; a symbol was the distorted form of
something that had been repressed. All symbols were sexual in meaning:
Elongated objects designated the male sexual organ, hollow objects designated the female sexual organ, etc. Symbols were only distorted signs or
designations for known things. Jung on the other hand saw symbols, not as
disguised or distorted signs, but as spontaneous expressions of the unconscious "background" of the psyche by way of revelatory images which,
unlike signs, pointed beyond, or transcended, the particular. Symbols
bridged the particular and the universal, they were both concrete and
abstract.[16] Moreover, symbols embraced both the affirmation and the negation of the symbolized,[17] they thus represented "the *tertium* that in logic
does not exist," that is, the excluded middle. Symbols, as described by
Jung, are exhibitive utterances. As described by Freud they are distorted
signs, parts of repressed hedonistic assertions.
    Were the symbols in Freud's "R" dream sexual? The coloring, or
discoloring, of R's beard in Freud's dream symbolized grief, such as the
grief that made Freud's father turn grey when his brother was jailed and the
grief of the brother that was jailed. The overly long face of the person in
the dream symbolized disappointment, such as the disappointment of R (and
Freud). The discoloring of the beard and the elongation of the face showed
Freud variations on a theme of disappointment and grief amongst victims of
prejudice. The dream itself is an exhibitive analysis. In assertive articulation, or what Freud called "dream analysis," it reaches its cognitive consummation, but not one limited by theory.
    Freud noted that there was one aspect of dreams which was not dis-
torted: the "mood" or affect of the dream never lies.[18] Therefore, when
interpreting a dream, we must remember to ask, "What was the mood of
the dream?" The mood will indicate if the dream content was happy or
sad, frightening or comforting, etc. The mood is not distorted because it is
not something "said" but mutely revealed or "felt." It is of course, pre-

cisely because Freud takes the remainder of the dream—everything except the mood—to be assertive, that he sees it as "distorted." Jung saw the mood or affect as a "feeling-tone" or *leitmotif* (comparable to the *leitmotif* in Wagnerian music) in that it denotes the meaning-core of the dream.[19] The mood is the nonassertive core of the dream. The dream context illuminates and elucidates the mood or feeling by exhibitive means, drawing out meanings that are implicit or unborn meanings until the dream takes on the role of a Socratic midwife giving them life. The mood then could be said to inform the query.

As Freud discovered, dreams do not close in on the *psyche*, lead into a *cul de sac* of nonsense; they open up to a vast area of the *psyche* which Freud called the "unconscious." Freud also felt that there is, in every dream, a part that cannot be unravelled by dream interpretation, a "core" or "unplumbable navel" of the dream, the point where the dream connects with the "unknown".[20] One could speculate that dreams perhaps open up to the "navel" or "umbilical cord" of "psychical productions" which connects these to the "physical productions," the flesh. We do sense that dreams are spontaneous and normal hallucinations made up of mostly visual, but also auditory images, and to some extent other sense impressions,[21] that the oneiric utterances of dreams are generated by deep-lying fears and desires—rather than being only "wish fulfillments," as was claimed by Freud[22]—the dreaming mind conjures up Gestalts, sensed wholes of experience. Dreams are not about clearly bounded individuals as is language, they are not solely or univocally about Freud's Uncle Joseph, his father or my brother Kaj, they are also, and importantly, about relational aspects of experience—as is art. Dreams do not make things the central and relations the marginal issue, but allow for an ontological parity that is not possible in assertion. Dreams reveal the relational aspect by the method of displacement. The dream may replace one's father by another authority figure. It may replace my brother with our dog because the dream is simultaneously and as centrally about such an easy, affectionate relationship as one can have with a brother and a dog in familiar surroundings, where the brother, the dog and the surroundings are part of the relational complex. In the dream I may be in a forest like those of my childhood, walking with my brother or our dog—the dream neglects to discriminate between them, but this is accepted within my oneiric set of mind. My walking companion is ambiguous; he may switch to boy or dog as the context demands or remain unspecified, or the dog may simply acquire speech when needed. The displacement frees the dreamer from the fixation on thing-concepts that belongs with assertive judgment. Dreams as exhibitive judgments restore what our linguistic assertive attitude obscures: the Gestalt of complex relations. Freud took the displacement in dreams to be a methodological obfuscation of the meaning of the dream, but it is just the opposite; it is a methodological clarification of the exhibitive meaning of the dream—of our exhibitive way of seeing in dreams.

Freud believed dreams to be like myths. Dreams and myths constituted distorted utterances of unconscious thoughts, of what could not be "said" in a more direct way—because of repression of the thought or thoughts at issue. I would agree with Freud that dreams and myths are utterances of what the dreamer or storyteller cannot "say" or state in assertive terms. I do not see these utterances as distortions or censored versions of assertions, or underlying verbal-logical thoughts, but as exhibitive utterances that constitute elucidations of meaning-complexes of a nonverbal kind. The function of dreams and myths is not to cover up or obscure what our logical thinking already possesses but chooses to disguise, but to uncover or elucidate what our linguistic-logical thinking does not possess because assertion is unable or less able to bring out nonassertive meanings or meaning-complexes.

In arguing that dreams are exhibitive judgments, I am suggesting that they function as metaphors do; a metaphor does not distort, it reveals by way of replacement. The dynamic transport of meaning, the revelation effected by the replacement, comes about through the freeing effect obtained by the shift in representation or "displacement." Making objects replaceable de-emphasizes them as objects, and brings out or emphasizes the relational field (the field dynamics) as what endures and is carried over between the two views as a focal issue, as what the dream is additionally about. Our concepts must be knocked over, not to disguise, but to disclose, to reveal what these encrusted concepts blind us to, to uncover what they cover up. The displacement occasions a radical shift in perspective, a shift not only of angles or points of view, but of the very mode of seeing or knowing.

Exhibitive concepts do not differentiate between universals and particulars. That is, "universal" and "particular" are assertive concepts and the exhibitive mode is innocent of such specifications. Furthermore, assertively functioning word-concepts draw a sharp line between things and relations. Assertive linguistic thinking eventually influences our experience of the world, how we "see" our world, how we judge our "concrete reality." Buchler points out that philosophers have held that what is directly confronted in experience is always something individual—the "thisness" Aristotle speaks of—which has wrongly been construed to mean that immediate experience discriminates individual objects from their relations. Buchler's ontology forbids us to make things prior to relations or to make the latter prior to the former, that is, it also forbids us to construe relation as prior to what is related. (ML 56) If assertion tends to make things prior or more real than relations, dreams and art restore the ontological parity of things and relations and of particulars and universals.

Notes

1. ML 3. See "List of Abbreviations" for Buchler's works, here p. xiii.

2. Proceiver is Buchler's categorial term for the human individual, a summed-up-self-in-process. See TGT, Ch. 1.

3. Henry Moore Exhibit, Hofstra University (Fall 1987).

4. Sigmund Freud, *The Ego and the Id, The Standard Edition of the Complete Works of Sigmund Freud* (London: The Hogarth Press, Vol. XIX. 1961. [Original 1923]), p. 181. (All references to Freud are to The Standard Edition.)

5. The reason for Freud's demand for full reducibility of all desire to libido was that he wanted to create a science on the model of the sciences of his time. Science employs analysis of the complex and opaque into simpler components, or simplification through systematic reduction. The Freudian reduction of all desire to libido is undertaken for the same reasons that scientists use reductive methods, that is, for clarity and control. If all desire reduces to sexual desire, then we have limited the scope of the too general word "desire," scaled it down to particularity and finiteness, and in fact made over "desire" into a more manageable concept. Also, "libido" implies psycho-biology, whereas "desire" has metaphysical implications. Freud does not want to become entangled in a metaphysical concept of general or infinite desire. The Freudian query is born of the kind of wonder that is generated by vexations and seeks to be appeased. According to the Freudian theory, all desire that does not seem to be sexual is merely "aim-inhibited libido," that is, displaced sexual desire. For Freud I am an ongoing act of dynamic libidinal forces from birth to death.

By now Darwinism has become well absorbed into our general picture of reality. The evolutionary theory is accepted foremost in the sophistic manner of reduction, i.e., man is "nothing but" a "wiser" ape or mammal. The Freudian reduction of the individual to the infant has also been received into the general consciousness of modern people. When what is less than man is offered as a full description of what man "really is," we have reduction. Gregory Bateson holds evolutionary change and somatic change, including thought and learning, to be fundamentally similar stochastic systems that are partly interactive and partly isolated from one another (Bateson, *Mind and Nature,* 1979, p. 165). If we were to use an evolutionary analog to Freud's reductive explanation of our complex adult desires as nothing but aim-inhibited infantile libido, then in a similar vein, perhaps legs, because they evolved from fins, could be said to be nothing but aim-inhibited fins. What would we gain and what would we lose by such a reductive "explanation" of legs? We would gain insight into the much neglected relationship between fins and legs. But we would gain that without giving up all that legs are and fins are not, by simply saying that legs have evolved from fins. Saying that legs are aim-inhibited fins implies that fin does what it ought to do, properly, while a leg is a kind of misplaced and deviant version of a fin. The analog is admittedly crude. I will nevertheless add a question in the form of another crude analogy: Do our infantile urges evolve into complex adult desires and aspirations "naturally," that is, as naturally as baby legs that kick the air grow into legs that support us and transport us around? And do cultures evolve naturally, or is a "culture" a deviation from an original natural precultural form that is more "sound"? Clearly answers to this have varied. Hegel would see such evolution of cultures or of individual behavior as life affirming and progressive while Freud would see both cases as deviations from original healthier forms, that is, as illnesses or neuroses of civilized man.

Ought we for this reason diagnose Freud as pathologically regressive, a product of an oppressive culture and an indulgent mother, a neurotic genius who regresses on a grand scale, pulling everyone down with him into the infantile, the precultural? No, clearly we ought to value both Hegel's and Freud's perspectives for their exhibitive insights and for the corrections each brings to bear on what the other view misses. The juxtaposing of views such as Hegel's view of culture as progressive against Freud's view of culture as oppressive or of Marx's view of humans as subject to external forces against Freud's view of humans as subject to internal forces and Aristotle's view of the human psyche as nonreducible to animal urges against Freud's reductive view, should emphasize the differences positively as legitimate but opposed perspectives. Their juxtaposing serves to enlighten us on the multidimensionality of our cognitive reality. As in a well represented collection of art, differing viewpoints ought not to confuse our understanding but add depth to it. If viewed exhibitively they will do so. Inquiry, active query and exhibitive query cooperate within what Buchler simply names "query." Query in this full meaning occurs only when no one of the separate modes of judgment is denied its import, but all are allotted ontological parity as modes of query that methodically contribute to the general query and thereby become one with the general query—as they were in Socratic query—and when seeking and finding are also allotted ontological parity and blend in the query.

6. Carl G. Jung, *The Portable Jung,* ed. Joseph Campbell (New York: Viking Press, 1971), p. xviii.

7. For Freud's account see *A Case of Hysteria, The Standard Edition,* Vol. VII (1955 [original 1905]). I would not claim that Dora's neurosis was "incorrectly" diagnosed by Freud: My reservation about Freud's handling of the "Dora" case is that he used an interpretation that was not helpful. Freud's interpretation consisted of an "academic" reduction in that its main function was to fit Dora's problem into Freud's pansexual theory. Freud's sexual readings of lust for father, for father's friend (as substitute for father) and for father's mistress (through identification with father) were "correct" within the Freudian paradigm. Freud's theory is a depth theory where all reality is seen as internalized in the patient. Outside reality is not what is focused on. This is of course the only way to deal with one's past—that

which cannot be changed. But Dora's problems lay in the present outside reality that needed acting on, not adjusting to. It is my contention that Adler, who saw the will to power rather than the libido as what drives us, would have been better suited than Freud to help Dora break out of the ungracious game in which she was used as a pawn.

8. Freud, *The Ego and the Id*, p. 15.

9. Ibid, p. 25.

10. Freud, *The Interpretation of Dreams, The Standard Edition*, Vol. IV (1953 [original, 1900]), pp. 261–266.

11. Freud, *Studies on Hysteria, The Standard Edition*, Vol. VII (1955), p. 30.

12. Freud, *The Interpretation of Dreams*, pp. 149, 219n, 283–4, 306–8.

13. Ibid, p. 219.

14. Ibid, pp. 652–3.

15. Ibid, pp. 137–142.

16. Carl G. Jung, *Psychology and Alchemy, The Collected Works of C.G. Jung*, Vol. 12 (Princeton: Princeton University Press, 1953. Revised 1968), p. 283. (Subsequent references to Jung are to *The Collected Works of C.G. Jung*.)

17. Jung, *Psychological Types, The Collected Works of C.G. Jung*, Vol. 6 (1971), p. 111.

18. Freud, *The Interpretation of Dreams*, p. 487.

19. Jung, "Dementia Praerox," *The Psychogenesis of Mental Disease, The Collected Works of C.G. Jung*, Vol. 3 (1960), p. 39, n.4.

20. Freud, *The Interpretation of Dreams*, p. 564, n.111.

21. Ibid, p. 49.

22. Ibid, pp. 122–134.

Buchler's Conception of Community

James Campbell

America has long been concerned with community. From her earliest settlements of Pilgrims and Puritans, through her revolution and early struggles for unity, through her many communistic societies and reform movements, up to her current attempts at reconstructing a troubled body politic, community has been the focal point of much of American thought and action, the goal of much of her longing.

America's concern for community has not been a matter solely for politicians and 'civil leaders'. Two of America's most famous thinkers—Josiah Royce and John Dewey—made community central to their understanding of humans and their world, and central as well to any attempts at improving human life. Dewey, for example, felt that our democratic form of government was based in our community structure, democracy being "the idea of community life itself." Historically, our "American democratic polity was developed out of genuine community life, that is, association in local and small centres where industry was mainly agricultural and where production was carried on mainly with hand tools." Since that time, however, we have lost touch with our communal roots through our failure to keep pace with the changing nature of modern life. Consequently, we have forgotten the value of our communities as places where each person has "a responsible share according to capacity in forming and directing the activities of the groups to which one belongs and in participating according to need in the values which the groups sustain;" and, unless we soon come to realize how significant local communities are to America and revitalize them, we will not be able to maintain our democracy. "Whatever the future may have in store," Dewey writes, "one thing is certain. Unless local communal life can be restored, the public cannot adequately resolve its most urgent problem: to find and identify itself." Our present state of disorientation may be transitional, Dewey suggests, but to hope for a better resultant state in the future—to hope that we will once again find ourselves—we must reconstruct our local communities. "Democracy must begin at home, and its home is the neighborly community."[1]

Royce also maintained that we need to make community central to our social philosophy. In fact, he once summed up his whole life's work as an increasingly self-conscious concern with community, remarking that "my deepest motives and problems have centered about the Idea of the Community, although this idea has only come gradually to my clear consciousness." The importance of the community for Royce was based in his belief in the vital role that community played in our understanding of ourselves and our neighbors, and in our attempts to overcome the isolation of individual existence. He wrote that "we are saved through the community," because community functions as a concrete and living focus for the loyalty that "we all, as human beings, need" and that is "chief amongst the moral goods of [human] life . . . " Without such a focus, the human individual has no meaning for his or her life: "The detached individual is an essentially lost being." Speaking at a time when the world was embroiled in the Great War, that America was soon to join, Royce turned the attention of the audience away from himself to the danger posed to the Community by the battles raging in Europe with the following question:

why should you give so kind an attention to me at a moment when the deepest, the most vital, and the most practical interest[s] of the whole community of mankind are indeed imperiled, when the spirit of mankind is overwhelmed with a cruel and undeserved sorrow, when the enemies of mankind often seems as if they were about to triumph?

Hoping "that we and the Community shall see better times together," Royce admitted that, without that hope, "I, for one, do not wish to survive the crisis," because for him life without hope of the "Great Community" was not worth living.[2]

I now turn from this sacral conception of community to that of Justus Buchler, who writes of community: "individuals who lead lives in some degree parallel, and who are subject to the same dominant commitment or allegiance, are in a state of community or experiential togetherness." (NJ 46) It is a long way from the 'eulogistic' or 'honorific tones' found in the discussion of community in Dewey and Royce to the merely descriptive definition which Buchler offers. Gone is the emotional aura of face-to-face communality. Gone is the foreboding implication that community is ephemeral. Gone is the requirement of work for stronger social organization. Gone, in fact, are the connotations of anything beyond the simple facts of human association of a certain sort.

Whether or not we should abandon the eulogistic sense of community for simple description I hold as a topic for later discussion. First, I wish to elaborate some aspects of Justus Buchler's conception of community. I will be restricting myself in this paper to *some* aspects because to discuss fully Buchler's position on community would require, among other considerations, a discussion of "reflexive community" which—though essential to the concept of "community" as Buchler sees it—under more traditional headings is a matter to be considered with discussions of personality or the self rather than community. Consequently, even though any position on associated existence implies a corollary position on the members of the group, I shall leave "reflexive community" at the level of an implication.[3]

As mentioned, questions as to how we can preserve or advance community are not of particular relevance to Buchler's consideration of the topic of community. Moreover, his consideration of the topic of community itself is not extensive. Questions about the nature of community are treated by Buchler only tangentially, and consequently we must tease out of his broad philosophic fabric the threads of this topic. These threads can then be rewoven into a new fabric using the framework and distinctions developed by other thinkers to whom community is a more central issue.

The potential value of such an endeavor is great. Even if community is not a central issue for Buchler, it is for others (some of us included). Whatever he might offer us then, either in challenge to, or sustenance of, our thinking would be welcome. In particular, his philosophy gives us a means of testing the acceptability of our basic conceptual approaches to, and of our various assumptions and conclusions about, community in a new light. His work offers us as well a possible means of uncovering insights which will be of advantage to us in furthering discussion. And from his viewpoint, of course, such an articulation of his work might offer further validation of the power of his philosophical system. Hence I undertake an explication of some aspects of community in the philosophy of Justus Buchler.

II

There are literally scores of definitions of the term 'community,' each carrying its own insights. It has even been suggested that their common core is nothing more than that "all the definitions deal with people. Beyond this common basis, there is no agreement."[4] Buchler suggests that there is something more to all the many definitions: besides dealing with people, these definitions deal with people in a special way—in their 'humanness' (as "proceivers"). Community, or experiential togetherness is, for Buchler, a state of relatedness among human individuals arising out of a shared life. This may seem to some imprecise and, no doubt, out of context it is quite vague. It is an initial attempt at an adequate definition of a concept whose edges are both naturally fuzzy and further tattered by philosophical wear and political abuse.

Elsewhere, Buchler offers another definition of community which at first seems much more precise: "A community is . . . a class of proceivers (necessary condition) for whom a given natural complex functions as a dominant procept (sufficient condition)." (TGT 39) Here we have given (and labeled) necessary and sufficient conditions for community. But, upon closer inspection, we realize that the terms of the definition neither admit to simple translations into 'ordinary' language nor, when replaced with equivalents from Buchler's own work, as I have done in the following, offer us a more precise definition of what community is than the one originally quoted:

> A community is . . . a class of [individuals taking part in a process of "forward propulsion and patient absorption" (TGT 4)] (necessary condition) for whom ["whatever is discriminated in any way" (MNC 31)] functions as a dominant ["part of" or factor in "the ongoing representation of the human aspect of the human animal" (TGT 7, 6)] (sufficient condition).

Has Buchler failed us here, offering definitions and terms which trade on still more definitions and terms, and they on others, until any definition of community becomes as elusive as the horizon? Not at all, considering what Buchler attempts to do in defining.

For Buchler, there are no simple definitions. Defining is a slow and intricate process which entails "marking out an area of relatedness, plotting boundaries . . . , as when we define a parcel of land or define the course of travel." (ML 106) He is not trying to settle the meaning of a term in as few words as possible, but rather to carefully display its full implications. Consequently, any one formulation for Buchler is seen as no more than an attempt at "the setting of bounds or limits" (MNC 162) on the concept. Any philosophical concept will admit of several formulations, each with its own emphases and limitations, each contributing to fuller understanding:

> To think of these actualizations as competitors in an attempt to produce the one precise definition is to miss their role as contributors to definition. Looking at any formulation in the "competitive" way increases suspicion of ambiguity. Looking at it in the "contributive" way enables us to put two and two together.

Hence, since there is no "one definitive version"[5] of a concept like 'community,' we must explore further the nature of community through

Buchler's eyes to see exactly how and where he does set the bounds and limits. His conception of community will thus grow clearer; the process of discussion becomes the process of definition. One good place to begin this process would be with a discussion of communication.

"Community is a necessary condition of communication," (NJ 45–46) Buchler writes at one point, because for him communication involves 'getting through to' another person. Before such communication is possible, there must be a prior community, "lives in some degree parallel," subject, as we have seen, "to the same dominant commitment or allegiance." (NJ 46) But Buchler also writes of communication that:

> whatever becomes a procept for the individual is communicated to him by nature or by art. The ocean communicates its vastness; history and the history of one's time communicate in the sense that they transmit symbols for proceptive assimilation. (TGT 29)

Here we have two different senses of communication that need to be reconciled. Buchler seems to be saying that the sea can converse with me more easily than my next door neighbor can. But this interpretation of his view depends upon the acceptance of two assumptions about community that are both denied by Buchler. The first is that I am not already in a deep state of community with my neighbor; the second, that the sea and I are equal partners in communication. Let us begin with a consideration of the latter.

For Buchler, though "the ocean communicates its vastness" to the individual, the individual communicates nothing to the ocean. "He cannot communicate to nature," Buchler writes, "because there is no individual, no direction that he can address or affect." (TGT 29–30) The communication that takes place between the ocean and the individual depends on the fact that the person is a proceiver, not on the fact that the ocean is vast, or the ocean would communicate its vastness to the shores as well. The sea and the person are not equal partners in communication; their communication is "asymmetrical." (TGT 30) But communication between proceivers has the potentiality of "mutuality." (TGT 29) Consequently, when Buchler writes that "[t]he communal bond eventuates in direct communication only contingently," (NJ 45) or that "[symmetrical communication] presupposes community and community presupposes sharing," (TGT 33) or that "[s]ymmetrical communication presupposes . . . joint manipulation and assimilation of signs correlated with the dominant procept," (TGT 34) what he is emphasizing is that for there to be any mutual communication at all there must be a common set of natural complexes functioning as signs that we can manipulate in our communication and a vast pool of perspectival similarities that we share to back up these signs. The communities of myself and my neighbor—either across the street or around the globe—are many and complex. Communication, our ability to 'get through to' others on the symbolic level, proves this.

One of the great problems in many discussions of community, Buchler suggests, and a problem that will be a major focus of my attention later, is the extent to which the moral overtones and sacral connotations of the concept tend to color the discussion. For if 'community' means more than just 'neighborhood' or if, on the contrary, living in a 'community' tends to be stifling to individuals, then we will have to restrict our use of 'community' to special cases of the intricate human interrelation on which we are focusing. Buchler rejects the need for such limitations because, for him, 'community' has neither positive nor negative connotations. For him, the ubiquitous fact of communication simply shows the pervasiveness of community in human experience. "What we generically call 'human experience' is not the mere multiplicity of all human happenings. . . . It is rather the tissue of likeness in individual human histories." This "tissue of likeness" is available to other persons, it "can be appropriated in some mode of judgment by one individual and another and still another." (NJ 129) The basis of this appropriation is that:

> there are real similarities between one individual and other individuals. The similarities obtain between spans of one individual history and spans of other individual histories. Similarity of this kind is proceptive parallelism. (NJ 128–129)

And it is this proceptive parallelism that gives rise to community.

This proceptive parallelism can be either generic (as in what Dewey calls "the basic identity of human nature"[6]) or specific (as in the common life of a married couple). This proceptive parallelism can be either spatially or temporally relevant (as with the inhabitants of a certain place or time span), or completely free of all space-time considerations (as with the many people who have pondered the meaning of life). This proceptive parallelism "prevents the atomization of the social" (NJ 129) by recognizing that human living has inherent similarities, not necessarily shared, but certainly sharable. Normally, many of these similarities flow silently beneath the surface of daily actions. But in times of great joy or great anguish they flower into a conscious realization of the extent to which all our lives run parallel to one another. On occasions like V-E Day or the Challenger explosion, people whose proceptive parallelism has been forged through years of common life suddenly recognize the extent of community among them. Yet this recognition just as quickly disappears, for consciousness of this interrelationship is not necessary for community. All that is necessary for community is the sharing of perspectives.

A perspective, for Buchler, is "a kind of order, that kind of order in which a given set of natural complexes function as procepts for a given proceiver or (distributively) for a community of proceivers." (TGT 124) From the definition of perspectives it is obvious that in his understanding a perspective is not something 'within' the individual (Cf. TGT 174); it is rather "a structure of conditions under which men produce." (CM 138) To see perspectivally for Buchler is therefore not the same as saying 'from my particular point-of-view,' but rather 'from a personal approach with elements shared by many.' The perspectives are public, either through the common heritage of man or through the overlap of others' lives with one's own. These perspectives are:

> either present for the experience of an individual or transmissible to an individual in the course of time. Common perspectives are available for the individual's participation; an aggregate of accumulated perspectives is available as a heritage for his assimilation. In the former case, the perspectives are there for him to share or adopt or recognize as already shared by him, voluntarily or involuntarily; in the latter, they are there for him to utilize and understand. (NJ 168–169)

In no case are these perspectives to be seen as harnesses which hold us together like a team of horses. They are, rather, the common roads we travel.

Not only are these perspectives not 'within' the individual, to a certain extent they are not even under his or her control. "We flatter ourselves too much on our power to give or withhold assent," Buchler writes in a different context (TGT 77), but his point is equally applicable here. Although perspectives are to some extent adoptable, and although a person "modifies in some degree what he acquires experientially," (NJ 169) the perspectives of a person's life are largely compulsive:

> Though perspectives are adoptable, the most influential and fundamental of them are . . . rarely held by a simple act of choice. They coalesce with the proceptive direction by the junction of many factors—the chances of the world, the powers of the social community, the flexibility of the proceiver, the nature and limits of all proceivers. (TGT 117)

A person's language, for example, "one of the bases of human parallelism," (NJ 46) carries with it conceptions, frameworks, and possible relations between that individual and all other speakers and nonspeakers over which he or she has little or no control. Language is not alone in this influence—we cannot "rule out innumerable forms of action, assertion, and contrivance besides those of language," (ML 19) that color contemporary human existence. The temper of the age, its philosophy and theology, its arts and sciences all are assimilated through perspectives.

These perspectives are most importantly sharable and "[t]he fact that perspectives can be shared makes social communication possible." (NJ 169) But, although "community of perspectives" remains "essential for communication," (TGT 114) individuals do not see everything in the same respect. A basic recognition of the rich diversity of humankind forces the admission that the extent of shared perspectives is limited:

> men cannot have all perspectives in common, for this would mean that each had the same proceptive direction as every other, and this in turn would mean, by the analysis of what an individual is, that there is only one individual. (TGT 115)

The amount of sharing of perspectives can be either broad or narrow depending on the amount of shared experience. But even the smallest amount of communality suffices: all instances of sharing of perspectives are instances of community. "When we say that the same object is a procept for different proceivers, we mean that they share at least one perspective: they judge or 'see' in the same respect," Buchler writes, "in that respect they are a distinctive community." (TGT 115)

The prior discussion seems to have filled in the general outlines of Buchler's conception of 'community.' Thus when we read that "individuals who lead lives in some degree parallel, and who are subject to the same dominant commitment or allegiance, are in a state of community or experiential togetherness," (NJ 46) we recognize Buchler to mean that individuals in community are individuals who participate in a common perspective as a result of living a shared life that need not be conscious or continuing or valued. Further clarification of Buchler's understanding of 'community' will come from contrasting his conception with other conceptions along lines hinted at earlier. In the next section, I will contrast his conception of 'community' with the natural sense of community to clarify more fully what traits a complex must display to be considered a 'community.' In section four, I will contrast Buchler's descriptive analysis with the eulogistic analysis to clarify more fully the nature of an adequate analysis of such concepts.

III

Traditionally, discussions of community have focussed upon 'natural' community, that is upon communities considered as permanent, locally based, face-to-face relationships like residential neighborhoods or small towns that carried with them an essential element of emotional attachment. An association that failed to have either of these two groups of qualities— for example, the group of people with whom one closely worked but to whom one was not emotionally attached, or the unknown number of individuals with whom one shared a love for the music of, say, Howard Hanson—was considered to be less than a community. There have been many who have recognized the limitations of this natural conception of community. From the historical point of view, for example, it is important to consider to what extent such warm and stable communities have really existed throughout human history.[7] And from our own contemporary standpoint, it is important to consider whether this emphasis upon natural community causes us to overlook other, more limited, possibilities. Are we unfairly downplaying, for example, the 'functional' community of a profession— with its common purposes and identity, its shared language, its authority and training functions, its distinctions between insiders and outsiders, and so on[8]—because of the primacy of our natural model?

Buchler's work is especially helpful if we attempt to transcend the narrowness of the natural approach because his analysis of community accepts neither the emphasis upon locality and permanence, nor that upon emotional attachment. We as members of communities do not necessarily know the members of the communities to which we belong—for example, the community of victims of violent crimes—nor do we necessarily have any emotional attachment to the communities to which we belong—for example, the community of faculty members and graduate students in a large academic department. For Buchler, all instances of community, all forms of shared perspectives, all examples of lives in some degree parallel with the same dominant commitment or allegiance, are of equal ontological status. None of them is prior to, or more basic or 'natural' than, any other.

This does not mean that Buchler cannot distinguish among different forms of community. He selects out two for special discussion: antecedent community and contingent community. "The antecedent mutuality of those who communicate is . . . their hereditary community—national language, customs, moral standards, prepared attitudes." This antecedent community has a permanence and an immutability arising from the one way influence of its hereditary nature: over this community "it is hardly possible to speak of control . . . " Contingent community on the other hand is highly plastic. A contingent community might rise out of "[s]imilar convictions shaped by a political atmosphere, joint involvement in a catastrophe, or chance bodily contact. . . . " (TGT 38)

Communities, whether antecedent or contingent, are equally communities. From the power and influence of the antecedent community, we may be able to understand why there has been the traditional emphasis on

natural community. Still, the various aspects of the natural community—
locality, permanence, affection—are not decisive factors of the existence of
community. For example, the locality aspect of community—the physical
place—is significant primarily as a focal point for the "national language,
customs, moral standards, prepared attitudes." Although a hereditary community must have a location, the significance of this location is not simply
as *a location* but as *a location for.* The local community has been the place
where most perspectives were shared. With changes made possible by
modern communication, we are now able to overcome this former limitation on community. But, by doing this, Buchler's analysis suggests that we
are not expanding locality, we are expanding the formerly locally based
perspectives.

In a similar fashion, Buchler's analysis of community rejects the re
quirement of permanence. A natural community is generally considered to
be an ongoing body of a fairly definite size (often small enough to allow for
individual recognition of all members) that maintains this size without too
great fluctuations. Along with the permanence goes a clear distinction between those who belong to the community and those who do not. With
Buchler, permanence as a requirement of community is abandoned as well.
For him, a community fluctuates in size because it is a function of judgment, in his broad conception of judgment as any "making, doing, or stating." (NJ 4) He continues:

> Judgment is a necessary condition of continuing community, as sheer
> social togetherness is a necessary condition of judgment. Significant
> relatedness among individuals implies common commitment in some
> form. (NJ 47)

This common commitment is what makes the community something distinct from an aggregation. The complexes which function as the communal
focal point must be ramified within each member's proceptive domain. This
judgment based character is also what distinguishes between what *might be*
or *could be* a community and what actually *is.* "The property of potential
connection, mutual availability, mutual involvement, enters as an aspect of
togetherness," (NJ 57); but this togetherness or aggregation becomes a
community only when there is judgment. Therefore, communities are constantly changing in size. "The bonds of a community, like the limits of a
proceptive domain, undulate." (TGT 45)

Depending on actual judgments, the size of a community grows and
diminishes; and, depending on how sharply one circumscribes the range of
these judgments, on how sharply one defines a community, the more
changeable it will be. Hence we could say that though perhaps the philo-

sophical community in general (for example, the dues paying members of
some national professional organization) remains fairly constant, the community of Buchler scholars constantly grows or diminishes, depending on
the judgments and articulations of particular philosophers familiar with his
work. If, as Buchler says, "Kant is necessarily a philosopher first and a
Kantian second," (NJ 192) it is at least partially because the community of
Kantians (or Buchlerians) is itself more changeable than the community
of philosophers.

Because of the fluctuating nature of communal boundaries, and the
fact that individuals belong to many communities at the same time, the
fringes of the Buchlerian community or any other community are consequently very hazy. There are those whose own philosophical work draws
primarily on Buchler's, while others might find only his notion of "prevalence" useful; those for whom membership in this community is central,
and those for whom it is only tangential. "[T]here must be for each individual a hierarchy of allegiances" (TGT 41), but no individual's allegiances
are entirely within a particular community. Nor, since there is a "tissue of
likeness" in human lives, can any individual's allegiances necessarily exclude entirely all of the aspects of any community.

Related to the emphases on locality and permanence in traditional
conceptions of community is an emphasis on conscious identification with,
or affection for, the community. Dewey, for example, denies the possibility
of community without a conscious recognition of other members:

> To have the same ideas about things which others have, to be like–
> minded with them, and thus to be really members of a social group, is
> therefore to attach the same meanings to things and to acts which
> others attach. Otherwise, there is no common understanding, and no
> community life. But in a shared activity, each person refers what he is
> doing to what the other is doing and *vice-versa*.[9]

Royce goes further, requiring the conscious identification of the community's work and one's own life:

> Men do not form a community, in our present restricted sense of that
> word, merely in so far as the men cooperate. They form a commu-
> nity . . . when they not only cooperate, but accompany this coopera-
> tion with that ideal extension of the lives of individuals whereby each
> cooperating member says: "This activity which we perform together,
> this work of ours, its past, its future, its sequence, its order, its
> sense,—all these enter into my life, and are the life of my own self
> writ large."[10]

For Buchler, on the other hand, the basis of community is not subjective at all. "Proceptive directions are irresistibly objective," he writes. "We stand in more communities than we know . . . " (TGT 42, 45) Moreover, oftentimes we do not even know the members of those of our communities of which we are conscious; for, although "[e]ach individual must also be a procept of the other," it in no way follows that "each must be 'directly aware' of the other." (TGT 34) Neither are we certain of our feelings of attachment to any community. We stand in these communities "with a firmness that is greater or less than we suspect." (TGT 45)

Put in a concise statement: "Membership in a community does not necessarily involve either conscious alliance or, as Royce supposed, loyalty." (TGT 42) All that is necessary for community is proceptive parallelism among the members, that individuals have the same 'approach' to a certain natural complex—whether that complex is the works of William Carlos Williams, the secrets of tomato growing, or the development of a particular industrial process. But subjective criteria, whether consciousness or loyalty, are irrelevant.

Now, if the existence of a community does not depend on consciousness or loyalty, the strength of a community cannot be dependent on affective identification or on felt agreement: "the strength of a community does not lie in the sense of union that happens to prevail . . . nor in the external symbols of unanimity; it lies rather in the strength of each of the parallel proceptive directions." (TGT 44) This proceptive parallelism moreover is not the result of the elimination of individuality, but rather the result of the importance to each individual of a certain complex. When a community is strong and vital:

> this is not because individuality is minimized but because the power of something common to individuals can be appropriated by each individual to conquer or alter his proceptive inertia, the course of his present self. (TGT 40–41)

A strong community is consequently a community that results from a large number of common life experiences and expectations which guarantee that there will be a great deal of sharing of perspectives, that the life of the community will not be "fragile." (TGT 44) But, just as community does not depend upon locality or permanence or affection, a strong community does not depend on a high degree of conscious identification or loyalty.

IV

I would like to turn at this point from the question of what sorts of human associations might qualify as communities to the related question of the adequate analysis of the concept of 'community.' This question of analysis will require us to focus upon the difference between those honorific conceptions of Community and the simple descriptive conceptions of community,[11] which in the present context can be seen in the distinction between Royce and Dewey's conception and Buchler's. Should we abandon their eulogistic conception of Community for the purely descriptive account that Buchler offers? Must we attempt to separate, in the interest of clarity, philosophical elaboration from widespread human longings for Community?

Both Dewey and Royce believe that the term 'community' is fundamentally ambiguous, applicable both descriptively to community and eulogistically to Community. For Dewey, Community is a sort of ideal state to which our present community should aspire; for Royce, we should attempt to integrate ourselves into the Great Community rather than remaining isolated in smaller groups. For both of them, 'community' is a concept similar to 'vacuum,' a term which has minimal existence conditions (to have a vacuum, the pressure need only be infinitely less than that of the prevailing atmosphere) yet impossible to satisfy perfection conditions (there is no perfect vacuum, nor is there likely to be). Descriptively, community for Royce and Dewey means a minimal level of association requiring a conscious common identity and common events and practices (existence conditions); yet, for both, Community holds out the promise of an ideal state (perfection conditions) that is to be sought although it is never to be reached, either because of the exigencies of human association (Dewey) or human weakness (Royce). Dewey and Royce use the term 'community' and its synonyms in either the eulogistic and descriptive senses, depending on what type of human association they are emphasizing at any given time.

Concentrating now on Dewey, we see that he has written that "the fact of association does not of itself make a society," emphasizing the distinction between a community and a Community. He sometimes talks about community descriptively—for example, "scattered communities" or "the business community"—and sometimes eulogistically—for example, "[w]e are born organic beings associated with others, but we are not born members of a community."[12] When he does so, Dewey believes that he is simply recognizing the dual meaning that is already present:

> The terms society, community, are thus ambiguous. They have both a eulogistic or normative sense, and a descriptive sense; a meaning *de jure* and a meaning *de facto*. In social philosophy, the former connotation is almost always uppermost. Society is conceived as one by its very nature. The qualities which accompany this unity, praiseworthy community of purpose and welfare, loyalty to public ends, mutuality of sympathy, are emphasized.

But, besides this eulogistic or honorific sense of association, replete with loyalty, sympathy, etc., there is the simple descriptive meaning—community *de facto:*

> when we look at the facts which the term *denotes* instead of confining our attention to its intrinsic *connotation,* we find not unity, but a plurality of societies, good and bad. Men banded together in a criminal conspiracy, business aggregations that prey upon the public while serving it, political machines held together by the interest of plunder are included.[13]

Such communities, however undesirable, must still be recognized as communities.

Having established the duality of the concept of community, Dewey then turns to developing criteria for evaluating communities. On the one hand, he writes, we must be realistic: "We cannot set up, out of our heads, something we regard as an ideal society. We must base our conception upon societies which actually exist, in order to have any assurance that our ideal is a practicable one." But, on the other hand, we cannot simply repeat without challenge the qualities present in these *de facto* communities. The ideal community, he continues, "cannot simply repeat the traits which are actually found. The problem is to extract the desirable traits of forms of community life which actually exist, and employ them to criticize undesirable features and suggest improvement." This dual procedure corresponds to the term's essential ambiguity—the same qualities required of an association to establish *community* will, when developed, result in *Community.*

The criteria themselves are two: "How numerous and varied are the interests which are consciously shared? How full and free is the interplay with other forms of association?" In any social group whatever, Dewey continues, "we find some interest held in common, and we find a certain amount of interaction and cooperative intercourse with other groups." But:

> If we apply these considerations to, say, a criminal band, we find that the ties which consciously hold the members together are few in number, reducible almost to a common interest in plunder; and that they are of such a nature as to isolate the group from other groups with respect to give and take of the values of life.

A criminal band consequently, while a community, is a weak or incomplete one because it possesses few of the qualities of community. Its common interests are limited in number and restricted in range, its interplay with other forms of association is negligible. But even a criminal band, for example, is not a totally worthless community because "each of these organizations, no matter how opposed to the interests of other groups, has something of the praiseworthy qualities of 'Society' which hold it together." We find in such limited communities "honor" and "fraternal feeling" and "intense loyalty."[14] A criminal band is thus a bad community, according to Dewey, because it is a bad example of community, because it has little community. It is good insofar as it has the traits of community, but it is a weak and narrow community. For Dewey, as for Royce, to the extent that any instance of association possesses the traits of community, it is good. Community itself, however partial, is good.

This aspect of the analysis of 'community' is troublesome to Buchler because the duality to which the work of Dewey and Royce points blends the questions of the strength of a community—powerful or weak—and its quality—good or bad—questions that Buchler maintains must be kept separate. Beginning with the question of quality, we recognize that for Buchler a community can be good or bad, but simply as an instance of community it is neither. Just as he rejects eulogistic analyses of such concepts as 'method,' 'unity,' 'intelligence,' 'imagination,' 'poetry' and 'humanity,'[15] Buchler rejects a eulogistic analysis of community. In some instances, community can lead to problems; in others, to benefits. Both saints and sinners, loving families and murdering hordes, can "lead lives in some degree parallel" and be "subject to the same dominant commitment or allegiance." Community itself, however, is amoral.[16]

Turning to the second issue, Buchler rejects the view of Dewey and Royce that quality and strength are related. A more powerful community is not necessarily a better community, nor a weaker, or worse. From his standpoint, to write this way is to overlook the fact that there are two distinct issues here, 1) the range or the impact of a natural complex, and 2) the worth of that complex, which must be sharply distinguished if clarity is to be achieved. This is also a fundamental theme for Buchler. He writes elsewhere, for example, that our analysis of human communication must distinguish carefully between its "extent" and its "value," (ML 19; cf. TGT 169) and also that "[w]hat the traits of discussion are and what the traits of a good discussion are appear to be two different questions."[17] Thus, when he describes the existence and the nature of associated life in his examinations of proceptive parallelism, communication, and so on, he still maintains that recognizing a community's existence and describing it is not the same as claiming value for it.

The term 'community' as Buchler understands it, simply does not have a dual meaning, it has two meanings. There is an order in which questions of strength are relevant, and another in which questions of quality are relevant. As such, community cannot be compared to a vacuum. A better comparison would seem to be atmospheric pressure. The fact that particles are in relation results in a pressure of some level, however high or low. This relation of particles is all it takes to create atmospheric pressure. So too, a particular relation of individuals results in community. Factors of the quality of the relation are not here relevant. When our focus is, with Buchler, purely descriptive, we cannot talk of a more or less perfect community any more than we can talk of a more or less perfect atmospheric pressure. The individual particles or persons are related or they are not. The nature of the relation, whether good or bad, is another issue.

We must not be hasty here and assume that Dewey or Royce are themselves confusing the 'good' and the 'real,' or that Buchler believes that they are. They are all too cognizant that the 'good' they seek is not yet 'real' and perhaps is unrealizable. Royce, for example, lamented during World War I that "[t]he outcome of the present struggle between good and ill remains still a mystery" and that "the lover of the ideal" is "wholly powerless" to determine "what shall be."[18] And, writing from a more metaphysical perspective, Dewey criticizes those who would simplify reality to make it more emotionally acceptable, complaining that in some analyses " 'reality' becomes what we wish existence to be, after we have analyzed its defects and decided upon what would remove them . . . "[19] Dewey and Royce, deliberately moral in their intent, are suggesting that instances of association bearing high levels of the traits of community are good and therefore that community needs to be sought out and expanded if human life is ever to improve. In addition, this goal of improvement, as Dewey writes, is morally pressing: "Nothing but the best, the richest and fullest experience possible, is good enough for man." Moreover, it is the primary job of philosophy "to clarify, liberate and extend the goods which inhere in the naturally generated functions of experience."[20]

Buchler recognizes the value of this social goal, yet as a commentator on their work he pushes on with his criticism because he believes that attempting to combine the analysis of the real with the pursuit of the good is likely to result in success in neither undertaking. Speaking of Royce's analysis of community, he writes for example, "the idea of community, while not an exclusively moral idea, is inherently honorific." (TGT 42) Of Dewey, Buchler writes that, because of categorial weaknesses and "blurred" distinctions, a "moral flavor" on occasion "crept into" his work, (NJ 104) and more strongly that Dewey's work suffered from "frequent jumbling of metaphysical and moral issues." (TGT xxxvi) Royce and Dewey were, of course, fully aware of the honorific or moral aspects of their work on community. They intended it to be this way. The difficulty that Buchler anticipates is that their unwillingness to distinguish here between issues of philosophical analysis and issues of moral worth will retard the efforts of those who use their work as guides.

Buchler's descriptive conception of community is a long way from the conceptions of Royce and Dewey, a distance which reflects a different conception of philosophy and of its role in society. The task of the philosopher, as Buchler sees it, is more narrowly intellectual. The philosopher is more concerned, he writes, with making the world "intelligible" than making it "manageable." (ML 124) In Buchler's own case, this search for intelligibility has focussed on attempts to investigate and elaborate conceptual or categorial programs, to comprehend if possible the full range of existence and of human existence. While recognizing that such "metaphysical query" is not all of "philosophic query,"[21] Buchler makes it his focus. The area of philosophical work that draws him is that of "the categorial struggle to encompass structures of indefinitely greater breadth." (TGT 81; cf. NJ 58) And within this struggle, even when the philosopher's focus moves from discriminating "generic complexes that have the widest possible scope" (MNC 38) to a more narrow concern with human beings through efforts "to discern the broadest and deepest aspects of human functioning" (TGT vii) or attempts "to sharpen the definition of man's status in nature," (NJ vii) the philosopher's task remains an intellectual one, distinct from directly meliorative social application.

Philosophical endeavor involves many intellectual qualities and skills: conceptual clarity, imagination, and insight, to name just three. It also requires a sharpened eye to enable the philosopher to distinguish the often painful facts of life from what we wish these facts were, and the ability to describe what is as-it-is and not in some sense as-it-should-be. Now, in order to prevent "the confusion of what prevails with what we want or do not want to have prevail," (MNC 117) and to maintain ontological parity— the view that no natural complex is "more 'real,' more 'natural,' more 'genuine,' or more 'ultimate' than any other" (MNC 31; cf. ML 126)— Buchler believes that the philosopher must always separate off value considerations from fundamental metaphysical analysis. Although, for example, community improvement may be in fact necessary for better human life, for Buchler, efforts to improve it are not essentially philosophical. When thinkers like Dewey and Royce advocate a dual approach to 'community,' they are, Buchler believes, undermining in those who would follow them the type of "metaphysical awareness"[22] that he advocates as a precondition for adequate philosophical analysis, and perhaps for eventual social improvement. Although all of us can tell that the wholesome and decent society we might have is sadly less real than what we do have, his work suggests that the longing after such a community is less likely to be satisfied if such ambiguity continues in our analyses.

I would not presume to attempt to settle the question of the adequate analysis of the concept of 'community' here. Such a settlement will require much more study and thought about the nature of community. It will also require important developments in the understanding of the normative implications of Buchler's work. Certainly, a normative ontology is by definition confused. But a social philosophy is necessarily normative, and Buchler recognizes functions of philosophy other than the metaphysical, even if he seldom undertakes them. Surely Buchler's attempt to eliminate *ontological* priority does not leave us without any means of evaluation. His discussions of the human process demonstrate some of his *desideranda:* for example, that societies that approximate Community are better societies. But a fuller understanding of the relationship between the results of Buchler's metaphysical query and social philosophy will take time to develop.

V

Buchler's elaboration of what he calls "a metaphysics of the human process' (MNC vii) demonstrates the parallelism and continuity of human life. The human self, he writes, "is connected with other selves and with the world by unseen ties—of obligation, intention, representation, conflict, memory, and love." (NJ 56) This connectedness to other selves is, as we have seen, the key to his analysis of community. His writings on the nature and importance of community, even if not an overriding concern throughout his work, remain a rich and powerful impetus to philosophical query in this area. With regard to his rejection of the natural model of community, we find in Buchler's broader understanding the possibility of encompassing more instances of parallelism. With regard to his rejection of the eulogistic model, we find in Buchler's descriptive understanding of community a powerful reminder of the potential dangers of human association and of the potential problems of combining metaphysical and value questions. It is a safe assumption that community will remain a major element in ongoing American attempts to advance toward a better future. Buchler's work will contribute to this advancement.[23]

Notes

1. *The Public and Its Problems* [1927] in *John Dewey: The Later Works,* vol. 2 (Carbondale: Southern Illinois University Press, 1984), pp. 328, 304, 327–328, 370, 368; cf. "Creative Democracy—The Task Before Us" [1939], in *John Dewey: The Later Works,* vol. 14 (Carbondale: Southern Illinois University Press, 1988), pp. 224–230.

2. *The Basic Writings of Josiah Royce*, ed. John J. McDermott (Chicago: University of Chicago Press, 1969), two vol., pp. 34–35, 876, 1154, 35.

3. For Buchler's discussion of "reflexive community" see NJ, 65–74 and TGT, Chapter 2. See "List of Abbreviations," here p. xiii, for Buchler's works.

4. George A. Hillery, Jr., "Definitions of Community: Areas of Agreement," *Rural Sociology* 20 (1955), p. 117; cf. p. 119.

5. "Reply to Singer: Alleged Ambiguities in the Metaphysics of Natural Complexes," SJP 68, in MNC [1989] 283; cf. MNC 22; TGT xii.

6. "Foreword to the 1930 Modern Library Edition" of *Human Nature and Conduct* in *John Dewey: The Middle Works*, vol. 14 (Carbondale: Southern Illinois University Press, 1983), p. 230.

7. Cf. Gerald D. Suttles, *The Social Construction of Communities* (Chicago: University of Chicago Press, 1972), p. 76.

8. Cf. William J. Goode, "Community within a Community: The Professions," *American Sociological Review* 22:2 (April 1957), pp. 194–200.

9. *Democracy and Education* [1916] in *John Dewey: The Middle Works*, vol. 9 (Carbondale: Southern Illinois University Press, 1980), p. 35; cf. pp. 7–9; *The Public and Its Problems*, p. 353.

10. Josiah Royce, *The Problem of Christianity* (Chicago: University of Chicago Press, [1918] 1968), p. 263.

11. To facilitate discussion in what follows, I have adopted (except in direct quotations) a distinction between 'community' and 'Community,' the latter being the sacral sense.

12. *The Public and Its Problems*, pp. 353, 306, 354, 331.

13. This and the next block quotation are from *Democracy and Education*, pp. 88–89.

14. Ibid.

15. Cf. CM 6, 50, 91, 133, 147; ML 10–14.

16. For Buchler, there is a moral aspect to every community, but it is not that aspect to which the eulogistic sense of community points. The moral aspect of associated existence for Buchler is the problem of ethical consensus. Human communities have "fundamental moral patterns" which are "communally binding and communally desirable," Buchler writes. "Moral similarity, the universal dominance of certain moral complexes," moreover, "is a possibility of any kind of community." (TGT 166) A community presupposes some level of agreement on what is right and wrong. The presupposition, what might be called ethical 'parallelism,' is an effect whether that community is a local neighborhood or a professional association.

17. Justus Buchler, "What is a Discussion?", *Journal of General Education* 8:1 (October, 1954), p. 7.

18. *The Basic Writings of Josiah Royce*, pp. 1145–1146.

19. *Experience and Nature* [1925] in *John Dewey: The Later Works*, vol. 1 (Carbondale: Southern Illinois University Press, 1981), p. 51; cf. *The Quest for Certainty* [1929] in *John Dewey: The Later Works*, vol. 4 (Carbondale: Southern Illinois University Press, 1984), pp. 7, 17.

20. *Experience and Nature*, pp. 308, 305.

21. "Reply to Greenlee: Philosophy and Exhibitive Judgment," SJP 139, in MNC [1989] 208.

22. "Reply to Greenlee," SJP 140, in MNC [1989] 208.

23. My attempts to formulate an analysis of Buchler's conception of community have benefited from the suggestions of Patrick J. Hill and Beth J. Singer, and from the guidance of the editors of this volume.

Buchler's Ordinal Metaphysics and Process Theology

Peter H. Hare and John Ryder

Hare:

Students of Whitehead can find much of interest in the metaphysics of Justus Buchler. Buchler, like Whitehead, subjects traditional substance–quality metaphysics to a devastating critique. If we regard, as surely we must, such rejection of substance–quality metaphysics as one of the distinguishing traits of process metaphysics, Buchler is a process metaphysician. But Buchler, again like Whitehead, does much more than find fault with traditional metaphysics—he elaborates an alternative system of categories.[1] Because his alternative categorial scheme is very different, the points Buchler makes in criticism of traditional metaphysics are interestingly different from those made by Whitehead. Indeed, though Buchler draws on the insights of various metaphysicians including Whitehead, his categories are genuinely original.[2] Consequently, Buchler's metaphysics offers to Whiteheadians the illumination of a novel perspective on the shared goal of the rejection of traditional substance. Furthermore, this shared rejection of substance–quality metaphysics leads to a shared rejection of classical Christian theology, and it is Buchler's original perspective on the rejection of such traditional theistic doctrines as creation *ex nihilo* which John Ryder explores below. After his account, I will explore the relevance of this account to the possible development of an ordinal, process theology based on Buchler's categories.

Ryder:

In his *Metaphysics of Natural Complexes,* Justus Buchler presents and develops the categorial framework of a general metaphysics. One of the primary functions of a system of this generality is its applicability to a wide range of more specific subject matters. A general ontology is designed to provide a framework for interpretation of such areas as experience, science, art, ethics, and religion. It is the task of this paper to consider some of the consequences of Buchler's ordinal metaphysics for one component of most religious systems, God. Our scope will in fact be limited to two specific issues: the existence of God and God as creator.

The discussion will be framed for the most part by the categories of natural complex, ordinality, prevalence, scope, contour, and integrity. For Buchler, everything is a natural complex, including such things as material objects, fictional characters, ideas, relations and laws. To say that something is a natural complex is to say that it is not simple, that it consists of subaltern traits. A natural complex is an order of complexes; it locates (i.e., it is a sphere of relatedness for) its subaltern traits. Not only does a complex locate traits, but it is itself a trait located. Every complex is an order that locates traits and is itself located in an order, a context. That every complex is located in some order or orders is Buchler's principle of ordinality. When a complex maintains traits in a particular ordinal location, it is said to prevail, to be prevalent, in that order.

Complexes may prevail in any number of orders, and for each order in which a complex prevails it has an integrity. A clock, for example, has an integrity as a time piece, a piece of furniture, and a wooden object, among others. The totality of a complex's integrities is its gross integrity, its contour. In addition to its integrities, a complex has subaltern traits which do not influence its ordinal locations. The individual splinters of wood in our clock are such constituents. These constituents fall within the scope of a complex. Each of the categories just discussed, i.e., complex, ordinality, prevalence, scope, contour, and integrity, will bear on the forthcoming discussion of God and God's characteristics.

In an ordinal metaphysics, "Whatever is, in whatever way, is a natural complex." (MNC 1) God, then, is a natural complex. This of course does not imply an affirmative answer to the question "Does God exist?" God is a natural complex in so far as it prevails in some order or another. The order in which it prevails might be the order of literature, or the order of complexes that have had an important influence on the course of human history. To say that God prevails in these orders would not provide the kind of answer called for by the question, "Does God exist?" The question must itself be understood in ordinal terms. To ask if God exists is to inquire into the ordinal locations of a discriminated complex. In particular, the question might concern the location of God in the order of complexes to which devotion is due, or the order of complexes that create other complexes. "Does God exist?" is a question that wishes to identify a specific integrity of the complex God.

Given the necessity of understanding the question "Does God exist?" within the terms and categorial framework of an ordinal metaphysics, it may be better to dispense with the question altogether—dispense with it, that is, only in the terms in which it is usually couched. In an ordinal metaphysics, existence outside of some order is an unintelligible notion. To ask if God exists is to ask whether God prevails in order x or order y. God is already discriminated, and to that extent must prevail in some order. To take the question of the existence of God at face value, we would have to answer yes to it. God does exist, at least in the order of myth, or that of symbol. But these are not the sorts of responses that fully satisfy the question. The question "Does God exist?" is not equivalent to the question "Does God prevail?" Outside of prevalence in some order, though, the term "existence" can have very little meaning in an ordinal metaphysics. Thus Buchler says that "the question whether God 'exists' or does not is a symptom of deficiency in the categorial equipment of a metaphysics." (MNC 8) It is better, i.e., less ambiguous and more clearly meaningful, to ask what orders God is located in rather than if God exists. A complete answer to this question would amount to an articulation of the contour of the complex God.

How can the question of the ordinal locations of God be answered? One way would be to look at several of the traditionally assigned attributes of God and consider whether these attributes can be consistently held along with the workings and conditions of ordinality. One such characteristic would be God as creator *ex nihilo*. If God is a creator *ex nihilo*, then certain things must be true. It must be true, for example, that at the point when God had not created the world, there was nothing other than God alone. If an ordinal metaphysics allows for this possibility, then it may allow for the possibility of God's being located in the order of complexes that create, or create *ex nihilo*. If this characteristic of God is found not to be possible in an ordinal metaphysics, then it is not possible that God is located in the order of complexes that create *ex nihilo*. If God cannot be located in this order, then God cannot be a creator. The same methodology must be applied to all the traditional traits of God. Once that is done, a picture will emerge of the nature of the God that an ordinal metaphysics can recognize. We will not pretend here to offer an exhaustive analysis of the characteristics of God. Rather we will treat only one of them. This will clarify at least a bit what an ordinal metaphysics does or does not allow for.

To say that God is a natural complex is to say a number of things, or a number of different kinds of things. Consequences follow in different branches of inquiry. One of the kinds of consequences that follows from God's being a natural complex is ontological. If God is a complex, then, by definition, God is not simple or indivisible. As a complex, God, to use an awkward phrase, is composed of constituent complexes. The constituent complexes are what constitute God. This in itself is contrary to one of the more prevalent features of the God of much of monotheism, *viz.*, its simplicity. Further consequences follow from this ontological point, one of which has to do with God as creator. If God is a creator *ex nihilo,* then there was a point where God had not yet produced his creation, or at least this is the popular conception. Leaving aside the difficult question of how there could be a "before" if time was not "yet" created, there are still difficulties in the notion of a creator God. Presumably, when God had not yet created the universe, there was nothing in existence other than God. But if God is a natural complex, there must be complexes other than God for there even to be God. If God is a complex, then this complex locates other subordinate complexes. That is, it has constituents. These constituents cannot be the same as God, since God, as a complex, is the order within which they are located. In order for God to be, certain subordinate complexes must be as well.

An ordinal metaphysics places further stipulations on the nature of any given complex. Not only must the complex locate subordinate subcomplexes, but it must be a subcomplex of another, perhaps more pervasive, complex. All complexes both locate and are located. If God is a complex, then God is located in at least one order. Here again, the image of God (as cause) standing alone, prior to everything else (its effects), is untenable. An order is defined by Buchler as "a sphere of (or for) relatedness. It is what 'provides' extent, conditions, and kinds of relatedness." (MNC 95) An order necessarily distinguishes complexes in certain ways and along certain lines; it necessarily delimits complexes and the relations among them. Complexes are what they are by virtue of their ordinal locations. The multiplicity of orders, which includes the idea of orders as delimiters, is what provides the many-faceted nature of complexes. The ordinal location or locations of a complex are what provide, or constitute, its integrity or integrities. The contour, or gross integrity, of a complex is what determines it as that and just that complex. Buchler characterizes identity as "the continuous relation that obtains between the contour of a complex and any of its integrities." (MNC 22) In an ordinal metaphysics, the very notion of identity, of a complex being the complex that it is, is a function of the stipulation that every complex must both locate traits and be located in an order of traits. For God to obtain at all, it is necessary that it both locate traits and be itself ordinally located. Neither of these conceptions seems to be compatible with a creator *ex nihilo.*

Even the principle of ontological parity creates trouble for a creator God. Much if not all of the more Platonic strain in the history of Christian thought turns to a large extent on a principle of ontological priority, but this is not the source of the trouble suggested here. Even though the principle of ontological priority has played such a crucial role in our philosophic and theological development, there is an equally strong tradition wherein the notion of degrees of being does not figure quite as prominently. The point at which the principle of ontological parity interferes with a creator God is in the context of the idea of existence itself. Whatever is, is a complex, and no complex "is" more than any other. Many things, and many different kinds of things, can be said "to be." It has become traditional philosophically to erect as a model of existence a rather crude spatiotemporal paradigm. But this is clearly too restrictive. There are many kinds of complexes that do not seem to fit this paradigm, but yet must be said "to be." Possibilities are one such kind of complex. There has also been a strong tendency in philosophy to consider "being" as in some sense equivalent to actuality. This conception places possibility in some sort of ontological limbo. A more coherent way of looking at all of this is to say that actuality "is" no more than possibility "is." A possibility is no less of a complex, with all the appropriate ordinal conditions, than is actuality. If either can be said "to be," then so must the other.

If God were a creator, then the possibility of what he creates obtains along with him. It would not do to suggest that God creates this possibility as well, since that would only push the question back one step. The question would then have to do with the possibility of *this* creation, and this could easily lead to an infinite regress of the possibility of the creation of the possibility of the creation of. . . . The possibility of creation must be understood as a complex, located in certain orders, and as obtaining along with, and in relation of some kind to, God. Again, the idea of a creator *ex nihilo* is severely hampered by the categorial demands of an ordinal metaphysics.

There is one further point that would be worth making here. It has to do with an issue already raised, *viz.*, the identity of a complex. It was pointed out earlier that Buchler locates the identity of a complex in the continuing relation "between the contour of a complex and any of its integrities." I will try to show why this way of characterizing identity is important for the coherence of an ordinal metaphysics, and in particular how identity in this sense allows for some of the more characteristic features of Buchler's treatment of the question of God. The issue of identity should also show the importance of a principle mentioned earlier, *viz.*, that all complexes must themselves be ordinally located.[3]

One of the more interesting points that Buchler makes in connection with God is that:

> In the metaphysics of natural complexes it could be said that God prevails, not for this reason or that, but because God is a complex

discriminated, and every complex prevails, each in its own way, whether as myth, historical event, symbol, or force; whether as actuality or possibility. (MNC 8)

On the basis of this, it would be appropriate to say that God prevails in the orders of literature, mythology, historical influences, etc. At the same time, there are orders in which God does not prevail, such as the order of complexes that create other complexes *ex nihilo.* The body of this paper has been an attempt to show that God could not possibly prevail in this order. The curious thing about this, though, is that the orders in which God cannot prevail are precisely those orders which seem to frame the historically most characteristic and persistent traits of God. If God cannot prevail in the order of complexes that create *ex nihilo,* as well as others which could be elaborated, then God cannot be a creator, etc.

    Yet it seems necessary, especially in light of the principle of ontological parity, to say that God does prevail in some of the other orders already mentioned. However, if God cannot create and do many of the other things customarily attributed to the Divinity, one wonders whether the God that does prevail in the orders of historical influences and literature is the same God that cannot prevail as creator, etc. If the two "Gods" are not one and the same, that is if we are doing something more than viewing the same complex in a number of its ordinal locations, then the point of saying that God *does* prevail in this or that order loses much of its force. Yet it does look as if it is not the same complex under discussion in the two cases. The complex "God" that prevails in these orders *is* the God who has created what is, who may perhaps preserve its prevalence and towards whom persons strive.

    It is crucial for an ordinal metaphysics to be able to show that the complex seen in terms of each of these orders, including those in which it prevails and in which it is not located at all, is the same one. This is accomplished by the particular way in which identity is characterized. Another point of considerable relevance here is that complexes are indefinitely ramifiable, which is to say they are amenable to indefinite inquiry and analysis. (MNC 24, 56 & 102) In so far as they are ordinally located they are relational, and in so far as they are relational, their traits and integrities are inexhaustible.

    What this point amounts to is that an elaboration of the traits of a complex must include both the traits of the complex in terms of each of its ordinal locations as well as each of its ordinal locations as among its traits. It would be curious to suggest that at a given point all the ordinal locations of a complex, all of its integrities, have been exhaustively delineated, since this would imply that all possibilities for the complex have ceased to obtain. If the integrities of a complex are indefinitely ramifiable, then so are its traits. The important implication of this, at least for our purposes, is that a discussion of the traits of a complex, if it hopes to achieve any sort of adequate scope, cannot limit itself to a consideration of a complex only in terms of one of its ordinal locations. A proper response to the question "What are the attributes (traits) of God?" must include those traits that obtain for the complex in terms of a number of its ordinal locations. God, then, could not be adequately characterized solely as a creator, preserver, judge, goal, etc. The description must include those traits relevant in other ordinal locations as well. God is also a major force in human political and social history, in literature, etc.

If one introduces at this point Buchler's account of the nature of identity, the question of the sameness of a complex across its ordinal locations should be answered. A complex has an integrity for each of its ordinal locations, and identity, to repeat a phrase cited twice already, is the "continuous relation that obtains between the contour of a complex and any of its integrities." The identity of a complex is not a function of this or that integrity. If it were, then we would be forced to say that a complex in one of its ordinal locations is not the same one as the complex considered in another of its locations. Since identity is a function of the relation between the contour, or gross integrity, of a complex and any of its integrities, the possibility of speaking of the "same" complex across ordinal locations is assured. Consequently, the categorial relations of an ordinal metaphysics allow us to say of God that while it cannot be a creator, etc., it, the same God, is locatable and identifiable in other ordinal locations.

It is clear, then, that whatever character an ordinal metaphysics may recognize God as having, it does not include God as a creator *ex nihilo*. As I have indicated earlier, it does not follow from this that it would be appropriate to say that "God does not exist." God prevails in any number of ordinal locations, but not as a creator. Peter H. Hare's remarks that follow consider in further detail the possibilities of examining the traits and functions that can be ascribed to God, which is to say the possibility of an ordinal theology.

Hare:

John Ryder has argued that Justus Buchler's metaphysical principles do not allow God to have at least some of the traits he is thought by traditional Christian theists to have. More specifically, using Buchler's categories of natural complex, ordinality, prevalence, scope, contour, integrity, and relation, he argues that God cannot be creator of the world. Ryder's careful account of the conflict between Buchler's metaphysics and the metaphysics of Christian theism is surprising. I find it surprising not because his exposition of Buchler's views is inaccurate. His exposition is faultless. Nor do I find it surprising because I do not think worthwhile the examination of the implications of Buchler's metaphysics. Certainly Buchler's ambitious and original categorial scheme deserves attention, much more attention than it has received. What I find surprising is that Ryder should consider it remarkable that the metaphysical principles of Buchler, or those of any other philosopher, are violated by Christian theology. In the history of metaphysics it has been *common*—it has been the *norm* even—to have metaphysical principles violated by Christian theology. For example, a metaphysician will commonly assert as sound metaphysical doctrine that every event has a cause, and yet will also assert, as a doctrine of Christian theology, that God's acts do not have causes. Or, as sound metaphysical doctrine it is asserted that everything that manifests design must have a designer, and yet as sound theological doctrine it is also asserted that the design manifested in God is without designer. Or, it is asserted as sound metaphysical doctrine that all existence is contingent, and yet as sound theology it is asserted that God's existence is necessary, that is, noncontingent. This fundamental sort of inconsistency seems to be *endemic* among metaphysicians.

In other words, it would have been remarkable if Buchler's metaphysics had *not* been found to contradict basic tenets of Christian theology. It would have been remarkable not just because Buchler is working in the tradition of American naturalism, but also because, as I have just pointed out, such a conflict is common among many sorts of metaphysicians, not just among naturalistic metaphysicians.

Although I applaud the accuracy of Ryder's account of the relations between some of the tenets of Christian theology and Buchler's categorial scheme, I worry that Ryder may unintentionally give the impression that Buchler's metaphysics is narrowly naturalistic and strongly antitheological in character when quite the opposite is the case. It seems to me that, all things considered, Buchler's categorial scheme is a naturalistic metaphysics that is unusually open to theological development. To be sure, Buchler's metaphysics quite appropriately rules out certain theological tenets of the sort Ryder describes. But Buchler's is not a militantly naturalistic metaphysics of the sort one finds espoused by Sidney Hook, for example. Indeed, I venture the opinion that Buchler's is the most broad and open naturalistic metaphysics yet produced. That breadth and openness is one of his system's most characteristic features, and I would not like to see that admirable breadth and openness obscured by Ryder's emphasis on the conflicts between Christian theology and Buchler's system of categories.

More than any other feature of his system it is Buchler's principle of ontological parity that ensures the openness of his metaphysics. According to that principle, "no complex is more 'real', more 'natural', more 'genuine', or more 'ultimate' than any other." (MNC 31) While this principle, of course, rules out any theology in which God is considered the *ultimate* reality, i.e., rules out traditional theism, it does not rule out other sorts of theology. When I speak of "other sorts of theology," I do not have in mind only a Deweyan or a Randallian sort of theology in which "God" is considered a human symbol of the unity of social ideals. It should go without saying that Buchler's metaphysics leaves room for religious humanism. Buchler's metaphysics, I am suggesting, leaves open the possibility of more than a humanistic sort of theology. I can find nothing in his metaphysics that requires that divine reality be reducible to human reality. It is a serious mistake to suppose that the fact that his metaphysical principles preclude traditional theism implies that they allow only humanistic conceptions of God. There is much metaphysical room between the extreme of traditional theism and the extreme of religious humanism. Humanism is by no means the only conceivable religion compatible with the principle of ontological parity. Let us consider the intriguing question of what nonhumanistic theologies Buchler's metaphysics will allow.

Whitehead advised us to seek a concept of God according to which he is the "chief exemplification" of our metaphysical principles, not an exception to those principles "invoked to save their collapse."[4] Whitehead may not have done a very good job of following his own advice, but it is good advice nonetheless. What might be the "chief exemplification" of Buchler's metaphysical principles? Couldn't we develop as such an exemplification a category of "divine proception?" "Proception" is the term Buchler uses to refer to the life-process of a human individual. I can find nothing in his principles which precludes a superhuman form of proception. There seems to be nothing in his characterization of individual experience that precludes a form of proception in which far greater than human powers are exercised. If proception in its human form involves the exercise of powers of assimilation and manipulation of natural complexes, could not a divine form of proception involve much greater powers of assimilation and manipulation? If the cumulative order of complexes which constitute the history of a human being is what Buchler calls the "proceptive domain," is it not metaphysically permissible to conceive of a much more inclusive proceptive domain, a "divine proceptive domain?" If human experience has what Buchler calls "proceptive direction," couldn't we suppose that much more influential forms of proceptive direction can be found—what might be thought of as a process form of Providence?

In short, I can find nothing in Buchler's metaphysics that rules out— or even discourages—the development of an ordinal, process theology. Of course, process theology is associated with the work of Whitehead, and

Whitehead has been severely criticized by Buchler for his arbitrary use of a principle of ontological priority.[5] Yet there seems to be nothing in the nature of process theology which requires that some entities be considered ''more real'' than others. If process theology were freed from Whitehead's ''strain of arbitrariness,'' it would seem to be compatible with Buchler's metaphysical principles.

The theological possibilities inherent in Buchler's metaphysics can, I think, be illustrated in other ways. For example, Buchler has said repeatedly that metaphysicians should cure themselves of the bad habit of treating the spatiotemporal complex as the fundamental entity. Surely this openness to realities that are not spatiotemporal invites the development of the notion of a divine reality that is located in various orders but not in a spatiotemporal order. If part of the motivation behind theistic theology lies in the need to believe that reality is not merely spatiotemporal, then a theology developed from Buchler's metaphysics would satisfy that need without committing the theologian to the metaphysical absurdity of a God that is not a natural complex.

Another feature of Buchler's metaphysics that invites theological development is his insistence on the reality of possibilities, a reality that follows from his principle of ontological parity. If part of the motivation behind traditional theology lies in the demand for a recognition of the genuine reality of possibilities and not merely the reality of here–and–now actualities, that demand could be satisfied without departing from Buchler's metaphysics of natural complexes.

My thesis, then, is that one of the remarkable features of Buchler's metaphysics is that it allows (by virtue of the principle of ontological parity) the development of a nonhumanistic theology, a development not allowed by other systems of metaphysics in the naturalistic tradition and a development that should be welcomed by process theologians.

Notes

1. For a comparison between Buchler's and Whitehead's critiques of traditional substance, see Beth J. Singer, ''Substitutes for Substances,'' *Modern Schoolman* 53 (November 1975), pp. 19–38. Here, pp. 73–91.

2. For helpful discussion of the relations between Buchler and many other metaphysicians, see Stephen David Ross, *Transition to an Ordinal Metaphysics* (Albany: State University of New York Press, 1980), passim.

3. For a detailed discussion of Buchler's treatment of identity, see Marjorie C. Miller, ''The Concept of Identity in Justus Buchler and Mahayana Buddhism,'' *International Philosophical Quarterly* 16:1 (1976), pp. 87–107. Here, pp. 93–113.

4. Alfred North Whitehead, *Process and Reality* (New York: MacMillan Company, 1929), p. 521. Free Press Paperback edition, 1957, p. 405. Corrected Edition, edited by David Ray Griffin and Donald Sherburne (New York: The Free Press, 1978), p. 343.

5. See Buchler's "On a Strain of Arbitrariness in Whitehead's System," *The Journal of Philosophy* 66 (1969), pp. 589–601, & Reprinted in *Explorations In Whitehead's Philosophy,* ed. Lewis S. Ford & George L. Kline (New York: Fordham University Press, 1983), pp. 280–294.

Ordinality and the Divine Natures

Robert S. Corrington

Introduction

Philosophical theology continues to be plagued by a lack of insight concerning its basic conceptual resources and a consequent inability to provide a compelling portrayal of the divine natures. On one side, process theology has extended and refined the categories of experience, event, and divine evolution, but has not been able to shed sufficient light on the ways in which the divine is embedded in the orders of nature. The implied panpsychism of Whitehead and Hartshorne privileges the traits of finite experience and overestimates the scope of psychic traits in nature. At the other philosophic extreme are those thinkers, enamored by the alleged free space provided by postmodernism, who reject all conceptual strategies that do not devolve into metaphors. Metaphoric language is held to free theology from the more difficult and prolonged process of validation. While the shift to metaphor, and the attendant elevation of aesthetic language, seems to advance philosophical theology, it actually masks a deeper theoretical impoverishment. Neither process theology nor the more recent metaphorical strategies contain sufficient categorial richness to sustain a generic exploration and articulation of the divine natures.

It does not follow from this that process thought will not continue to provide some of the concepts needed for a more generic articulation of the divine. Nor is it denied that metaphoric language can often enhance the richness and evocative power of a conceptual portrayal. What does follow is that process categories need to be located within a more generic perspective that does not privilege consciousness and its contingent features. Further, metaphoric language must be shown to serve extrametaphoric interests. The creative tension between categorial articulation and metaphoric expression remains central to the present task.

Throughout this paper, a number of key concepts of ordinal metaphysics are employed to create a more adequate way of understanding the divine natures. At several key junctures in the analysis it will be necessary to reconstruct or even reject some of the features of the ordinal perspective.

Buchler did not create a detailed conception of the divine even though he
provided a metaphysical framework that makes such a conception possible.
I am persuaded that one of the most important tests of any philosophic
perspective is its ability to probe into the various dimensions of God. At the
same time, any philosophic encounter with God may put creative pressure
back on the very categories used to explore the divine. We do not simply fit
God into an antecedent framework. There are striking senses in which God
will be an exception to any basic conceptual perspective. While Buchler
would reject the notion that God violates some aspects of ordinality, he sets
the tone for my exploration as follows:

> Nothing jeopardizes the strong uniqueness of this complex [i.e.,
> God]. Historically and persistently, there attaches to it a customary
> formal scheme of traits. This scheme, adhered to in its essentials by
> widely differing philosophers, serves to maintain a level of gravity
> and primacy for the idea of God. It predetermines the complex to be
> interpreted, however different the interpretations otherwise may be. It
> provides the "rules" with which all versions are to accord. Thus men
> have recognized in effect that to God belongs great pervasiveness,
> inexhaustible value as a paradigm, symbolic richness, "supremacy."
> Such traits prescribe the sphere of relevance, the formula as it were,
> for ceaseless translation of the idea. Translation presupposes an
> "original;" so that when a philosopher wishes to use and adapt the
> concept of God, but fails to grasp the sense of the schematic require-
> ment and fails to grasp the compulsion behind it, he achieves not the
> metaphysical or poetic perception he might have sought, but a some-
> what hollow categorial freedom.[1]

It is important to note that ordinal metaphysics can facilitate more than one
conception of God. Any given portrayal of the divine natures represents one
"translation of the idea," and must establish its claims to adequacy through
its ability to become relevant to all the dimensions of religious experience.
Further, such a portrayal must remain in creative tension with traditional
conceptions of God and provide mechanisms for moving past and through
perspectives that continue to remain compelling. The current enterprise is
ultimately concerned with reshaping Christian theology so that it can free
itself from some of its idiosyncratic and nongeneric commitments and
thereby liberate Christology from a provincial and self-serving perspective.

The Dimensions Of Nature

If we assume that God is in process then it follows that the divine is
in some sense finite and in need of further growth and self-articulation. In

this protracted process of self-expansion, God overcomes its previous limitations and moves toward a more complete state. While process theologians, in acknowledging the growth of the divine, distinguish between the primordial and the consequent natures of God, it is necessary to transform their perspective to clarify more precisely those ways in which God is located in nature and the orders of history. More importantly, it is necessary to examine the respects in which the divine is eclipsed by a reality that provides the goad and lure for its own eternal self-surpassing. In what follows, I delineate four divine dimensions and contrast them to more traditional formulations. This entails a redefinition of trinitarian structures along the lines of this four-fold analysis. My ultimate objective is to show that there are conceptual impulses within Christianity that provide an Encompassing perspective within which Christianity can be relocated and redefined. Process theology, with all of its innovations, has only explored and refined several of these impulses.

To say that God is in some respect finite is to affirm the sheer locatedness of God in the innumerable orders of nature. Nature, as itself without an outer circumference or ultimate contour, is in many respects a more encompassing reality than God. It makes no sense to say that nature is some sort of "collection" of individuals or that it is bound by an eternal outer limit within which all complexes prevail. It is more compelling to understand nature as without any limitations or extrinsic framework. This is not to say, however, that nature is completely bereft of observable aspects. There are two fundamental dimensions to nature, as noted by Buchler. The first is *natura naturata* or nature natured. In this dimension we can speak of nature or world as the "sum" of all complexes. While it is impossible to enumerate and encompass these complexes, it is important to recognize that nothing can prevail that is not a complex in relation to other complexes. While a given complex may have more scope or comprehensiveness than another, it will still be located and limited by other complexes. The second dimension of nature is *natura naturans* or nature in its naturing. In this dimension, nature lives as the protean and active source for all of the complexes in the first dimension. The innumerable complexes manifest as nature natured are themselves located and ordered by the sheer power of nature in its naturing. In the words of Buchler:

> If *natura naturata* is "the world" or "the Universe," then *natura naturans* is the order of provision and determination. It is reflected in the fertility of any complex whatever. Nature is not so much the order which contains or even includes all other orders as the order which permeates them all; not the order within which but by which new orders are discriminable and explorable, whether through assertion,

action, or contrivance. Only such an order can make possible and justify the indefinite continuation of query. (MNC 100)

This fundamental distinction will function as the basic categorial structure that enables us to articulate the four divine natures. Nature in its naturing permeates the divine orders as well as the nondivine and lives as the sheer "providingness" of the innumerable complexes of the world.

Invoking more traditional language, we can see nature natured as equivalent to the orders of creation. These orders have a certain autonomy from the creative impulses that sustain them. Nature in its naturing can be understood as the continuing acts of creation by and through which the world is sustained against the recurrent threats of nonbeing. Not all acts of creation are temporal although many are. The inner correlation between the creation and the creative power of nature will rule out in principle the earlier Christian view of this relation that insisted on a radical creation out of nothing. The doctrine of *creatio ex nihilo* will prove to be misguided when we probe into the third dimension of the divine.

Turning to our analysis of the divine natures themselves, I assert that the first and second divine aspects prevail within the dimension of nature as natured. The third aspect can be partially equated with nature naturing while the fourth aspect will relocate this fundamental distinction from the standpoint of the Encompassing. The distinctions among God, nature, and that which encompasses both will emerge more fully as the analysis unfolds.

First Divine Dimension

God in its first dimension is one complex among the innumerable complexes of nature. In the words of Buchler, "If the concept of God is thought of as viable metaphysically, and not blankly endured as a stimulus to animism, it must signify a natural complex." (MNC 6) As such, God is finite and embedded in a nature that transcends its scope and power. In this dimension the divine is fragmented and splintered by the orders within which it must appear. This fragmentation is deepened by the fact that nondivine complexes have their own spheres of power and sovereignty that limit the ways in which God may become manifest. In this sense, God is fully wedded to the time process and evolves and grows within the fitful and fragmentary forces of history. God may be more strongly present in some orders than in others, although the expression of this presence will be fraught with ambiguity. The fragmentary and plurally located forces of history and nature make it impossible for God to have a clear and distinct manifestation. Any theophany (divine appearance) will be part of a time process that will distend and regionalize that appearance.

God, as a natural complex, will contain alescent traits, or represent alescent traits within a complex. Whenever a given complex becomes permeable to the divine potency, that power will represent an alescent trait within the complex. The complex will admit this divine potency into its trait constitution. If the presence of God as fragmented origin—that is, God in its first dimension—adds to the meaning, power, and value of a complex, then we can see God as contributing to an augmentative alescence. The complex, in becoming the locus of part of the divine potency, enhances both its scope and its integrity. Its scope is broadened to include a fragment of the indefinite potency of God. Its gross integrity or contour is radically redefined to include at least one specific integrity that is ordered and shaped by the divine potency.

By the same token, God can live as one or more possibilities that prevail for any given complex. In a strong sense, human freedom is preserved by its ability to actualize or ignore those possibilities that are preserved by God. Of course, these possibilities must be ordinally located and "belong" to the person as part of his or her contour. God thus becomes part of the "prefinition" of many complexes. More generally:

> The prefinition is that which is intrinsic to the complex as it prevails, *that* complex, that order of traits. The *order*, with its makeup of traits, is what basically prefines. It is represented by its prefinitions or possibilities. . . . Possibilities, therefore, it [the complex] always has, whether they vary in their general pattern or continue intact. (MNC 167)

Some of these possibilities, of course, are related to nondivine complexes. My contour as a person is changed whenever a possibility is actualized or when another ceases to be available for actualization. The most strongly relevant prefinitions are those that emerge from the divine. These possibilities are not free-floating any more than they are nonlocated. A possibility, even when divine, is always of and for a complex. By the same token, God's possibilities are partly determined by the possibilities and actualities that prevail in nondivine complexes. The orders of the world help to shape and define the possibilities available to God. This redefinition of divine possibilities makes it possible to overcome those frameworks that would force us to locate possibilities in some alleged eternal mind of God beyond the orders of the world.

If we say, following Tillich, that God appears in works of art, we must also say that this manifestation will vary in strength and purity from one perspectival order to another. By the same token, this presence will depend upon the spiritual capacities of the governing culture and its nonreligious horizons. Individual interpreters may be unable to see the divine presence within a given painting or piece of music and thereby ignore their own insensitivity to the higher spiritual presence. Patterns of expectation often foreclose our ability to respond to the presence of the divine. So-called "realist" conceptions of art might close off our understanding of a nonrepresentative work of art such as a color field painting by Rothko, where a striking sense of the spirit is present. Sheer hermeneutic drift and spiritual opacity frustrate God's desire to appear in the orders of nature and history. God may affect the scope and integrity of a complex in ways that remain just beyond the reach of finite interpreters. In a striking sense, God coaxes us beyond current limits. We will see this most clearly in exhibiting the third divine dimension.

God is thus a prevalence that must recognize the limits of its power. Since God is in some respects a natural order, it follows that God cannot be omnipotent in this first dimension. That is, God remains bound and measured by innumerable other orders of nature and must respond to their own forms of prevalence. God's power is limited by the sheer density and resistance of other complexes of nature, and experiences profound limits to its scope and efficacy. In this first dimension, God must wait upon the diverse and fragmented forces of life and history in order to enrich and deepen its own contour. The concept of "life" refers to those complexes of nature characterized by an inner dynamism that has its own momentum and power.

In biblical terms, this is a dimension of the spirit that moves through and among the orders of nature. "The wind [*pneuma*] blows where it wills; you hear the sound of it, but you do not know where it comes from, or where it is going. So with everyone who is born from spirit." (John 3:8) Spirit is limited in the form and manner of its appearance even though, from our finite perspective, spirit seems to move wherever its internal impulses lead it. God as spirit is the finite God that suffers and labors within the innumerable orders of nature. In this dimension, God is self-surpassing and timebound. Put differently, God in its first dimension suffers with the orders of creation and labors with them toward an elusive wholeness and harmony. Finite power and sheer embeddedness limit the expansive presence of the divine.

If God suffers with the orders of creation and experiences limits to its power because of the freedom and autonomy of many of these orders, then it follows that God is sympathetic to the travails of creation. God does not need to be a person to be sympathetic to suffering orders. The language of "sympathy" and "suffering," is applied analogically to the divine. The continuity between the divine and the nondivine provides the "space" within which the prepersonal power of God can become relevant to persons. A God that is embedded in the orders of creation, as one order among others, knows of the demonic forces that destroy harmony and integrity. In this first divine aspect, God manifests its eternal sympathy for all suffering creatures. As noted by Hartshorne, this sympathy extends to God's willingness to cosuffer with creation. God participates in our lives and gathers our suffering to itself. In the words of Hartshorne:

> The chief novelty of the New Testament is that divine love, which seems plainly affirmed in the prophetic doctrine of a merciful deity concerned with the fate of the helpless and unfortunate, is carried to the point of participation in creaturely suffering, symbolized by the Cross taken together with the doctrine of the Incarnation.[2]

Insofar as God remains embedded within the emergent orders of creation (nature natured), God fully participates in the pain and suffering of all orders. This ever active and expanding divine sympathy can be felt by conscious beings whenever the power of spirit breaks through the concresced shells of personal or social life.

A God bereft of omnipotence must also be unable to eradicate evil from the orders of nature and history. William James understood this dimension clearly when he affirmed that God requires human aid if the structures and forces of evil are to be overcome or weakened. Further, as repeatedly noted by Hartshorne, the concept of finite freedom requires that we acknowledge built-in limits to God's omnipotence. Put logically, God cannot but allow for evil. God can and does preserve possibilities for proceivers, but cannot legislate whether and how they will be actualized. If God is part of numerous temporal and spatial structures, as well as of those that are neither spatial nor temporal, it follows that those orders have nondivine traits that limit the efficacy of the divine. God is fully cognizant of the intrinsic tragedy of the world and its conflicting orders.

Second Divine Dimension

In the second dimension, God lives as the lure and goad to personal and social transformation. In terms of Boston Personalism, God works tirelessly to empower all selves with the dignity of an autonomous personality. The evolution from the prepersonal to the personal stage is made possible by the dynamic and propulsive energy of God. In its second aspect, the divine must contend with the recalcitrance of the inorganic and organic realms. But within these orders lie many possibilities for growth and the emergence of self-consciousness. Nature struggles to give birth to selves.

Each self leaps out of the oblivion of its genus and gains its own autonomy and uniqueness. Whenever an order of nature adds the trait of personality it becomes more fully and internally related to the actuality of God.

If the movement toward selfhood, what the poet Gerard Manley Hopkins calls "selving," is found throughout the orders of nature, it follows that this precarious gift must itself be nurtured from a source outside of itself.[3] The power behind an internal entelechy comes from selving and no personal entelechy can long prevail that is bereft of divine support. God lives as the sustaining presence that protects each personality from the forces of inertia and decay. Tillich forcefully argued that God is not itself a person, except by analogy, but lives as the ground for those acts of individuation that make personality possible. In his *Systematic Theology* he exhibits this distinction:

> "Personal God" does not mean that God is *a* person. It means that God is the ground of everything personal and that he carries within himself the ontological power of personality. He is not a person, but he is not less than personal.[4]

God cannot be less than personal because the impulse toward personality must come from an ontological potency that understands the full manifestation of the self. "Selving" is a gift of that dimension of God that drives toward the future and the manifestation of greater actuality and consciousness. This propulsive and eschatological dimension of the divine is most clearly manifest in the emergence of centers of personality. We call this aspect the eschatological aspect because of the priority of the future in the evolution of personality from the prepersonal matrix. Within the opening created by the future, the nascent self can find the room within which to satisfy its inner longing for expansion and articulation. Such centers are what they are through the divine lure that empowers growth and unending transformation.

In Buchler's terms, although not applied in this way in his perspective, this would mean that God enhances the scope and richness of our proceptive domains. These domains represent the cumulative "reach" of the self within its various worlds. Buchler defines these domains:

> The *gross* proceptive domain comprises all that belongs to the individual's living makeup, the segment of nature within which he functions, the past that is actually or potentially alive for him, the sum of his suppositions, guiding principles, commitments, and peculiarities. The gross domain is the class of all his interrelated procepts. The *floating* proceptive domain represents the summed-up self or pro-

ceiver within a given situation. . . . Finally, the *immanent* proceptive domain comprises all that is present to—that is, available for—the proceiver at a given moment; it is the gross domain represented in minimal cross section. (TGT 8–9)

The relative value or relevance of past, present, and potential procepts, is to some extent derived from the divine potencies that operate in some procepts. These "epiphanies of power," a conception not used by Buchler, stand as traces of the inclusion of the divine within the various proceptive domains. Religious query consists, to some extent, in the exploration of those procepts that give the gross, floating, and immanent proceptive domains some sense of a transcending potency that cannot be reduced to the nondivine powers of nature. The self is transformed whenever it assimilates procepts that exhibit traces of the divine.

The proceptive direction is perhaps even more clearly permeable to the first divine dimension. The self finds a new depth and source of meaning whenever its proceptive direction is modified by the assimilation of the divine life. The religious concept of conversion points to the possibility of a profound change in the proceptive direction. God, as the fragmented origin, compels the self to acknowledge traits and powers not of its own making. Nor are these traits the "natural" product of nondivine complexes. In more traditional language, the proceptive direction receives an intimation of a theonomous core that lives as the true measure for the movement and growth of the self.

Can we extend the concepts of proceptive domain and proceptive direction to the divine itself? Peter Hare argues that such an extension is strongly suggested by the ordinal perspective. He argues that God has its own proceptive domain and that God's proceptive direction is manifest as "providence." Hare states:

"Proception" is the term Buchler uses to refer to the life-process of a human individual. I can find nothing in his principles which precludes a superhuman form of proception. . . . If human experience has what Buchler calls "proceptive direction," couldn't we suppose that much more influential forms of proceptive direction can be found—what might be thought of as a process form of Providence?[5]

This extension or projection of proceptive domain and direction to the divine natures does violate several key principles of ordinality. For one thing, the concepts pertaining to proception are specifically designed to deal with the unique features of the human process and reflect forms of relation and embeddedness that are not necessarily found in the divine. For another, there are senses in which God is not part of a time process and thus cannot be exhaustively understood in terms of floating domains or specific forms of directionality.

God is still finite in this dimension of its nature. The evolution and growth of personal centers of power is as precarious and time bound as any other natural process. God can no more create a center of personality than such a center can create itself. Rather, both God and the finite self condition each other as they struggle beyond the opacity of the prepersonal stage. God can provide a lure within which the finite self may find strength to overcome Its previous limitations, but God cannot force the self toward a transformed and deepened autonomy. A self attains autonomy when it provides the law (*nomos*) for its own (*autos*) being.

The depth dimension of autonomy is the theonomy that is rooted in the divine. A self attains theonomy when its self-law is rooted in the divine (*theos*) law (*nomos*). This law is not a pregiven rule of life, but a gift of meaning that regrounds the self. As each finite self finds its theonomous center it comes closer to living with the divine lure. This lure is most fully manifest in the eschatological core of personal and social transformation. The animating center of hope is the movement of God toward the community of selves in which all heteronomy (alien law) is transformed into a true theonomy. The divine lure is persuasive rather than coercive, as noted by Hartshorne, and cannot be omnipotent. By the same token, God in this second dimension is not the force of "providence" if "providence" is understood as a divine ordering of natural and historical events. The movement of selving, which evolves from a fragmented autonomy toward an integral theonomy, is a movement fully embedded in the fissures and disruptions of the world. Such a "fissure" is manifest, for example, when we confront radical evil that cannot be explained through any of the moral categories at our disposal.

The spirit also lives within this second dimension. If the first dimension is the fragmented God of history, then the second is the emancipatory God of human community. The spirit lives and moves within the eschatological impulses of personal and social orders and enables some of these orders to transcend their conditions of origin. The spirit moves through the orders of nature quickening some of them toward the status of selves. But no personal transformation can succeed if it fails to become gathered into the more encompassing structures of communal transformation. As Josiah Royce and others have argued, the very meaning of personal existence is derived from the pervasive features of the community of interpretation.[6] The spirit operates within the community of interpreters, moving them toward meaningful and just social convergence. These communal orders are empowered by the spirit of interpretation that guides each finite hermeneutic act and helps such acts toward a convergence with the manifestation of God. The divine works to enliven personal centers of value and meaning within those orders that transcend the mere enumeration of all finite selves. The soteriological (salvific) impulses manifest in emancipatory communities come from the second divine dimension. While God in its first dimension is broken and sundered by the forces of history, even while struggling with and against them for wholeness, God in its second dimension arches out over the selving process to comfort and embolden human transformation. Spirit works throughout prepersonal orders to find its own in the elusive impulses of personality.

Shifting to metaphorical language, we can see the most concrete expression of this second divine aspect in the symbol of the kingdom of God. Such a kingdom, perhaps more properly called a "community of the spirit," lies both within and beyond history. It is facile to privilege either realized or future eschatology. Both dimensions must be present in order for the "community of the spirit" to prevail within the orders of life. In some respects this "community" is realized in the spirit–filled lives of some of its members. Yet in other respects this "community" lies beyond all human acts and experiences and thereby judges the finite social and political orders. The "community of the spirit" is both realized and in the future but in different respects. Put differently, this "community" is both personal and social and neither aspect can long prevail without the other. St. Paul came to focus more clearly on these tensions as his theology matured under the pressure of the delayed *Parousia* (second coming of Christ).

Third Divine Dimension

The finitude of God is more clearly manifest when we explore the other side of the natured/naturing divide and gain insight into the non-finite dimension of God. When we go beyond God's status as an order within nature, that is, as one of nature's products, we penetrate into the deeper mystery of God as the eternal power of naturing. In this third divine aspect, God is most properly understood as the power that sustains the innumerable orders of nature. Of course, complexes sustain each other without the divine and we move beyond the ordinal perspective when we speak of the third divine dimension.

It is impossible to prove that the third divine dimension "exists," if by "proof" one means entailment from pre-established categories or other forms of evidential compulsion. Two more indirect forms of argument make this conception compelling. The first, more negative argument, states that the concept of "natural complex," with the codependent concepts of ordinal location and discontinuity, fails to describe the infinite scope of God.

All other natural complexes are located in other complexes and are discontinuous with some others. God, on the other hand, is not discontinuous with any complex but has a scope that is limited only by the Encompassing. This sense of God's continuity with each and "every" natural complex converges with the second argument. The second indirect argument, derived from the general argumentative strategy of Schleiermacher, moves from the traits of lived experience to that which makes such experience possible. This type of argument does not impose traits derived from the human process onto the divine. It is a type of transcendental argument moving from what is the case to what we must suppose as its enabling condition. Schleiermacher's concept of "absolute dependence" expresses that quality of experience that cannot be derived from any given natural complex or group of complexes. Our experience of grace, the more traditional term for absolute dependence, can only be possible if experience is permeable to the third divine dimension. These two indirect arguments provide their own type of "evidence" and force us to admit those senses in which God is not a natural complex.

In this dimension, God is most unlike the order of personality and most like an impersonal potency that can never be adequately rendered in finite analogies or concrete metaphors. From the standpoint of the ordinal perspective, such a God would be an unlocated power that does not actualize or realize possibilities. Buchler would reject this metaphoric and conceptual extension of his perspective. As noted, other philosophical and theological concerns makes such an extension compelling and these will emerge more fully as we proceed. As the power that sustains the infinite orders of the world, God is not merely a natural complex or a part of the time process. While time is itself an order and thus located within some orders and not others, time is not a trait of nature as a whole. By the same token, space, while applicable to some orders, is not applicable to all orders. Some orders are temporal and/or spatial and some are not. In exhibiting the characteristics of God in this third dimension it is important not to assume that God has traits derived from aspects of nature as natured. Consequently, God's third aspect cannot be part of a temporal process or confined to specific spatial locations. It is more conceptually compelling to see God as the quiet and still self-effacing origin that makes nature and worldhood possible. This origin is self-effacing in that it is not a first principle or natural primitive from which complexes can be derived, either logically or causally. Rather, such an origin, unlike any other kind of origin, refuses to intrude its presence into the orders that it sustains. Consequently, God in this dimension is omnipotent in only a derivative sense. This power cannot be defined as a "power over" or as a "power against" but as an enabling power that frees its "objects" from a dependence on a demonic or devouring origin. The metaphor of "devouring origin" evokes the neo-Platonic idea that emanated orders are pulled back into the emanating power, thus destroying their independence and any principle of individuation. From the standpoint of the human process, the third divine dimension is felt in the sheer difference between given complexes and meaning horizons on the one hand, and the indefinite and awe–inspiring scope of God on the other. The movement of thought and proception is freed from constriction by an encounter with the third divine dimension. Buchler, speaking out of a very different philosophic context, describes one sense in which the divine provides us with a sense of contrast:

> If God were understood in part as that complex of nature which preserves overwhelming contrast with the finite, then to God might be ascribed perpetual consummations of a related kind—delimiting all other complexes, opening human ways beyond prevailing limits, and constantly renewing in the experiental orders of the world (in the perspectives of man) that sensitivity to the similar and the different which lies at the base of query. (MNC 7–8)

God, as a complex discriminated, stands over and against the other orders of the world. Thus the divine complex has a unique status within the metaphysics of natural complexes. On the one hand, God is clearly a natural complex and is thus located "within" the innumerable orders of the world. Yet, on the other hand, God is one of the most striking manifestations of nature naturing, of "providingness." This tension within the divine natures locates God on both sides of the ontological difference. In Heideggerian terms, the ontological difference is that between Being and a being. In ordinal terms, the ontological difference is between natural complexes and "providingness."[7] Buchler would resist this extension of the ordinal perspective because it seems to put God in the dubious position of violating the basic traits of any complex. Yet the ordinal perspective is itself ambiguous concerning the notion of that dimension of nature that is not commensurate with the concept of complexes. God is thus both a complex within nature (first, second, and fourth dimensions) and the sheer "providingness," Tillich's "power of Being," for the innumerable orders of the world.[8] As noted above, God is not to be equated with sheer prevalence alone. Not only is God an alescent trait within many complexes, but God also "contains" alescent traits within its own natures. Insofar as God becomes permeable to that which is novel or which lies outside of the scope of its power, it must allow alescent traits into its contour. This reinforces the process notion that God can be surprised in time and can thus respond to and become aware of that which is not prefigured in antecedent traits.

In Tillich's well known, and well worn, formulation, this dimension of the divine can be seen as the ground of "Being" that overcomes the forces of absolute and dialectical "nonbeing." In his *Systematic Theology* he redefines this category in terms of the maternal. He states:

> In so far as it [the ground of Being] is symbolical, it points to the mother-quality of giving birth, carrying, and embracing, and, at the same time, of calling back, resisting independence of the created, and swallowing it.[9]

Here is adumbrated his recurrent preoccupation with the polarity of mysticism and guilt consciousness. Tillich perhaps goes too far in his personification of the forces of emanation and return but does, nonetheless, focus on the inner logic of this third divine aspect. God as nature naturing equally sustains all offspring no matter what their specific ontological or ethical status. The lament of Job points to the profound mystery surrounding the seeming indifference of the divine to the radical difference between good and evil. It is no longer possible to fall back on the notion that evil is a mere diminution of good or that evil is a necessary enrichment of the cosmic process. While God struggles against evil in its first two dimensions, the third dimension is detached from these struggles. The counter pressure to emanation is not the "swallowing" envisioned by Tillich, but the advance of finite autonomy and creative evolution. In this dimension, God is beyond good and evil and lives as both ground and abyss for all of the orders of nature. To say that God is both ground and abyss is to reaffirm that God is a self-effacing origin. The metaphor of "ground" evokes the sustaining power of the divine, while the metaphor of "abyss" evokes the sheer otherness and indifference of the divine.

In scholastic trinitarian language, we can call this dimension the dimension of God the Father. Needless to say, both paternal and maternal analogies cloud the conceptual structure and intrude traits that are simply inappropriate at this level of generality. If the first and second dimensions of the divine represent the orders of spirit, then this third and ubiquitous dimension represents the sheer sustaining power of God as the ground and abyss of nature's innumerable orders. Such a "power," as noted, cannot be understood as an omnipotent or causal efficacy that somehow alters the trait configuration of complexes. It is a reticent power that lives only insofar as it gives all of its power away. The eternal giving over of this power is, as noted, to some degree analogous to the neo–Platonic force of emanation but is far less bound to that which is ventured forth than the emanated is from its emanating source. Nature as natured is free of origin even while receiving its very freedom from that elusive origin. Historically this harks back to Meister Eckhart's concept of *Abgeschiedenheit* (detachment or letting be).

The relationship between God and nature has been understood in three broad ways in the tradition. Classical theism, especially as manifest in such thinkers as Kierkegaard and Barth, sees God as radically divorced from all created orders and as merely interacting in the form of miracles that violate the causal order or in the form of the Incarnation that is a once and for all intrusion of God *qua* Christ into an otherwise nondivine world. Of course, traditional perspectives, such as that of Aquinas, also affirm the dependence of the world of God and thereby brook confusion concerning the dependency relation between God and the world. At the other extreme is a pantheism that equates God with the innumerable orders of nature. Such a perspective often relies on the category of substance (Spinoza) as its universal term of designation. The third conception of the God/nature correlation is that of panentheism, which struggles to find the ways in which God both is and is not to be equated with the orders of nature. Pan–entheism, particularly as developed by Hartshorne, is conceptually far richer than its two competing perspectives even though its own inner logic has not been fully explored. By sharpening the distinction between nature natured and nature naturing it is possible to refine the general panentheistic framework.

As stated above, God cannot be understood to create the innumerable complexes of the world out of nothing. In its first two dimensions, God is a natural complex that is to be found within the orders of nature. In the words of John Ryder, "For God to obtain at all, it is necessary that it both locate traits and be itself ordinally located. Neither of these conceptions seems to be compatible with a creator *ex nihilo*."[10] It is clear that an ordi-nally located God cannot be the creator of "all" complexes. On a deeper level, the very concept of a totality of complexes is rendered deeply prob-lematic by the ordinal perspective. God, *qua* natural complex, is as much a product of nature in its naturing as are all other complexes. And, according to the principle of ontological parity, God cannot be more real than any other complex even if God has greater scope and power than any other complex.

The third divine dimension, God as Providingness, as ordinality, is also far removed from the traditional notion of God the creator. While God's scope is coextensive with the scope of the world, God is not separa-ble from those complexes sustained by divine presence and power. Meta-phorically we can say that God is more the sustainer and preserver of the world than its creator. To talk of a time before ordinality or before Provid-ingness is to misunderstand the nature of these categories. Nor does it help to talk of the cocreation of time and world as if such a portrayal could reach into the heart of ordinality. Again it must be pointed out that time and creation are categories of more limited scope and only apply to specific orders in specific respects. Neither category can be exhaustively applied to the world or innumerable complexes.

God is identical to nature in its naturing in the sense that God lives as the enabling and sustaining source for all of the orders of the world. This source is, as noted, more than a bare origin, or grounding substance, and lives as the potency guaranteeing freedom for all ventured forth orders. It is a misguided extension of the ordinal framework to simply equate God with all of the orders of the world. God transcends creation. But this transcendence is not that expressed by a bare theism that would insist on a wholly other God. To use a paradoxical formulation, we can say that this is an immanent transcendence in which God never removes itself from the orders of nature. God, as sustaining love, is present to all complexes. But this presence does not interfere with the traits structure of any order. God's presence is as gentle as it is eternal.

Thus God is both finite and infinite, but in different respects. Insofar as God is an order within nature, and thereby contains its own suborders, God is finite and located by the nondivine. Insofar as God is that which sustains the orders of nature, while eternally refraining from altering their trait constitution, God is infinite. God's eternal growth and self-surpassing is manifest in the first and second divine aspects as these participate in the plenitude of the world and its various time processes. What has not been articulated in the above account is that dimension which makes such self-surpassability possible in the first place.

Fourth Divine Dimension

As is well known, Hartshorne reworks the surpassability thesis to allow for God's own growth and continual renewal in the face of the nondivine.[11] In affirming that God is that than which no greater can be conceived we are also saying that God is not complete and self-contained in its natures and thus can achieve greater scope and richness for its own complex life. From this we are compelled to conclude that God, in addition to confronting its "other" in the nondivine complexes of nature, confronts an ultimate other which is not an order within nature. This ultimate "other" or divine alterity is that which gives the divine natures the "space" within which to grow and expand. Put differently, the eternal possibility for divine growth cannot be guaranteed by the world's complexes any more than it can emerge as a product of nature. God cannot be both the growth and the clearing within which that growth occurs. There remains an elusive reality that lives as the lure for God's own self-surpassing. Analogous to the divine

lure that God presents to personal and social transformation, this ultimate
lure preserves the clearing within which God may become more fully what
it is. Insofar as God has an entelechy, that internal goal is quickened and
deepened by that which encompasses both nature natured and nature in its
naturing. This "other" is perhaps best termed the Encompassing itself. The
concept of the "Encompassing" is firmly denied by Buchler as it seems to
evoke something that cannot be explored or that does not have any kind of
ordinal location. For Buchler, such a concept can only have value in linguistic orders.

The concept of the Encompassing is well known from the writings of
Karl Jaspers.[12] Unfortunately, Jaspers frequently failed to distinguish the
Encompassing from the reality of Transcendence (i.e., God). In his understanding of religion and the life of faith, Jaspers struggles to find that which
radically transcends all intraworldly pictures of the divine. In his *Philosophical Faith and Revelation* he gives this account of the evolution of
religious consciousness from the primitive stage of natural forces to the
evocation of the Godhead:

> The liberation of man proceeds from dark, savage forces to personal
> gods, from gods beyond good and evil to moral gods, from the gods
> to the one God, and on to the ultimate freedom of recognizing the
> one personal God as a cipher. We may call this last liberation the
> ascent from God to the Godhead, from the ciphers to what makes
> them speak. It is our liberation from the hobbles with which our own
> conceptions and thoughts prevent us from reaching the truth that halts
> all thinking.[13]

A cipher is a transparent symbol that effaces itself before something that is
not delimited by content or form. The Godhead, as understood by Jaspers,
is not a personal God and cannot be understood in any of the usual categories of theology or philosophy. It would not be inappropriate to see the term
"Godhead" as analogous to the term Encompassing. The Encompassing is
not a reality that lies within the divine nature and cannot be equated with
God. The distinction between God and the Godhead is thus similar to that
between God and the Encompassing. Thus, in articulating the fourth divine
aspect, we must make the distinction between God and the Encompassing
sharp and total.

God's sense of its own incompletion is maintained by the Encompassing that is not an order of nature and cannot be equated with the "sum" of
all worldly orders. Nor can the Encompassing be understood through the
analogy of the horizon. By definition, a horizon, as a prethematic structure
of meaning and truth, prevails as only one horizon among others. Any

given horizon will contain its own content and have its own internal traits. More importantly, such a horizon will have referential structures that illuminate, in however attenuated a fashion, orders outside of itself. The Encompassing lies beyond all horizons, be they finite or divine, and has no hermeneutic or semiotic content. As sheer alterity the Encompassing is that which is ever receding from the grasp of horizonal structures. From the divine standpoint, the Encompassing lives as the lure that creates an eternal restlessness within the divine life. God cannot rest on its plenitude or indefinite complexity. Rather, the divine natures all live under the impress of that which encompasses such plenitude. The Encompassing, as void of all plenitude, ever empties itself in the face of that which would grasp it.

We must further clarify the differences among nature, God, and the Encompassing. Nature, as noted, is itself constituted by two fundamental dimensions, namely, that of nature as natured and nature naturing. Nature natured is the "sum" of all orders, including the order known as God. As such, this dimension of nature is encompassed by nature naturing. Since nature naturing is partially equivalent to the third divine aspect, it follows that the God that lives within the power of naturing encompasses its own finite dimensions as manifest in nature natured. That is, God in its first two dimensions is encompassed by nature as a "whole." The infinite divine aspect encompasses the finite divine dimensions and gathers them under the gentle power of nature naturing. Thus God both encompasses and is encompassed. This seeming paradox vanishes when it is understood that one is talking of distinct aspects of God.

But it is not sufficient to trace out the ways in which nature naturing encompasses all orders, including the order known as God. Conceptual clarity is only attained when it is recognized that the Encompassing is that which transcends even nature in its naturing. Insofar as nature naturing has its manifestation in the orders of nature natured, it can not be the Encompassing. God, in its first three dimensions cannot fill in the Encompassing or give it some kind of delimited quality. The urgency behind God's incompletion in all divine aspects, is a gift of the Encompassing. God must be restless and self-surpassing under the loving pressure of that which encompasses its nature. Hence the fourth divine dimension is filled with longing for eternal self-expansion in the face of the void that stands before it. Returning to the language of Jaspers and Meister Eckhart, God longs to become absorbed into the Godhead even though such an absorption is an impossibility. The continual death and rebirth of God is only possible because of the love of the Encompassing for that which is encompassed.

God becomes crucified under the power of the Encompassing. Put differently, God is forced to let go of its fullness and power in the light of that which can never be encompassed by its own reach. The Encompassing humbles the divine and shows it its own locatedness. Divine compassion for the suffering orders of the world has its ultimate source in God's recognition of its own incompletion in the face of the Encompassing.

Yet God's experience of its own crucifixion is gathered under the deeper experience of its eternal resurrection. The Encompassing not only shows the divine its fragmented and limited reality but gives the divine continual hope and renewal. This renewal is the gift of the Encompassing to God as the divine struggles to overcome the bifurcation between and among its other natures. God's quest for wholeness is secured in the lure of the Encompassing that refuses to let God become subject to a self-satisfied closure.

In trinitarian terms, this final divine aspect is the Christological dimension in which God becomes a child to itself. That is, God, in giving birth to new possibilities within its life of eternal self-surpassing, experiences the mystery of that which gives birth to itself. This continual crucifixion and resurrection is the universal actuality that empowers the finite transformations in the worldly orders. The Encompassing is thus the midwife for God's self-transcendence, and through this the hidden potency behind natural and historical evolution.

The Divine Life

All four divine aspects belong together within the divine life itself. The Encompassing gathers and secures each dimension against a bifurcation that would destroy divine unity. God lives with its own lack of power and endures the shocks and diremptions of nature and history. At the same time, God lives in the lure of hope that quickens and transforms personal and social reality. Suffering and hope are themselves gathered under the quiet and eternal power of nature naturing and preserved in their actuality. In a very real sense, God lives in the infinite complexity of its own death and transfiguration in which the Encompassing holds open the highest love of all. God lives in the gift of the love that comes both from its creatures and from the Encompassing. In light of this dual love, God can endure the suffering of the world and its orders.

Christian theology, as bound to the self-giving of God in the Christ, becomes permeable to the power of the Encompassing that locates and radically alters the reality of Christhood. If, using the language of Tillich, we wish to see Christ as the New Being that overcomes the estrangement of essence and existence, then we can see the Encompassing as the ultimate clearing within which the Old Being becomes redeemed and the New Being remakes the world. Seen in this light, the Christocentric moment belongs to the innumerable orders of nature and not to a time–bound human community.

Notes

1. MNC 6–7. See "List of Abbreviations" for Buchler's works, p. xiii.

2. Charles Hartshorne, *A Natural Theology for Our Time* (La Salle, Illinois: The Open Court Publishing Company, 1967), pp. 104–05.

3. For a more detailed treatment of Hopkins' analysis of selfhood, see my, "The Christhood of Things," *The Drew Gateway* 52 (Fall 1981), pp. 41–47.

4. Paul Tillich, *Systematic Theology* (Chicago: University of Chicago Press, 1967), vol. 1, p. 245.

5. Peter H. Hare and John Ryder, "Buchler's Ordinal Metaphysics and Process Theology," *Process Studies,* 10: 3 & 4 (Fall–Winter 1980), pp. 127–128. Here pp. 343.

6. The nature of these communal structures has been worked out in my book, *The Community of Interpreters* (Macon, Georgia: Mercer University Press, 1987).

7. For further analysis on this issue, see my, "Naturalism, Measure, and the Ontological Difference," *The Southern Journal of Philosophy,* 23: 1 (1985), pp. 19–32.

8. For Buchler's criticisms of such an extension of his perspective, with particular reference to Tillich, see, "Conversation Between Justus Buchler and Robert S. Corrington," *The Journal of Speculative Philosophy* 3: 4 (1989), pp. 261–274.

9. Paul Tillich, *Systematic Theology,* vol. 3, pp. 293–94.

10. Hare, Ryder, op. cit., p. 123, here, p. 338.

11. For more detailed criticism of Hartshorne, see my, "Toward a Transformation of Neoclassical Theism," *International Philosophical Quarterly,* 28: 4 (1987), pp. 391–406.

12. In particular see his, *Philosophy of Existence,* trans. by Richard F. Grabau (Philadelphia: University of Pennsylvania Press, 1971), *Reason and Existenz,* trans. by William Earle (New York: Noonday Press, 1955), and *Von der Wahrheit* (Munich: R. Piper, 1947).

13. Karl Jaspers, *Philosophical Faith and Revelation,* trans. by E. B. Ashton (New York: Harper & Row, 1967), p. 284.

Contributors

Richard J. Bernstein is Vera List Professor of Philosophy at the Graduate Faculty of the New School for Social Research. His books include *Philosophical Profiles, Beyond Objectivism and Relativism, The Restructuring of Social and Political Theory,* and *Praxis and Action.* He studied with Justus Buchler during the 1950s.

Lawrence E. Cahoone received his B.A. from Clark University and his Ph.D. in philosophy from State University of New York at Stony Brook. He is Assistant Professor of Philosophy at Boston University, and the author of *The Dilemma of Modernity: Philosophy, Culture and Anti-Culture.*

James Campbell works primarily in the areas of the history of American philosophy and of social and political philosophy. He is a graduate of both Temple University and the State University of New York at Stony Brook. He is currently Associate Professor of Philosophy at the University of Toledo.

Robert S. Corrington is visiting Associate Professor of Philosophical Theology in the Graduate and Theological Schools of Drew University. He has published over twenty articles in the areas of American philosophy, philosophy of religion, and semiotics. He is co-editor of *Pragmatism Considers Phenomenology,* and of the second, expanded edition of Buchler's *Metaphysics of Natural Complexes.* He is the author of *The Community of Interpreters* (1987). He has recently completed his second book, *Nature and Spirit: An Essay in Ordinal Phenomenology.* He is the recipient of the Church Divinity, Greenlee, and John William Miller Prizes.

Abraham Edel is Research Professor of Philosophy, University of Pennsylvania, and Distinguished Professor Emeritus of the Graduate School of the City University of New York. He has authored more than a dozen books, including: *Analyzing Concepts in Social Science* (1979), *Exploring Fact and Value* (1980), *Aristotle and His Philosophy* (1982), *Interpreting Education* (1985), *The Struggle for Academic Democracy* (1990), and *Relating Humanities and Social Thought* (1990).

Roland Garrett is Professor of Philosophy at Montclair State College. He received his Ph.D. from Columbia University where he wrote a dissertation on John Dewey's metaphysics with Buchler. He has published articles on metaphysics, John Dewey, Plato, social philosophy, ethics, philosophy of sport, the nature of philosophy and topics on education and literature.

Sidney Gelber is Leading Professor of Philosophy, Distinguished Service Professor, Provost Emeritus and Director of the Stony Brook Collegium at the State University of New York at Stony Brook. He studied and later worked with Justus Buchler in the 1940s and 1950s. At Columbia University he was chairman of the Contemporary Civilization Editorial Committee. He has written on issues in higher education and on the work of Justus Buchler.

Peter H. Hare is Professor and Chairperson of the Philosophy Department at the State University of New York at Buffalo where he has taught since 1962. He earned a B.A. from Yale University and a Ph.D. from Columbia University (with a dissertation under Buchler on G. H. Mead's metaphysics). He is author or co-author, editor or co-editor of *Evil and the Concept of God, Causing, Perceiving and Believing: An Examination of the Philosophy of C. J. Ducasse, Religion and Spiritual Democracy, Naturalism and Rationality, Doing Philosophy Historically,* and a biography of anthropologist Elsie Clews Parsons. He is president of the Society for the Advancement of American Philosophy and the editor of the *Transactions of the Charles S. Peirce Society: A Quarterly Journal in American Philosophy.*

Matthew Lipman holds a B.S. and Ph.D. from Columbia University, where he was also a professor of philosophy for eighteen years. Since 1972, he has been Professor of Philosophy and Director of the Institute for the Advancement of Philosophy for Children at Montclair State College. He has authored twelve books, and co-authored nine books. His works have been translated into more than a dozen languages. In addition, he is the editor of *Thinking,* an academic quarterly, and he is an honorary fellow of the Center for Critical Thinking and Moral Critique at Sonoma State University.

Armen Marsoobian is Associate Professor of Philosophy at Southern Connecticut State University. He is Articles Editor for the journal *Metaphilosophy.* He has written on aesthetics, metaphysics and American philosophy. He co-edited the second, expanded edition of the *Metaphysics of Natural Complexes* and is currently working on two books, one on the metaphysics of John Dewey and another on a general theory of aesthetic meaning.

Marjorie Cantor Miller currently serves as Associate Dean for General Education at the State University of New York College at Purchase, where she holds the rank of Associate Professor of Philosophy. Other publications dealing with Buchler's work in light of Oriental philosophic traditions include: "Method and System in Justus Buchler and Chu Hsi: A Comparison," in *Journal of Chinese Philosophy* 14 (1987): 209–235. Dr. Miller's current philosophic interests grow out of her earlier work, but presently focus on the metaphysics of decision-making, particularly as decision making is formalized in decision support systems. Recent analyses in these areas use Buchler's categories in conjunction with discussions of C. S. Peirce: cf. "The Principle of Continuity in Charles Sanders Peirce and Contemporary Decision Support Technology" (forthcoming, *Texas A & M Studies in American Philosophy*).

I. A. Richards was an English critic, poet, playwright, editor, semanticist, and one of the most influential figures in modern literary criticism. His theories uniting the principles of science and literature are fundamental precepts of formalist criticism. He also had a continuing interest in language and semantic theory which he explored in several books and essays. It was after a long career devoted to the exegesis of literature that Richards began to write poetry. His subtly rendered verse evidences his finely honored critical sense and his delight in the power and pleasure of the written word. (Taken from *Contemporary Literary Criticism* Volume 14. Edited by Dedria Bryfonski and Laurie Lanzen Harris. Gale Research Company, Michigan, 1980.)

John Ryder is Associate Professor of Philosophy at the State University of New York, College at Cortland. His specialties include systematic metaphysics, the history of American philosophy, and Marxist philosophy. He is currently completing a study of Soviet writings on the history of American philosophy.

Beth J. Singer is Professor of Philosophy at Brooklyn College. Her publications include *Ordinal Naturalism: An Introduction to the Philosophy of Justus Buchler*, other writings on Buchler, Santayana, Dewey, G. H. Mead, and John Herman Randall, Jr., and papers on metaphysics, sign–theory, the concept of community, and the theory of rights.

Ann-Mari Wallen Wachter is Adjunct Assistant Professor of Philosophy at Hofstra University. She studied at the Technical College of Helsinki and received her doctorate in philosophy from the State University of New York at Stony Brook where she studied for a short time with Justus Buchler. She is revising her dissertation, "Ways of Seeing and Modes of Knowing," and is also preparing a manuscript, "From Personal and Social Ethics to a Bioethic: Broadening our Moral Concerns."

Kathleen Wallace is Associate Professor of Philosophy at Hofstra University. She has written on Santayana, Buchler, and the problem of validation in metaphysics. She wrote the introduction and co-edited the second, expanded edition of Buchler's *Metaphysics of Natural Complexes*. She is currently working on a book on the concept of self and morality.

Phil Weiss is the father of two children, Darshan of Congregation B'nai Brith of Somerville, Mass. and Assistant Professor of Philosophy, Wheelock College.

Bibliography of Secondary Works on Justus Buchler

Adelman, G.
    1955 "Review of *Nature and Judgment*." *Library Journal* 80 (November 1955):2516.

Aiken, H. D.
    1952 "Review of *Toward a General Theory of Human Judgment*." *Nation* 174 (March 1952):282.

Allers, Rudolf.
    1959 "Judgment, Culture, and Conduct." *The Journal of Philosophy* 61:5 (February 1959):214–220.

Anton, John P.
    1976 "Categorial Thought: Buchler's Natural Complex and Aristotle's *Ousia*." (With reply by Buchler), *The Southern Journal of Philosophy* 14:1 (Spring 1976):69–90.

Arnett, Willard E.
    1959 "Reflections on Justus Buchler's Theory of Meaning." *The Journal of Philosophy* 61:5 (February 1959):220–233.

Barzun, Jacques.
    1962 "Review of *The Concept of Method*." *American Scholar* 31:3 (1962): 468–472.

Baum, Archie J.
    1962 "Review of *Metaphysics of Natural Complexes*." *Philosophy and Phenomenological Research* 28 (1967):292–293.

Beardsley, Monroe.
    1954 "Categories." *The Review of Metaphysics* 8 (September 1954):3–29.

Belaief, Gail.
    1977 "Philosophy and the Special Sciences." *Journal of Critical Analysis* 6 (1977):101–109.

Bernstein, Richard J.
1956   "Review of *Nature and Judgment.*" *The Review of Metaphysics* 9 (1956):517.

1967   "Buchler's Metaphysics." *The Journal of Philosophy* 64:22 (November 1967):751–770.

Brown, Donald G.
1956   "Review of *Toward a General Theory of Human Judgment.*" *Mind* 65 (1956):274–279.

Cahoone, Lawrence E.
1989   "Buchler and Habermas on Modernity." *The Southern Journal of Philosophy* 27:4 (Winter 1989):461–477.

Churchill, Jordan.
1959   "Validation." *The Journal of Philosophy* 61:5 (February 1959): 200–208.

Clayton, Stafford A.
1963   "Review of *The Concept of Method.*" *Studies in the Philosophy of Education* 3 (Summer 1963):36–41.

Collins, James.
1953   "Review of *Toward a General Theory of Human Judgment.*" *Thought* 28 (1953):287.

1956   "Review of *Nature and Judgment.*" *Thought* 31 (1956):134.

Corrington, Robert S.
1982   "Horizonal Hermeneutics and the Actual Infinite." *Graduate Faculty Philosophy Journal of the New School* 8:1 & 2 (Spring 1982):36–97.

1985   "Naturalism, Measure, and the Ontological Difference." *The Southern Journal of Philosophy* 23:1 (Spring 1985):19–32.

1985   "Justus Buchler's Ordinal Metaphysics and the Eclipse of Foundationalism." *International Philosophical Quarterly* 25:3 (September 1985):289–298.

1987   "Finitude and Transcendence in the Thought of Justus Buchler." *The Southern Journal of Philosophy* 25:4 (Winter 1987):445–459.

1989   "Conversation Between Justus Buchler and Robert S. Corrington." *The Journal of Speculative Philosophy* 3:4 (1989):261–274.

Cua, Antonio S.
1987   "Comments on Marjorie Miller's 'Method and System in Justus Buchler and Chu Hsi: A Comparison.' " *Journal of Chinese Philosophy* 14 (1987):227–231.

Bibliography 373

Donmeyer, F. C.
  1963 "Review of *The Concept of Method.*" *Philosophical Review* 72 (January 1963):113–114.

Durfee, P.
  1975 "Review of *The Main of Light.*" *The Review of Metaphysics* 29:2 (1975):337.

Feibleman, James.
  1940 "Review of *Charles Peirce's Empiricism.*" *Science and Society* 4 (1940):233–235.

Foot, Philippa.
  1957 "Review of *Nature and Judgment.*" *Philosophy* 32 (1957):372–373.

Francis, R. G.
  1962 "Review of *The Concept of Method.*" *American Journal of Sociology* 68 (July 1962):146.

Gallagher, N. A.
  1962 "Review of *The Concept of Method.*" *The Review of Metaphysics* 15 (1962):524.

Garlan, Edwin.
  1957 "Review of *Nature and Judgment.*" *The Journal of Philosophy* 54:20 (September 1957):620.

Garrett, Roland.
  1989 "The Limits of Generalization in Metaphysics: The Case of Justus Buchler." *The Southern Journal of Philosophy* 27:1 (Spring 1989):1–28.

Gelber, Sidney
  1959 "Toward a Radical Naturalism." *The Journal of Philosophy* 61:5 (February 1959):193–199.

  1986 "Justus Buchler: Nature, Power, and Prospect." (with Kathleen Wallace), *Process Studies* 15:2 (Summer 1986):106–119.

Goudge, Thomas G.
  1940 "Review of *Charles Peirce's Empiricism.*" *The Journal of Philosophy* 37 (1940):274–276.

Greenlee, Douglas.
  1974 "Particulars and Ontological Parity." *Metaphilosophy* 5:3 (July 1974):216–231.

  1975 "Review of *The Main of Light.*" *Journal of Aesthetics and Art Criticism* 33 (Spring 1975):358–361.

1976   "The Problem of Exhibitive Judgment in Philosophy." (With reply by Buchler), *The Southern Journal of Philosophy* 14 (Spring 1976):129–143.

1980   "Buchler and the Concept of Poetry." *The British Journal of Aesthetics* 20:1 (Winter 1980):54–66.

Gross, M. W.
1952   "Review of *Toward a General Theory of Human Judgment.*" *The Journal of Philosophy* 49 (November 1952):748.

Hare, Peter H.
1980   "Buchler's Ordinal Metaphysics and Process Theology." (With John Ryder), *Process Studies* 10:3 & 4 (Fall-Winter 1980):120–129.

Hartshorne, Charles.
1970   "Ontological Primacy: A Reply to Buchler." *The Journal of Philosophy* 67:23 (December 1970):979–986. Reprinted in *Explorations in Whitehead's Philosophy,* ed. Lewis S. Ford and George L. Kline (New York: Fordham University Press, 1983):295–303.

1984   "Neville on Creation and Buchler on Natural Complexes." *Creativity in American Philosophy* (Albany: SUNY Press 1984):265–276.

Heinemann, F. H.
1952   "Review of *Toward a General Theory of Human Judgment.*" *Hibbert Journal* 51 (October 1952):85.

Johnstone, Henry, Jr.
1962   "Review of *The Concept of Method.*" *Philosophy and Phenomenological Research* 23:2 (1962):286–287.

Kadish, Mortimer R.
1952   "Review of *Toward a General Theory of Human Judgment.*" *Philosophical Review* 61 (1952):426–428.

Keeles, J.
1948   "Review of *Introduction to Contemporary Civilization in the West.*" (et al) *Thought* 23 (1948):242.

Keeton, Morris.
1956   "Review of *Nature and Judgment.*" *Antioch Review* 16 (1956):256.

Kivy, P.
1976   "Review of *The Main of Light.*" *Philosophical Review* 85:1 (1976):109–111.

Kuhns, Richard.
1976   "Some Observations on Justus Buchler's Theory of Poetry." (With reply by Buchler), *The Southern Journal of Philosophy* 14 (Spring 1976): 111–127.

Laird, John.
1940 "Review of *Charles Peirce's Empiricism.*" *Philosophy* 15 (1940): 208–209.

1941 "Review of *The Philosophy of Peirce.*" *Philosophy* 16 (1941):434.

Landesman, Charles.
1962 "Metaphysics and Human Nature." *The Review of Metaphysics* 15 (June 1962):656–671.

Leclerc, Ivor.
1971 "A Rejoinder to Justus Buchler." *Process Studies* 1:2 (Fall 1971): 55–59.

Lipman, Matthew.
1959 "Natural Obligation, Natural Appropriation." *The Journal of Philosophy* 61:5 (February 1959):246–252.

Long, Wilbur.
1954 "Review of *Toward a General Theory of Human Judgment.*" *Personalist* 35 (1954):163.

1957 "Review of *Nature and Judgment.*" *Personalist* 38 (1957):404.

1962 "Review of *The Concept of Method.*" *Personalist* 43 (1962):267.

Macdonald, M.
1941 "Review of *Charles Peirce's Empiricism.*" *Mind* 50 (1941):81–83.

Marsoobian, Armen.
1987 "Review of Beth J. Singer's, *Ordinal Naturalism: An Introduction to the Philosophy of Justus Buchler.*" *The Journal of Speculative Philosophy* 1:2 (1987):172–175.

1991 "Signification Without Reference: C. S. Peirce and Justus Buchler on Interpretation." *Texas A & M Studies in American Philosophy* 2 (1991).

Medina, A.
1967 "Review of *Metaphysics of Natural Complexes.*" *The Review of Metaphysics* 20 (1967):713–714.

Miller, Marjorie C.
1976 "The Concept of Identity in Justus Buchler and Mahayana Buddhism." *International Philosophical Quarterly* 16:1 (March 1976):87–107.

1982 "Review of Stephen David Ross, *Transition to an Ordinal Metaphysics.*" *The Review of Metaphysics* 35:4 (1982):900–901.

1987 "Method and System in Justus Buchler and Chu Hsi: A Comparison." *Journal of Chinese Philosophy* 14 (1987):209–225.

Mischel, Theodore.
1959 "Some Questions Concerning Exhibitive Judgment." *The Journal of Philosophy* 61:5 (February 1959):233–246.

Olson, Robert G.
1959 "Two Questions on the Definition of Man's Status in Nature." *The Journal of Philosophy* 61:5 (February 1959): 208–214.

Palau, Joseph F.
1986 "Review of Beth J. Singer's *Ordinal Naturalism: An Introduction to the Philosophy of Justus Buchler.*" *International Studies in Philosophy* 18:3 (1986):95–96.

Pasch, Alan.
1964 "Review of *The Concept of Method.*" *The Journal of Philosophy* 61 (1964):372–375.

Prosch, Harry.
1984 "Review of Beth J. Singer's, *Ordinal Naturalism: An Introduction to the Philosophy of Justus Buchler.*" *The Review of Metaphysics* 38:2 (1984):404–405.

Reck, Andrew.
1968 *The New American Philosophers.* (Baton Rouge: LSU Press, 1968). (Chapter entitled, "The Humanistic Naturalism of Justus Buchler":149–163.)

1972 "Contemporary American Speculative Philosophy." *Revue Internationale de Philosophie* 26 (1972):149–171.

1976 "Categories and Justus Buchler." (With a reply by Buchler), *The Southern Journal of Philosophy* 14:1 (Spring 1976):31–54.

1986 "Review of Beth J. Singer's *Ordinal Naturalism: An Introduction to the Philosophy of Justus Buchler.*" *Man and World* 19:4 (1986):471–478.

Richards, I. A.
1974 "Review of *The Main of Light.*" *Times Literary Supplement* (November 29, 1974):1343.

Rohatyn, Dennis.
1985 "Review of Beth J. Singer's *Ordinal Naturalism: An Introduction to the Philosophy of Justus Buchler.*" *Modern Schoolman* 62:3 (1985):216–217.

Ross, Stephen David.
1973 "The Inexhaustibility of Nature." *Journal of Value Inquiry* 8:4 (1973):241–53.

1976 "Complexities of Judgment." (With reply by Buchler), *The Southern Journal of Philosophy* 14:1 (Spring 1976):91–109.

1977 "Translation as Judgment." *Translation in the Humanities,* M. Ross ed., (SUNY-Binghamton, 1977).

1980   *Transition to an Ordinal Metaphysics.* (Albany: SUNY Press, 1980). 164 pgs.

Ryder, John.
1980   "Buchler's Ordinal Metaphysics and Process Theology." (With Peter Hare), *Process Studies* 10:3 & 4 (Fall–Winter 1980):120–129.

Shapiro, Gary.
1976   "Review of *The Main of Light.*" *The Journal of Philosophy* 73 (1976):546–550.

Shuford, H. R.
1952   "Review of *Toward a General Theory of Human Judgment.*" *Philosophy and Phenomenological Research* 13 (1952):264–265.

Singer, Beth J.
1975   "Substitutes for Substances." *Modern Schoolman* 53 (November 1975):19–38.

1976   "Introduction to the Philosophy of Justus Buchler." *The Southern Journal of Philosophy* 14:1 (Spring 1976):3–30.

1976   "Some Ambiguities in the Metaphysics of Natural Complexes." (With a reply by Buchler), *The Southern Journal of Philosophy* 14:1 (Spring 1976):55–68.

1983   *Ordinal Naturalism: An Introduction to the Philosophy of Justus Buchler.* (Lewisburg: Bucknell University Press, 1983). 232 pgs.

1985   "Art, Poetry, and the Sense of Prevalence: Some Implications of Buchler's Theory of Poetry." *International Philosophical Quarterly* 24:3 (1985):267–282.

Smith, R. N. W.
1953   "Review of *Toward a General Theory of Human Judgment.*" *Philosophical Quarterly* 3 (1953):375–376.

Snyder, William S.
1957   "Review of *Philosophical Writings of Peirce.*" *Personalist* 38 (1957):81.

Tejera, Victor.
1980   "The Human Sciences in Dewey, Foucault and Buchler." *The Southern Journal of Philosophy* 18 (Summer 1980):221–235.

1986   "Communication and Meaning: Theories of Buchler and Habermas." *Symbolic Interaction* 9:1 (1986):83–104.

Thompson, M.
1957   "Review of *Nature and Judgment.*" *Ethics* 68 (1957):65–66.

[TLS]
1940   Unsigned Review of *Charles Peirce's Empiricism. Times Literary Supplement* (February 10, 1940):68.

Van Der Veer, Garrett L.
1967 "Review of *Metaphysics of Natural Complexes.*" *Philosophical Quarterly* 17 (1967):370–371.

Vivas, E.
1940 "Review of *Charles Peirce's Empiricism.*" *Nation* 151 (1940):483–484.

Wallace, Kathleen.
1982 "Review of Stephen David Ross, *Transition to an Ordinal Metaphysics.*" *The Journal of Philosophy* 79:4 (1982):222–227.

1986 "Justus Buchler: Nature, Power, and Prospect." (With Sidney Gelber), *Process Studies* 15:2 (Summer 1986):106–119.

1988 "Making Categories or Making Worlds." *The Journal of Speculative Philosophy* 2:4 (1988):322–327.

1990 "Making Categories or Making Worlds, II." *Texas A&M Studies in American Philosophy* 1 (1990).

1991 "Metaphysics and Validation." *Antifoundationalism: Old and New,* Thomas Rockmore and Beth J. Singer eds., Temple University Press.

Weiss, Paul.
1940 "Review of *Charles Peirce's Empiricism.*" *Philosophical Review* 49 (1940):595.

1942 "Review of *The Philosophy of Peirce.*" *Philosophy and Phenomenological Research* 2 (1942):259–261.

Weiss, Phil.
1980 "Possibility: Three Recent Ontologies." *International Philosophical Quarterly* 20:2 (June 1980):199–219.

Wohlstetter, Albert.
1940 "Review of *Charles Peirce's Empiricism.*" *Isis* 32 (1940):399–403.

Zarecor, William D.
1962 "Review of *The Concept of Method.*" *Western Humanities Review* 16 (1962):283.

Dissertations on Buchler

Brahinsky, David Melvin.
1976 "Metaphysical Generality and the Principle of Ontological Parity: An Examination of the Ontology of Justus Buchler in Comparison with the Cosmology of Alfred North Whitehead." (SUNY at Binghamton 1976). DDJ76–19793.

Calore, Gary.
1986 "Temporality and Radical Naturalism." (Bryn Mawr College 1986). DE586–17151.

Coutant, Raymond G.
1977 "The Rhetorical Dimension: An Articulation of the Philosophy of Justus Buchler." (Ohio University 1977). DDJ77–23460.

Gold, Jon.
1981 "Complexity, Ordinality and Logic." (SUNY at Stony at Stony Brook 1981). DDJ81–27109.

Hopkins, Richard Lee.
1980 "Reconstructive Query: Dewey, Buchler, and Merleau-Ponty as Guides to an Epistemology of Experiential Learning." (Boston University School of Education 1980). DDJ80–13326.

Miller, Marjorie Cantor.
1980 "The Concept of Identity in Aristotle, Locke, and Buchler." (SUNY at Stony Brook 1980). DDJ80–19740.

Norman, James J.
1986 "Some Implications of Justus Buchler's Thought for a Philosophy of Education." (Rutgers University, Department of Education 1986). DES86–13876.

Palau, Joseph Francis.
1978 "Ontological Parity and Reciprocal Constitution in Buchler's System." (SUNY at Binghamton 1978). DDJ78–18055.

Ryder, John Joseph.
1983 "Ordinality, Language Games and Sunyata: Their Implications for Religion." (SUNY at Stony Brook 1983). DEP83–01436.

Zampini, Philip R.
1984 "The Metaphysics of Social Inquiry: An Objective–Relativist Perspective." (Miami University of Ohio, Department of Political Science 1984). DER84–25422.

Name Index

Subject Index